AUTHORITARIAN RULE OF LAW

Two common assumptions are made about the rule of law: that authoritarianism and rule of law are mutually incompatible, and that free markets and rule of law must tip authoritarian societies in a liberal direction. This book shows both assumptions are wrong. Jothie Rajah demonstrates how Singapore has created that most improbable coupling – the authoritarian rule of law. Through a close and engaging analysis of several key moments in Singapore's history, *Authoritarian Rule of Law* shows how prosperity, public discourse, and a rigorous observance of legal procedure enable a reconfigured rule of law that is liberal in form but illiberal in content. Rajah alerts us to ways institutions and processes at the bedrock of rule of law and liberal democracy become tools to constrain dissenting citizens while protecting those in political power, even as the national and international legitimacy of the state is secured. With China seeing in Singapore a model for its own development, as do any number of regimes that hope to replicate Singapore's economic success and compliant citizenry, this book overturns conventional understandings of law and politics. This volume reveals a configuration of law, power, and legitimacy that may have far-reaching consequences for theory and politics worldwide.

Jothie Rajah is a Research Professor at the American Bar Foundation, Chicago. She obtained her PhD at the Melbourne Law School, Australia, where she was awarded the University's 2010 Chancellor's Award and the Law School's 2010 Harold Luntz Graduate Research Thesis Prize for excellence. For her doctoral dissertation she was awarded an honorable mention by the Law & Society Association, U.S.A. She is the author of several articles on the history and politics of legislation. She has taught at the Melbourne Law School; the National University of Singapore; and the Institute of Education, Singapore. Her current research focuses on global discourses on the rule of law and colonial constructions of Hindu law in the Straits Settlements.

CAMBRIDGE STUDIES IN LAW AND SOCIETY

Cambridge Studies in Law and Society aims to publish the best scholarly work on legal discourse and practice in its social and institutional contexts, combining theoretical insights and empirical research.

The fields that it covers are: studies of law in action; the sociology of law; the anthropology of law; cultural studies of law, including the role of legal discourses in social formations; law and economics; law and politics; and studies of governance. The books consider all forms of legal discourse across societies, rather than being limited to lawyers' discourses alone.

The series editors come from a range of disciplines: academic law, socio-legal studies, sociology and anthropology. All have been actively involved in teaching and writing about law in context.

Books in the series

Diseases of the Will
Mariana Valverde

The Politics of Truth and Reconciliation in South Africa: Legitimizing the Post-Apartheid State
Richard A. Wilson

Modernism and the Grounds of Law
Peter Fitzpatrick

Unemployment and Government: Genealogies of the Social
William Walters

(*continued after Index*)

Authoritarian Rule of Law

LEGISLATION, DISCOURSE AND LEGITIMACY IN SINGAPORE

Jothie Rajah

American Bar Foundation

CAMBRIDGE UNIVERSITY PRESS
Cambridge, New York, Melbourne, Madrid, Cape Town,
Singapore, São Paulo, Delhi, Mexico City

Cambridge University Press
32 Avenue of the Americas, New York, NY 10013-2473, USA

www.cambridge.org
Information on this title: www.cambridge.org/9781107634169

First published 2012

Printed in the United States of America

A catalog record for this publication is available from the British Library.

Library of Congress Cataloging in Publication data
Rajah, Jothie, 1963–
Authoritarian rule of law : legislation, discourse and legitimacy in Singapore / Jothie Sauntharajah.
p. cm. – (Cambridge studies in law and society)
Revised version of thesis (Ph.D.)–University of Melbourne, Melbourne Law School, 2010, issued under the title Legislating illiberalism.
Includes bibliographical references and index.
ISBN 978-1-107-01241-7 (hardback) – ISBN 978-1-107-63416-9 (pbk.)
1. Rule of law – Singapore. 2. Freedom of expression – Singapore.
3. Authoritarianism – Singapore. 4. Law reform – Singapore. 5. Singapore – Politics and government. I. Title.
KPP169.7.R35 2012
340′.11–dc23 2011048127

ISBN 978-1-107-01241-7 Hardback
ISBN 978-1-107-63416-9 Paperback

For my father, K. S. Rajah, who believed in the Rule of Law

3 March 1930–17 June 2010

CONTENTS

AN INSIDER'S PREFACE ON 'RULE OF LAW' CONFUSIONS

In 1983 Singapore's then Prime Minister, Lee Kuan Yew, said it was a problem for Singapore that graduate women were not marrying at the same rate as non-graduate women; and when they did marry, they weren't having as many children.[1] This meant, he argued, that Singapore's next generations were losing out on the genetic talent pool.[2] It was, of course, a highly controversial speech.[3]

At the time of Lee's speech, I was a second-year law student at the National University of Singapore. I wrote a parody, the "Procreation Encouragement Act", for the Student Union magazine. I modelled the "Procreation Encouragement Act" very closely on the legislation we were studying. The national coat of arms, margin notes, tortured legislative language – apart from its obviously satirical content, my "Act" looked and read like a product of Parliament. I conscientiously acknowledged the idea I was borrowing: my constitutional law tutor, Dr Hugh Rawlings, had referred to an imaginary "Procreation Encouragement Act" in a tutorial problem he set us. I asked for his permission, took the title and wrote the "Act".

[1] "PM's National Day Rally Speech", *Straits Times* (15 August 1983).

[2] Ibid.

[3] For a fuller discussion, see Lenore Lyons-Lee, "The 'Graduate Woman' Phenomenon: Changing Constructions of the Family in Singapore" (1998) 13:2 *Sojourn: Journal of Social Issues in Southeast Asia* 1.

To my surprise, this two-page student effort was faxed across lawyers' offices throughout Singapore. It even crossed the causeway into neighbouring Malaysia. Three weeks or so after the magazine came out, there was a notice pinned on the Law Faculty notice board – the Student Liaison Officer wanted to see me.

She was very pleasant, but I was terrified by the thirty minutes I spent in her room. She started by telling me that a senior official of the University had asked her to speak to me – information which located insignificant me on an intimidating scale of downward scrutiny. Her next move was to establish that I had broken the law. Did I know that it was an offence to reproduce the Singapore coat of arms without official permission? I didn't. I was wrong and already guilty. Mostly, though, she wanted to know the extent of Dr Rawlings's involvement. Had he read drafts, had he made suggestions? She asked again and again about my tutor, and I repeated my story with an increasing sense of panic and bewilderment. In about six weeks, the whole thing thankfully died down. I never again produced legal parody.

Instead, twenty-two years later, I embarked on a dissertation on the relationship between legislation, public discourse and state legitimacy in Singapore, wrestling with the way in which the ambivalences inherent to the category 'law' – between a rights-protecting 'rule of law' and an instrumental, state-serving 'rule by law' – have unfolded in Singapore. My project has uncovered variations on the state's fifty-year-old theme of dangerous foreigners, so that I finally understand the University's need to determine Dr Rawlings's role in the "Procreation Encouragement Act".

Until moving to the University of Melbourne's Law School to undertake doctoral studies, I lived and was educated in Singapore. I received a legal education in which I was taught that Singapore was a 'rule of law' 'nation' in which the *Constitution* was supreme. As first-year law students, we were taught stern rules articulated through instructive case law about the high standards of conduct expected of lawyers, who must, first and foremost, be officers of The Court and serve Justice. The extent to which a legal professional identity pervaded every facet of one's existence was brought home to us by a memorable case in which a lawyer was found to have engaged in conduct unbecoming of an advocate and solicitor of the Supreme Court of Singapore. This lawyer, a man, in order to do a favour for a friend, sold "women's dresses and brassieres" from his hotel room while on a professional trip to his Kuching office.[4]

The almost religious exaltation of the 'rule of law' expressed in my legal education was consistent with the screen heroes I had been exposed to as a child – Gregory Peck as Atticus Finch in *To Kill a Mockingbird*, Paul Scofield as Sir Thomas More in *A Man for All Seasons* – just two of the handsome and compelling personifications of what I was being socialised to regard as the exemplary (somehow male) virtue of 'law'. The disjuncture between the ideals I was taught and the anxiety I imbued from my environment – the government should not be displeased or challenged – was something that confused me, even as I (mostly) conformed. It was not until just after I had graduated that the detentions, televised confessions and courtroom disappointments of the so-called Marxist conspiracy (events that included a classmate from the Law Faculty and a quiet woman whose principled conduct had won her the respect of law students at the time) that I saw what earlier generations had already witnessed – the state's readiness to turn to coercion and its capacity to silence, if not demonise, counter-narratives.

This study is informed by my desire to unpack the complexities and paradoxical co-existence of 'rule of law' and 'rule by law' voices in Singapore. Through a focus on legislation, I have been led to state discourse and notions of the 'rule of law' which have constructed a mode of authoritarianism[5] that has generated widespread legitimacy for the Singapore state. Shaped by the very polity I examine, I have found it invaluable to exit the ideological fortress that Singapore can sometimes be in order to peel off, layer by layer, some of the assumptions embedded in Singapore-speak – assumptions that have, until recently, been invisible

[4] *Re An Advocate* (1963), [1964] 1 M.L.J. 1 (Kuching).

[5] Garry Rodan, *Transparency and Authoritarian Rule in Southeast Asia: Singapore and Malaysia* (London: Routledge Curzon, 2004).

to me. Through a determined decoding of state text, I have untangled complex bundles of meaning conveyed by apparently simple declarations. The process has been revelatory of a dynamic between 'rule of' and 'rule by' 'law' that has led me to texts and histories I did not originally anticipate as destinations.

A striking constant, when presenting papers at conferences and in my own analytical processes, has been the issue of the space for critical scholarship on Singapore, especially for those who consider themselves Singaporean. There is little doubt that Singapore's pervasive environment of self-censorship[6] influences and contextualises the academy. Yet, paradoxically, a measure of academic freedom also clearly exists,[7] and the official, declared position of the state is that academic freedom is supported and must flourish.[8] In addition to building upon the scholarship of those who are not Singapore nationals, this project builds upon the critical scholarship of those who identify as Singaporean, who are located within Singapore institutions, and who have built their careers and reputations as Singapore scholars. The critically engaged work of Chua Beng Huat, Cherian George, Hong Lysa, Nirmala PuruShotam, Li-ann Thio and many, many others precedes and informs my project. Like these scholars, I identify as Singaporean and hope to establish a long critical engagement with this fascinating, contradictory and complex social space that is also home.

[6] Cherian George, "Consolidating Authoritarian Rule: Calibrated Coercion in Singapore" (2007) 20:2 *Pacific Review* 127.

[7] Chapter 8's argument on the manner in which spokespersons, alliances and transcendences appear to be viewed as great dangers may account for this paradox.

[8] Sing., *Parliamentary Debates*, vol. 47, col. 474 (17 March 1986).

ACKNOWLEDGEMENTS

I am in the happy position of having received a great deal of support throughout this project from friends, family and colleagues in Singapore, Melbourne and elsewhere. Pip Nicholson, Abdullah Saeed and Li-ann Thio have supplied valuable guidance and asked important questions, for which I am very grateful. My very particular thanks go to Pip Nicholson for sustained, generous and consistent mentoring.

Many senior scholars have been extremely generous with their expertise. Hong Lysa has guided me through explorations of Singapore histories and I am deeply grateful to her. Anoma Pieris's probing questions have taught me much about inter-disciplinarity, as have Nirmala PuruShotam's lucid lessons on sociological thinking and methodologies. Warm thanks also to Shaun McVeigh who articulated that improbable coupling – authoritarian rule of law – that has become this book's title. The three wise men who lead the legal complex and political liberalism project, Terence Halliday, Lucien Karpik and Malcolm Feeley, have supported this study in a range of valuable ways. William Neilson and Terence Halliday have read the penultimate draft of this manuscript with particular care and I have benefited tremendously from their invaluable advice. Others who have made time, despite the (often urgent) demands of their own teaching and research schedules, are Anthony Anghie, Michael Barr, Jennifer Beard, Sarah Biddulph, Mark Brown, Chris Dent, Carolyn Evans, Cherian George, Michael Hor, Tim Lindsey, Don Miller, Frank Munger, Debbie Ong, Juliet Rogers, Kevin Y. L. Tan, Tang Hung Wu,

Arun Thiruvengadam, Geoff Wade, Helena Whalen-Bridge and Amanda Whiting. I am also indebted to an inspiring and passionate teacher from my undergraduate education who taught me to see law through different eyes, Professor Yash Ghai and to three anonymous reviewers. My warm and deep thanks to all.

Institutional support has also been generous and forthcoming. The Melbourne Law School and the Asian Law Centre have supplied a lively and collegial community of researchers and an environment in which students receive mentoring and resources at many levels, including funding that makes attending overseas conferences possible. Professor Tan Cheng Han, Dean of the Faculty of Law of the National University of Singapore, and the staff of his office extended much kind assistance and an ongoing welcome on my frequent research trips to NUS, as did Eleanor Wong and the Legal Analysis, Writing and Research team. Carolyn Wee and the staff of the C. J. Koh Law Library were similarly welcoming and helpful. The libraries and research facilitators of the Institute of South East Asian Studies, the New York City Bar, the International Press Institute, Lawyers Rights Watch Canada and Amnesty International have also extended assistance. My thanks to them all.

Many friends have supplied warm and invaluable companionship. My particular thanks go to Eve Lester, Daniel Muriu and Yoriko Otomo, partners on this scholarly journey in many important ways. Other dear friends who have thoughtfully extended help and support throughout are Elizabeth Brophy, Naomita Royan, Helen Pausacker, Laura Griffin, Sanjay Pala Krishnan, Niloshan Vijayalingam, Cate Read and Sonja Zivak.

My family has also been an important source of support. My daughter, Shrimoyee, has asked valuable questions; my father, K. S. Rajah, and my son, Ravindran, kept an alert eye out for current affairs relating to my research, and were thoughtful and careful readers of my draft chapters; my mother, Gnanam, has been an invaluable and constant source of care and support, and I am very grateful. My final and deepest acknowledgements go to my children, Shrimoyee and Ravindran, whose love, encouragement and support have sustained me in the time I have spent away from them.

1 LAW, ILLIBERALISM AND THE SINGAPORE CASE

IN OCTOBER 2007, FOUR THOUSAND LAWYERS from more than 120 countries converged upon Singapore for the International Bar Association's (IBA)[1] annual conference.[2] The selection of Singapore as a venue had been controversial, with some members[3] and Singapore dissidents[4] protesting that the IBA was lending legitimacy to a regime that had systematically violated the rule of law. The conference aired these and other issues from the air-conditioned comfort of Singapore's technologically superior conference facilities.[5]

[1] The IBA describes itself as the world's leading organisation of international legal practitioners, bar associations and law societies with a membership of thirty thousand individual lawyers worldwide; online: "About the IBA", <http://www.ibanet.org/About_the_IBA/About_the_IBA.aspx>.

[2] "4,000 Delegates from 120 Countries", *Straits Times* (16 October 2007).

[3] K. C. Vijayan, "Global Law Meeting Will Tackle Heavy Issues", *Straits Times* (12 October 2007), notes that "some European-based legislators … initially objected to the choice of Singapore as conference host on rule-of-law grounds."

[4] Chee Soon Juan, an opposition politician who is Secretary-General of the Singapore Democratic Party, wrote to the President of the IBA in February 2007 asking him to reconsider Singapore as the venue because of Singapore's repressive practices towards political opponents; online: "SDP Writes to International Bar Association About Its Conference in Singapore", <http://www.singaporedemocrat.org/articleiba.html>.

[5] Hailin Qu, Lan Li & Gilder Kei Tat Chu, "The Comparative Analysis of Hong Kong as an International Conference Destination in Southeast Asia" (2000) 21 *Tourism Management* 643.

Singapore's elder statesman, Lee Kuan Yew,[6] delivered the keynote address at the opening session of the conference.[7] Lee's address was followed by a question-and-answer session at which Lee was asked to account for Singapore's problematic standing with regard to the rule of law.[8] Lee's response to this challenge was to pull out a series of tables[9] citing Singapore's high rankings in rule of law and governance indicators as proof of the existence of the rule of law in Singapore.[10] According to press reports, the listening IBA members responded by bursting into laughter.[11]

[6] Lee Kuan Yew was Prime Minister of Singapore from 1959 to 1990. His successor, Goh Chok Tong, was selected by Lee to head a cabinet from 1990 to 2004, in which Lee held the newly created cabinet position of Senior Minister. When Goh was succeeded as Prime Minister by Lee's son, Lee Hsien Loong, in 2004, Goh became Senior Minister. Lee Kuan Yew continued to be a member of cabinet, holding another newly created position, that of Minister Mentor, until May 2011 when both Lee and Goh retired from government following a general election in which the highest number (to date) of opposition members (6 in an 87 seat Parliament) were voted in.

[7] Vijayan, *supra* note 3; Lee Kuan Yew, "Why Singapore Is What It Is", *Straits Times* (15 October 2007) [*Why Singapore Is What It Is*].

[8] Rachel Evans, "Singapore Leader Rejects Amnesty", *International Financial Law Review* (18 October 2007), online: <http://www.iflr.com/Article/1983342/Singapore-leader-rejects-Amnesty.html>.

[9] Evans (ibid.) mentions that the sources Lee cited included World Bank and Transparency International. Loh Chee Kong, "What Price, This Success? MM Asked Whether Singapore Sacrificed Democracy", *Today* (15 October 2007), describes Lee as "rattling off the favourable rankings of Singapore's legal framework by International Institute for Management Development, Political and Economic Risk Consultancy and the Economist Intelligence Unit". In addition to these, the state typically refers to the rankings produced by the World Competitiveness Yearbook, the World Economic Forum Global Competitiveness Report, the World Bank Report on Governance, the Transparency International Corruption Perception Index, and the Business Environment Risk Intelligence (BERI) reports. These were some of the reports Lee referred to in order to support his claim of the quality of Singapore's 'rule of law' in a 2000 lecture, "For Third World Leaders: Hope or Despair?" (delivered at JFK School of Government, Harvard University, 17 October 2000), online: <http://www.gov.sg/sprinter/search.htm>. Chapter 8 discusses the state's use of statistics in its construction of legitimacy.

[10] Evans, *supra* note 8.

[11] Ibid. Lawyers Rights Watch Canada released a very prompt repudiation of Lee's claim that Singapore observed the 'rule of law': Kelley Bryan, "Rule of Law in

That laughter could mean many things, of course – from admiration for the preparedness of a man who was Prime Minister for thirty-one years, to incredulity at the discursive minimisation of the 'rule of law' from a qualitative ideal to schemas that rank and quantify. This laughter, and the range of meanings held within it, point to a Singapore paradox: A regime that has systematically undercut 'rule of law' freedoms has managed to be acclaimed as a 'rule of law' state.

The Singapore state's strategic management of 'law' forms the primary focus of this study. In particular, I examine the ways in which legislative text and public discourse have been used to reconstitute the meanings of 'law'. My concern is to excavate the often-submerged policing and politics of 'law' in Singapore. This excavation leads to an exploration of a broader question: How has the Singapore state constructed legitimacy for itself despite methodically eroding rights through legislation even as it claims to be a Westminster-model democracy?[12]

This book builds on that strand of socio-legal studies that "examines law as a discourse that shapes consciousness by creating the categories through which the social world is made meaningful.... [L]aw is part of social life, not an entity that stands above, beyond, or outside of it".[13] My methodological approach is detailed in Chapter 2. Briefly, I examine legislative and state discourse through the lens of language as social practice, uncovering how notions of the 'rule of law' and state legitimacy have been constructed in Singapore, arguing that though the state claims the

Singapore: Independence of the Judiciary and the Legal Profession in Singapore" (22 October 2007), online: Lawyers' Rights Watch Canada <http://www.lrwc.org/pub1.php >.

12 The state's description of itself as Westminster is, as Rodan has noted, insistent: Garry Rodan, "Westminster in Singapore: Now You See It, Now You Don't", in Haig Patapan, John Wanna & Patrick Weller, eds., *Westminster Legacies: Democracy and Responsible Government in Asia and the Pacific* (Sydney: UNSW Press, 2005) 109 at 110 [*Westminster in Singapore*].

13 Mark Kessler, "Lawyers and Social Change in the Postmodern World" (1995) 29:4 *Law & Soc'y Rev.* 769 at 772. Kessler's article presents discursive studies of 'law' as an alternative to traditional law and society studies requiring "scientific, empirical research" (at 771).

liberalism of the 'rule of law', its instrumentalist legalism is more properly labelled 'rule by law'.[14]

I use the binaries 'rule of law' / 'rule by law' as shorthands for these two modes of 'law'. Briefly, 'rule of law' signifies 'law' which, in content[15] and in institutional arrangements,[16] prevents "arbitrary power and excludes wide discretionary authority".[17] In contrast, 'rule by law' signifies 'law' which, in content and institutional execution, is susceptible to power such that the rights content of 'law', and restraints on and scrutiny of state power, are undermined. I expand upon my use of these terms and address some of the contestations around 'rule of law' later in this chapter. I should also explain that, in keeping with sociological conventions, I mark with single quotation marks the terms I problematise as social constructs[18] – terms such as 'law', 'nation' and 'race', along with other, related concepts.

WHY SINGAPORE MATTERS

Singapore's troubling success lies in the way markets, 'politics' and 'law' have been managed such that the state is pervasive, constitutional processes have been substantively erased,[19] yet national and international

[14] Li-ann Thio, "Lex Rex or Rex Lex? Competing Conceptions of the Rule of Law in Singapore" (2002) 20 *UCLA Pac. Basin L.J.* 1 at 75 [*Lex Rex or Rex Lex?*]; Kanishka Jayasuriya, "The Exception Becomes the Norm: Law and Regimes of Exception in East Asia" (2001) 2:1 *Asian Pac. L. & Pol'y J.* 108 at 118 [*The Exception Becomes the Norm*].

[15] Brian Z. Tamanaha, *On the Rule of Law: History, Politics, Theory* (Cambridge: Cambridge University Press, 2004) 114.

[16] David Clark, "The Many Meanings of the Rule of Law", in Kanishka Jayasuriya, ed., *Law, Capitalism and Power in Asia: The Rule of Law and Legal Institutions* (London: Routledge, 1999) 28 at 30.

[17] Ibid.

[18] Social categories and constructs are some of the "deeper classification schemes that organise experience, perception and interpretation, structure communication and are reflected upon, articulated, brought to awareness and made into objects of conflict by discourse": Piet Strydom, *Discourse and Knowledge: The Making of Enlightenment Sociology* (Liverpool: Liverpool University Press, 2000) at 10.

[19] Rodan, *Westminster in Singapore*, *supra* note 12 at 110.

legitimacy[20] for the state has been sustained. In 2007, when the Australian National University conferred an honorary doctorate on Lee Kuan Yew, one protestor's placard read, "What next? Masters for Mugabe?"[21] This provocation prompts difficult questions: Does it matter if a regime that secures and sustains general prosperity has also decimated political opponents and prevented institutional autonomy in the media, the courts and civil society? Does the delivery of employment, infrastructure and social order make for some sort of realpolitik balance sheet in which the political violence visited upon a few is set off against general contentment? To even begin to address this conundrum – a normative quagmire – requires a nuanced appreciation of a legal system poised to become a model for other jurisdictions, including, most notably, China.[22] In addition to states[23]

[20] I use the term 'legitimacy' in a broad sense to connote the kind of embedded, everyday acceptability – national and international – that Singapore enjoys, such that events like the IBA are well attended and well organised, subordinating the critique of Singapore's 'rule by law'.

[21] Emma Macdonald, "ANU Protesters to Corner Lee", *Canberra Times* (28 March 2007).

[22] Gordon Silverstein, "Singapore: The Exception That Proves Rules Matter", in Tom Ginsburg & Tamir Moustafa, eds., *Rule by Law* (Cambridge: Cambridge University Press, 2008) 73 at 98 [*The Exception That Proves Rules Matter*]; Lee Kuan Yew, *From Third World to First: The Singapore Story, 1965–2000* (Singapore: Times Editions, 2000), 718 [*From Third World to First*]. Hilton L. Root & Karen May, "Judicial Systems and Economic Development", in Tom Ginsburg & Tamir Moustafa, eds., *Rule by Law: The Politics of Courts in Authoritarian Regimes* (New York: Cambridge University Press, 2008) 304. Rodan notes how Vietnam and China have set out to emulate Singapore's regulatory model for Internet control: Garry Rodan, "The Internet and Political Control in Singapore" (1998) 113:1 *Political Science Quarterly* 63 at 87–88. The contemporary scholarship on the 'rule of law' is increasingly alert to the exportability of 'rule by law' and the manner in which 'Western' formulations of 'rule of law' attributes contribute to this emerging trend: Gordon Silverstein, "Globalisation and the Rule of Law: 'A Machine That Runs of Itself?' " (2003) 1:3 *International Journal of Constitutional Law* 427. See also the Ministry of Law's website: "Visit by Delegation from China's State Intellectual Property Office" (26 November 2008) and "Visit by Deputy Commissioner of the State Intellectual Property Office, People's Republic of China" (24 November 2010), http://app2.mlaw.gov.sg/News/tabid/204/ctgy/Visit/currentpage/2/Default.aspx#mlato.

[23] Some other states that appear to be studying Singapore's management of 'law' are Qatar, United Arab Emirates, and Cambodia; http://app2.mlaw.gov.sg/News/tabid/204/ctgy/Visit/currentpage/2/Default.aspx#mlatop.

such as China[24] and Vietnam,[25] institutions such as the World Bank have been lauding Singapore's legal system.[26] In short, despite being a tiny island of just 720 square kilometres[27] with a population of about 5.08 million,[28] Singapore matters because it has powerful admirers who are seeking to adopt and replicate the Singapore model of 'law'.

The appeal of Singapore's legal system to China and Vietnam is particularly significant given that Singapore has a certain fluency in the 'rule of law' derived from having been a British colony. As a former British colony, Singapore stepped into independence equipped with institutions and structures for the 'common law' and Westminster government.[29] Singapore is thus positioned to instruct states without the same legal history, or the same sophistication in media management,[30] on how to structure a version of the 'rule of law' that negotiates international acceptability alongside high levels of state control of social actors with

[24] See references at supra note 22.

[25] "Vietnam to Bolster Singapore Ties, Particularly on Law", *Thai News Service* (21 August 2007); Ministry of Law press releases archived online: Ministry of Law <http://app2.mlaw.gov.sg>: "Singapore and Vietnam Sign Agreement on Legal and Judicial Cooperation" (12 March 2008); "Vietnam Ministry of Justice Delegation Visits MinLaw" (30 June 2008); "Vietnam Ministry of Justice Delegation Visits MinLaw (16 June 2009); "Visit by Dr. Dinh Trung Tung, Vice Minister from the Ministry of Justice, Vietnam (8 July 2009); "Visit by the Vietnam Lawyers' Association" (23 September 2009).

[26] Waleed Haider Malik, *Judiciary-Led Reforms in Singapore: Frameworks, Strategies, and Lessons* (Washington, DC: World Bank, 2007).

[27] Rodolphe De Konick, Julie Drolet & Marc Girard, *Singapore: An Atlas of Perpetual Territorial Transformation* (Singapore: NUS Press, 2008) 86. Singapore has added about 140 square kilometres to its territory through land reclamation.

[28] This figure is for 2010. Singapore Department of Statistics Press Release: http://www.singstat.gov.sg/news/press31082010pdf.

[29] Rodan, *Westminster in Singapore*, *supra* note 12.

[30] Jonathan Woodier argues that the Singapore state offers a model for authoritarian regimes on how to skilfully manage a media image that projects the state as more liberal than it is and sustains regime longevity: Jonathan Woodier, "Securing Singapore/Managing Perceptions: From Shooting the Messenger to Dodging the Question" (2006) 23 *Copenhagen Journal of Asian Studies* 57. The ironic and rather damning facets of this argument appear to have been misunderstood in at least one mainstream media representation of it: Jeremy Au Yong, "Singapore Govt Wins Kudos for Smart PR", *Straits Times* (24 July 2008).

(actual or potential) political presence. In other words, Singapore is poised to export a version of 'rule *by* law' that serves state power while managing perceptions of legitimacy. In unpacking legislation and public discourse in Singapore, this study presents an argument that is about both why and how. Why is 'law' so central to Singapore's presentation of itself and how has it managed to construct what may seem an oxymoron: authoritarian legitimacy?

AUTHORITARIAN LEGITIMACY

It is important to note that if today's Singapore is regarded by some as authoritarian,[31] authoritarianism was not how the Singapore story began. The monopoly of politics,[32] the institutionalisation of the ruling party[33] – these are outcomes of the past fifty years of government by one party, the People's Action Party. And the nature of authoritarianism in Singapore is not straightforward either. While the state describes itself as a Westminster-model democracy,[34] scholars have assessed Singapore differently. The range of descriptions applied include authoritarian,[35] semi-authoritarian,[36] soft authoritarian,[37] Asian democracy,[38]

[31] Garry Rodan, *Transparency and Authoritarian Rule in Southeast Asia: Singapore and Malaysia* (London: Routledge Curzon, 2004) [*Authoritarian Rule*]; Daniel A. Bell, "A Communitarian Critique of Authoritarianism: The Case of Singapore" (1997) 25:1 *Political Theory* 6.

[32] Rodan, *Authoritarian Rule*, *supra* note 31 at 1.

[33] Rodan, *Westminster in Singapore*, *supra* note 12.

[34] See, for example, Chief Justice Chan Sek Keong, Keynote Address to New York State Bar Association Seasonal Meeting (27 October 2009), online: Supreme Court of Singapore <www.supcourt.gov.sg> at paragraphs 17 and 18. See also Rodan, *Westminster in Singapore*, *supra* note 12. Rodan notes the state's "insistence" that it is Westminster-style government at 110.

[35] Rodan, *Authoritarian Rule*, *supra* note 31; Bell, *supra* note 31.

[36] Shanthi Kalathil & Taylor C. Boas, *Open Networks; Closed Regimes: The Impact of the Internet on Authoritarian Rule* (Washington, DC: Carnegie Endowment for International Peace, 2003).

[37] Cherian George, *Contentious Journalism and the Internet: Towards Democratic Discourse in Malaysia and Singapore* (Singapore: Singapore University Press, 2006) at 27.

[38] Ibid.

semi-democracy,[39] illiberal democracy,[40] communitarian democracy,[41] dictatorship,[42] pseudo-democracy,[43] limited democracy,[44] mandatory democracy,[45] despotic state,[46] "decent, non-democratic state",[47] and hegemonic electoral authoritarian.[48] This plethora of descriptors embracing the poles of despotism and democracy, alongside multiple qualifiers, signals the complexity of Singapore as a regime type. For purposes of this study, I treat Singapore as authoritarian because it is "characterised by a concentration of power and the obstruction of serious political competition with, or scrutiny of, that power".[49] The case studies of this project illustrate the ways in which Singapore authoritarianism expresses itself through 'law', with legislation removing constraints upon state power and reinforcing the hegemony of the "virtual one-party state".[50]

Given that Singapore is an authoritarian polity, it becomes important to highlight that authoritarianism and the 'rule of law' are not mutually incompatible. Indeed, "the rule of law ideal initially developed in non-liberal societies".[51] In these non-liberal polities, rights and liberties existed,

[39] Ibid.

[40] Ibid.

[41] Beng-Huat Chua, *Communitarian Ideology and Democracy in Singapore* (London: Routledge, 1995); Li-ann Thio, "Rule of Law Within a Non-Liberal 'Communitarian' Democracy: The Singapore Experience", in Randall Peerenboom, ed., *Asian Discourses of Rule of Law* (London: Routledge, 2004) 183 [*Rule of Law*].

[42] George, *supra* note 38.

[43] Eugene K. B. Tan, " 'WE' v. 'I': Communitarian Legalism in Singapore" (2002) 4 *Australian Journal of Asian Law* 1.

[44] Ibid.

[45] Ibid.

[46] Ibid.

[47] Ibid.

[48] Larry Diamond, "Thinking About Hybrid Regimes" (2002) 13:2 *Journal of Democracy* 21.

[49] Rodan, *Authoritarian Rule*, *supra* note 31 at 1.

[50] Rodan, *Westminster in Singapore*, *supra* note 12.

[51] Tamanaha, *supra* note 15 at 5.

but as grants that "depended on the consent of sovereign power".[52] In the non-liberal societies which gave birth to the 'rule of law', if rights were somehow contingent, restraints on state power were not.[53] Even in the authoritarianism of the pre-liberal state, the 'rule of law' was understood as government limited by law.[54] After the American and French revolutions, the place of rights in 'law' shifted so that

> rights are recognized as existing prior to the power of the sovereign ... lead[ing] to the establishment of a new form of political rule, one which contains at its core the necessity of maintaining and protecting the "natural rights" of individuals.[55]

If individual rights are at the heart of liberal conceptions of the 'rule of law',[56] this exaltation of individual freedoms builds upon the pre-liberal "widespread and unquestioned belief in the rule of law, in the inviolability of certain fundamental legal restraints on government ... attitudes *about* law provide the limits".[57] The data scrutinised by this study – legislation and state discourse on 'law' – capture the essence of an authoritarian state's attitudes about 'law' and show that the Singapore state neither adheres to the pre-liberal constraints on government, nor regards individual rights as inviolable. Just as the state has appropriated and emasculated Westminster institutions and ideologies as "an adjunct to, rather than as a constraint against" state authoritarianism,[58] this study demonstrates the manner in which Singapore has selectively performed emasculated facets of the 'rule of law', facets which lack that core capacity to limit state power.

[52] Martin Loughlin, *Sword and Scales: An Examination of the Relationship Between Law and Politics* (Oxford: Hart 2000) at 202.

[53] Ibid. at 29.

[54] Tamanaha, *supra* note 15 at 58.

[55] Loughlin, *supra* note 52 at 198.

[56] Tamanaha, *supra* note 15 at 32.

[57] Ibid. at 58.

[58] Rodan, *Westminster in Singapore*, *supra* note 12 at 109. See also Andrew Harding, "The 'Westminster Model' Constitution Overseas: Transplantation, Adaptation and Development in Commonwealth States" (2004) 4 *Oxford Commonwealth Law Journal* 143.

As a study of 'law' in an authoritarian state, this project extends the body of scholarship on how the 'rule of law' is dismantled.[59] In contrast to the extensive scholarly and institutional attention given to building the 'rule of law', there is very little literature on how its dismantling occurs.[60] The small body of literature on how the 'rule of law' has been dismantled touches on one or another fragment of this process: how courts in authoritarian regimes perform a range of governance, social control and regime legitimation functions;[61] how failures by the bar to mobilise for the protection of judicial autonomy leave the judiciary vulnerable to attack;[62] how strategies of governance mask the dismantling of judicial independence;[63] how a legal system driven by the political economy creates courts ideologically aligned to the state[64]; how the formal and procedural regularities of 'law' can constitute a minimum and legitimising

[59] Extending Rodan's arguments (*Westminster in Singapore, supra* note 12), it is arguable that liberal 'rule of law' ideas and institutions have perhaps held a brief place in the history of Singapore. The lively political pluralism of the post–World War II period has been noted by a range of other scholars as well. See, for example, Tim Harper, "Lim Chin Siong and the 'Singapore Story,' " in Tan Jing Quee & Jomo K.S., eds., *Comet in Our Sky: Lim Chin Siong in History* (Kuala Lumpur: Insan, 2001) 3; Hong Lysa & Huang Jianli, *The Scripting of a National History: Singapore and Its Pasts* (Singapore: NUS Press, 2008); and Michael D. Barr & Carl A. Trocki, eds., *Paths Not Taken: Political Pluralism in Post-War Singapore* (Singapore: NUS Press, 2008).

[60] Peerenboom makes a parallel point, noting that the voluminous literature on 'rule of law' in 'Western' contexts is in "striking contrast to the ... relatively little work ... clarifying alternative conceptions of rule of law in other parts of the world, including Asia": Randall Peerenboom, "Varieties of Rule of Law: An Introduction and Provisional Conclusion", in Randall Peerenboom, ed., *Asian Discourses of Rule of Law* (London: Routledge, 2004) 1 at 5.

[61] Tom Ginsburg & Tamir Moustafa, eds., *Rule by Law: The Politics of Courts in Authoritarian Regimes* (New York: Cambridge University Press, 2008).

[62] Terence C. Halliday & Lucien Karpik, "Politics Matter: A New Framework for the Comparative and Historical Study of Legal Professions", in Terence C. Halliday & Lucien Karpik, eds., *Lawyers and the Rise of Western Political Liberalism* (Oxford: Clarendon Press, 1997) 15.

[63] Ross Worthington, *Governance in Singapore* (London: Routledge Curzon, 2003).

[64] Kanishka Jayasuriya, ed., *Law, Capitalism and Power in Asia: The Rule of Law and Legal Institutions* (London: Routledge, 1999) [*Law, Capitalism and Power*]; Silverstein, *The Exception That Proves Rules Matter, supra* 22 at 98.

'thin rule of law'[65]; and how socialist states create their own legalities and reinterpret the 'rule of law'.[66]

Although establishing a valuable foundation, none of these works or other scholarship on contemporary authoritarianism offers a comprehensive account of a sustained and successful dismantling of the 'rule of law'. Even scholarship on Singapore authoritarianism,[67] while providing a valuable foundation for this project, has not offered a systematic treatment of the role of legislation and public discourse in dismantling and reconfiguring the 'rule of law'. This project applies discourse theory to

[65] Peerenboom, *supra* note 60; Thio, *Rule of Law*, *supra* note 41 at 183.

[66] John Gillespie & Pip Nicholson, "The Diversity and Dynamism of Legal Change in Socialist China and Vietnam", in John Gillespie & Pip Nicholson, eds., *Asian Socialism and Legal Change* (Canberra: Asia Pacific Press, 2005) 1; Sarah Biddulph, *Legal Reform and Administrative Detention Powers in China* (Cambridge: Cambridge University Press, 2007); Mark Sidel, *Law and Society in Vietnam* (Cambridge: Cambridge University Press, 2008); John Gillespie, "Understanding Legality in Vietnam", in Stephanie Balme & Mark Sidel, eds., *Vietnam's New Order* (New York: Palgrave Macmillan, 2007) 137; Pip Nicholson, "Vietnamese Courts: Contemporary Interactions Between Party-State and Law", in Stephanie Balme & Mark Sidel, eds., *Vietnam's New Order* (New York: Palgrave Macmillan, 2007) 178; Randall Peerenboom, "Competing Conceptions of Rule of Law in China", in Randall Peerenboom, ed., *Asian Discourses of Rule of Law* (London: Routledge, 2004) 113; Pip Nicholson, *Borrowing Court Systems* (Leiden: Martinus Nijhoff, 2007) (Part Four in particular traces links and departures between the Soviet and the Vietnamese court systems); William A. W. Neilson, "Reforming Commercial Laws in Asia: Strategies and Realities for Donor Agencies", in Timothy Lindsey, ed., *Indonesia: Bankruptcy, Law Reform and the Commercial Court* (Sydney: Desert Pea Press, 2000) 15.

[67] Chua, *supra* note 41; Li-ann Thio, "'Pragmatism and Realism Do Not Mean Abdication': A Critical and Empirical Inquiry into Singapore's Engagement with International Human Rights Law" (2004) 8 *Singapore Year Book of International Law* 41 [Pragmatism and Realism]; Thio, *Rule of Law*, *supra* note 41; Christopher Tremewan, *The Political Economy of Social Control* (Hampshire: Macmillan Press, 1994); Garry Rodan, "Singapore 'Exceptionalism'? Authoritarian Rule and State Transformation", in Edward Friedman & Joseph Wong, eds., *Political Transitions in Dominant Party Systems: Learning to Lose* (London: Routledge, 2008) 231; Rodan, *Authoritarian Rule*, *supra* note 31; Rodan, *Westminster in Singapore*, *supra* note 12; Manuel Castells, "The Developmental City-State in an Open World Economy: The Singapore Experience" (Berkeley: University of California, 1988), online: <http://brie.berkeley.edu/publications/working_papers.html>.

legislation in order to repair this gap in the scholarship while excavating the political processes underpinning the formulation and application of enactments. While there is a well-established scholarly literature on Singapore as an authoritarian state (as noted) and although the role of courts in Singapore has also been well studied,[68] the political processes by which legislation has been formulated, justified and applied have received almost no attention.[69]

In studying the operations of 'law' through a focus on legislation and state discourse, this project is explicitly directed at "law imposed by a political superior onto a political inferior".[70] This focus on the source and speech of political power is surely necessary in studying a de facto one-party state. A focus on legislation is important for another reason: As text, legislation has an oddly clean, ahistorical appearance. Judgments, that other primary source of 'law' in a 'common law' system, reveal argument and challenges to interpretation in a way that legislation does not. Legislation sits on the statute books stripped of histories and skirmishes that may have informed and resisted the language that has come to be 'law'. By approaching legislation as textual moments in a narrative of state power, this study counters the ahistorical appearance of legislation and draws attention to forgotten contestations that have marked the making of 'law' – contestations rendered absent and invisible in legislation's final text.

Reading legislation in tandem with contextual discourse allows me to trace the history of the state's construction of a discursive definition of 'law'. This study reveals a pattern: Facilitated by state dominance of the

[68] Worthington, *supra* note 63; Jayasuriya, *Law, Capitalism and Power*, *supra* note 64; Thio, *Rule of Law*, *supra* note 41; Ginsburg & Moustafa, *supra* note 61; Silverstein, *The Exception That Proves Rules Matter*, *supra* note 22.

[69] In addition to drawing on the legal texts of judgments and legislation, I have drawn on other sources which capture state discourse, such as parliamentary debates, Select Committee Hearings and newspaper reports.

[70] Margaret Davies, *Asking the Law Question: The Dissolution of Legal Theory* (Sydney: Lawbook, 2002) 27.

public domain, the state's meanings become entrenched in three related steps. First, state meanings are institutionalised through legislation; second, they are normalised through reiteration in the public domain; and finally, when the state's inherently ideological definitions are adopted by the courts, they become even more legitimised and are given the appearance of 'neutral' and self-evident 'truths'.

Singapore's complex and contingent discourses on 'law' are so central to the analysis and argument presented that I ground the case studies and the methodological discussion in a genealogy for 'rule of law' and 'rule by law' in Singapore. Before launching into this genealogy for Singapore 'law', however, I will account for the choice of legislation examined by this project.

CASE STUDIES OF 'LAWS' THAT SILENCE

The five enactments which form the empirical heart of this project – the *Vandalism Act*, the *Press Act*, the 1986 amendments to the *Legal Profession Act*, the *Religious Harmony Act*, and the *Public Order Act* – demonstrate that the state has enacted 'law' in response to moments of contestation in the public domain. More importantly, these 'laws' have been instrumental in silencing critique emanating from non-state actors and institutions while sustaining the government's standing as a 'rule of law' regime. In this way, legislation has been central to effecting illiberalism.

Illiberalism, as the Other of liberalism, might be understood in terms of the absences, fractures and subversions of political liberalism. If political liberalism[71] is disaggregated as, first, the existence and protection of

[71] I adopt the "legal concept of political liberalism": Terence C. Halliday, Lucien Karpik & Malcolm Feeley, "Introduction: The Legal Complex in Struggles for Political Liberalism", in Terence C. Halliday, Lucien Karpik & Malcolm Feeley, eds., *Fighting for Political Freedom: Comparative Studies of the Legal Complex for Political Change* (Oxford: Hart, 2007) 1 at 10–11.

the basic legal freedoms of individuals, second, the moderation of state power (most crucially by autonomous courts) and, third, civil society,[72] then these Acts might be understood as augmenting state power by undermining these features of political liberalism. Basic legal freedoms are those freedoms that

> reside in the core rights of citizenship ... [and] rest upon the granting of legal personality to a citizen and the protection of all residents within a sovereign legal jurisdiction. These freedoms include the institutionalisation of juridical rights (eg, rights to due process in law, habeas corpus, legal representation and access to justice, freedom from arbitrary arrest, torture and death) ... and the protection of foundational political freedoms (eg, speech, faith, travel, association).[73]

The case studies illustrate a range of ways in which the courts have been constrained, civil society dismantled and basic legal freedoms disregarded. Put differently, these Acts have silenced non-state actors that, in conditions of political liberalism, would enable advocates for 'law' (such as the legal professions and civil society) to moderate state power.[74] In brief, the legislation I study illustrates that 'law' has been the state's instrument for silencing critique.

A second reason for selecting these Acts is that they demonstrate how, despite a 'rule of law' procedural correctness in their enactment, crucial legislative terms have taken on (often oppressive) ideological meanings peculiar to Singapore. In other words, legislative language lacks the clarity and autonomy from the state that it should, in 'rule of law' terms, exemplify. This feature of the Acts is particularly ironic given Lee's 2007 assertion to the IBA that Singapore 'law' was characterised

[72] Ibid.
[73] Ibid.
[74] Ibid.

by "clear laws".[75] A third reason determining my selection of legislation relates to the manner in which 'law' is routinely discursively presented alongside an invocation of 'nation'. The legislation I study was enacted in the first fifty years of Singapore's existence as a nation-state. All five Acts construct, reinscribe and consolidate the connectedness of 'law' and 'nation'. These enactments and the discourses in which they are situated illustrate the thematic consistency of the Singapore state's insistence that 'law' must ensure the security, prosperity and social order of the 'nation'.

This project is concerned primarily with covert, rather than overt, modes of illiberalism and does not claim to comprehensively survey the corpus of Singapore 'law' for the range of ways in which 'law' is illiberal. Indeed, two particularly notorious instances of Singapore's legal illiberalism – defamation proceedings against political opponents and the *Internal Security Act* (enabling detention without trial) – are not studied. These illiberal facets of 'law', while beyond the parameters of this study, are related issues.

The *Internal Security Act*[76] (*ISA*) is the nation-state's reformulation of the colonial state's *Emergency Regulations*. The *Emergency Regulations* were originally designed to enable detention without trial during the Malayan Emergency (1948–60), the colonial state's response to the Malayan Communist Party's decision to take up an armed struggle.[77] The *ISA* has, unfortunately, become a fixed feature of the Singapore

[75] Lee, *Why Singapore Is What It Is*, *supra* note 7.

[76] *Internal Security Act* (Cap. 143, 1985 Rev. Ed. Sing.).

[77] Yeo and Lau note that the Emergency Regulations, by prohibiting all public meetings except at election times, and empowering the police screening of union leaders cleared the political arena of left-wing politicians unacceptable to the colonial state: Yeo Kim Wah & Albert Lau, "From Colonialism to Independence, 1945–1965", in Ernest Chew & Edwin Lee eds., *A History of Singapore* (Singapore: Oxford University Press, 1991) 117 at 124. See also C. C. Chin & Karl Hack, eds., *Dialogues with Chin Peng: New Light on the Malayan Communist Party*, 2nd ed. (Singapore: Singapore University Press, 2005).

scene. The crude 'rule of law' violations of the *ISA* have been well noted in scholarly literature,[78] as have the Act's applications against political opponents of the state.[79]

[78] For a sampling, see Li-Ann Thio, "Taking Rights Seriously? Human Rights Law in Singapore", in Randall Peerenboom & Andrew Chen, eds., *Human Rights in Asia* (London: Routledge Curzon, 2006) 158; Michael Hor, "Law and Terror: Singapore Stories and Malaysian Dilemmas", in Michael Hor, Victor Ramraj & Kent Roach, eds., *Global Anti-Terrorism Law and Policy* (Cambridge: Cambridge University Press, 2005) 273; Michael Hor, "Terrorism and the Criminal Law: Singapore's Solution" (2002) *S.J.L.S.* 30; Damien Chong, "Enhancing National Security Through the Rule of Law: Singapore's Recasting of the Internal Security Act as an Anti-Terrorism Legislation" (2005) 5 *AsiaRights Journal* 1; Simon Tay, "Human Rights, Culture and the Singapore Example" (1996) 41 *McGill L.J.* 743; H. F. Rawlings, "Habeas Corpus and Preventive Detention in Singapore and Malaysia" (1983) 25 *Mal. L. Rev.* 324; Tan Yock Lin, "Some Aspects of Executive Detention in Malaysia and Singapore" (1987) 29 *Mal. L. Rev.* 237; S. Jayakumar, "Emergency Powers in Malaysia, Development of the Law, 1957–1977" (1978) 1 *M.L.J.* ix; Low Hop Bing, "Habeas Corpus in Malaysia and Singapore" (1977) 2 *M.L.J.* iv; Rowena Daw, "Preventive Detention in Singapore: A Comment on the Case of Lee Mau Seng" (1972) 14 *Mal. L. Rev.* 276; R. H. Hickling, "Some Aspects of Fundamental Liberties Under the Constitution of the Federation of Malaya" (1963) 2 *M.L.J.* xiv; R. H. Hickling, "The First Five Years of the Federation of Malaya Constitution" (1962) 4 *Mal. L. Rev.* 183; Francis Seow, *The Media Enthralled: Singapore Revisited* (Boulder: Lynne Rienner, 1998); Jayasuriya, *Law, Capitalism and Power, supra* note 64; Silverstein, *The Exception That Proves Rules, supra* note 22; Thio, *Pragmatism and Realism supra* note 67; Rodan, *Authoritarian Rule, supra* note 31; Tremewan, *supra* note 67. Geoff Wade, "Operation Cold Store: A Key Event in the Creation of Malaysia and in the Origins of Modern Singapore", Paper presented at the 21st Conference of the International Association of Historians of Asia, 21–25 June 2010.

[79] For a sampling see J. B. Jeyaretnam, "The Rule of Law in Singapore", in *The Rule of Law and Human Rights in Malaysia and Singapore: A Report of the Conference Held at the European Parliament* (Limelette, 1989) 37; Fong Hoe Fang, ed., *That We May Dream Again* (Singapore: Ethos, 2009); Tan Jing Quee, Teo Soh Lung & Koh Kay Yew, eds., *Our Thoughts Are Free: Poems and Prose on Imprisonment and Exile* (Singapore: Ethos, 2009); Said Zahari, *The Long Nightmare: My 17 Years as a Political Prisoner* (Kuala Lumpur: Utusan, 2007); Chris Lydgate, *Lee's Law: How Singapore Crushes Dissent* (Melbourne: Scribe, 2003); Asia Watch, *Silencing All Critics: Human Rights Violations in Singapore* (Washington, DC, 1989); Lawyers Rights Watch Canada, "Singapore: Independence of the Judiciary and the Legal Profession in Singapore" (17 October 2007); Chee Soon Juan, *Dare to Change: An Alternative Vision for Singapore* (Singapore: Singapore Democratic Party, 1994); Teo Soh Lung, *Beyond the Blue Gate: Recollections of a Political Prisoner* (Singapore: Ethos, 2010); Poh Soo Kai, Tan Jing Quee & Koh Kay Yew eds., *The Fajar Generation: The University Socialist Club and*

My excluding the *ISA* as a case study has, however, been ironically subverted by the insidious persistence of internal security detentions in the sub-strata of events relating to three of the four Acts studied: the *Press Act*, the *Legal Profession Act* and the *Religious Harmony Act*. Additionally, the core illiberalisms displayed by the five Acts might be read as the *ISA* writ large in three crucial ways. First, like the *ISA*, all five case studies reveal the exclusion or containment of the courts. Second, like the *ISA*, all five case studies involve legislative text that facilitates an interpretive imprecision weighted in favour of the state's accusatory characterisations, transforming dissent into a security threat. And third, as in the case of the *ISA*, the state's accusations need never be scrutinised or substantiated because the state claims to be preventing and pre-empting an emergency.

There is, however, an important distinguishing feature that sets the five enactments I study apart from the *ISA*. The case studies of this project, unlike the *ISA*, are not obvious 'rule by law' instruments encoding the legal exceptionalism through which the state manages extreme threats. The legislative instruments I study *conceal* their 'rule by law' nature. Bearing in mind the alarming attainment of legitimacy for the Singapore state's 'rule by law', the masking of legislation as a tool of repression warrants attention. The instruments I study construct a homogenised public domain, incrementally and almost invisibly. Alongside the crude repression of the *ISA*, it is covert 'rule by law' that appears to have facilitated the legitimacy of the Singapore state.

If the *ISA* is one illiberal facet of Singapore 'law' that has most widely and most consistently earned the state a measure of notoriety, then the use of defamation proceedings against opposition politicians and critics of the state is another. Defamation 'law' in Singapore is, broadly speaking, the 'common law' conception of defamation,[80] although Singapore

the Politics of Postwar Malaya and Singapore (Petaling Jaya: Strategic Information and Research Development Centre, 2010).

[80] Doris Chia & Rueben Mathiavaranam, *Evans on Defamation in Singapore and Malaysia*, 3rd ed. (Singapore: LexisNexis, 2008) 3.

courts have developed a uniquely Singaporean formulation with regard to damages[81] and have limited the applicability of 'common law' defamation in certain ways.[82] In contrast to the standard common law parameters for damages, in which public figures are expected to be able to deal with a degree of public criticism, Singapore courts have adopted the state's reasoning in holding that the reputations of political leaders are especially vulnerable to public opinion[83] and thus warrant a higher accounting of damages than when calculating damages for ordinary people.[84] Jurisprudence on the related offence of scandalising the court has also generated a uniquely Singaporean standard that inhibits

[81] Michael Hor, "The Freedom of Speech and Defamation" (1992) *S.J.L.S.* 542; Li-ann Thio, "Singapore: Regulating Political Speech and the Commitment 'to Build a Democratic Society' " (2003) 1 *International Journal of Constitutional Law* 516 at 523–24 [*Regulating Political Speech*]; Tsun Hung Tey, "Confining the Freedom of the Press in Singapore: A 'Pragmatic' Press for 'Nation-Building'?" (2008) 30:4 *Hum. Rts. Q.* 876 at 902; Tsun Hung Tey, "Singapore's Jurisprudence of Political Defamation and Its Triple-Whammy Impact on Political Speech" (2008) *Public Law.* 452; Cameron Sim, "The Singapore Chill: Political Defamation and the Normalisation of a Statist Rule of Law" (2011) 20:2 *Pac. Rim L. & Pol'y J.* 319; *Lee Kuan Yew v. J. B. Jeyaretnam*, [1979] 1 M.L.J. 281; *Lee Kuan Yew v. Seow Khee Leng*, [1989] 1 M.L.J. 172; *Lee Kuan Yew v. Derek Gwynn Davies & Ors.* [1990] 1 M.L.J. 390; *Lee Kuan Yew & Anor. v. Vinocur & Ors. & Another Action*, [1995] 3 Sing. L.R. 477; *Goh Chok Tong v. Jeyaretnam Joshua Benjamin*, [1998] 1 Sing. L.R. (upheld in *Goh Chok Tong v. Jeyaretnam Joshua Benjamin & Another Action*, [1998] 3 Sing. L.R. 337 (C.A.)); *Goh Chok Tong v. Chee Soon Juan (No. 2)*, [2005] 1 Sing. L.R. 573; *Lee Kuan Yew v. Chee Soon Juan (No. 2)*, [2005] 1 Sing. L.R. 552. See also jurisprudence cited at note 230 below.

[82] In *Attorney-General v. Wain and Others (No.1)* [1991] 1 Sing.L.R. 383, the High Court limited the applicability of English 'common law' on defamation and contempt to the pre-1981 position, citing developments in statute 'law' and the European Court of Human Rights as reasons to exclude post-1981 English decisions. Jurisprudence from a range of other 'common law' and Commonwealth jurisdictions was also excluded for a various reasons that were not especially convincing.

[83] A Deputy Prime Minister who also holds the office of Minister for Home Affairs reiterated the state's position recently when he said that the government "must robustly defend the integrity of our institutions of justice and law enforcement when anyone maliciously attacks and undermines the public confidence and trust which have been earned over the years." S. Ramesh, "Why S'pore Must 'Robustly' Defend Its Courts, Police Force", *Today* (4 August 2010).

[84] Ibid.

free speech.[85] As with the *ISA*, this feature of Singapore 'law' has been well studied.[86]

The legislation I study points to a different strand of state legal practices in two important ways. First, defamation proceedings have (inter alia) been directed at individuals who enter the public domain as explicit political opponents.[87] In contrast, none of the Acts featured as case studies in my project have acknowledged their targets as political opponents.

[85] Thio Li-ann, "Legal Systems in Singapore: Chapter 3 – Government and the State", Legal Systems in ASEAN, online: <http://www.aseanlawassociation.org/legal-sing.html>, 13–14; Tsun Hung Tey, "Singapore's Jurisprudence of Defamation and Scandalising the Judiciary", Paper presented at the Centre for Media and Communications Law Conference, Melbourne Law School, November 2008 (unpublished); Thio Li-ann, "The Virtual and the Real: Article 14, Political Speech and the Calibrated Management of Deliberative Democracy in Singapore" (2008) *Sing. J.L.S.* 25; Cameron Sim, "The Singapore Chill: Political Defamation and the Normalisation of a Statist Rule of Law" (2011) 20:2 *Pac. Rim L. & Pol'y J.* 319.

[86] Chia & Mathiavaranam, *supra* note 80; Hor, *supra* note 81; Thio, *Regulating Political Speech*, *supra* note 81, Tey, *supra* note 82; Michael Hor & Collin Seah, "Selected Issues in the Freedom of Speech and Expression in Singapore" (1991) 12 *Sing. L. Rev.* 296; Michael Hor, "Civil Disobedience and the Licensing of Speech in Singapore" (1999) *Lawasia Journal* 1.

[87] Singapore's leaders have used defamation against political opponents since 1960, when a split within the ruling PAP precipitated Lee Kuan Yew's threat to bring defamation proceedings against a cabinet minister and fellow PAP member, Ong Eng Guan: "Singapore: Its History", in Singapore Year Book 1966, reprinted in Verinder Grover, ed., *Singapore: Government and Politics* (New Delhi: Deep & Deep, 2000) 33 at 63. All of the cases cited at *supra* note 81 involve actions brought by state actors against opposition politicians. See also Gail Davidson & Howard Rubin, Q.C., for Lawyers Rights Watch Canada, "Defamation in Singapore: In the Matter of J. B. Jeyaretnam" (July 2001), online: <http://www.lrwc.org/news/report2.php>; Kelley Bryan & Howard Rubin for Lawyers Rights Watch Canada, "The Misuse of Bankruptcy Law in Singapore: An Analysis of the Matter of Re Joshua Benjamin Jeyaretnam, ex parte Indra Krishnan" (October 2004), online: <http://www.lrwc.org/documents/Misuse%20of%20Bankruptcy%20Law.Bryan& Rubin.22.10.04.pdf>; Howard Rubin for Lawyers Rights Watch Canada, "In the Matter of an Addendum to the Report to Lawyers Rights Watch on the Trial of J. B. Jeyaretnam as a Result of Observations on the Trial of Chee Soon Juan" (March 2003), online: <http://www.lrwc.org/documents/Addendum.Chee.Soon.Juan.trial.Mar.03.pdf>; Report of the Special Rapporteur on the Independence of Judges and Lawyers, UN Commission on Human Rights, 52d Sess., UN Doc. E/CN.4/1996/37.

Second, in contrast to the visibility and attention invited by defamation proceedings and internal security detentions, the enactments I study attract relatively little national or international notice. It is surely no accident that three of the five Acts studied deploy muted technologies of control enveloped within administrative and regulatory mechanisms. This enveloping that ensures the state's controlling measures lack the dramatic flourish of court proceedings or detention without trial and thus does not enter the public domain with the same demand for attention. In other words, the legislative technologies through which silencing is effected are themselves almost silent.

FROM BACKWATER TO METROPOLIS: PROSPERITY, 'RACE' AND 'LAW'

The state's account of Singapore history (an account I refer to as the national narrative) might be regarded as the primary context for 'law' with reference to 'nation'. [88] In turn, the national narrative locates various permutations of 'law' – colonial 'law', national 'law', 'English law', customary 'law', Dicey's concept of 'rule of law' – as markers of development. Unsurprisingly, the national narrative does not name 'rule by law'. Together with the strands of 'law' the national narrative does name, 'rule by law' weaves into a discursive fabric constructing and reinforcing the authority of the state. These compound and complex meanings attaching to 'law' in Singapore, indicate that 'law' sits within a context in which discourse, legal and otherwise, is marked by the recurrence of certain categories of social identity, in particular 'race',[89] 'language'[90] and

[88] Discussing the overwhelming dominance of the state's account of Singapore history, Hong and Huang (perhaps in a parody of *From Third World to First*, the title of the second volume of *The Singapore Story*, Lee Kuan Yew's two-volume memoir) write of "the 'from mangrove backwater to metropolis' line [of history], with Raffles and Lee Kuan Yew as the transformers": Hong & Huang, *supra* note 59 at 15.

[89] Geoffrey Benjamin, "The Cultural Logic of Singapore's Multiculturalism", in Riaz Hassan, ed., *Singapore: Society in Transition* (Kuala Lumpur: Oxford University Press, 1976) 115.

[90] Nirmala Srirekam PuruShotam, *Negotiating Language, Constructing Race: Disciplining Difference in Singapore* (Berlin: Mouton de Gruyter, 1998) 30–55.

'religion',[91] all framed by the category 'nation'.[92] In Singapore's national narrative, history, prosperity, 'race' and 'law'[93] entwine to produce the state's claims that, first, Singapore is a 'rule of law' state in the 'English' tradition and, second, that Singapore must, in the interests of 'nation', script departures from that same 'English' 'rule of law'. The state's pervasive narrative of national vulnerability[94] tends to be at the heart of the state's arguments as to why 'law' must be modified. When Lee Kuan Yew addressed the IBA, for example, he opened his address by characterising Singapore as a disadvantaged terrain with traumatic origins:

> [W]e were suddenly thrown out of the Federation of Malaysia.[95] ... We faced a bleak future. We had no natural resources. A small island-nation in the middle of newly independent and nationalistic countries of Indonesia and Malaysia. To survive, we had to create a Singapore different from our neighbours – clean, more efficient, more secure, with quality infrastructure and good living conditions.[96]

The trauma of an imposed nationhood layers onto other events in Singapore's past to augment the trope of vulnerability: the Japanese

[91] Tong Chee Kiong, *Rationalising Religion: Religious Conversion, Revivalism and Competition in Singapore Society* (Leiden: Brill, 2007).

[92] In Singapore, as in other former colonies, social categories such as 'race', 'religion', 'law' and 'nation' are vehicles of concepts and belief systems "authored and authorised by colonialism and Western domination" but adopted and renewed by the nation-state: Gyan Prakash, 'Subaltern Studies as Postcolonial Criticism' (1994) 99:5 *American Historical Review* 1475.

[93] For a succinct summary of the arguments on the centrality of 'law' to 'nation', see Peter Fitzpatrick, "Introduction", in Peter Fitzpatrick, ed., *Nationalism, Racism and the Rule of Law* (Aldershot: Dartmouth, 1995) xiii at xv–xvii.

[94] The uses and effects of the state's narrative of national vulnerability inform scholarship in a range of other disciplines. For a sampling see PuruShotam's sociological study, *supra* note 90; a collection of essays produced by scholars in the social sciences and the humanities, Anne Pakir & Tong Chee Kiong, eds., *Imagining Singapore*, 2nd ed. (Singapore: Eastern Universities Press, 2004); a foreign policy study, Michael Leiffer, *Singapore's Foreign Policy: Coping with Vulnerability* (Abingdon: Routledge, 2000); and from the perspective of historians, Hong & Huang, *supra* note 59.

[95] In an arrangement brokered by the departing British colonial state, Singapore was granted independence as a state in the newly formed Federation of Malaysia in 1963. In 1965, Malaysia ejected Singapore from the Federation.

[96] Lee, *Why Singapore Is What It Is*, *supra* note 7.

Occupation (1942–45)[97]; Konfrontasi with Indonesia (1962–66), which took the form of military aggression[98] and sabotage[99] and riots in Singapore and Malaysia, which are typically presented as mob violence precipitated by irresolvable differences centring on 'race' and 'religion'.[100] It is probable that the enduring efficacy of the narrative of national vulnerability rests, in part, on its resonance with the lived experience of Singaporeans of a certain generation. Vulnerability chimes with "the middle sort of knowledge"[101] and social memory.

[97] The Japanese Imperial Army was a violent occupying force. The Occupation is remembered for large-scale massacres, starvation, torture and general terror. The inhumane treatment of Australian, New Zealand and British prisoners of war, many of whom lost their lives while interred at Changi Prison or while building the so-called Death Railway through the Thai/Burmese jungles, is part of the military history that links Singapore to these countries. The Occupation has been widely written about. For a sampling, see Lee Geok Boi, *The Syonan Years: Singapore under Japanese Rule, 1942–1945* (Singapore: Epigram, 2005) and Kevin Blackburn, "Reminiscence and War Trauma: Recalling the Japanese Occupation of Singapore, 1942–1945" (2005) 33:2 *Oral History* 91.

[98] The dominant national narrative in Singapore recounts Konfrontasi (or Confrontation) as Indonesia's objection to the 1963 constitution of the Federation of Malaysia as a "neo-colonialist plot": Yeo Kim Wah & Albert Lau, "From Colonialism to Independence, 1945–1965", in Ernest C. T. Chew & Edwin Lee, eds., *A History of Singapore* (Singapore: Oxford University Press, 1991) 117 at 142–43. The Federation consisted of peninsula Malaysia, the British Borneo territories of Sabah and Sarawak, as well as Singapore. Sukarno is generally cast as the initiator of Konfrontasi. The British were heavily involved in the formation of the Federation of Malaysia. Recent scholarship reveals that the British had been covertly involved militarily in attempts to destabilise Sukarno's regime and may have been motivated to secure the Federation as a way of countering Communism in the region: Tony Stockwell, "Forging Singapore and Malaysia: Colonialism, Decolonization and Nation-Building", in Wang Gungwu, ed., *Nation-Building: Five Southeast Asian Histories* (Singapore: Institute of Southeast Asian Studies, 2005) 191 at 200–209.

[99] Harun Said Osman Hj Mohd Ali, Jackie Sam, Philip Khoo, Cheong Yip Seng, Abdul Fazil, Roderik Pestana, & Gabriel Lee, "Terror Bomb Kills 2 Girls at Bank", *Straits Times* (11 March 1965).

[100] Syed Muhd Khairudin Aljunied, *Colonialism, Violence and Muslims in Southeast Asia* (London: Routledge, 2009); Lai, Ah Eng, *Beyond Rituals and Riots: Ethnic Pluralism and Social Cohesion in Singapore* (Singapore: Eastern Universities Press, 2004); Albert Lau, *A Moment of Anguish: Singapore in Malaysia and the Politics of Disengagement* (Singapore: Times Academic Press, 2000).

[101] Colin Gordon, "Introduction", in James D. Faubion, ed., *Michel Foucault: Power* (London: Penguin, 1994) xviii.

The trope of national vulnerability has been framed by a regional context in which violence and disorder precipitated by power struggles, often linked to the Cold War (such as the Vietnam War, the Korean War, the Cultural Revolution in China, the coup in Indonesia and the long years of violence in Cambodia), 'race' politics (such as the Sri Lankan civil war),[102] periodic violence in India presented as 'religious' clashes[103] and the bewildering lack of civility periodically displayed by Taiwanese parliamentarians when they abandon debate and resort to fisticuffs.[104]

When regarded in this light, the political, social and economic stability of Singapore appears extraordinary. The state-scripted national narrative explains the Singapore success story as a product wrought through the wisdom, foresight and virtuous diligence of its leaders,[105] with emphatic attention to the inescapable vulnerability of the nation-state. In terms of 'law' and 'nation', national vulnerability is typically presented as a legitimising rationale for two further features of the Singapore legal system: first, legal exceptionalism (ousting judicial review and concentrating power in the executive on the grounds of national security); and second, dual state legality.[106] Singapore is a dual state in that it matches the 'law' of the liberal 'West' in the commercial arena while repressing civil and political individual rights.[107] The bifurcation of Singapore's legal system is so distinct that the Canadian courts have recently specified that Singapore courts have parity with Canadian courts in commercial matters,[108] a specification that might be seen as implicit acknowledgement of different standards in other realms of 'law'. In a similar vein, the World Justice

102 See, for example, Zakir Hussain, "Religious Harmony: 20 Years of Keeping the Peace", *Straits Times* (24 July 2009).

103 Ibid.

104 Chin Ko-lin, *Heijin: Organized Crime, Business, and Politics in Taiwan* (Armonk, New York: MESharp 2003).

105 Hong & Huang, *supra* note 59.

106 Kanishka Jayasuriya, "Introduction", in Jayasuriya, *Law, Capitalism and Power*, *supra* note 64 [*Introduction*].

107 Ibid.

108 *Oakwell Engineering Ltd. v. Enernorth Industries Inc.*, 2005 CanLII 2218 ON Sup. Ct. 7 B.L.R. (4th) 256.

Project has ranked Singapore first among its socio-economic peers for access to civil justice and order and security, while ranking it last in terms of open government and fundamental rights.[109]

Lee's address to the IBA was consistent with employing dual state legality to justify the state's use of legal exceptionalism. He described Singapore's legal system as "similar to" London and New York in terms of "laws relating to financial services", while characterising repressive, rights-violating legislation, such as the *Internal Security Act*[110] and the *Maintenance of Religious Harmony Act*,[111] as "special legislation to meet our needs".[112] The instrumental applications of the state's accounts of Singapore's history featuring the tropes of Singapore exceptionalism and Singapore vulnerability are best understood through the dominant account of how Singapore came to be.

Singapore tells its history in a particular way, and there is a particular significance to the choice of a launching point for this history. According to the national narrative, the island was populated by a few pirates and fisher folk until 'discovered' by the British East India Company's Raffles in 1819.[113] Recounting Singapore's history in this manner is consistent with the colonial account of Singapore as an insignificant space until it

[109] Mark David Agrast, Juan Carlos Botero, & Alejandro Ponce, *WJP Rule of Law Index* (Washington, DC: World Justice Project, 2010) at 78.

[110] *Internal Security Act* (Cap. 143, 1985 Rev. Ed. Sing.).

[111] *Maintenance of Religious Harmony Act* (Cap. 167A, 2001 Rev. Ed. Sing.).

[112] Lee, *Why Singapore Is What It Is*, *supra* note 7.

[113] It is impossible to overstate the overwhelming dominance of the state's account of Singapore history. Not only does it feature in the education system in terms of content taught in History, the National Education project involves presenting the national narrative as content across the curriculum; online: Ministry of Education <http://www.ne.edu.sg/>. See also Hong & Huang, *supra* note 59 at 15–29. The ruling party has been alert to the power of narrating its account of history from as early as 1961: Harper, *supra* note 59 at 4.

In addition to socialising effected through schools, compulsory military service (for all male citizens and permanent residents), as well as the annual National Day celebrations (which typically involve a re-telling of the national narrative), become platforms for the national narrative. See also Trocki & Barr, *supra* note 59 at 1 on efforts to complement "the standard 'Singapore Story' sponsored by the regime", and the references therein.

came into colonial hands.[114] Both the colonial and the national narratives credit Sir Stamford Raffles with having transformed Singapore into a thriving entrepôt, drawing immigrants seeking a better life from China, India and the surrounding Malay archipelago.

The People's Action Party (PAP) government has ruled Singapore since the first moments of independence in 1959 and has based much of its legitimacy on the delivery of prosperity.[115] In the colonial framing of Singapore as an insignificant fishing village until Raffles,[116] all prosperity in Singapore-the-nation is necessarily tied to this genesis of

[114] For example, "Singapore when occupied by Sir Stamford Raffles on the 6th of February 1819 … was covered by dense primeval jungle … with a few fishermen (of piratical habits).… [A]t the end of 1822, … Raffles …[wrote,] 'In little more than three years it has rise[n] from an insignificant fishing village, to a large and prosperous town, containing at least 10,000 inhabitant of all nations, actively engaged in commercial pursuits, which afford to each and all a handsome livelihood and abundant profit'." W. J. Napier, "An Introduction to the Study of the Law Administered in the Colony of the Straits Settlements" (1898), reprinted in (1974) 16:1 *Mal. L. Rev*. 4. Sir Walter Napier was Attorney General of the Straits Settlements from 1907 to 1909. His description of Singapore as a territory echoes the preamble of the document through which the reception of 'English law' is traced, the "Letters Patent Establishing the Court of Judicature at Prince of Wales Island, Singapore and Malacca in the East-Indies" (1826), known as the Second Charter of Justice.

[115] Kevin Y. L. Tan, "Economic Development, Legal Reform and Rights in Singapore and Taiwan", in Joanne R. Bauer & Daniel A. Bell, eds., *The East Asian Challenge for Human Rights* (Cambridge: Cambridge University Press, 1999) 264; Linda Low, *The Political Economy of a City-State: Government-Made Singapore* (Singapore: Oxford University Press, 1998). One scholar describes the Singapore government's determinations of the interests of citizens as "nearly completely materialistic" and the government as "now one of the wealthiest in the world, with massive financial assets both at home and abroad." Ian Austin, "Singapore in Transition: Economic Change and Political Consequences", Paper presented at the 17th Biennial Conference of the Asian Studies Association of Australia, July 2008. The legitimising effect of prosperity is not, of course, limited to Singapore as a polity. Loughlin, for example, writing in general on the modern state, notes that "the political administrative system is legitimated by its achievement in bringing about substantial improvements in material conditions. It delivered the goods. Consequently, throughout much of the twentieth century, when living standards for the majority were improving, the nature of the political-administrative system was not called into question." Martin Loughlin, "Law, Ideologies, and the Political-Administrative System" (1989) 16:1 *J. L. & Soc'y* 21 at 22.

[116] On the manner in which the ruling party resolves and presents its post-colonial credentials despite valorising colonisation, see Hong & Huang, *supra* note 59 at 16–18.

Singapore-the-colony. Selecting as history's Day One the moment of Singapore's entry into global capital (as it then was) is ideologically consistent with Singapore's development "from a colonial entrepot economy to one based on trade and foreign investments in manufacturing".[117] If the colonial project was primarily about trade[118] and managing populations so as to generate wealth for the colonial coffers,[119] then the national project shares the colonial state's focus on wealth and social order[120] but remedies the colonial state's neglect of social welfare.[121]

Locating the beginnings of Singapore in 1819 is also significant in terms of 'race'.[122] It is British colonial rule that has led to Singapore's 'racially' plural population and the dominance of 'race' as a social category.[123] Singapore-the-nation has adopted colonial 'race' categories and has extended the meanings and applications of 'race'.[124] The population of Singapore has been predominantly 'Chinese' since 1836 (45.6%).[125] Today, 'Chinese' consist of about 74% of the population, with

[117] Ibid. at 3.

[118] J. S. Furnivall, *Colonial Policy and Practice: A Comparative Study of Burma and Netherlands India* (Cambridge: Cambridge University Press, 1948).

[119] Ibid.

[120] See generally Part One of Lee, *From Third World to First*, *supra* note 22.

[121] In hailing Singapore's "remarkable achievements in economic growth and social welfare", Doshi and Coclanis echo the many admiring assessments of Singapore's progress since independence: Tilak Doshi & Peter Coclanis, "The Economic Architect: Goh Keng Swee", in Lam Peng Er & Kevin Y. L. Tan, eds., *Lee's Lieutenants: Singapore's Old Guard* (St. Leonards: Allen & Unwin, 1999) 24. The text I have quoted is from note 20 at 208. For a sampling of evaluations of Singapore's economy, see World Bank, *The East Asian Miracle* (New York: Oxford University Press for World Bank, 1993) and W. G. Huff, *The Economic Growth of Singapore: Trade and Development in the Twentieth Century* (Cambridge: Cambridge University Press, 1994). Vasoo and Lee point out that social welfare has been incorporated into, and treated as a factor of, economic development: S. Vasoo & James Lee, "Singapore: Social Development, Housing and the Central Provident Fund" (2001: 10) *International Journal of Social Welfare* 276. See also Beng-Huat Chua, *Political Legitimacy and Housing: Stakeholding in Singapore* (London: Routledge, 1997).

[122] PuruShotam, *supra* note 90.

[123] Ibid.

[124] Ibid.; Benjamin, *supra* note 89.

[125] PuruShotam, *supra* 90, note 3 at 41.

a significant 'Malay' minority (13%) and an 'Indian' population of about 9.2%.[126] To start the Singapore story in 1819 is a way of constructing the island as becoming economically viable only with the arrival of a range of outsiders: first, the foreign British, who then facilitated immigration, resulting in prosperity. 'Race' and 'prosperity' are thus enmeshed and inter-dependent categories.

This narrative focus on prosperity deflects attention from a core instability in Singapore nationhood – the inability of the majority 'Chinese' population to claim legitimacy from being 'of the land'; a mode of legitimacy that resides in the 'raced' bodies of the minority, but crucially indigenous 'Malays'. A national narrative that celebrates colonisation is thus a narrative that validates the presence of the non-indigenous, attributing prosperity to colonialism and 'racial' pluralism and vesting legitimacy in material attainments, thereby augmenting the state's narrative of its virtuous rule.[127]

Celebrating colonisation also cements the place of 'law' in the 'nation'. Typically, the state's description of Singapore 'law' simultaneously elevates the colonial past and the national legal system, as in this example: "The Singapore legal system, which is closely modelled after the English legal system, is a legacy from Singapore's colonial past".[128] The characterisation

[126] Government of Singapore Census of Population 2010 Press Release online: <http://www.singstat.gov.sg/news/news/press31082010.pdf>.

[127] Harper, *supra* note 59.

[128] Sharon Koh, Gillian Koh Tan & Low Wan Jun Tammy, eds., *Speeches and Judgments of Chief Justice Yong Pung How*, vol. 1, 2nd ed. (Singapore: SNP, 2006) 18. Yong was Chief Justice from 1989 to 2006. Other instances of this simultaneous claim to inheriting English 'law' and building a sound legal system might be seen in Lee, *Why Singapore Is What It Is*, *supra* note 7; Chan, *supra* note 34; and the state's self-description in Singapore's Initial Report to the UN Committee for the Convention on the Elimination of All Forms of Discrimination Against Women (1999) 21 [CEDAW Report]a state report to the United Nations. The received status of this account of Singapore's legal history is also reflected in authoritative scholarship, for example, Kevin Tan, Yeo Tiong Min & Lee Kiat Seng, *Constitutional Law in Malaysia and Singapore* (Singapore: Malayan Law Journal, 1991); Li-ann Thio, "Government and the State", in Legal Systems in ASEAN, online: <http://www.aseanlawassociation.org/legal-sing.html>; Li-ann Thio and Kevin Y. L. Tan eds., *Evolution of a Revolution: 40 Years of the Singapore Constitution* (Abingdon: Routledge Cavendish, 2008).

of 'English' or 'British law' as "legacy"[129] or "heritage"[130] builds on the adoption of the colonial account of Singapore history[131] by adopting the colonial presentation of 'law' as "the gift we gave them".[132] Thus, in crucial ways, the national narrative perpetuates colonial constructs.

Just as the nation-state's accounts of history constitute the 'nation' as already-always 'Western',[133] the language, concepts and vision of 'law' are a similarly foundational claim to a 'Western' mode of state legitimacy. Indeed, the public, declaratory and symbolic legal texts of Singapore, such as the *Constitution*[134] and the *Proclamation of Singapore*,[135] bring the 'nation' into being as an entity shaped by explicitly 'Western' notions of legitimacy and political liberalism:[136]

[129] Koh, Tan & Low, *supra* note 128.

[130] Lee, *Why Singapore Is What It Is*, supra note 7.

[131] *Supra* notes 93 and 94.

[132] Peter Fitzpatrick, "Custom as Imperialism", in Jamil M. Abun-Nasr, Ulrich Spellenbert & Ulrike Wanitzek, eds., *Law, Society and National Identity in Africa* (Hamburg: Helmut Buske, 1990) 15.

[133] Ien Ang & John Stratton, "The Singapore Way of Multiculturalism: Western Concepts/Asian Cultures" (1995) 10 *Sojourn: Journal of Social Issues in Southeast Asia* 1.

[134] *Constitution of the Republic of Singapore* (1999 Rev. Ed. Sing.) [*Constitution*]. The *Constitution* declares itself to be "the supreme law of the Republic of Singapore" (Art. 4), thereby explicitly "opposing political absolutism": Thio, *Lex Rex or Rex Lex? supra* note 14 at 1. The Fundamental Liberties section of the *Constitution* (Part IV) imports liberal values by guaranteeing the freedoms of speech, assembly, association, movement, religion and equality before the law. It protects against retrospective criminal laws and repeated trials, prohibits banishment, slavery and forced labour. These constitutional promises, however, are qualified in a range of ways, such that, generally, human rights practice and policy in Singapore are "ultimately informed by overriding state objectives and national development goals prioritising economic growth and social order": Thio, *Pragmatism and Realism, supra* note 67 at 43. On the dereliction of the ideal of the supremacy of the *Constitution* in Singapore's nearly one-party Parliament, see Benedict Sheehey, "Singapore, 'Shared Values' and Law: Non East versus West Constitutional Hermeneutic" (2004) 67 *Hong Kong L.J.* 74.

[135] *Independence of Singapore Agreement 1965* (1985 Rev. Ed. Sing.) [*Proclamation*].

[136] An enormous literature, a review of which is beyond the scope of this project, tracks the long history of liberalism embedded within 'rule of law'. A recent and accessible account is Tamanaha, *On the Rule of Law*, supra note 15. A succinct summation of the history of liberalism's inseparable connection with 'common law' and the location of that 'common law' in Singapore is available in Michael Rutter, *The Applicable Law in Singapore and Malaysia* (Singapore: Malayan Law Journal, 1989).

> Now I Lee Kuan Yew Prime Minister of Singapore, do hereby proclaim and declare on behalf of the people and the Government of Singapore that as from today the ninth day of August in the year one thousand nine hundred and sixty-five Singapore shall be forever a sovereign democratic and independent nation, founded upon the principles of liberty and justice and ever seeking the welfare and happiness of her people in a more just and equal society.[137]

As the voice of the 'nation', Lee marked Singapore's genesis through proclaiming 'democracy', 'independence', 'liberty', 'justice' and 'equality' as founding principles. The proclamation of these values, consistent with constructing the emerging 'nation' along the lines of a 'Western' model, shows that the complex links and entanglements between 'law', political liberalism and legitimacy[138] inform the category 'rule of law' in Singapore. The 'nation' is, in a sense, constituted by a liberal account of 'law'.

The enduring power of this strand of Singapore 'law' is signalled, for example, by Lee Kuan Yew's 2007 address to the IBA. Here, too, the description was "Singapore inherited a sound legal system from the British.... The common law heritage and its developed contract law are known to and have helped attract investors".[139] It is noteworthy that, for Lee, the value of 'English law' is exemplified by commercial advantage. Augmenting the presentation of institutional inheritance, Lee highlights his unassailable personal authority arising from education and immersion in 'English law':

> I studied law in the Cambridge Law School and am a barrister of Middle Temple, an English inn of Court. I practised law for a decade

[137] *Proclamation, supra* note 135.

[138] As previously set out, while acknowledging the many contestations around these terms, I adopt the parameters for "a legal concept of political liberalism rather than a suffrage-based model of liberalism" identified as basic legal freedoms, a moderate state and civil society: Halliday, Karpik & Feeley, *supra* note 71.

[139] Lee, *Why Singapore Is What It Is, supra* note 7. Lee has identified the protection of intellectual property rights and the 'rule of law' as the two crucial ways in which Singapore had a competitive advantage over China: Chew Xiang, "IP Rights, Rule of Law Our Competitive Edge: MM Lee", *Business Times* (20 October 2009).

> before I took office in 1959 as prime minister of self-governing Singapore. Therefore I knew the rule of law would give Singapore an advantage in the centre of South-east Asia.[140]

In claiming 'English law', 'British law' and 'common law' as part of the genealogy of Singapore 'law', it is as if the state signals the pedigree, so to speak, of its modernity. The inter-textuality of language[141] lends richly legitimising associations to this claim of a shared parentage in 'English law', for England is "the acknowledged birthplace of liberalism and the bastion of the rule of law".[142] Thus, just as the national narrative links prosperity to colonial rule and 'racial' pluralism, the pedigreed modernity of 'British law' becomes an important legitimising trope in the Singapore account of 'law'. The apparent contradiction between declaratory texts asserting 'Western' liberal values, and everyday discourse and legislative text recoding these values into a Singapore mode of illiberalism, points, I would argue, to subterranean anxieties relating to 'race' and legitimacy.

Subterranean Anxieties

When the majority of Singapore's population bears a 'race' name – 'Chinese' – that precludes claiming power on the basis of a timeless, ancestral connection to the land,[143] then 'British law' and 'common law' become vital to a post-colonial construction of legitimacy. 'British law', structuring 'nation' in ways that vest rights in humanity and citizenship rather than ancestry, prevents an interrogation of the right to rule for those who

[140] Lee, *Why Singapore Is What It Is*, *supra* note 7.

[141] In the terms employed by Critical Discourse Analysis, "texts always exist in intertextual relations with other texts … [requiring] us to view discourses and texts from a historical perspective": Norman Fairclough, *Language and Power* (London: Longman, 1989) at 155.

[142] Tamanaha, *supra* note 15 at 56.

[143] The title of Regnier's monograph reflects the 'racial' dislocation that underpins state, and popular, conceptions of Singapore's existence: Philippe Regnier, *Singapore: A Chinese City State in a Malay World*, trans. Christopher Hurst (London: Hurst, 1991).

are not, so to speak, 'of the land'.[144] In adopting the legal-administrative apparatus put in place by the British, the 'nation' deflects possible claims to prior legal systems, claims which would necessarily import alternative histories and alternative legitimacies (the place of 'customary law' within the official legal system is discussed later in this section).

Read through the lens of the legitimising project of the national narrative,[145] the state's discourse on 'law' might be understood as a constant endeavour to authorise itself, to the exclusion of all others, to speak on 'law'. When speaking, the state repeatedly prescribes the basis for a uniquely Singapore account of the 'rule of law'. This account typically frames Singapore, and Singapore 'law', as an exception to some generalised 'Western' notion of 'rule of law'. For example:

> Singapore's legal system is largely founded upon the British legal system which has since been modified and adapted to suit the nation's needs and circumstances. It is within this legal framework whereby human rights are protected. Any persons who are of the view that their legal rights have been infringed upon can bring an action in the local courts which will then adjudicate upon the issue according to the applicable law in Singapore.[146]

However, the discursive double-bind for the state is that the 'nation' has been explicitly shaped by 'Western' ideals and values that valorise a 'Western', liberal 'rule of law' (as demonstrated by the text of the *Proclamation*, for example). And yet the same state that has framed

[144] Hong argues that because of the immigrant composition of the population, Singapore's nationalist leaders initially steered clear of references to the past immediately prior to colonial rule, because "[t]he glories of a mythical past did not suit the purposes of a Singapore leadership ruling over an immigrant, plural society. They claimed to be harbingers of a new society rather than the reincarnation of essentialist cultural icons". Lysa Hong, "Making the History of Singapore: S. Rajaratnam and C. V. Devan Nair", in Lam Peng Er & Kevin Y. L. Tan, eds., *Lee's Lieutenants: Singapore's Old Guard* (St. Leonards: Allen & Unwin, 1999) 96 at 98–99.

[145] Hong & Huang, *supra* note 59; Harper, *supra* note 59 at 3–55; Philip Holden, "A Man and an Island: Gender and Nation in Lee Kuan Yew's Singapore Story" (2001) 24:2 *Biography: An Interdisciplinary Quarterly* 410.

[146] CEDAW Report, *supra* note 128.

'nation' as 'Western' (probably so as to avoid the problematic issue of political legitimacy arising from an ancestral connection to land) insistently departs from a 'Western' standard for 'law' with reference to civil and political rights.[147] This double-bind has led to the state's efforts to be the sole author on 'law' and legitimacy, a project requiring endless reiteration and constant refinement.

DISCIPLINING DIFFERENCE THROUGH 'LAW'

The manner in which the categories 'law', 'race' and 'nation' come together in Singapore state discourse is captured by this address delivered by independent Singapore's first Head of State, the Yang Di-Pertuan Negara,[148] presiding over the 1965 opening of the first sitting of the first Parliament of the very new Republic of Singapore:

> Our survival as a people … depends upon … our perseverance in seeking long-term solutions to the problems of finding a new balance of forces in this part of the world, a task made more difficult by the migration of different racial groups into South-East Asia during the period of European domination.… [I]ndependence offers us the greater authority to bring about what we have always thought necessary, a tolerant society, multi-racial, multi-lingual, multi-religious, welded ever closer together by ties of common experience into a satisfying society, satisfying both for the indigenous peoples and for those migrant stock who came during the period of British rule.

[147] Jayasuriya, *The Exception Becomes the Norm*, *supra* note 14, at 118; Jayasuriya, *Introduction*, supra note 107 at 1; Agrast, Botero & Ponce, *supra* note 109.

[148] Singapore has maintained the Westminster practice of a Head of State delivering an address on behalf of government on the occasion of the opening of Parliament. 'Yang Di-Pertuan Negara' is the formal title for the Head of State in the Malay language. Malay is officially, and as provided in Art. 153A(2) of the *Constitution*, the national language of Singapore. In what must have been obeisance to the symbolic power of language, Singapore's head of state went by the title 'Yang Di-Pertuan Negara' from 1959 to 1970. With the death of Singapore's first Head of State, the 'Malay' Yusof bin Isyak, and the appointment of the second Head of State, the 'Eurasian' Benjamin Sheares, the title changed to 'President'.

> Whilst the best guarantee of our future as a distinct and separate people in South-East Asia is the creation of a tolerant multi-racial society, we must however expect obstruction and resistance to this from groups inside ... and outside Singapore. They are the Communalists and the Communists.... Needless to say, the more extreme any community is about one race, one language and one religion, the more likely it is to arouse counter chauvinism amongst the other communities to the detriment of all.
>
> ... [W]e must never allow ourselves the luxury of forgetting that survival depends upon rallying and strengthening the forces ... who are for a secular, rational and multi-racial approach to the problems of economic backwardness and the legacy of unbalanced development in the colonial era.[149]

When this speech was made, in 1965, issues of 'race' and tensions about the place of Singapore in the Federation of Malaysia[150] had precipitated the ejection of Singapore from the Federation.[151] Issues of 'race', identity and the legitimacy to reside in and rule the territory of Singapore therefore launched Singapore's very existence as a nation-state. And 'British law', embedding (in the state's terms) secularism, modernity and rationality, was presented as the vehicle that de-clawed the dangerous beasts of difference: 'race', 'language' and 'religion'.

The importance of a 'Western' mode of legality for Singapore 'law' is reflected in another way: the absence, within the official legal system, of 'customary law'.[152] In using the term 'customary law', I adopt the colonial

[149] Sing., *Parliamentary Debates*, vol. 24, cols. 5–14 (8 December 1965) (Yang Di-Pertuan Negara Encik Yusof Ishak).

[150] Hong & Huang, *supra* note 59 at 88–95.

[151] Rogers M. Smith, ed., *Southeast Asia Documents of Political Development and Change* (Ithaca, N.Y.: Cornell University Press, 1974) at 266–76.

[152] It is not my intention to perpetuate essentialising oppositions of 'Western law' and 'customary law'. Rather, I point to a colonial history of differentiated categories – in particular, 'English law' as against 'customary' or 'personal law'. These terms were used by the British to draw a distinction between the domains in which 'English' law would apply (for example, contract, property and taxation) and the domain of "personal law" (such as marriage and inheritance): M. B. Hooker, *Laws of Southeast Asia* (Singapore: Butterworths, 1986). Article 12(3) of the *Constitution* may appear to enable personal law in the colonial sense, but the case law (discussed later) suggests otherwise.

state's category for 'law' tied to custom and tradition.[153] While there is a limited legal pluralism represented by the operation of the *Administration of Muslim Law Act*[154] and the history of even the colonial ruler accommodating some measure of 'customary law[155] within the hegemony of 'English law',[156] the nation-state has policed 'law' in a manner that minimises, to the point of exclusion, a non-'Western' 'law'.

The official legal system of Singapore-the-nation-state is extremely wary of claims made by citizens that legal consequences should follow from customary practices. In a 2002 decision, *OHC on behalf of TPC v. TTMJ*,[157] the Tribunal for the Maintenance of Parents refused to recognise an adoption conducted by Chinese customary rituals, holding that only adoptions consistent with the bureaucratic requirements of the *Adoption of Children Act*[158] could be recognised as valid. In the 1995 High Court decision of *Sonia Chataram Aswani v. Haresh Jaikishin Buxani*,[159] the court refused to recognise a marriage that was conducted in accordance

[153] Hooker, *supra* note 152; H. Patrick Glenn, *Legal Traditions of the World: Sustainable Diversity in Law* (Oxford: Oxford University Press, 2004).

[154] *Administration of Muslim Law Act* (Cap. 3, 1999 Rev. Ed. Sing.) [*AMLA*]. Although state discourse presents *AMLA* as unproblematically 'Muslim', the statute is very much a colonial construct (Hooker, *supra* note 152). *AMLA* constitutes an administrative body, the Majlis Ugama Islam, "to administer matters relating to the Muslim religion and Muslims in Singapore" (s. 3(2)(b)) and limits the operation of 'Muslim law' to the areas of marriage, divorce, inheritance, charitable trusts and the administrative aspects of Islam, such as the certification of halal food, the regulation of Haj services and goods. *AMLA* was passed in 1966, a year after Singapore became an independent republic. *AMLA* reworks the colonial *Muslim and Hindu Endowments Ordinance*, which was enacted by the British in 1905; see "Chronological Table of the Ordinances Enacted From 1st April, 1867 to 30th April, 1955", *The Laws of the Colony of Singapore* (1955 Rev. Ed.), vol. VIII, 206.

[155] Hooker, *supra* note 152.

[156] Hence the description of a "fused administration of justice". Geoffrey Bartholomew, "Introduction", *Tables of the Written Laws of the Republic of Singapore, 1819–1971* (Singapore: Malaya Law Review, University of Singapore, 1972).

[157] [2002] SGTMP 3. The decisions of the Tribunal for the Maintenance of Parents are available at the electronic database produced by the Singapore Academy of Law, LawNet.

[158] Cap. 4, 1985 Rev. Ed. Sing.

[159] [1995] 3 Sing.L.R. 627.

with Hindu rites but not registered as a monogamous marriage within the terms of the *Women's Charter*.[160] In both these decisions, the national legal system's need for bureaucratic homogeneity was asserted over the unpredictable diversity of prior legal traditions.[161]

The fact that these cases are among the very few in which Singapore citizens have attempted to seek recognition for 'customary law' as legally valid reflects perhaps the overwhelming success of the nationalist legal project. Legal traditions that pre-date colonial rule and that might still operate in the everyday realities of people's lives are not traditions the 'nation' is ready to recognise as 'law'. In other words, Singapore-the-nation has appropriated 'law' in such a manner that only textual 'law' consistent with 'common law' categories of cases and legislation is recognised. In closing off the limited accommodation of 'personal law' afforded by the colonial system, there may be less 'customary law' in Singapore-the-nation than there was in Singapore-the-colony. The state's vigilant exclusion of 'customary law' from the Singapore legal system points to a crucial homogenising role played by 'law' in the 'nation'.[162]

That 'law' should be tied to the homogenising project of 'nation' is unsurprising. National legal systems have a long history of "pointing to the exclusivity of state sources of law ... instrumentally directed towards the process of creating binding law, which can be uniformly enforced within the defined territory of the state".[163] In tracing this history, Glenn argues that "[s]tate law had to bind because otherwise there would be

160 Cap. 353, 1997 Rev. Ed. Sing.

161 On the enduring nature of legal traditions, see Glenn, *supra* note 153.

162 This homogenising effect was possibly augmented by a 2004 High Court decision on an appeal from a ruling of the Fatwa Committee constituted by the *AMLA*. In this decision, the High Court held that "it was an important principle of Western as well as Muslim jurisprudence that a person could not be a judge in his own case", with the possible consequence that Syariah courts will be subject to supervision by civil courts in issues of natural justice: *Mohammed Ismail bin Ibrahim and Another v. Mohammed Taha bin Ibrahim* [2004] 4 Sing.L.R. 756 at 779.

163 H. Patrick Glenn, "The Nationalist Heritage", in Pierre Legrand & Roderick Munday, eds., *Comparative Legal Studies: Traditions and Transitions* (Cambridge: Cambridge University Press, 2003) 76 at 83.

no state law, and no state'."[164] Even allowing for the centrality of 'law' to marking and consolidating the boundaries of 'nation', the resistance to 'customary law' sits oddly with Singapore's avowed and explicit plural political model of the nation-state.[165] The contradiction inherent to rejecting 'customary law' while presenting the modern, rational 'nation' as a guardian of multi-racial, multi-religious difference[166] is an ongoing (but underlying) tension within Singapore public discourse on 'law'.[167] Chapter 4 on the *Press Act* and Chapter 6 on the *Religious Harmony Act* show how 'race', 'language' and religion' have been appropriated by the state in certain ways, delegitimising any attempt on the part of the citizen to invest these categories with claims for rights.

If 'law' in Singapore has been used to shape legal homogeneity for citizens marked notionally and bureaucratically different in terms of 'language', 'religion' and 'race', then this project shows how 'law' has been used to erase the expression of another kind of difference – ideological/political difference. Through interrogating and contextualising legislation, this project shows how the state has reserved unto itself the authority to manage the discursive ambivalence of 'law'. The inaugurating Proclamation of Independence (quoted earlier) inter-textually[168] invokes "a legal concept of political liberalism"[169] that is inherently and explicitly

[164] Ibid. at 80.

[165] The state has, from the outset, declared itself to be building a 'nation' on the principles of being multi-racial, non-Communist, non-aligned, and democratic socialist: Chan Heng Chee, "Political Developments, 1965–1979", in Ernest Chew & Edwin Lee, eds., *A History of Singapore* (Singapore: Oxford University Press, 1991) 157 at 158.

[166] The promises of the plural political model are perhaps best exemplified by Art. 12 of the *Constitution*. Article 12(1) guarantees that "[a]ll persons are equal before the law and entitled to the equal protection of the law". At the same time, this guarantee is qualified by Art. 12(2), which paves the way for positive discrimination for 'Malays' (Art. 152), and Art. 12(3), which preserves the regulation of "personal law" and restrictions to employment in religious affairs.

[167] Sing., *Parliamentary Debates*, vol. 86 (19 August 2009) (Lee Kuan Yew); Clarissa Oon, "MM Rebuts NMP's Notion of Race Equality", *Straits Times* (20 August 2009).

[168] Fairclough, *supra* note 141.

[169] Halliday, Karpik & Feeley, *supra* note 71.

'Western'. This political liberalism is then moderated by qualifications and constraints the state positions itself, and only itself, as authorised to determine. In the process, as the case studies illustrate, the state delegitimises actors who challenge the state's prescriptions for Singapore 'law'. The vehemence with which the state rejects and silences critique is consistent with the inaugural anxiety of 'nation'. The state's hyper-vigilant policing of the standing to speak on 'law' papers over the fragility of a state that can claim neither the authority of 'race' nor (as I argue later in this chapter) the authority of an unambiguous electoral victory. The leaders of the state cannot claim that third legitimising banner of post-colonialism, that of having led an anti-colonial battle for independence (a point discussed later). As the discussion in Chapter 3 elaborates, this is a state that has come into power through a complicit relationship with the coloniser, relying on coercion, surveillance and a violence legitimated by legal exceptionalism so as to secure power and control.

'RULE OF LAW': THICK, THIN, DUAL AND DICEY

It is consistent with the state's claim that its legal system originates in 'British law' that the category 'rule of law' has rich, legitimising resonances in the Singapore public domain. The Diceyan notion of the 'rule of law' offers a reference point for one of the main ways in which the category 'rule of law' is used in Singapore public discourse. The Victorian jurist A. V. Dicey is generally considered to have framed "the seminal modern definition of the 'rule of law'".[170] Dicey's definition requires, first, that punishment should be only according to existing 'laws', which 'laws' should be enforced by ordinary courts rather than special tribunals or government officials exercising discretion; second, that everyone be regarded as equal before the 'law', with a particular emphasis on the subordination of public officials to 'law'; and third, in the common law

[170] Rachel Kleinfeld, "Competing Definitions of the Rule of Law", in Thomas Carothers, ed., *Promoting the Rule of Law Abroad* (Washington. DC: Carnegie Endowment for International Peace, 2006) 31 at 38.

tradition, that rights should be enforceable through courts.[171] Diceyan notions of 'rule of law' are applicable in Singapore through the 'common law',[172] which, as I have shown, the state celebrates as part of Singapore's "heritage" from 'colony'.[173] Additionally, Singapore state actors describe Singapore as complying with Dicey's formulation of the 'rule of law', as this recent excerpt from a speech delivered by Chief Justice Chan Sek Keong illustrates:

> Singapore has a robust criminal justice system under the rule of law. English law and English justice, the epitome of the rule of law as conceived by A V Dicey, was the foundation for the Singapore legal system.[174]

Not only are Dicey's parameters for the 'rule of law' typically claimed as a foundational Singapore feature by state actors, Dicey is also presented as relevant to Singapore 'law' by the standard texts of legal education.[175] In addition to explicit references, the Diceyan formulation is repeatedly alluded to in Singapore state discourse.[176] Examples of these discursive allusions are presented in the Chapter 3 discussion of the Fay case, in the state's insistence that it punishes according to the 'law',[177] that all are equal before the 'law' in Singapore[178] and that Singapore courts are

[171] Tamanaha, *supra* note 15 at 63–65.

[172] Rutter, *supra* note 136.

[173] Lee, Why Singapore Is What It Is, *supra* note 7.

[174] Chan, *supra* note 34. Zakir Hussain, "Raffles, MM Lee and the Rule of Law: CJ", *Straits Times* (28 October 2009).

[175] Significantly, a leading Singapore constitutional law textbook offers students three definitions of 'rule of law': Dicey's, de Q. Walker's, and Raz's; Tan, Yeo & Lee, *supra* note 129. See also Jaclyn Ling-Chien Neo & Yvonne C. L. Lee, "Constitutional Supremacy: Still a Little Dicey", in Li-ann Thio & Kevin Y. L. Tan, eds., *Evolution of a Revolution: 40 Years of the Singapore Constitution* (Abingdon: Routledge, 2009) 153.

[176] Lee Kuan Yew's IBA address is an example: Lee, *Why Singapore Is What It Is*, *supra* note 7. In his October 2009 address to the New York State Bar Association Seasonal Meeting, Chief Justice Chan Sek Keong claimed that "English law and English justice, the epitome of the rule of law as conceived by A.V. Dicey, was the foundation for the Singapore legal system"; Chan, *supra* note 34.

[177] See Chapter 3.

[178] Ibid.

independent.[179] The state's description of the legal system as protective of human rights[180] and as facilitating the enforcement of rights in courts (as illustrated in the earlier quote from the state's report to CEDAW) also alludes to Diceyan principles.

The Diceyan ideals are perhaps most symbolically captured by the constitutional enshrinement of the supremacy of 'law',[181] the equality of all before the 'law'[182] and the structures of governance designed to maintain the separation of powers and the independence of the courts.[183] In this, 'law' in Singapore conforms to the fundamental and foundational notion of the 'rule of law' as "a government of laws, the supremacy of the law, and the equality of all before the law".[184] And if the 'common law', which the state claims as the applicable 'law' in Singapore, is inextricably "a law of liberty"[185] informed by "the philosophy which places the highest value upon the right of the individual to life, liberty and security",[186] how has Singapore 'law' come to be characterised by illiberalism?

When Lee Kuan Yew gave his 2007 address to the IBA, in reciting laudatory rankings and assessments he was equating the demonstrable success of Singapore 'law' with technocratic efficiency[187] and "institutional attributes",[188] such as the "necessary" laws, a "well-functioning" judiciary and a "good" law enforcement apparatus.[189] If, as Peerenboom argues,[190] such institutional attributes are at the foundation of a functional 'rule of

[179] Ibid.
[180] CEDAW Report, *supra* note 128.
[181] *Constitution*, Art. 4.
[182] Ibid.
[183] Ibid., Parts V, VI and VII.
[184] Peerenboom, "Introduction," *supra* note 60 at 2.
[185] Rutter, *supra* note 136 at 574.
[186] Ibid. at 575.
[187] Kleinfeld, *supra* note 170 at 32, notes the World Bank's focus on "providing computers to courts, printing laws, and establishing magistrates' schools to create its technocratic vision of the rule of law as efficient and predictable justice".
[188] Kleinfeld, *supra* note 170 at 33.
[189] Ibid.
[190] Peerenboom, "Introduction," *supra* note 60 at 2–46.

law', does that mean the Singapore legal system is already and adequately 'rule of law'? This question is best explored through Peerenboom's conception of a 'rule of law' continuum, articulated as 'thin' and 'thick' conceptions of 'rule of law'.

Peerenboom argues that in order for 'rule of law' to be a meaningful category enabling the commensurability of comparative study, 'rule of law' conceptions must be divided into 'thin' and 'thick' accounts of the 'rule of law'.[191] At its most basic, a 'thin rule of law' conceives of 'law' in formal or instrumental terms,[192] whereas a 'thick rule of law' involves embedding the formal operations of 'law' within "a particular institutional, cultural and values complex".[193] A 'thin rule of law' displays the following features, which, Peerenboom argues, represent "core ... and basic elements" of 'rule of law' for which there is broad consensus:[194] meaningful restraints on state actors; rules determining which entities may validly make 'law'; public accessibility and general applicability of 'law'; clear, consistent 'laws'; stable and generally prospective 'laws'.[195] Additionally, 'laws' must be enforced and be reasonably acceptable to a majority of the population.[196] Peerenboom presents these features as general markers, not absolutes, stressing that "[w]hile marginal deviations are acceptable, legal systems that fall far short are likely to be dysfunctional".[197] Broad functionality, then, is a key determinant of a realised 'thin rule of law'. The conspicuous efficiency of the Singapore legal system,[198] he argues, means that with reference to Singapore, contestation centres on "competing thick conceptions rather than thin rule of law concerns".[199]

The analysis presented by this project supports Peerenboom's evaluation that 'rule of law' critique in Singapore focuses on the state's

[191] Ibid. at 2.
[192] Ibid.
[193] Ibid. at 5.
[194] Ibid. at 2.
[195] Ibid.
[196] Ibid.
[197] Ibid. at 3.
[198] Thio, *Rule of Law*, *supra* note 41 at 183.
[199] Peerenboom, "Introduction," *supra* note 60 at 18.

"particular non-liberal thick conception".[200] However, my project illustrates two crucial refinements of his evaluation. First, contrary to Peerenboom's assessment,[201] the state's own 'thick' conceptions are not simplistically non-liberal. The state's discourse and the key legal texts of 'nation' present 'Western' liberalism as *generally applicable* to Singapore 'law' (as demonstrated by the *Proclamation* and the *Constitution*). It is vital to note that liberalism, or the claim to liberal democratic statehood, is the Singapore state's opening position on 'law'. Second, facets of 'thick rule of law' generate problematic uncertainties in the realm of 'thin rule of law' in a manner that undermines even Peerenboom's core and basic elements for 'thin rule of law'. For example, the state's ideology of Singapore exceptionalism, and its readiness to instrumentally appropriate legal forms and procedures, point to ways in which the formal, 'thin' functionality of the legal system is tainted by its susceptibility to power. Even Peerenboom identifies meaningful restraints on state actors as a primary constitutive feature of a 'thin rule of law',[202] yet as these case studies show, the Singapore state's incursions into individuals' rights leave citizens without meaningful and substantive redress or methods of restraining the state. Legal instrumentalism cannot be treated as value-neutral.

Thio's position that Singapore adheres to a formal, 'thin rule of law' bolstered by a 'thick' communitarian conception of the 'rule of law'[203] is an argument that supports Peerenboom's model. But the reading of power relations informing legal text and state discourse that I engage in through this project suggests otherwise. The detail of this study demonstrates that, despite Peerenboom's caution that "legitimate differences in values [are] at stake" in 'Asian' discourses on 'rule of law',[204] it is impossible, in the context of Singapore, to divorce state formulations of values from political

[200] Ibid. at 5.
[201] Ibid.
[202] Ibid. at 2.
[203] Thio, *Rule of Law*, *supra* note 41.
[204] Randall Peerenboom, "Preface", in Randall Peerenboom, ed., *Asian Discourses of Rule of Law* (London: Routledge, 2004) at x.

motivations. Even if operating within the parameters of Peerenboom's general markers for a 'thin rule of law', the case studies show how an instrumental 'thin rule of law' selectively obstructs the public accessibility and general applicability of 'law', discards meaningful restraints on state actors and strategically scripts opaque and uncertain 'laws'. Both 'thin' and 'thick' accounts of 'rule of law' and the dynamic interpellations between formal rules ('thin rule of law') and ideological justifications ('thick rule of law') are vividly demonstrated in the data of discourse, legislation and contextual events presented by the case studies.

A related difficulty is Peerenboom's claim that a 'thin rule of law' is "ideologically neutral".[205] Through this project, I argue that Singapore's attention to a high-functioning, "institutional attributes"[206] account of 'law' is inextricably ideological. Singapore's 'thin rule of law' is ideologically invested in at least three ways. First, 'law' is central to Singapore's conception of 'nation'; second, 'British law', 'common law' and 'rule of law' (categories replete with liberal legitimacy) are claimed as foundational features of the Singapore legal system; and third, 'law' pertaining to foreign investment, trade and the economy is on par with 'Western' liberal democracies while 'law' pertaining to civil and political rights is repressive.[207] It is this ideological dichotomy within 'law' that has led Jayasuriya to characterise Singapore as a dual state.[208]

'LAW' AND THE DUAL STATE

In his compelling analysis of Singapore's legal system, Jayasuriya adopts Fraenkel's concept of the Nazi dual state, combining "the rational

[205] Peerenboom, "Introduction," *supra* note 60 at 33.

[206] Kleinfeld, *supra* note 170 at 33.

[207] Jayasuriya, *Introduction*, *supra* note 106.

[208] Peerenboom's critique of Jayasuriya's model of legal statism relates to three points: Jayasuriya's focus on state discourse, the failure to account for the diversity of legal systems within Asia and the failure to apply the model to the full range of Asian jurisdictions: Peerenboom, "Introduction," *supra* note 60 at 48. This critique does not diminish the value and applicability of Jayasuriya's model to Singapore.

calculation demanded by the operation of the capitalist economy within the authoritarian shell of the state"[209] to argue that Singapore exemplifies a contemporary dual state in which "economic liberalism is enjoined to political illiberalism".[210] Jayasuriya presents Singapore's dual state legality as building upon the normalisation of legal exceptionalism. Legal exceptionalism (understood as the authoritarian primacy of executive power through a suspension of individual rights and standard legal processes) entered the Singapore legal system through colonial ordinances designed for the Malayan Emergency.[211] Jayasuriya argues that, building on the colonial model of state authoritarianism, the post-colonial Singapore state has frequently deployed executive power "in the name of public order and national unity"[212] in a manner that constructs a culture of political and ideological homogeneity in Singapore, dismantling the autonomy of the judiciary in political matters.[213]

Jayasuriya's characterisation of Singapore as a legal regime in which "the 'rule of law' applies to the economy but not to the political arena"[214] frames the argument of this study. With regard to the overarching question of the Singapore state's legitimacy despite violations of the 'rule of law', dual state legality accounts for one of the strategies that has sustained

[209] Jayasuriya, *The Exception Becomes the Norm*, *supra* note 14.

[210] Ibid. at 120.

[211] Ibid.

[212] Ibid. at 109.

[213] Ibid. at 128. With reference to Dicey's parameters for 'rule of law', this dismantling of judicial autonomy results in a failure of the principle of the equality before the 'law' when state practices and the courts interpret 'law' so as to secure state hegemony: Thio, *Regulating Political Speech*, *supra* note 81 at 516; Li-ann Thio, "Beyond the 'Four Walls' in an Age of Transnational Judicial Conversations Civil Liberties, Rights Theories, and Constitutional Adjudication in Malaysia and Singapore" (2006) 19 *Colum. J. Asian Law* 428; Li-ann Thio, *Pragmatism and Realism*, *supra* note 67. Li-ann Thio, "The Secular Trumps the Sacred: Constitutional Issues Arising from *Colin Chan v Public Prosecutor*" (1995) 16 *Sing. L. Rev.* 26; Ross Worthington, "Between Hermes and Themis: An Empirical Study of the Contemporary Judiciary in Singapore" (2001) 28:4 *J. L. & Soc'y* 490; Sheehey, *supra* note 134.

[214] Jayasuriya, *The Exception Becomes the Norm*, *supra* note 14 at 124.

legitimacy for the state. The dual state nature of Singapore 'law' also accounts for the confusion and complexity that mark discourse on 'law', such that a critique of the state's violations of individual liberties might be deflected and thrown into doubt by presenting World Bank rankings of legal efficiency, as Lee did when addressing the IBA.[215]

While the focus of this project is on legislation, the role of the courts in enabling illiberal legislation cannot be ignored. Singapore's courts have not, generally speaking, shown themselves to be advocates for the 'rule of law'.[216] Jayasuriya contextualises the operation of liberal courts as requiring "a liberal state and an autonomous civil society, whereas statist legalism is located within a corporatist state and a managed civil society".[217] The case studies of this project demonstrate the extent to which Singapore courts are located within the shaping context for statist courts – a context which predetermines the impossibility of liberal courts.

In summary, in this discussion of the category 'rule of law', I have argued that important and inaugural legal texts, such as the *Proclamation* and the *Constitution*, have imported into Singapore discourse the liberal values and ideals inherent to understanding the 'rule of law' as "a venerable part of Western political philosophy".[218] Ongoing state descriptions of Singapore's legal system as shaped by 'British law', 'common law', and Diceyan ideals build on these key texts to construct the 'rule of law' as a content-rich ideal, signifying the protection of individual rights and liberties.[219] In short, a liberal account of 'rule of law' informs Singapore's very existence as a nation-state and is incontrovertibly a part of Singapore discourse.

[215] Lee, *Why Singapore Is What It Is*, *supra* note 7.

[216] See, generally, references at *supra* notes 67 and 68, as well as the references on the applications of the *Internal Security Act* and defamation law: notes 78, 79, 80, 81, and 230.

[217] Kanishka Jayasuriya, "Corporatism and Judicial Independence within Statist Legal Institutions in East Asia", in Kanishka Jayasuriya, ed., *Law, Capitalism and Power in Asia* (London: Routledge, 1999) 173 [*Statist Legal Institutions*].

[218] Thomas Carothers, "The Rule-of-Law Revival", in Thomas Carothers, ed., *Promoting the Rule of Law Abroad: In Search of Knowledge* (Washington, DC: Carnegie Endowment for International Peace, 2006) 4.

[219] Kleinfeld, *supra* note 170 at 36.

Through these textual claims to a 'Western' mode of 'thick rule of law' and through the state's delivery of 'thin rule of law' in the shape of efficient[220] and corruption-free[221] legal operations, the 'nation' has sought parity and comity with 'Western' states. And as Lee Kuan Yew's 2007 engagement with the IBA demonstrates, the state continues to claim membership of an international league of legitimacy. The state's retention and reiteration of 'rule of law' in its discourse[222] conveys the continuing importance of 'rule of law' as a key category in the state's management of its legitimacy.

'LAW', POLITICAL LIBERALISM AND THE MODERATE STATE

If the category 'rule of law' (as deployed in Singapore discourse) is a vehicle for the values and meanings of political liberalism, then part of what is claimed via the state's references to 'British law', the 'common law' and the Westminster-model separation of powers is the desirable dispersal of power characteristic of the moderate state.[223] The moderate state is a state where power is internally, systemically dispersed (for instance, through judicial independence), providing for "ordered or

[220] The World Economic Forum Global Competitiveness Report 2008 ranks Singapore second out of 134 in terms of efficiency of legal framework; online: <http://www.weforum.org>. See also the Chapter 8 discussion of the manner in which the Singapore state uses these assessments and tables.

[221] "The World Bank's governance indicators place Singapore in the top percentile (90% to 100%) with reference to control of corruption, rule of law, government effectiveness and regulatory quality"; "Governance Matters 2009"; online: <http//info.worldbank.org/governance/wgi>.

[222] K. C. Vijayan, "Singapore Gets Top Marks in Global Law Survey", *Straits Times* (7 January 2011) reports on Chief Justice Chan Sek Keong's speech on the occasion of the opening of the legal year in which Chan highlighted the fact that Singapore had been ranked first among its socio-economic peers in terms of access to civil justice in the World Justice Project's Rule of Law Index. Neither the Chief Justice nor the press report acknowledged that the same index had ranked Singapore last in terms of fundamental rights and transparency of government.

[223] Halliday, Karpik & Feeley, *supra* note 71 at 10–12.

constitutionally-structured contestation among elements of the state'.[224] Within the legal principles that frame the 'nation', citizens are meant to be protected against abuses of state power through constitutional provisions for the separation of powers. In other words, power in the moderate state[225] is reliably moderated by non-state centres of power.

By focusing on state measures to silence actors who seek the scrutiny and containment of state power, this study extends the Halliday, Karpik and Feeley theorising on the relationship between state power and advocacy for political liberalism.[226] While the analysis of the state's intimidation of lawyers (presented in Chapter 5) is explicitly within the Halliday et al. contemplation of legal professions as advocates for political liberalism,[227] the overarching attention of this project to the state's discursive and legislative delineations of 'law' demonstrates Singapore's institutional subversions of the moderate state. With authoritarian rule of law, legislation has been a key tool effecting the decimation of opposition parties (Chapter 3), the dismantling of independent media (Chapter 4) and the thwarting of an autonomous civil society (Chapters 5–7). In other words, 'law' has been central to consolidating the state, thus simultaneously subverting the dispersal of power characteristic of the moderate state. Despite the declaratory promises of political liberalism in founding legal texts like the *Constitution* and the *Proclamation*, legal and institutional practices have effected a "naked merging of state and party".[228]

Given the absolutist nature of the Singapore state,[229] its insistence that it is institutionally observant of the Westminster separation of powers is significant. The many defamation and contempt of court proceedings

[224] Ibid. at 10.

[225] Jayasuriya's parameters for the liberal state also highlight the presence of an autonomous civil society; *Statist Legal Institutions*, *supra* note 217.

[226] Halliday, Karpik & Feeley, *supra* note 71.

[227] Ibid.

[228] Rodan, *Westminster in Singapore*, *supra* note 12 at 114.

[229] Jayasuriya, *The Exception Becomes the Norm*, *supra* note 14.

initiated by the state to defend itself against allegations of executive interference in the judiciary[230] testify to the importance accorded by the state to being perceived as governing through the separation of powers. And yet the state is known for "the politicization of the legal system and the use of law to undermine political opposition, limit civil society and advance the conservative, statist substantive agenda of the People's Action Party".[231] Augmenting the close association between state and the judiciary is the conflation between the executive and Parliament.[232] An institutional division of powers does not appear to be a reality in the context of Singapore. Instead,

> [a]spects of Westminster-style government such as accountability of ministers to parliament, a non-partisan public bureaucracy and the tolerance of a loyal opposition were all casualties in the ... establishment of a virtual one-party state by the ruling People's Action Party.... [A]ppearances of at least some aspects of Westminster remain important to the ideological defence of the political system ....[reflecting]

[230] The state has brought cases in defamation and scandalising the judiciary against parties who have explicitly or implicitly suggested that the courts are not independent of political pressure: *Lee Kuan Yew v. J.B. Jeyaretnam*, [1979] 1 M.L.J. 281; *Lee Kuan Yew v. Seow Khee Leng*, [1986] 1 M.L.J. 11; *Lee Kuan Yew v. Seow Khee Leng* [1989] 1 M.L.J. 172; *Lee Kuan Yew v. Derek Gwynn Davies & Ors.* [1990] 1 M.L.J. 390; *Lee Kuan Yew v. Jeyaretnam J.B. (No. 1)* [1990] Sing. L.R. 688; *Lee Kuan Yew & Anor v. Vinocur & Ors. & Another Action* [1995] 3 Sing. L.R. 477; *Lee Kuan Yew v. Tang Liang Hong (No. 1)*, [1997] 2 Sing.L.R. 97; *Lee Kuan Yew v. Tang Liang Hong (No. 2)*, [1997] 2 Sing.L.R. 833; *Lee Kuan Yew v. Tang Liang Hong (No. 3)*, [1997] 2 Sing.L.R. 841; *Goh Chok Tong v. Jeyaretnam Joshua Benjamin* [1998] 1 Sing.L.R. (upheld in *Goh Chok Tong v. Jeyaretnam Joshua Benjamin & Another Action*, [1998] 3 Sing.L.R. 337 (C.A.)); *Goh Chok Tong v. Chee Soon Juan (No. 2)*, [2005] 1 Sing.L.R. 573; *Lee Kuan Yew v. Chee Soon Juan (No. 2)*, [2005] 1 Sing.L.R. 552; *Lee Hsien Loong v. Singapore Democratic Party & Ors.* [2007] 1 Sing.L.R. 675; *Attorney-General v. Hertzberg Daniel* [2009] 1 Sing.L.R. 1103; *Lee Hsien Loong v. Review Publishing Company* [2009] 1 Sing.L.R. 167; *Review Publishing Company Ltd. and another v. Lee Hsien Loong and another appeal* [2010] 1 Sing.L.R. 52; *Attorney-General v. Shadrake Alan* [2010] SGHC 327 read with *Attorney-General v. Shadrake Alan* [2010] SGHC 339.

[231] Peerenboom, "Introduction," *supra* note 60 at 18.

[232] Chan Heng Chee, "Politics in an Administrative State: Where Has the Politics Gone?" in Seah Chee Meow, ed., *Trends in Singapore* (Singapore: Institute of Southeast Asian Studies, 1975) 51.

> the deliberate practice of trying to harness historically liberal institutions to authoritarian ends.[233]

Rodan points out that in addition to selected performative facets of liberal institutions, the rhetoric of liberalism has been harnessed by the PAP in its rise to power with the Lee Kuan Yew of 1955 attacking detention without trial and restraints on free expression until the eve of the PAP's rise to power.[234] In other words, the PAP has exalted the 'rule of law', but in an instrumental manner. Alongside strategic uses of discourse and institutions, Lee managed an "uneasy but powerful alliance" between the two major factions of the PAP: the middle-class, 'English-educated' PAP leadership, and the working-class, 'Chinese-educated' leftists and nationalists of the labour movement. Lee managed this uneasy alliance until his party came to power in 1959.[235] Once the party was in government, a 1961 split between the two factions led to the founding of the opposition Barisan Sosialis. This split exposed Lee's faction as "but a shell of a party"[236] without strong links to the working class or to organisations and networks on the ground. It was the instrumental power of 'law' that enabled the PAP leadership to recover from this moment of weakness

> through exploiting its executive power systematically to obstruct its opponents, embedding the party within the structures of the State, and building a new electoral base through social and economic reforms. In particular, both the formal political institutions through which political competition was channelled, as well as the broader civil society institutions needed to render that competition meaningful, were to undergo major modifications. Repressive laws to block free expression and curtail independent collective organisations engaged in political activities combined with various initiatives to build up extensive structures of political co-option that saw a naked merging of state and party.[237]

[233] Rodan, *Westminster in Singapore*, *supra* note 12 at 110.
[234] Ibid.
[235] Ibid.
[236] Rodan, *Westminster in Singapore*, *supra* note 12 at 114.
[237] Ibid.

Others have noted that it was an alliance between the right-wing faction of the PAP and the colonial state that facilitated this early turn to repressive executive power –culminating perhaps in Operation Coldstore, the detention without trial of more than a hundred left-wing Socialists, trade unionists and journalists in the crucial lead up to the 1963 general elections.[238] Operation Coldstore decimated the leadership of the opposition Barisan Sosialis[239] and eviscerated the Left.[240] The party was never to regain its strength or its promise.[241]

If a pre-condition of the moderate state is party political contestation, then all the case studies illustrate how the Singapore state has undermined this crucial pre-condition. Civil society is another major moderator of state power, but in Singapore, associations that had been autonomous of the colonial state were dismantled by the new nation-state,[242] resulting in a quiescent and co-opted civil society without the capacity or the will to contest the state in the public domain.[243] The studies of the *Legal Profession Act*, the *Religious Harmony Act* and the *Public Order Act* illustrate how an embryonic civil society leadership attaching to the Law Society, the Catholic Church and an opposition politician has been repressed and removed. Media also has the capacity to moderate state power. With print media, as with civil society, the PAP dismantled media autonomy early in its rule and extended its policing of print media at a crucial juncture in the mid-1980s (Chapter 4).[244]

[238] Hong & Huang, *supra* note 59 at 18; Harper, *supra* note 59, Barr & Trocki *supra* note 59.

[239] Ibid.

[240] Wade, *supra* note 78.

[241] Ibid.

[242] Kay Gillis, *Singapore Civil Society and British Power* (Singapore: Talisman, 2005).

[243] Terence Chong, *Civil Society in Singapore: Reviewing Concepts in the Literature* (Singapore: Institute of Southeast Asian Studies, 2005); Terence Lee, "The Politics of Civil Society in Singapore" (2002) 26:1 *Asian Studies Review* 97; Gary Rodan, "Civil Society and Other Political Possibilities in Southeast Asia" (1997) 27:2 *Journal of Contemporary Asia* 14.

[244] The Singapore formulation of defamation has further attenuated the independence of media.

'RULE *BY* LAW': PRACTICES OF ILLIBERALISM

This project is, in part, an excavation of the Singapore state's development of a measure of legitimacy for its brand of 'rule by law'. I use the term 'rule by law' as the Other, so to speak, of 'rule of law'. 'Rule by law', conveying the impoverishment of power-serving instrumentalism, is not an expression used by the Singapore state. It is, however, an expression used by scholars tracking modes of state legality characterised by the subordination of 'law' to political power.[245] Peerenboom, for example, describes 'rule by law' as operating when "states ... rely on law to govern but do not accept that basic requirement that law bind the state and state actors".[246] Thio concludes that in the context of state authoritarianism and one-party dominance, the Singapore state's subordination of liberal democratic values to "statist goals like stability and economic growth ... is more accurately characterised as ... the rule *by* law".[247] And as Neilson points out with reference to another one-party state, "*rule of law* ... might better be described as *rule by law* in a single party state because questions of constitutionality, due process and official illegality are not reviewable by an independent judiciary".[248] In Singapore, if the 'rule of law' occupies resonant public and declaratory spaces (the *Constitution*, the *Proclamation*), then 'rule by law' is contained within the tedious detail of legal text and practice – detail through which the Singapore state effects a rescripting of the 'rule of law' content of the promise of 'nation'. It is the strategic rescripting of the 'rule of law' into 'rule by law', while sustaining state legitimacy, that this study tracks and reveals.

It is befitting of the complexity carried by the many meanings of 'law' that if 'rule of law' attaches to Singapore's colonial history, so too does 'rule by law'. The colonial legal system governed through modernist,

[245] Thio, *Lex Rex or Rex Lex? supra* note 14 at 75; Jayasuriya, *The Exception Becomes the Norm*, *supra* note 14 at 113.

[246] Peerenboom, "Introduction," *supra* note 60 at 2.

[247] Thio, *Rule of Law*, *supra* note 41 at 75.

[248] Neilson, *supra* note 66 at 15.

bureaucratic technologies that were, in essence, power-serving 'rule by law'.[249] Colonial legal instruments typify 'law' as governance: state control through licensing, co-option and, from 1915, surveillance.[250] Lee's assertion to the IBA that Singapore had inherited and built upon an "English' legal system is an interesting mis-description. The legal system by which the British governed their colonies arrived in Singapore via India[251] and had been tailored for colonial purposes.[252]

There is thus, for Singapore, an important disjunction relating to 'law' vis-à-vis 'nation'. Through colonisation and tutelage to independence, features of the modern nation-state, such as sovereignty, were transplanted. However, the more enduring structures of modern statehood entrenched by the colonial project derive from the "powerful illiberal ideological traditions"[253] drawn from the absolutist state:

> [T]he colonial state ... facilitated the development of notions of executive power rooted in ideas of 'state prerogatives' that were formed within the womb of the absolutist state. The colonial state was pre-eminently an 'executive state' defined by the 'reason of state' juristic tradition.... The development of the post-colonial state in East Asia also has been greatly influenced by those aspects [a high degree of hegemony and autonomy] of the colonial state. For example, in Singapore the state has tended to justify the use of executive power in a manner reminiscent of the colonial state.... [T]he post-colonial state could continue to be characterised as an executive state. [254]

For Singapore, the executive state characteristics of colonial rule have been augmented by two further historical events: the legal exceptionalism of

[249] Hooker, *supra* note 152; Furnivall, *supra* note 118.

[250] Ban Kah Choon, *Absent History: The Untold Story of Special Branch Operations in Singapore, 1915–1942* (Singapore: Horizon, 2002).

[251] Hooker, *supra* note 152. McQueen and Pue also note that 'law' in the colonies, because of adaptations, misapplications and different institutional support, inevitably differed from 'law' in the metropolitan centre: Rob McQueen & W. Wesley Pue, eds., *Misplaced Traditions: British Lawyers, Colonial Peoples* (Sydney: Federation Press, 1999) 1.

[252] Furnivall, *supra* note 118; Hooker, *supra* note 152.

[253] Jayasuriya, *The Exception Becomes the Norm*, *supra* note 14 at 114.

[254] Jayasuriya, "Statist Legal Institutions", *supra* note 217 at 178.

the Malayan Emergency[255] and the Cold War context in which Singapore became a 'nation'. The studies of the *Vandalism Act* (Chapter 3), the *Press Act* (Chapter 4) and the *Religious Harmony* Act (Chapter 6) reveal the legal-discursive continuities between Emergency and Cold War exceptionalism, on the one hand, and contemporary 'law', on the other. In other words, Singapore's 'rule by law' core has been uninterrupted in the passage from 'colony' to 'nation'.

The one defining event that might have ruptured colonial 'rule by law' and generated a groundswell of awareness for 'rule of law' individual rights – an anti-colonial battle for independence – did not occur in Singapore. The closest thing to a liberation movement was represented by the left-wing Socialists and the Communists in post–World War II Singapore.[256] But because of the Cold War anxieties of the time, the British allied with the pro-'West' PAP to repress the left wing, smoothing the way for ideological continuity between the colonial state and the nation-state.[257]

Thus it is that 'rule by law' has had a long and powerful presence in Singapore. The liberal humanism of the *Constitution* and the *Proclamation* sits like a thin, extremely fragile veneer upon deeply rooted structures that counter and devalue the proclaimed democracy, liberty, justice and equality. 'Rule by law' has a far deeper legal tradition in Singapore than 'rule of law' – a tradition which possibly accounts for the sustained expression of 'rule by law' in the 'nation'.[258] The post-Communist account of the 'rule

[255] Singapore's most notoriously illiberal legal instrument, the *Internal Security Act*, is an adoption and extension of the colonial *Emergency Regulations*. The *Emergency Regulations* were enacted to enable detention without trial as a state strategy to repress the anti-colonial activity of the Malayan Communist Party.

[256] Hong & Huang, *supra* note 59; Harper, *supra* note 59; Geoff Wade, "Suppression of the Left in Singapore, 1945–1963: Domestic and Regional Contexts in the Southeast Asian Cold War", Paper presented at the 5th European Association of Southeast Asian Studies (EUROSEAS) Conference, University of Naples 'L'Orientale', Italy, 12–15 September 2007); Kevin Hewison & Garry Rodan, "The Decline of the Left in Southeast Asia" (1994) *Socialist Register* 235; Rodan, *Authoritarian Rule supra* note 31.

[257] Ibid.

[258] Glenn, *Legal Traditions of the World*, *supra* note 153, argues that newer legal institutions and practices are reinterpreted, driven and determined by deeper and longer established traditions.

of law' as a technocratic assemblage of institutional attributes[259] seamlessly extends Singapore's 'rule by law' into a new era of relevance and legitimacy without resolving the founding disjuncture between 'rule of' and 'rule by' law, a disjuncture arising from the critical difference between the colonial project and the national project: 'Colony' did not promise democracy, independence, liberty, justice and equality. It is the project of 'nation' that has made these promises. 'Rule of law' indicators that privilege efficiency and commerce, and contemporary theorising on 'rule of law', such as Peerenboom's 'thin' to 'thick' 'rule of law' continuum, generate additional ways of attending to function first, thus relegating values and ideals to a secondary place in evaluations of 'law'.

Inevitably, my project's scrutiny of 'law' in Singapore raises the issue of whether my study argues from a normative position on the 'rule of law'. In tracing the discursive excursions of the Singapore state in, through and around the category 'law', my goal has been to avoid an unreflective treatment of the 'rule of law'. The close reading of text required by discourse analysis grounds my conclusions in the detail of history, language and social encounters. While I have done my best to resist polarising positions, I ought to declare my own normative inclinations towards a 'rule of law' that protects and upholds political liberalism.

[259] Kleinfeld, *supra* note 170 at 33.

2 LAW AS DISCOURSE

Theoretical and Definitional Parameters

THE TERM 'DISCOURSE' AND THE IDEA OF discursive constructions of knowledge have become commonplace in scholarly writing, although 'discourse' has been used largely in a taken-for-granted manner. In order to be clear on what I mean by 'discourse' (a term so expansive and inclusive in its meanings and applications "that [it] should be marked 'Danger'"),[1] I first outline the definitions and parameters of discourse and discourse theory that shape my analysis.

Foucaultian scholar Gary Wickham describes discourses as "visible 'systems of thought'" such that, for example,

> the legal discourses involved in the regulation of gambling involve much thought, but we do not and should not look for the 'source' of the thinking 'inside' some head or heads. We are presented with the surfaces of appearance of this thinking in written judgments and regulations, in the design of casinos and other gambling venues, in the comportment and conversations of the gamblers and the staff at the venues, in policing arrangements and practices, and so on. This is discourse – quotidian not mysterious.[2]

[1] Gary Wickham, "Foucault and Law", in Reza Banakar & Max Travers, eds., *An Introduction to Law and Social Theory* (Oxford: Hart, 2002) 249 at 256.

[2] Ibid. at 257.

Discourse is thus evident, everyday and mundane. It is also inextricably part of social processes and practices.[3] In one influential form of theorising on discourse that is informed, in part, by Foucault's work, Critical Discourse Analysis,[4] 'discourse' is described as a term that signals recognition that language use is socially determined.[5] The social determination of language is disaggregated as meaning

> [f]irstly, that language is a part of society and not somehow external to it. Secondly, that language is a social process. And thirdly, that language is a socially conditioned process, conditioned that is by other (non-linguistic) parts of society.[6]

In Critical Discourse Analysis, language choices and power relations in society are seen as co-determined such that an analysis of communication in a particular social institution ties together the macro-analysis of society with the micro-analysis of particular texts.[7] Thus, a close reading of a legislative text, its conditions and contexts validly enables a reading of 'law' and power relations in the Singapore state.

The recent cross-disciplinary focus on narrative, persuasion and rhetoric[8] has meant that there is no single, neatly contained theoretical model of discourse theory.[9] Indeed, the plurality of approaches and applications is consistent with the post-modernist reflexivity that informs

[3] Norman Fairclough, *Language and Power* (London: Longman, 1989) [*Language and Power*] at 23.

[4] Ibid. I rely broadly on the approach known as Critical Discourse Analysis introduced by Fairclough's *Language and Power* and developed primarily in his *Discourse and Social Change* (Cambridge: Polity Press, 1992) and *Media Discourse* (London: Edward Arnold, 1995) and in Lilie Chouliaraki & Norman Fairclough, *Discourse in Late Modernity: Rethinking Critical Discourse Analysis* (Edinburgh: Edinburgh University Press, 1999).

[5] Fairclough, *Language and Power*, *supra* note 3 at 21.

[6] Ibid. at 22.

[7] Christopher Candlin, "Preface", in Fairclough, *Language and Power*, *supra* note 3 at x.

[8] Fairclough, *Language and Power*, *supra* note 3 at 109.

[9] Chouliaraki and Fairclough perceive Critical Discourse Analysis "as contributing to a field of critical research on late modernity [rather than] a particular theory or narrative": *supra* note 4 at 3.

scholarly attention to the unfolding processes of communication, for which language is a vehicle. Post-modernist awareness dismantles the barriers that formerly held between disciplinary fields, adding to the richness with which language is understood as constituting, constructing and reconstructing society.[10] With discourse theory shaping my analysis, I attend to legislative text, the conditions of production and interpretation of each enactment and the ways in which language use relating to 'law' has been, and is, socially determined. Each enactment, read through discourse theory, is an instance of the ways in which people construct and reconstruct social knowledge and power, via legal discourse, in the collective space of society.

I adopt the assumption central to Critical Discourse Analysis: that this collective space, society, is marked by a "dynamic formation of relationships and practices constituted in large measure by struggles for power".[11] In other words, power in society is not equally distributed, nor is its distribution fixed. In terms of power relations, 'law' occupies a particular niche in the complex discursive networks of society. If, in modern societies, it is through discourse (rather than coercion) that the steering of social processes takes place,[12] then 'law', as the "uniquely authorised discourse for the state",[13] has a particular capacity to be the means by which social processes are steered. Put differently, while all discourse is a vehicle for the reiteration, contestation and negotiation of social categories and socially constructed knowledge,[14] legal discourse is especially expressive of elite formulations of social knowledge and elite efforts to manage contestations and negotiations. Given that 'law' is a discursive field especially contiguous with power, dismantling the positivist isolation of 'law'

[10] Fairclough, *Language and Power*, *supra* note 3 at 108.

[11] Candlin, *supra* note 7 at vi.

[12] Piet Strydom, *Discourse and Knowledge: The Making of Enlightenment Sociology* (Liverpool: Liverpool University Press, 2000) at 9.

[13] Robert Post, "Introduction: The Relatively Autonomous Discourse of Law", in Robert Post, ed., *Law and the Order of Culture* (Berkeley: University of California Press, 1991) at vii.

[14] Strydom, *supra* note 12 at 1.

becomes especially important when reading legal texts as expressions of state management of legitimacy through 'law'.

Legal scholarship has recently come to approach 'law' as not just interacting with society, but being in a relationship with society "mediated by or even constituted by language itself".[15] As Conley and O'Barr have put it, "[L]anguage is the essential mechanism through which the power of the law is realized, exercised, reproduced, and occasionally challenged and subverted".[16] The analytical approach to discourse in terms of text, interaction and context (required through Critical Discourse Analysis)[17] also means that I attend to the arenas and actors involved in the discursive moments I study, with particular reference to how language captures and performs the relative positions of power of social actors.[18]

Literature in the field expresses the struggle inherent in approaching 'law' as discourse. Fundamental questions have arisen as to whether "conditions for a field of study of or for 'law as communication'"[19] even exist. Reviews of existing work on 'law' and discourse note that it is interdisciplinary fields (such as law and language, law and literature and the semiotics of law) that set out to examine law as communication.[20] In adopting an inter-disciplinary approach, I perceive the fluidity inherent to a 'law' and discourse approach as a rich resource. This fluidity is a 'problem' only if theory is expected to provide "a circumscribed explanation of its object that is universally valid in all circumstances".[21] If, on

[15] David Nelken, "Can There Be a Sociology of Legal Meaning?" in David Nelken, ed., *Law as Communication* (Dartmouth: Ashgate, 1996) 107 at 108 [*Can There Be a Sociology of Legal Meaning?*].

[16] Jon M. Conley & William M. O'Barr, *Just Words: Law, Language and Power*, 2nd ed. (Chicago: University of Chicago Press, 2005) at 129.

[17] Fairclough, *Language and Power*, *supra* note 3 at 22–27.

[18] Ibid.

[19] David Nelken, "Law as Communication: Constituting the Field", in David Nelken, ed., *Law as Communication* (Dartmouth: Ashgate, 1996) at 3.

[20] Ibid. at 5–13.

[21] Ben Golder & Peter Fitzpatrick, *Foucault's Law* (Abingdon: Routledge, 2009) at 3.

the other hand, 'law' and discourse are approached as offering "a situated 'analytics' of power in diverse social practices",[22] then the absence of fixity might be perceived as a strength.

To approach 'law' as discourse involves some measure of engagement with the theories and concepts that inform these inter-disciplinary fields, notably the work of modern and post-modern social theorists who have focused on communication and discourse, such as Habermas, Bourdieu, Luhmann and Foucault.[23] Arguably, it is the work of the social theorists Foucault and Habermas that has been most influential in launching the contemporary scholarly attention to discourse.[24] The Habermasian emphasis on the role of public discourse in securing democratic legitimacy,[25] and Habermas's ideal of a "social system that guarantees basic civil rights and enables meaningful participation by all those affected by a decision",[26] make a close application of his conception of discourse problematic in the context of Singapore's carefully managed public domain and minimally participatory democracy.[27] In addition, the colonial history of Singapore and the impact of the particular events on state responses to 'law' and the public domain (such as the Indian Mutiny/Rebellion on state responses to 'religion'[28] or the Malayan Emergency on

[22] Ibid. at 4.

[23] Nelken, *Can There Be a Sociology of Legal Meaning? supra* note 15 at 4; Fairclough, *Language and Power*, *supra* note 3 at 12–15.

[24] For a comprehensive and rigorous survey of scholarship on discourse, see Strydom, *supra* note 12.

[25] Jürgen Harbermas, *Between Facts and Norms: Contributions to a Discourse Theory of Law and Democracy*, trans. by William Rehg (Cambridge, MA: MIT Press, 1995).

[26] A. Michael Froomkin, "Habermas@Discourse.Net: Towards a Critical Theory of Cyberspace" (2003) 116:3 *Harv. L. Rev.* 751 at 752.

[27] Beng-Huat Chua, *Communitarian Ideology and Democracy in Singapore* (London: Routledge, 1995); Cherian George, *Singapore the Air-Conditioned Nation: Essays on the Politics of Comfort and Control* (Singapore: Landmark, 2000); Christopher Tremewan, *The Political Economy of Social Control in Singapore* (New York: St. Martin's Press, 1994); Ho Khai Leong, *Shared Responsibilities, Unshared Power: The Politics of Policy-Making in Singapore* (Singapore: Marshall Cavendish, 2003).

[28] 1858 Proclamation of Queen Victoria, *Straits Government Gazette* no. 47 (19 November 1858) 245.

state responses to 'law') speak of a different trajectory from that assumed in Habermas's work.[29]

There is also the risk that "under conditions of Western hegemony, Habermas's 'impartial' procedures and 'universally binding' communicative rationality ... may mask both Western hegemony and non-Western cultural extinction"[30] – a risk that perhaps accounts for the relatively small pool of scholarship applying Habermasian democratic theory to the political contexts of the developing world.[31] I must, however, note that Habermas's "crucial insight ... that a public sphere is constituted as a particular way of using language in public"[32] informs this analysis of legal text and the attendant focus on state and public discourse, and the configuration of 'law' through the public domain.

A FOUCAULTIAN TOOLKIT

In contrast to Habermasian theorising, Foucault's conception of discourse seems particularly suited to understanding Singapore because of the focus

[29] Jürgen Habermas, "Religion in the Public Sphere" (2006) 14:1 *European Journal of Philosophy* 1.

[30] Ilan Kapoor, "Deliberative Democracy or Agonistic Pluralism? The Relevance of the Habermas–Mouffe Debate for Third World Politics" (2002) 27:4 *Alternatives: Global, Local, Political* 459 at 470. There is a large literature softening and broadening the application of Habermasian theory on 'law', discourse and democracy, which space constraints prevent me from engaging with here. Some recent samples are: Karl-Otto Apel, "2 Discourse Ethics, Democracy, and International Law: Towards a Globalization of Practical Reason" (2007) 66:1 *American Journal of Economics & Sociology* 49; Pauline Johnson, *Habermas: Rescuing the Public Sphere* (Oxford: Routledge, 2006); John P. McCormick, *Weber, Habermas and Transformations of the European State: Constitutional, Social and Supranational Democracy* (Cambridge: Cambridge University Press, 2007); David L. Prychitko & Virgil Henry Storr, "Communicative Action and the Radical Constitution: The Habermasian Challenge to Hayek, Mises and Their Descendents" (2007) 31:2 *Cambridge Journal of Economics* 255; and Rene Von Schomberg & Kenneth Baynes, eds., *Discourse and Democracy: Essays on Habermas's "Between Facts and Norms"* (Albany: State University of New York Press, 2002).

[31] A recent example of the application and adaptation of Habermas to the third world is John Gillespie, *Transplanting Commercial Law Reform: Developing a Rule of Law in Vietnam* (Aldershot: Ashgate, 2006). See also Kapoor, *supra* note 30.

[32] Chouliaraki & Fairclough, *supra* note 4 at 5.

on historical specificity and on how power informs discourse.[33] I should, however, explicate the manner in which Foucaultian theorising informs this project. In their important new work, *Foucault's Law*,[34] Golder and Fitzpatrick identify two approaches to Foucault in legal scholarship. The first has been called an "exegetical or interpretive" approach, which seeks to "locate the position of law within Foucault's existing (and indeed posthumously expanding) body of work" and "synthesise Foucault's disparate statements on law or to explicitly (re)construct his overall position on law as a precondition to using his work".[35] The second approach, which Golder and Fitzpatrick call "applied" or "appropriative",

> seeks to employ Foucaultian concepts and methodologies in the critical study of law ... unencumbered by the exegetical debates around whether and to what extent, Foucault theorised law.... In doing so, they have developed a piecemeal Foucaultian jurisprudence which addresses a wide range of legal topics.... Such an approach is entirely consistent with Foucault's oft-repeated methodological pronouncements on how he wished his work to be used – that is, as a 'toolkit' for activists, scholars and writers.[36]

I locate my scholarship within the second approach: applied or appropriative use of Foucaultian concepts and methodologies. In the same spirit of valuing and adopting the conceptual 'toolkit' generated by prior scholarship, I use the term 'hegemony' in a broad, everyday sense (to mean dominance) without engaging in the debates surrounding the strictly Gramscian sense of the term,[37] just as I employ the concept of the public domain without engaging in the Foucault–Habermas debate. Instead, my

[33] Strydom, *supra* note 12 at 50.

[34] Golder & Fitzpatrick, *supra* note 21 at 5.

[35] Ibid.

[36] Ibid.

[37] I should, however, note Castell's argument that while Singapore is clearly authoritarian, it is not simplistically a dictatorship but rather a hegemonic state in the Gramscian sense because it is based on consensus as well as coercion: Manuel Castells, "The Developmental City-State in an Open World Economy: The Singapore Experience" (Berkeley: University of California, 1988), online: <http://brie.berkeley.edu/publications/working_papers.html>.

focus is on Foucaultian approaches because the Foucaultian alertness to forms of knowledge and power that might be subjugated, disguised or hidden by dominant discourses is a particularly enabling approach in the context of the high level of state hegemony in Singapore.[38]

In keeping with a Foucaultian understanding of discourse, I also employ Foucault's concepts of genealogy, conditions of possibility, disciplinary power and governmentality. Given the focus of this project on the state's reframing of the 'rule of law', governmentality – the "calculating preoccupation with activities directed at shaping, channelling and guiding the conduct of others"[39] – is a concept that seems especially useful. The term 'governmentality' is "an amalgam of 'government' and 'mentality'"[40] and involves thinking about "law as another means of, and another location for the exercise of, government. Law is not a special 'external force'."[41] Instead, 'law' is one among many "forms of modern political rationality"[42] that leads individuals to "govern themselves outside of institutions."[43] In explaining governmentality, Foucault described power as expressing itself in a dynamic that is triangular: "[W]e have a triangle: sovereignty, discipline, and governmental management, which has population as its main target and apparatuses of security as its essential mechanism."[44] In short, governmentality represents a complex and diffuse post-monarchical form of power by which people govern themselves and others.[45] Indeed, Hunt and Wickham argue that "all operations of law are instances of governance."[46]

[38] On the range and reach of the Singapore state hegemony, in addition to Castell (ibid.), see references in Chapter 1's discussion of Singapore as a regime type.

[39] Alan Hunt & Gary Wickham, *Foucault and Law: Towards a Sociology of Law as Governance* (London: Pluto Press, 1994) at 26.

[40] Wickam, *supra* note 1 at 261.

[41] Ibid. at 263.

[42] Golder & Fitzpatrick, *supra* note 21 at 12.

[43] Ibid. at 30.

[44] Ibid. at 219–20.

[45] Michel Foucault, "Governmentality," in *Michel Foucault: Power, Essential Works of Foucault, 1954–1984*, ed. by James D. Faubion (London: Penguin, 2002) vol. 3 at 201.

[46] Hunt & Wickham, *supra* note 39 at 99.

Governmentality includes a range of ways in which states target populations[47] and acknowledges "the multiplicity of forces acting on a given individual in any activity".[48] The governmentality power complex is constituted by "institutions, procedures, analyses, and reflections ... calculations and tactics"[49] and results in the construction of "specific governmental apparatuses alongside the development of complexes of knowledge, all of which are geared towards the state's control and management of populations".[50] An important feature of governmentality relating to a study of 'law' and discourse is that governmentality embraces

> both the (self-)governance of individuals (through internalised controls and the individual's discursive constitution – the conduct of conduct) and multiple government rationalities that are engaged in order to govern the population.[51]

One expression of governmentality is the state appropriation of the "political technology of pastoral power"[52] embedded in "the pastoral promise of material salvation within the frame of the modern administrative state".[53] An application of Foucault's concept of governmentality is therefore especially suited for a study of legislation and discourse in Singapore because, as the case studies highlight, the Singapore state assumes an overtly pedagogical stance towards a population it discursively infantalises.

Augmenting the ascendancy the state accords itself is the state's consistent rehearsal of the discourse of national vulnerability. This discourse of perpetual territorial vulnerability is typically tied to the state's discursive promise that 'rule by law' measures will ensure continuing prosperity for the fragile 'nation'. The state's narratives of a 'nation' under siege (whether in the territorial, moral or economic sense) become legitimising

[47] Ibid.

[48] Chris Dent, "Copyright, Governmentality and Problematisation: An Exploration" (2009) 18:1 *Griffith Law Review* 134 at 135.

[49] Foucault, *supra* note 45 at 219.

[50] Ibid. at 208.

[51] Dent, *supra* note 48.

[52] Golder & Fitzpatrick, *supra* note 21 at 30.

[53] Ibid. at 31.

tropes when enacting 'law'. In other words, as shepherd, the state presents itself as the only social actor equipped to lead the vulnerable 'nation' to the protected pastures of wealth, security and social order.

However, I should note the caution of Foucaultian scholar Dent that, in Singapore's case, history and the sustained political dominance of a single personality (Lee Kuan Yew) may come together to create a form of governmentality that departs from standard analyses in two regards. First, "in most governmentalist analyses, there is no entity called the 'state' that consciously acts upon the population"[54]; and second, strong features of the precursor to the governmentalist state, the administrativist state, are apparent in the governance practices of Singapore.[55] Dent cautions that Foucault's concept of governmentality is situated in a different social, historical and geo-political context from Singapore, and suggests that while, typically, notions of governmentality do not centre on the state, given the specifics of Singapore, it may be possible

> to consider the state, or at least specific organs of the state, as an actor itself; an actor that has appropriated some governmentalist practices (such as encouraging the self-regulating (economic) practices of *homo oeconomicus*) but has retained that degree of separation necessary to act upon the population in certain limited but specific areas.[56]

Bearing in mind both Dent's caution and the continuing presence of the technologies, ideologies and practices of the colonial administrative state in contemporary Singapore,[57] and in keeping with my "appropriative"[58] approach to Foucaultian tools, I retain the term 'governmentality' in my analysis.

[54] Chris Dent, "The Administrativist State and Questions of Governmentality" (2009) (unpublished paper).

[55] Ibid.

[56] Ibid.

[57] Kanishka Jayasuriya, "The Exception Becomes the Norm: Law and Regimes of Exception in East Asia" (2001) 2:1 *Asian Pac. L. & Pol'y J.* 108 at 118; and "Corporatism and Judicial Independence Within Statist Legal Institutions in East Asia", in Kanishka Jayasuriya, ed., *Law, Capitalism and Power in Asia* (London: Routledge, 1999) 173.

[58] Golder & Fitzpatrick, *supra* note 21 at 5.

3 PUNISHING BODIES, SECURING THE NATION

1966 Vandalism Act

THE *VANDALISM ACT*[1] WAS THE FIRST legislative instrument enacted in the 'nation' to prescribe mandatory corporal punishment. The state discourse of the time, directed at legitimising corporal punishment, is therefore central to a particular construction of the role of 'lawful' violent punishment in the vulnerable Singapore 'nation'. At the time it was enacted, through context and sub-text, the state used the *Vandalism Act* to demarcate certain expressions of opposition politics as criminal and anti-national – thus consolidating the state's power over the space of 'nation', in both material and discursive terms. But the 1994 use of the *Vandalism Act* (discussed in the second half of this chapter) reveals that, in addition to being a vehicle for repressive technologies (corporal punishment, incarceration and heightened surveillance), the Act has become a vehicle for state pedagogy, such that the 'citizen' is instructed on how to constitute individual identity in terms of 'good' citizenship, virtuous conduct and 'Asian values'.

Both the 1966 enactment and the 1994 enforcement of the Act are marked by a thematic constant in state discourse: the insistence that Singapore is an exceptionally vulnerable nation with exceptional circumstances necessitating 'tough laws' (symbolised by violent punishment) in order that the always vulnerable Singapore 'nation' might be rendered

[1] Cap. 341, 1985 Rev. Ed. Sing.

less vulnerable. This theme, cast in the rhetoric of nationalism, masks an appropriation of 'law' in the service of pedagogy such that, even if conducted behind prison walls, caning becomes instructive public spectacle. It is the high degree of violence and the state's capacity to legitimise this violence that serve to control the (notionally) watching citizen. This chapter traces some of the expansive and malleable ways in which, through the *Vandalism Act*, 'law' as governance has manifested so as to reconfigure 'rule of law' ideals into a form of 'rule by law' that maintains legitimacy for state violence.

The *Vandalism Act* was originally entitled the *Punishment for Vandalism Act* and was intended, as stated in its preamble, "to provide exemplary punishment for vandalism". The Act provides for mandatory caning upon conviction and was a significant departure from the then-existing punishment for comparable conduct – a fine of S$50.[2] The Act was, at the time, a significant departure from penal practices in one other way – it prescribed a violent punishment for a property offence.[3] The original title (amended in the 1970 revised edition of the Statutes to the abbreviated *Vandalism Act*) placed attention squarely on the instructive power of punishment. I use the original title when discussing the Act in 1966 and the revised title when discussing the Act in 1994 in order to retain the significance of the original focus on punishment.

POLITICS AND VANDALISM IN 1966

The *Punishment for Vandalism Bill* was presented to Parliament in August 1966, not by the Minister for Law, but by the Minister of State for Defence.[4] How was vandalism an issue within the purview of the Ministry for Defence and why did a one-year-old nation-state, beset by all the

[2] *Minor Offences Ordinance* (Cap. 117, 1936 Rev. Ed. Sing.) s. 11(1).

[3] Sing., *Parliamentary Debates*, vol. 25, col. 298 (26 August 1966) (Mr. E. W. Barker). See also Mark Lim Fung Chian, "An Appeal to Use the Rod Sparingly: A Dispassionate Analysis of the Use of Caning in Singapore" (1994) 15:3 *Singapore Law Review* 20.

[4] Sing., *Parliamentary Debates*, vol. 25, cols. 291–93 (26 August 1966) (Wee Toon Boon).

concerns of a tiny third-world country in a politically volatile region, set out to address vandalism as a priority? The events of 1966, the sub-text of the parliamentary debates on the Act[5] and the early prosecutions[6] reveal that the *Vandalism Act*, in its original formulation, was not really about vandalism but about the visible expression of opposition politics in the public domain – politics that was pro-Vietcong, anti-US, and left wing.

The *Punishment for Vandalism Bill* was first read in Parliament on 17 August 1966, a year, almost to the day, from 9 August 1965, when Singapore had an unexpected nationhood thrust upon it.[7] At the time the Bill was presented to Parliament, Singapore's leadership was extremely anxious about a range of issues pertaining to the survival and viability of Singapore as a nation-state: the economy, the sudden Separation from the Federation, Konfrontasi (Confrontation) with Indonesia,[8] inescapable geographical proximity to the war in Indochina and continuing defence dependency on Britain, Australia and New Zealand.[9] The Cold War context of the period, the high level of Communist activity in the

[5] Sing., *Parliamentary Debates*, vol. 25, cols. 291–305 (26 August 1966).

[6] Discussed below at "A Fragmentary Jurisprudence of Vandalism."

[7] In the brief account of Singapore history that Lee presented to the IBA, Separation features as a key moment. The two defining moments relating to the Federation, that of becoming a state within it in September 1963 and that of being cast out of the Federation in August 1965, are conventionally referred to as "Merger" and "Separation". See, for example, two books aimed at a popular readership: *Singapore: Journey into Nationhood* (Singapore: National Heritage Board & Landmark, 1998) and *10 Years That Shaped a Nation* (Singapore: National Archives of Singapore, 2008). The August 1965 Separation from the Federation of Malaysia (a disentanglement Singapore did not seek, resulting from a decision of the central government in Malaysia) is presented in the national narrative as a moment of trauma, defining "a national predicament and a national watchword of vulnerability": Michael Leiffer, *Singapore's Foreign Policy: Coping with Vulnerability* (London: Routledge, 2000) at 14. For the dominant account of Separation, see Lee Kuan Yew, *From Third World to First: The Singapore Story, 1965–2000* (Singapore: Times Editions, 2000) 19–25.

[8] See note 98, Chapter 1.

[9] The anxieties are perhaps best captured by a speech made by the Head of State, the Yang Di-Pertuan Negara, upon the opening of the first Parliament of the Republic of Singapore: Sing., *Parliamentary Debates*, vol. 24, cols. 5–14 (8 December 1965). This speech is discussed in Chapter 1.

region, as well as within Singapore and Malaysia,[10] made Singapore a new nation whose declared anti-Communism was of international geopolitical significance.[11]

To summarise a point that has been made in critical readings of Singapore's history, in the Cold War climate in which Singapore became a 'nation', with 'Communist' constructed as a marginalising and demonising category, the PAP and the British allied to remove much of the left wing from the political and public spheres.[12] If the PAP represented a pro-West, capitalist, right-wing party, then the more overtly anti-colonialist, Socialist, political actor was the left-wing Barisan Sosialis, the party that represented the main opposition to the PAP. The Barisan Sosialis[13] (meaning Socialist Front, referred to hereafter as "Barisan"), formed largely by a splinter faction of the PAP,[14] had already been severely undermined by the notorious Operation Coldstore of 1963, in which, eight months before the September 1963 elections, at least 107 left-wing trade unionists and

[10] See, for example, "Troops for Border", *Straits Times* (11 August 1966) 1 (reporting the movement of Malaysian army and police reinforcements to the Thai border "to counter any resurgence of Communist terrorism") or Chan Beng Soon, "10 Die in Thai Border Ambush", *Straits Times* (9 August 1966) 1.

[11] In the post–World War II period, the British were convinced that Singapore was the centre of "an international conspiracy aimed at destabilising the region": T. N. Harper, "Lim Chin Siong and the 'Singapore Story'", in Tan Jin Quee & Jomo, K. S. eds., *Comet in Our Sky: Lim Chin Siong in History* (Kuala Lumpur: Insan, 2001) 3 at 12. See also Geoff Wade, "Suppression of the Left in Singapore, 1945–1963: Domestic and Regional Contexts in the Southeast Asian Cold War", Paper presented at the 5th European Association of Southeast Asian Studies (EUROSEAS) Conference, University of Naples 'L'Orientale', Italy, 12–15 September 2007) (unpublished).

[12] Hong Lysa & Huang Jianli, *The Scripting of a National History: Singapore and Its Pasts* (Singapore: NUS Press, 2008); Christopher Tremewan, *The Political Economy of Social Control in Singapore* (New York: St. Martin's Press, 1994); Harper, *supra* note 11. Said Zahari, a Coldstore detainee who was held for seventeen years, presents his analysis of the PAP–British complicity in *The Long Nightmare: My 17 Years as a Political Prisoner* (Kuala Lumpur: Utusan, 2007) 3–16.

[13] The Barisan was formed in August 1961 as a result of a split between left- and right-wing elements within the PAP: Hussin Mutalib, *Parties and Politics: A Study of Opposition Parties and the PAP in Singapore* (Singapore: Marshall Cavendish International, 2005) at 75.

[14] Ibid.

opposition activists had been detained without trial, and thus prevented from contesting the elections.[15] The Barisan still managed to win thirteen seats in Parliament, but three of the victorious Barisan candidates were arrested and another two fled Singapore to escape arrest, leaving just eight Barisan Members of Parliament.[16] Seven Barisan-affiliated trade unions were also threatened with de-registration.[17] Ideologically opposed to detention without trial[18] and disgusted with the state's repressive use of 'law', the Barisan boycotted Parliament, declaring that Singapore's independence was spurious[19] and that it would take its cause to the streets.[20]

In 1966, despite being absent from Parliament and weakened by 'anti-Communist' measures, the Barisan appears to have been perceived by the PAP as a not insignificant challenge to PAP power.[21] At the very least, the Barisan impinged upon a growing PAP management of the public domain by presenting accounts of events that were alternatives to, and dissented from, accounts generated by the PAP. Within this context, the *Punishment for Vandalism Act* was, I would argue, a state response to a specific event involving Barisan expressions of dissent: a Barisan-led campaign against the US military presence in Vietnam.

THE "AID VIETNAM" CAMPAIGN

In April 1966, for the first time in Singapore's history, US troops who had been serving in South Vietnam arrived in Singapore for rest and

[15] See references at *supra* notes 11, 12 and 13.

[16] Hong & Huang, *supra* note 12 at xiii.

[17] Mutalib, *supra* note 13 at 102.

[18] Harper, *supra* note 11 at 47.

[19] Hong & Huang, *supra* note 12 at xiii.

[20] Mutalib, *supra* note 13 at 106–107.

[21] One scholar assesses the Barisan as having "emerged as a potential alternative government to the PAP" between 1961 and February 1963 (Harper, *supra* note 11 at 25), while another despairs of the Barisan as a viable leftist party (C. C. Chin, "The United Front Strategy of the Malayan Communist Party in Singapore, 1950s–1960s", in Michael D. Barr & Carl A. Trocki, eds., *Paths Not Taken: Political Pluralism in Post-War Singapore* [Singapore: NUS Press, 2008] 58 at 72). Mutalib concludes that, initially at least, the Barisan was a formidable political foe: *supra* note 13 at 82–84.

recreation leave.[22] In response, a campaign against the presence of US troops in Singapore[23] and against US military action in Vietnam was launched by the Barisan and left-wing trade unions.[24] As part of this campaign, the Barisan put together a display of "pictures and newspaper clippings about alleged American atrocities in Vietnam",[25] a markedly opposing view of the US engagement from that of the PAP.[26]

The PAP-state was not passive in response to these Barisan initiatives. The Barisan was already being squeezed out of the public domain – the *Straits Times* coverage of the Barisan campaigns was patchy, and state actions directed at containing the Barisan must often be discerned from reporting on other matters.[27] The state also turned to strategies of governance in a range of ways to manage opposition activity, banning rallies in public places and finding Barisan activities illegal.[28] Unsurprisingly, therefore, much of the "Aid Vietnam" campaign took the shape of

22 "100 US Troops in S'pore for Rest", *Straits Times* (6 April 1966) 5.

23 "Anti-US Slogans Daubed on Bus Shelters", *Straits Times* (14 April 1966) 9.

24 "Society illegal, Dr Lee is Warned", *Straits Times* (10 April 1966) 2; "'Aid Vietnam' Display by Barisan", *Straits Times* (11 April 1966) 4; "Anti-US Name Campaign", *Straits Times* (19 May 1966) 11; "Barisan to Hold Meetings Against Police", *Straits Times* (22 May 1966) 3.

25 "'Aid Vietnam' Display by Barisan", *supra* note 24 at 4.

26 The *Straits Times* gave prominence to its reports on the US military engagement in Indochina. The Vietcong was represented as cruel and ruthless, the United States as a selfless warrior for freedom and democracy. See, for example, "Mobs Out for US Blood", *Straits Times* (9 April 1966) 1; "Worst Week in Air War for US", *Straits Times* (15 August 1966) 1.

27 For example, a three-paragraph article reporting on the statements issued by the University of Singapore Socialist Club and the Singapore Polytechnic Political Society, that the government should remove the ban it had placed on Nanyang University students who agitated against the reorganisation of Nanyang University, discloses in its last three lines that the government has declared the "Aid Vietnam against US Aggression" committee illegal: "Reinstate Expelled Students", *Straits Times* (19 April 1966) 5. Another example of this 'discreet' reporting is "Aid-Vietnam Posters Hint of May Day Violence", *Straits Times* (24 April 1966) 1 (which mentions that all public places have been barred from rallies).

28 "Society Illegal, Dr Lee warned", *Straits Times* (10 April 1966) 2; "Reinstate Expelled Students" at 5; "May Day: Police on Emergency Alert", *Straits Times* (2 May 1966) 9; *May Day* "Putting up Posters: 23 Charged", *Straits Times* (4 May 1966) 4.

slogans and posters which were painted and put up covertly, in the middle of the night.[29]

Recent scholarship has noted that the PAP-state had, from at least 1962, adopted a strategy designed to frustrate the Barisan into abandoning a 'lawful' engagement in politics: "[A] Special Branch Paper ... suggested a two-phase programme of action. In the first phase, the Barisan would be harassed by the police and the government. This was designed to provoke it into unconstitutional action".[30] It is probable that in 1966 the state had retained this strategy. On 13 April 1966, the city woke to discover red, anti-American slogans had been painted on bus-stops and walls while most people had been asleep.[31] Two days later, two top leaders of the Barisan were arrested on a sedition charge relating to an article that had been published five months earlier,[32] with the state unable to explain why it had taken so long to press charges for so serious an offence.[33] The timing of this arrest, 16 April, was also significant with regard to another event in the public domain: Labour Day on 1 May.

A week before Labour Day, state discourse anticipated left-wing Labour Day activity in terms of violence and disorder.[34] On Labour Day itself, police visibility was high: Left-wing unions were placed under police surveillance, platoons of policemen stood at the intersections of roads and the American Embassy was heavily guarded. The state constrained the left wing's capacity to use Labour Day to make its presence felt: The roads around the site of a strike, the Hotel Singapura, were closed to prevent left-wing unionists from expressing solidarity with the twenty-two striking workers there, and public announcements were made every thirty minutes to warn the public against participating in

29 "Anti-US Slogans Daubed on Bus Shelters", *supra* note 23 at 9; "Aid-Vietnam Posters Hint of May Day Violence", *supra* note 27 at 1.

30 Harper, *supra* note 11 at 37.

31 "Anti-US Slogans Daubed on Bus Shelters", *supra* note 23 at 9.

32 "Two Barisan Leaders Arrested on Sedition Charge", *Straits Times* (16 April 1966) 1.

33 "The Barisan Sedition Case Takes New Turn", *Straits Times* (26 April 1966) 1.

34 "Aid-Vietnam Posters Hint of May Day Violence", *supra* note 27 at 1.

rallies or demonstrations.[35] And yet, despite these measures, the streets leading to the American Embassy and outside the left-wing unions bore "Yankees, Go Home" posters.[36] Two days after Labour Day, twenty-three men and boys were charged with putting up posters, notices and banners on 30 April and 1 May.[37]

Police permission for the Labour Day Rally of the left-wing trade unions was granted at the very last minute, on the eve of Labour Day,[38] timing which must have obstructed planning, organisation and publicity for the left-wing rally. In sharp contrast to the constraints the Barisan was operating under, the PAP-affiliated National Trades Unions Congress rally was a lavish affair supported by the resources of the state:

> The Deputy Prime Minister, Dr Toh Chin Chye, will officially declare open the $140,000 fountain in the grounds of the National Theatre, as part of the Labour Day celebrations on May 1.
>
> Announcing this today, the National Trades Union Congress, which is organising the Republic's Labour Day celebrations, said that the opening ceremony would coincide with a massive carnival and a mammoth rally to be held in the same grounds, and the theatre proper on that day. The opening ceremony will begin at 6:30 PM with a march-past, and a display by the People's Association Band. About the same time, hundreds of trade union leaders will leave the theatre after attending a Labour Day rally to assemble around the fountain.[39]

Lexically, this report conflates the PAP with 'nation': The venue for the event is a new *national* monument, the National Theatre; the organising trade union, instead of declaring its political affiliation to the PAP, describes itself as a *national* trade union; and the celebration it is managing is presented as the *Republic*'s celebration.

35 *Supra* note 33; "May Day", supranote 28.

36 "May Day: Police on Emergency Alert", *supra* note 28 at 9.

37 "Putting up Posters: 23 Charged", *supra* note 28 at 4; "Reasons Behind the Vandalism Bill ...", *Straits Times* (25 August 1966) 4.

38 "May Day Rally Approved", *Straits Times* (30 April 1966) 1.

39 "A $140,000 Fountain to Be Opened by Toh on May Day", *Straits Times* (20 April 1966) 6.

Just as Labour Day became an occasion upon which political contestation played out in the public domain in a manner which conflated 'nation' and PAP (with the highly visible deployment of policemen implicating the left wing as somehow criminal), a similar dynamic played out later that year. Three days before Singapore's first National Day on 9 August 1966, internal security officers raided the Barisan's headquarters and seized what were described as "anti-Singapore posters":

> Internal Security officers raided the Barisan Sosialis headquarters in Victoria Street today. A sackful of documents and anti-Singapore posters were seized. The ISD [Internal Security Department] men burst into the premises while a meeting was going on just before 4 PM – soon after police announced that action would be taken against those putting up illegal posters or writing slogans in public places.
>
> The police secretary, Mr T Chelliah, said in a statement; "it has come to the knowledge of the police that the Barisan Sosialis and Partai Rakyat Singapore[40] intend to stick up posters and write slogans in public places in Singapore over the next three days. "This is an offence under the law and members of the public are requested to co-operate with the police by dialling 999 should they see anyone committing this offence."
>
> The Barisan Sosialis, together with Partai Rakyat, has planned a "phoney independence' rally at Hong Lim on National Day. [41]

The validity of patriotism is denied to the Barisan when the posters, probably anti-PAP, are characterised as "anti-Singapore". The urgency and forcefulness of the terms "raided", "seized" and "burst into" valorise the police even as they radicalise the Barisan. It was not weapons or illegal drugs that were being "seized"; it was documents and posters. The police and the media report characterised the Barisan's posters and slogans as such an alarming illegality that citizens were told to dial the emergency

[40] Said Zahari writes of how the alliance between the Barisan, Partai Rakyat Singapura (Singapore People's Party) and Partai Pekerja Singapura (Singapore Workers' Party) alarmed the PAP and the British: *supra* note12 at 6.

[41] "Security Men Raid Barisan Office", *Sunday Times* (7 August 1966).

number, 999, if they witnessed 'vandalism' in action. Ten days after this 'raid' was reported, the *Punishment for Vandalism Bill* had its first reading in Parliament.

EXEMPLARY PUNISHMENT AND THE VULNERABLE NATION

When the government presented the *Punishment for Vandalism Bill* to Parliament, it did not explicitly acknowledge that the Bill was a response to the "Aid Vietnam Against US Aggression" campaign or the planned "phoney independence" rally. Instead, it was the examples of 'vandalism' the government offered that revealed the connection. Prime Minister Lee Kuan Yew described vandalism as "a particularly vicious social misdemeanour, like taking a pot of paint and going to every bus stand and chalking up anti-American or anti-British or pro-Vietcong slogans",[42] while the Minister who presented the Bill to Parliament said:

> Members will be aware of the reasons for this Bill, for we have witnessed the sorry spectacle of people of ill-will smearing and defacing our fair city. The writing of slogans, drawing of pictures, painting and marking or inscribing on public and private property has been rampant. Indeed, even the sides of drains have been used by anti-social and anti-national elements in the name of democracy.[43]

These examples, offering definitions of 'vandalism' that relate to the "Aid Vietnam" campaign, demonstrate that 'vandalism' was a cipher for opposition politics, or at least the kind of opposition politics that could not be contained by police permits. The February 1963 Coldstore detentions demonstrated that the nation-state had already adopted the colonial state's practices in two ways: first, characterising political opposition as public disorder,[44] and second, utilising the legal exceptionalism of detention without trial to manage dissent.[45] But by using 'vandalism' as a

[42] Sing., *Parliamentary Debates*, vol. 25, col. 295 (26 August 1966) (Lee Kuan Yew).

[43] Sing., *Parliamentary Debates*, vol. 25, col. 291 (26 August 1966) (Wee Toon Boon).

[44] Peter Fitzpatrick, *Law and State in Papua New Guinea* (London: Academic Press, 1980).

[45] Detention without trial in the Singapore legal system has been contextualised in the discussion of the PAP–British alliance in Chapter 1.

cipher for visible left-wing dissent, the nation-state exceeded the colonial state's legal exceptionalism by criminalising opposition activity that had resorted to acts of disobedience in the face of a government machinery determined to obstruct 'lawful' dissent.

Augmenting the nation-state's criminalisation of dissent was another reinvention of colonial practices, this time relating to corporal punishment. Under the colonial state, sanguinary punishment (by which I mean punishment targeted at the body, such as corporal and capital punishment) appears to have been regarded as a justifiable penal response to violent crime.[46] The nation-state was aware it was departing from a standard in prescribing violent punishment for a minor offence relating to property.[47] Prime Minister Lee justified the mandatory corporal punishment in terms that revealed, yet again, that the conduct the state sought to contain was not conventional 'vandalism':

> [A] fine will not deter the type of criminal we are facing here. He is quite prepared to go to gaol having defaced public buildings with red paint. Flaunting the values of his ideology, he is quite prepared to make a martyr of himself and go to gaol. He will not pay the fine and make a demonstration of his martyrdom.
>
> But if he knows he is going to get three of the best, I think he will lose a great deal of enthusiasm, because there is little glory attached to the rather humiliating experience of having to be caned.[48]

The 'vandal', by this account, is motivated by political ideology, yet is categorised as a criminal, not a political, actor. If the 'vandal' were acknowledged to be a political actor, his or her citizen's right to dissent must be acknowledged or the state must contain him or her through preventive detention – detention by which the 'vandal' would acquire the

[46] Mark Brown, "Ethnology and Colonial Administration in Nineteenth-Century British India: The Question of Native Crime and Criminality" (2003) 36:2 *British Journal for the History of Science* 201–19; Anand A. Yang, "Indian Convict Workers in Southeast Asia in the Late Eighteenth and Early Nineteenth Centuries" (2003) 14:2 *Journal of World History* 179–208. Jörg Fisch, *Cheap Lives and Dear Limbs: The British Transformation of the Bengal Criminal Law, 1769–1817* (Wiesbaden: Franz Steiner Verlag, 1983).

[47] Sing., *Parliamentary Debates*, vol. 25, col. 298 (26 August 1966) (E. W. Barker).

[48] Sing., *Parliamentary Debates*, vol. 25, cols. 296–97 (26 August 1966) (Lee Kuan Yew).

moral status of a martyr. The state, however, does not want to accord the status of 'martyr' to the 'vandal'. And so, through legal text, the category 'vandal' is constructed, the offence 'vandalism' is distorted and the punishment of caning is mandated, so as to humiliate, so as to bring the visceral experience of pain to bear upon the body of the person with a different ideology – a use of pain that might be called torture.[49]

In 1966 enacting a 'law' that punished through caning was regressive, as even the state recognised.[50] Violent punishment therefore needed its own legitimising arguments. In addition, because containing the opposition was a masked purpose of the 'law', the *Punishment for Vandalism Bill* had to be justified in other ways, and the justification the state chose to present was that caning was an appropriate disciplinary practice for protecting "the people's money" that had gone into public property.[51] In making this argument, the Minister valorised not only punitive violence but also the state's dismantling of the elements required for guilt in criminal law:

> An important feature of the Bill is the fact that not only the person or persons who actually do these acts will be punished but also those who cause such acts to be done. It is common knowledge to Members that anti-national elements use children and other young persons to smear and mar public and private property. These young people may not be expected to understand their acts and they could be disciplined by their elders giving them a good spanking. However, the person actually responsible for these acts has hitherto got away with it. This Bill now gives the power to use the rod effectively on those who are really behind such acts of vandalism. Indeed, the punishment which would normally be meted out to children can now be meted out to the adult delinquents actually responsible for wanton acts of vandalism.[52]

The Minister does not acknowledge the Bill's departure from the general principle that a criminal conviction requires guilt in terms of both action

[49] Robert Cover, "Violence and the Word" (1985) 95 *Yale L.J.* 1601.

[50] Sing., *Parliamentary Debates*, vol. 25, cols. 295–98 (26 August 1966).

[51] Sing., *Parliamentary Debates*, vol. 25, col. 291 (26 August 1966) (Wee Toon Boon).

[52] Ibid. at col. 293.

and intention. An unsubstantiated and sweeping assertion, as if of a 'truth', is made to justify the dual targeting ("It is common knowledge to Members that anti-national elements use children and other young persons"). The characterisation "anti-national" becomes a rhetorical justification for dismantling the legal principle, as if to imply that when the 'nation' is at stake, exceptions must be made to general principles – exceptions that subordinate the protection of individuals to the protection of the 'nation'.

Building on the characterisation "anti-national", the Minister presents the instigators as doubly sinister: They are concealed in their criminality, and the instrument of their concealment is a violation of those who are innocent – "children and other young persons". However, the fact that these young actors do not bear guilty intention does not excuse them from punishment.[53] Violence upon the body of the actor innocent of ill-intent is legitimised and normalised through a parallel to other social institutions – the family and, possibly, the school ("they could be disciplined by their elders giving them a good spanking"). From this assertion that the violence of adults successfully regulates the behaviour of children, the Minister makes an argument that appears to rely on word association, likening the state's violence upon the body of the concealed criminal adult instigator of 'vandalism' to the disciplining of children by elders.

> This Bill now gives the power to use the rod effectively on those who are really behind such acts of vandalism. Indeed, the punishment which would normally be meted out to children can now be meted out to the adult delinquents actually responsible.[54]

The lexical chain invoking a just and proportionate retribution ("those who are really behind", "punishment", "normally meted out") builds the

[53] In *Ang Chin Sang v. Public Prosecutor*, [1970] 2 M.L.J. 6 [*Ang Chin Sang*], the Singapore High Court upheld the Magistrate Court's sentencing of a fifteen-year-old to three months of imprisonment and three strokes of the cane for vandalism, rejecting defence counsel's argument that the caning was ultra vires s. 55(3) of the *Children and Young Persons' Ordinance*, which provided that only the High Court could sentence someone younger than sixteen years of age to corporal punishment.

[54] *Supra* note 51 at col. 293.

claim of a legitimate violence. The language of classroom discipline ("a good spanking", "use the rod" and, later in the speech, "clean and tidy") augments the adult–child/state–vandal analogy. In making its argument for mandatory caning, the state effectively infantilises "the people", recalling and reinscribing in the national legal system the colonial subordination of a subject (non-citizen) Other. The rhetoric of nationalism masks the nation-state's perpetuation of colonial penal practices[55] – practices rooted in dehumanising constructions of an irrational Other that must be managed through the fear generated by violence.[56]

The expression "the people" is available to an inclusive nationalism but constitutes as its counterpart "anti-social and anti-national elements", delineating a section of "the people" as *not* the 'nation'. The implication is that the state may lash out, literally and metaphorically, at certain citizens, denied their individuality by state insistence on their membership in a criminalised category. The slippage, for "the people", rests in how membership in these categories, 'the people' and 'anti-national, anti-social elements', is assigned. In exposing certain categories of citizens to the violence of 'law', perhaps the Singapore state becomes a dual state in a second way:

> [T]he modern "dual state" ... may have a perfectly fair and principled private law system, and also a harsh, erratic criminal control system, but it is a "dual state" because some of its population is simply declared to be subhuman, and a public danger, and as such excluded from the legal order entirely.[57]

The sub-text of the *Punishment for Vandalism Act* suggests that the distinguishing feature of the population declared to be "subhuman and a

[55] Brown, *supra* note 46; Yang, *supra* note 46; Fisch *supra* note 46.

[56] Ibid.

[57] Judith N. Shklar, "Political Theory and the Rule of Law", in Allan C. Hutchinson & Patrick Monahan, eds., *The Rule of Law: Ideal or Ideology* (Toronto: Carswell, 1987) 1. For analysis of "dual state" conduct with reference to commercial law and individual rights, see Kanishka Jayasuriya, "The Exception Becomes the Norm: Law and Regimes of Exception in East Asia" (2001) 2 *Asian Pac. L. & Pol'y J.* 108.

public danger" is ideological dissent. The question thus becomes: Is ideological compliance to the ruling party necessary for membership in the category 'the people' and the resulting protection of the 'nation'? The parameters set for the category 'vandalism' refuse to recognise the slogans, pictures and markings as expressions of political dissent. If certain modes of 'politics' are illegal and thus excluded from legitimate visibility in the public domain, then slogans and anti-US posters might be read as modes of resistance that reveal the limits of the 'nation'. For those who do not submit to state hegemony, is the 'nation' a disempowering and marginalising space necessitating a resort to disobedience amounting to illegality in order to express dissent in the public sphere?

The 1966 *Punishment for Vandalism Act* reformulated what had been one sub-section of the 1906 colonial *Minor Offences Ordinance* on nuisance.[58] The crucial difference between the *Minor Offences Ordinance* and the *Punishment for Vandalism Act* is that the *Punishment for Vandalism Act* selects what has been a minor nuisance and names it 'vandalism', thereby creating a new category of criminal conduct. The new enactment reinscribes 'vandalism' in three significant ways.

First, 'vandalism' is classified as a non-bailable offence (along with offences punishable by death and life imprisonment, for example).[59] Second, the *Punishment for Vandalism Act* was underpinned by a state insistence that severe punishment was needed to counter this "serious" offence. Thus, while under the *Minor Offences Ordinance* the maximum penalty was a S$50 fine and a week in jail, under the *Punishment for Vandalism Act* the fines increased to S$2,000, the prison term increased to three years and, most crucially, the offender would be caned a minimum of three strokes, up to a maximum of eight strokes.[60] The state's ideological attention to punishment is also proclaimed by the inclusion of the term 'Punishment' in the title of the Act. Third, the *Punishment for Vandalism Act* expands upon the parameters of the offence in a manner

[58] *Minor Offences Ordinance* (Cap. 117, 1936 Rev. Ed. Sing.) s. 11 (1).
[59] *Criminal Procedure Code* (Cap. 68, 1985 Rev. Ed. Sing.) sch. A, cols. 3, 5.
[60] *Vandalism Act* (Cap. 341, 1985 Rev. Ed. Sing.) s. 3.

that focuses on visible markings that convey meaning. Under the *Minor Offences Ordinance*, it was the act of marking a surface or putting up a bill or poster that constituted the nuisance. Nothing in the *Minor Offences Ordinance* paid attention to the message that was being written or the communication conveyed by a mark upon a surface, but the *Punishment for Vandalism Act* is very specific:

> any word, slogan, caricature, drawing, mark, symbol; affixing or displaying any poster, placard, advertisement, bill, notice, paper or other document; hanging, suspending, hoisting, affixing or displaying any flag, bunting, standard, banner or the like.[61]

These are lists that target visible communication, focusing upon content and communication so as to police the 'nation'. Words, slogans and symbols become dangers that must be eliminated, rendering the space of 'nation' free of ideological contestation. Politically, the *Punishment for Vandalism Act* served to homogenise the visible, built space of 'nation'. The 'rule of law' expectation of a plural political domain generating ideological and political choice for the 'citizen' has been reframed by the 'rule by law' definition of 'vandalism'. Given that this Act was passed a year after Singapore became a republic, the *Punishment for Vandalism Act* is clearly a crucial early marker of what has become an enduring feature of PAP rule: the conflation of 'nation' and PAP, such that opposition to the PAP becomes characterised as 'anti-national'.

A FRAGMENTARY JURISPRUDENCE OF VANDALISM

The record of the early instances of the enforcement of the Act is rather fragmentary because Singapore's subordinate courts did not begin to collect their judgments until the late 1970s.[62] I therefore rely primarily on reports in the *Straits Times* for a discussion of the early applications of the Act.

[61] Ibid. at s. 2.

[62] I am grateful to Carolyn Wee of the C. J. Koh Law Library, Faculty of Law, National University of Singapore for this information.

As the discussion so far has shown, the "Aid Vietnam" campaign (April 1966) and the ideological contestation marking both Labour Day (1 May 1966) and the first National Day (9 August 1966) became flash points for slogans and posters in public space. Acts of 'vandalism' appear to have been prompted in the following two years (1967 and 1968) by two events: Singapore's second National Day in August 1967 and the enactment of the *Employment Act*[63] in 1968. In July and August 1967, repeated charges were brought against young people for acts of 'vandalism' such as painting slogans in red paint in public spaces[64] and, in one case, marking "two black smudges" on a National Day celebration arch.[65] Some of the reports do not detail the nature of the 'vandalism',[66] but it is striking that the reports consistently refer to the youth of the accused – characterising them as "girls", "boys" or "youths".[67]

The sub-text of political opposition to the PAP is present in the references to red paint[68] and the targeting of symbols of National Day, such as the decorative arches.[69] The extreme frustration of Barisan activists with the conflation between state and party is also suggested by the conduct of certain "youths": A seventeen-year-old and an eighteen-year-old damaged two wooden courtroom benches and were charged with 'vandalism'.[70] The report does not explain the context for this damage, but the benches were damaged in the same courtroom in which, just the day before, a painter of red slogans had been discharged for one 'vandalism' offence, then immediately re-arrested and charged, in a neighbouring

[63] Cap. 91, 2009 Rev. Ed. Sing.

[64] "Two Remanded on Vandalism Charge", *Straits Times* (8 July 1967) 5; "Two Girls Remanded", *Straits Times* (11 July 1967) 6; "Girl Fined $200", *Straits Times* (2 August 1967) 11; "Jail, Rotan for Act of Vandalism", *Straits Times* (23 March 1968) 22. Although reported only in March 1968, this sentence relates to a twenty-one-year-old who had painted slogans in red paint on a bus shelter on 20 May 1967, that is, just ten days before Labour Day on 1 May.

[65] "Vandal Charge: Bail Refused to Girl, 18", *Straits Times* (11 August 1967) 11.

[66] "Freed, Then Re-arrested", *Straits Times* (1 August 1967) 8.

[67] See references at *supra* notes 64–66.

[68] *Supra* note 64.

[69] *Supra* note 65.

[70] "Damaging Court Benches: 2 Charged", *Straits Times* (2 August 1967) 8.

courtroom, for another 'vandalism' offence.[71] The press reports show that the young people were repeatedly refused bail.[72] Held by the police until charged in court, these young people are likely to have been subjected to interrogation.

A final round of ideologically motivated 'vandalism' appears to have been precipitated by the state's moves to emasculate trade unions and consolidate state control over labour through legislation on employment.[73] On 15 May 1968, barely a month after the general elections of 13 May 1968, the *Employment Bill* had its first reading in Parliament.[74] On 20 June, an unemployed twenty-year-old was caught while trying to affix an anti–*Employment Bill* poster to a lamp-post in the early hours of the morning.[75] Six others were putting up posters, hanging banners and painting slogans, but the police managed to catch only one of the group.[76]

'Vandalism' was again the state's weapon against the Barisan in October 1968. A total of 262 Barisan members and supporters were charged with continuing an assembly outside Changi Prison on 13 June 1968 despite being ordered to disperse by police.[77] When they appeared in court in September on this charge, they tore up numbered identification cards and were then charged with 'vandalism'. This charge was eventually altered to the "less severe charge of contempt of court".[78]

In this fragmentary jurisprudence of 'vandalism', two cases are particularly noteworthy. Both cases bear a striking similarity in that young

[71] *Supra* note 66.

[72] *Supra* notes 64–66 and note 70.

[73] The emasculation of autonomous and Left-leaning trade unions in Singapore, in part through legislation, is another early instance of illiberal legislation: Tremewan, *supra* note 12.

[74] The legislative history of the *Employment Act*, setting out the dates of the Bill's readings in Parliament, is appended to the Act.

[75] "Youth Gets Four Months for Vandalism", *Straits Times* (18 July 1968) 6.

[76] Ibid.

[77] "Counsel Fails in Bid to Have Case Heard by Another Court", *Straits Times* (25 October 1968).

[78] "96 Barisans Get 4 Months for Contempt", *Straits Times* (21 December 1967) 4.

boys – a fifteen-year-old and a sixteen-year-old – were the accused persons. In the parliamentary debates, as I have already noted, the state argued that the terms of the Act would enable the state to punish the "adult delinquents" who were using "children and other young persons to smear and mar public and private property".[79] However, the early cases suggest that it was the "children and other young persons" who were being caught and punished, with the state claiming that these young people were but tools of hidden adult instigators.[80] Indeed, not only were the events precipitating the Act connected to the Barisan, the primary supporters of the opposition party appear to have been the young:

> Some 1,000 supporters this morning crammed into the small zinc-and-plank premises of the Barisan's Jalan Alsagoff branch to "protest" against Singapore's "phoney independence". For three sweltering hours, the supporters, mainly teen-age boys and girls, heard their leaders condemn the Singapore Government, the Americans, the British – and the atom and hydrogen bombs.[81]

The state's parliamentary analogies between punishment and the disciplining of wayward children take on a slightly sinister cast in view of this demographic profile of the major opposition party. While the *Sedition Act* was unleashed on a Barisan leadership,[82] the *Punishment for Vandalism Act*'s disproportionate and violent punishment attacked the grassroots foundations of the Barisan's activists. Both the existing and a successor generation of Barisan leaders and followers were being skilfully dismantled through 'law'. It is hard not to see the *Punishment for Vandalism Act* as a 'law' scripted and enforced in a manner designed to secure greater power for the ruling party. The role played by the courts in facilitating this outcome is illustrated by the *Liu Tong Ban* case.

[79] Sing., *Parliamentary Debates*, vol. 25, col. 293 (26 August 1966) (Wee Toon Boon).

[80] The state's minimisation of the agency of the young people is interesting given that teenagers in 'Chinese' schools at the time were highly politicised and were at the forefront of the anti-colonial movement: Hong & Huang, *supra* note 12 at 138–39.

[81] "Barisan Hits at 'Phoney Freedom'", *Straits Times* (10 August 1966) 5.

[82] *Supra* note 32.

Public Prosecutor v. Liu Tong Ban[83] was heard on 24 August 1966, a week after the first reading of the Bill but before the Bill was debated and passed in Parliament – that is, before the *Punishment for Vandalism Act* actually became 'law'. This case, however, is highly significant because it reflects a judicial responsiveness to the anticipated 'law' that speaks of an ideological convergence between the judiciary and the government. In other words, this case offers an early example of statist courts.

The case was a High Court appeal brought by the state against the Magistrate's Courts' having given an absolute discharge to a sixteen-year-old goldsmith's apprentice, Liu Tong Ban. Liu had been charged with the section 11 offence of nuisance under the *Minor Offences Ordinance* for having put up an anti-American poster in Chinese characters on an electric main box along a major road in the centre of the city on 27 April. The poster was related to the forthcoming Labour Day on 1 May, and it contained what the *Straits Times* report allusively called "an appeal",[84] as well as an anti-American slogan with the words "Yankees, go home".[85]

The High Court heard the case when the parliamentary debate on the Bill had not yet taken place. Yet the Bill was central to the arguments made by the Deputy Public Prosecutor, who persuaded the High Court to revise the absolute discharge on the basis of the "probable reasons" for the terms of punishment set out by the Bill.[86] The Deputy Public Prosecutor also told the High Court that the state was "dissatisfied" with the leniency of the absolute discharge, that one of the possible reasons for the introduction of the Bill was that "the lower courts might not fully appreciate the serious nature of such offences, which include putting up unauthorised posters on public or private buildings".[87]

[83] Reports on this case at both the Magistrates' Court and the High Court are not available. I rely on press reports for the details of this case: "Reasons Behind the Vandalism Bill ...", *supra* note 37.

[84] It is probable that the press was replicating the Prosecutor's language and that the Prosecutor was avoiding going into the facts of the poster's content.

[85] *Supra* note 37.

[86] Ibid.

[87] Ibid.

There are two facets to this 'argument': first, that the lower courts needed to be managed and disciplined by the parliamentary provision of mandatory sentencing[88]; and second, that the High Court, being the High Court, had a greater capacity to grasp complexity and to "fully appreciate" what the lower courts could not and, therefore, to correct the lower courts' mistakes.

In order to support his claim that the offence was "serious", the Prosecutor told the High Court of the severe punishments provided for by the Bill – punishments which contrasted sharply with the penalties under the existing terms of the *Minor Offence Ordinance*.[89] The implicit (rather than explicit) rationale of this argument was that the severity of the proposed punishments was the indicia of the "serious" nature of the offence. The Prosecutor was unable to articulate how "putting up unauthorised posters" was an offence of a "serious nature". Instead, in an inversion of the concern of modernist 'law' for rational proportionality between crime and punishment,[90] it was the very severity of punishment that proved the seriousness of the offence.

The Prosecutor relied on allusion and coded references to construct an argument as to how and why the putting up of unauthorised posters was a "serious" crime. The trial Magistrate, according to the Prosecutor, had apparently "closed his mind" to topical events; he had paid more attention to the individual offender than to the offence and completely ignored "the hidden hand behind the offence".[91] It is probable that these radicalising allusions to shadowy and hidden actors serving conspiratorial forces could be invoked only through allusion because the state could not prove their existence. Putting up unauthorised posters was not a basis for detention under the *Internal Security Act*. Thus, the provisions of the *Minor Offences Ordinance*, reinterpreted through the lens of the state's

[88] The press report does not refer to mandatory sentencing, but the provision of mandatory sentencing in the Bill appears to inform the Prosecutor's arguments.

[89] *Supra* note 37.

[90] Brown, *supra* note 46; Yang, *supra* note 46. Fisch, *supra* note 46.

[91] *Supra* note 37.

proposed 'law' on the "serious" offence of 'vandalism', became the heart of the Prosecutor's argument that this sixteen-year-old should not be let off with an absolute discharge that the Magistrate had granted.

The High Court accepted the Prosecutor's sentencing proposal and imposed a fine of S$25 or one week of imprisonment. This response of the High Court suggests that the Prosecutor's coded references to "hidden hands" and "topical events" were successfully received by the Court. These two legal actors, state Prosecutor and High Court judge, spoke the same coded language and colluded to punish Liu, not for the act of putting up an unauthorised poster, but for the content of that poster. Liu's offence was not the offence of 'vandalism' but that of being the tool of anti-American "hidden hands". In Liu's prosecution and sentencing, the sub-text of the *Punishment for Vandalism Bill* was being extracted and enforced even before the Bill had become an Act.

ANG CHIN SANG V. PUBLIC PROSECUTOR

In 1967, a year after the *Vandalism Act* was passed, a Magistrate's Court convicted a fifteen-year-old for vandalism and sentenced him to three months' imprisonment and three strokes of the cane.[92] On 14 August 1967, Ang had thrown egg shells containing green paint at a decorative arch.[93] Given the timing of the prosecution, just days after National Day, and the fact that the police had been on hand to apprehend Ang at 11 PM,[94] it is probable that the decorative arch was one marking National Day.

The appeal against this sentence was heard in the High Court by the Chief Justice. Counsel for the fifteen-year-old argued that in sentencing the fifteen-year-old to caning, the Magistrate's Court had been acting ultra vires, because the *Children and Young Persons Ordinance* provided that

92 *Ang Chin Sang*, *supra* note 53.

93 "Father Denounces Son as 'Incorrigible'", *Straits Times* (15 August 1967) 6.

94 Ibid.

only the High Court could sentence a youth less than sixteen to corporal punishment.[95] Caning under the *Punishment for Vandalism Act* is subject to the *Criminal Procedure Code*, which provides that women, men sentenced to death and men older than fifty cannot be sentenced to caning.[96] The material provisions of both the *Punishment for Vandalism Act* and the *Children and Young Persons Ordinance* included this exception: "notwithstanding the provisions of any other written law". In the *Punishment for Vandalism Act* it was as follows:

> Notwithstanding the provisions of any other written law, any person who commits any act of vandalism or attempts to do any such act or causes any such act to [be] done shall be guilty of an offence under this Act and shall be liable to ... subject to the provisions of s 274 of the Criminal Procedure Code, be punished with caning.[97]

Under the *Children and Young Persons Ordinance*:

> Notwithstanding the provisions of any other written law no child or young person shall be sentenced by any court other than the High Court to corporal punishment.[98]

Faced with these two "notwithstanding" provisions, the Chief Justice held that the provisions of the *Criminal Procedure Code*, excepting from corporal punishment women, men older than fifty and men who had been sentenced to death, were a clear enactment of general application – no court could ever sentence a woman, a man older than fifty or a man on death row to caning. The *Children and Young Persons Ordinance* was not, he held, of the same general application because the High Court could

[95] At the time, the reference was to the *Children and Young Persons Ordinance* (Cap. 128, 1955 Rev. Ed. Sing.) s. 55 (3). The current *Children and Young Persons Act* (Cap. 38, 2001 Rev. Ed. Sing.) does not have an equivalent provision.

[96] At the time, the reference was to the *Criminal Procedure Code* (Cap. 231, 1955 Rev. Ed. Sing.) s. 231. Section 231 in the current *Criminal Procedure Code* (Cap. 68, 1985 Rev. Ed. Sing.) is identical to the provision considered in the case.

[97] *Punishment for Vandalism Act* (No. 38 of 1966, Sing.) s. 3. Section 3 of the current *Vandalism Act* is the identical provision.

[98] *Children and Young Persons Ordinance* (Cap. 128, 1955 Rev. Ed. Sing.) s. 55 (3).

sentence a youth younger than sixteen to caning. On this basis and on the basis that the Court must give effect to legislative intent "to provide for exemplary punishment for acts of vandalism",[99] the Chief Justice dismissed the appeal and upheld the sentence of caning.

What is striking about this judgment is the refusal of the court to see the appellant as a child. The mandatory sentencing provisions are applied to this fifteen-year-old – jail and caning – as if he were already criminal, already adult.[100] The Chief Justice, hearing the appeal in 1967, months after Prime Minister Lee had, from Parliament, instructed the judiciary to "apply the letter of the law in such a spirit that society is able to protect itself", is completely compliant to the state's account of what amounts to 'vandalism' and becomes the tool of the state's precept that severe punishment is the necessary response to this especially "serious" offence.

The jurisprudence of 'vandalism' in Singapore illustrates the discursive continuity between judicial text and state discourse on 'vandalism' and is remarkable for the absence of judicial questioning of the Act's terms and parameters. The judiciary complied with the state's articulations of 'nation' and 'citizen' in a manner that fostered 'rule by law' penal violence upon the bodies of fifteen- and sixteen-year-olds. The text of the *Punishment for Vandalism Act*, together with the interpretations delivered by the courts, result in the 'law' becoming a tool through which the state constrains the ideological space of 'nation'. This jurisprudence of 'vandalism' demonstrates the acuity of Jayasuriya's characterisation of Singapore's courts as statist. The statism of Singapore's courts, as early as 1966, was such that judicial actors were alive and responsive to the subtextual politics of illiberal legislation.

In the years after 1968, politically motivated 'vandalism' appears to have disappeared from the public space of 'nation'. Instead, it the theft and damage of public property prompted prosecutions for 'vandalism'.

[99] *Ang Chin Sang, supra* note 53

[100] Ibid.

The Barisan, already weakened by Operation Coldstore in early 1963, appears to have been well and truly decimated through the early applications of the *Punishment for Vandalism Act.*

'VANDALISM' AND CANING IN A POST–COLD WAR WORLD

Almost thirty years after the 1966 enactment of the *Punishment for Vandalism Act*, in a post–Cold War world in which Singapore had achieved spectacular economic prosperity,[101] corporal punishment for 'vandalism' became revitalised and relegitimised when Michael Fay, a US national, was punished for 'vandalism'. In both 1966 and 1994, the state employed public discourse to reframe the 'rule of law' in a manner that denuded the rights of the individual in an encounter with 'law'. At both these moments, the state invoked the narrative of national vulnerability to legitimise violent punishment, presenting itself as resorting to penal violence in the service of the 'nation'. In 1994, when eighteen-year-old Fay and a sixteen-year-old Hong Kong national, Shiu Chi Ho, were sentenced to imprisonment and caning for having spray-painted some cars, a fifteen-year-old Malaysian national, Harun Sharudin bin Sufian Saufi, who had been with Shiu and Fay was treated as a juvenile. He was not named in the media reports and was not sentenced to caning because of his age. Instead, he served two months detention in a juvenile home. In the post–Cold War world of 1994, this fifteen-year-old boy was spray-painting cars, not putting up anti-American posters, and perhaps this was why he was treated as a 'child'. A few months' difference in age meant, unluckily for Fay and Shiu, that they were, for purposes of the *Vandalism Act*, adults.

[101] "Singapore's per capita income of USD 14,637 in 1990 was close to, or even higher than, that of many Organisation for Economic Co-operation and Development (OECD) countries": Manu Bhaskaran, "Transforming the Engines of Growth", in Bridget Welsh et al., eds., *Impressions of the Goh Chok Tong Years in Singapore* (Singapore: NUS Press, 2009) 201.

Fay pleaded guilty to two counts of vandalism involving spraying paint on cars.[102] He was sentenced to six strokes of the cane.[103] The Fay case launched a state-scripted version of events in which 'vandalism' became symbolic of the decline of the 'West' and corporal punishment a protective, disciplinary mechanism conveying the 'national' corrective to 'Western' moral decay. In this post–Cold War context, the original subtext of opposition activism was abandoned, but the state's insistence on the nation's vulnerability, a vulnerability countered by corporal punishment, remained.

Because Fay was a US national, his conviction and punishment attracted a high level of media attention in the United States and internationally. Much of this attention was critical of caning as a cruel and disproportionate punishment. In other words, the critique emanating from the 'West' was framed in somewhat essentialising 'rule of law' terms. While the *Straits Times* coverage dwelt primarily on the state's defence of the 'lawfulness' of the Singapore legal system and of Singapore 'law' as an expression of sovereign autonomy, the Fay case inevitably drew attention in the Singapore public domain to how the rest of the world viewed corporal punishment.

The state responded to this spotlight on penal caning by reformulating the Fay case, employing, first, 'rule of law' rhetoric to assert the legitimacy of Singapore 'law' and, second, the category 'Asian values' to renew the justification of legal exceptionalism. Arguably, 'Asian values' was used to explain the Fay case as emblematic of 'Western' moral and

[102] *Michael Peter Fay v. Public Prosecutor* (3 March 1994) M/A No. 48/94/01 (Sing. Subordinate Cts.) [*Fay v. PP*]. Fay was also sentenced to four months' imprisonment for mischief causing damage and for the dishonest retention of stolen property and fined S$3,500 for throwing eggs at a car and switching its license plate, as well as throwing eggs at another car and damaging its right front door. See also "Teen Vandal Gets Jail and Cane", *Straits Times* (4 March 1994) 1; and *Fay v. Public Prosecutor*, [1994] 2 Sing. L.R. 154 (H.C.).

[103] The caning was later reduced to four strokes to accommodate President Clinton's request that clemency be shown. "Caning Sentence on Fay to Stay", *Straits Times* (5 May 1994).

social disintegration in order to deflect public attention away from the issue of the legitimacy of violent punishment. In the process, the 'rule by law' history of the *Vandalism Act* (detailed earlier) was occluded.

Shiu Chi Ho, the sixteen-year-old Hong Kong national who was accused of having committed the vandalism and mischief with Fay,[104] was to play an important role in the state's reformulation of the Fay case. Shiu's 'Asian' identity, a convenient 'racial' Other to Fay's 'Caucasian' identity, became a narrative hook upon which the Fay case became an 'Asian values' story. While the rhetorical devices of the state's discourse around this 1994 expression of the *Vandalism Act* might appear to be very different from the 1966 discourses surrounding the original scripting and early enforcements of the Act, the state's re-narrativisation of the Fay case through 'Asian values' might be perceived as leading to the same end – an infantalisation of the citizenry – as the parliamentary justifications of corporal punishment delivered in 1966. But before I address the manner in which the 1994 enforcement of the *Vandalism Act* renewed the state's subordination of citizens, I first set out the public discourse on the *Fay* and *Shiu* cases.

PUBLIC DISCOURSE ON 'VANDALISM' IN 1994

Three consistent features of the public discourse on the Fay case were, first, a use of language (by the press and the police) characterised by 'excess'[105]; second, a construction of the police as efficient and effective 'law' enforcers; and third, an Othering (primarily 'racial') of the boys involved.

104 Shiu pleaded not guilty but was, at the close of his trial, convicted and sentenced to twelve strokes of the cane and eight months in jail. His sentence was later reduced to six strokes and six months following an appeal for clemency to President Ong: *Shiu Chi Ho v. Public Prosecutor* (25 April 1994) M/A 93/94/01 (Sing. Subordinate Cts.) [*Shiu v. PP*]; "Hongkonger Convicted of Vandalism to Get 6 Strokes", *Straits Times* (19 June 1994) 1.

105 Yao argues convincingly that the Singapore state employs "excess" as a strategic mode of engaging with or responding to a range of issues so as to maintain its hegemony: Souchou Yao, *Singapore: The State and the Culture of Excess* (Oxford: Routledge, 2007).

The language of excess that characterised state discourse in the Fay case is in continuity with the state's discourse in 1966 in which 'vandalism' was characterised as "extremely serious" and "anti-national".[106] The presentation and re-presentation of 'vandalism' as unambiguously criminal fed into the legitimation of corporal punishment in public discourse (as shown later). Alongside the construction of 'vandalism' as a "serious crime", public discourse focused on the role of the police. The police were consistently presented as an effective, efficient agency for 'law' enforcement – a presentation recalling Kleinfeld's description of the "institutional attributes" definition of the 'rule of law'.[107] In performing police efficiency, the Singapore state was perhaps asserting its capacity to deliver 'law and order' in a manner consistent with, if not exceeding, the standards of efficiency of the 'rule of law' exemplar: the 'West'.

The efficiency of the police was constructed, in part, by the manner in which the 'vandalism' of cars was reported in the press. The opening moment in the re-emergence of 'vandalism' in the Singapore public domain was a news report that cars had been vandalised.[108] The police had received reports of cars having been sprayed with paint and pelted with eggs as early as 18 September,[109] but these "attacks on cars"[110] were not relayed as news until some three weeks later, on 6 October, when the *Straits Times* reported that "[s]ome Caucasian teenagers" were suspected of being behind a spate of car vandalism cases in a neighbourhood in the vicinity of the Singapore American School.[111] The very next day, 7 October, the press was able to report police success.[112] Two

106 Sing., *Parliamentary Debates*, vol. 25 col. 291 (26 August 1966) (Mr. Wee Toon Boon).

107 Rachel Kleinfeld, "Competing Definitions of the Rule of Law", in Thomas Carothers, ed., *Promoting the Rule of Law Abroad* (Washington, DC: Carnegie Endowment for International Peace, 2006) 31 at 47.

108 "At Pine Grove: Vandalism on Cars", *Straits Times* (6 October 1993) 22.

109 "9 Foreign Students Held for Vandalism", *Straits Times* (7 October 1993) 25.

110 Ibid.

111 *Supra* note 106.

112 *Supra* note 107.

sixteen-year-olds had been caught in a police ambush.[113] Under police questioning, the two boys supplied the names of seven others.

The *Straits Times*'s reports are characterised by the excess[114] that came to typify media discourse on the case: The police itemisation of what they found added up to a damning "50 stolen items",[115] and the homes of the nine were "raided" (rather than searched).[116] Fay was first charged with two counts of retaining stolen property,[117] then a week later with an alarming fifty-one counts of vandalism and mischief.[118] When Fay was charged with two counts of retaining stolen property, he had already been in custody and subject to extensive questioning for more than forty-eight hours.[119] He was held in police custody for a further week, the court having denied bail in response to the police prosecutor's claim that further investigations and questioning of Fay were necessary in order to trace the owners of the stolen property and facilitate their investigations into the incidents of vandalism.

This police conduct was not recognised as excessive in the public domain. No questions were raised as to why sixteen-year-old boys had been held for forty-eight hours[120] or whether their parents or counsel had had access to them. There was no suggestion that the vulnerability of these young people, forced into an intimidating encounter with state authority, had been mitigated or mediated in any way. The boys

113 "Vandal Case: HK Boy Gave Names of Others", *Straits Times* (16 March 1994) 2.

114 Yao, *supra* note 105.

115 *Supra* note 106.

116 Ibid.

117 These were trophy-like items that the teenagers had marked with their initials; they included Singapore flags, fire extinguishers and signs such as "In case of fire do not use lift": "9 Foreign Students Held for Vandalism", *supra* note 109 at 25; "American Teenager Charged with Keeping Stolen Goods", *Straits Times* (9 October 1993) 1.

118 "Vandalism Case: American Teen Faces More Than 40 Charges", *Straits Times* (15 October 1993) 3.

119 "American Teenager Charged with Keeping Stolen Goods", *Straits Times* (9 October 1993) 1.

120 The police may hold a person for up to forty-eight hours without a warrant: *Criminal Procedure Code* (Cap. 68, 1985 Rev. Ed. Sing.) s. 36(1).

were caught in an uncertain space before the 'law' along the continuum of 'child'/ 'minor'/ 'juvenile'/ 'adult', an uncertainty reflected by the media's use of shifting descriptors: "teenagers", "students", "boys". The police, by detaining the boys for forty-eight hours for initial questioning, were handling the boys as already dangerous, already criminal, already adult.

Singapore 'law' (at the time) marked twenty-one as the age of majority.[121] Eighteen-year-olds can marry[122] and be sentenced to death.[123] Sixteen is the age of consent for (hetero)sexual activity.[124] As we have seen, fifteen-year-olds have been considered old enough to be subject to penal caning, a punishment which cannot apply to women and men older than fifty.[125] The absence of critical questioning of the police handling of these boys, boys who were still children in many ways – living in their parents' homes as dependents, full-time students yet to graduate from high school or secondary school – is a striking absence in the media construction of the public response. In a 'rule by law' strategy, the boys were dealt with in a manner that served police efficiency, minimising the 'rule of law' claims to rights and protections against state power. The absence of questioning is a potent reflection of the absence of rights awareness in the Singapore public domain.

The press presentation of police efficiency was supported by the detail of how much the police had already uncovered from their initial investigations:

[121] *Bahadur Singh & Anor v. Bank of India* [1993] 1 Sing. L.R. 634 (H.C.); *Bank of India v. Bahadur Singh & Anor.* [1994] Sing.L.R. 328 (C.A.). See also Leong Wai Kum, *Principles of Family Law in Singapore* (Singapore: Butterworths, 1997) at 485–526. In March 2009, however, a legislative amendment came into effect, lowering the age of full contractual capacity, and the capacity to bring and defend legal proceedings, to eighteen (with some exceptions). The Act refers to "minors who have attained 18 years of age": *Civil Law Act* (Cap. 43, 1999 Rev. Ed. Sing.) s. 35, s. 36.

[122] *Women's Charter* (Cap. 353, 1997 Rev. Ed. Sing.) s. 9.

[123] *Criminal Procedure Code* (Cap. 68, 1985 Rev. Ed. Sing.) s. 213.

[124] *Women's Charter* (Cap. 353, 1997 Rev. Ed. Sing.) s. 140(1)(i). Homosexuality is criminalised under the *Penal Code* (Cap. 224, 2008 Rev. Ed. Sing.) s. 377A.

[125] *Criminal Procedure Code* (Cap. 68, 1985 Rev. Ed. Sing.) s. 213.

> They sprayed paint and pelted eggs on at least 67 cars, smashed a windscreen and stole road signs, flags, fire extinguishers – and even a public telephone booth. But the trail of vandalism left by nine foreign teenagers, mostly Caucasians, ended when detectives arrested them yesterday.[126]

The next day, 8 October, the *Straits Times* carried a report which encapsulated two themes – racial/national Othering and a celebration of severity in punishment. This report recounted public outrage:

> Members of the public yesterday called the police and The Straits Times to express their outrage at the multiple acts of vandalism allegedly committed by nine foreign students....
>
> Businessman Joseph Wong, 38, told The Straits Times NewsLine the students should be punished severely. "Such social behaviour should not be imported into our country," he said. Student Tan Geok Mui, 19 said, "As guests staying here, they should observe the law and not tarnish the image of their own countries."
>
> The students, aged 16 to 19, comprise three Americans, two Malaysians, a Belgian, an Australian a Thai and a Hongkonger.... Tanglin Police Commander, Superintendent Lum Hon Fye, said several people had called the police about the vandalism.
>
> "We would like to assure them that the police are viewing this matter very seriously," he said. The police have said they intend to press multiple charges.... Said Supt Lum: "The suspects may be foreigners from well-to-do families but they will not get any preferential treatment. The police will treat them like any Singaporean offender".[127]

Letters to the editor over the next weeks congratulated the police on their resolve, typically recommending that the "foreign student vandals" be "caned and jailed, then deported".[128] An overwhelming proportion

[126] *Supra* note 109.

[127] Tan Ooi Boon, "Vandalism Spree Provokes Outraged Reaction from Public", *Straits Times* (8 October 1993).

[128] Leong Hong Chiew, Letter to the editor, *Straits Times* (8 October 1993); see also Derek Ee Ming Chong "Be Strict, Not Harsh, on Vandals – Local or Foreign", *Straits Times* (9 October 1993).

of the public responses reproduced by the *Straits Times* advocated punishing the boys. The popular concern, or perhaps more accurately the media construction of public concern,[129] was that the Otherness of the students (in terms of race, nationality and class privilege) should not exempt them from the 'law'. This was a concern the police were quick to respond to in their assurance that the "foreign students" would be treated "like any Singaporean offender". In this way, the discourse constructed a public demand for 'justice' – a 'justice' that involved subjecting the "foreigners" to severe punishment. By discursively presenting the demand as one generated by outraged and patriotic members of the 'nation', the state-managed media discourse[130] constructed a legitimising popular consent within the 'nation' for violent punishment – a consent that necessarily meant citizens, too, should be subject to violent and retributive punishment.

The media presentation of a public demand that the students be caned, jailed and deported replicates the state's assumption that severe punishment is an appropriate response to 'vandalism'.[131] The invocation of severe punishment, along with the media's selection of public opinion (these "guests ... should observe the law" is a typical example), presages

[129] See also the *Straits Times* of 12 March 1994, in which the editor reported having received forty letters on the Fay case after Fay had been sentenced, and published a selection of those letters, most of which approved of the penalty and Singapore's right to apply its laws. Soon after this, the paper reproduced a selection of the international media's approving opinion pieces on the penalty: "Lesson on Crime from S'pore", *Straits Times* (18 March 1994).

[130] Cherian George, *Contentious Journalism and the Internet: Towards Democratic Discourse in Malaysia and Singapore* (Singapore: Singapore University Press, 2006).

[131] The impenetrable texture of this ideology and rhetoric is reflected in the 2010 prosecution for vandalism of a Swiss national who had broken into a depot and spray-painted the sides of a mass rapid transit train. In sentencing Oliver Fricker to five months' imprisonment and three strokes of the cane, the court said, "Our laws apply with equal force to all and the courts' sentencing policies reflect this", while the prosecutor argued that "such serious, flagrant breach of the law cannot be taken lightly or viewed as a mere prank": Elena Chong, "Accused Had No 'Noble Aim' in Exposing Lapses", *Straits Times* (26 June 2010); *Public Prosecutor v. Oliver Fricker*, Singapore Subordinate Courts DAC0024677/2010.

the following Ministry of Home Affairs statement, made some five months later (on the evening of the day on which Fay had been sentenced):

> Singaporeans and foreigners are subject to the same laws here and tough laws against anti-social crimes have kept the country orderly and relatively crime-free.... Unlike some other societies which may tolerate acts of vandalism, Singapore has its own standards of social order, as reflected in our laws.
>
> ... [O]f the 14 people aged 18 to 21 convicted of vandalism and ordered to be caned in the last five years, 12 were Singaporeans. The law provided for a range of punishments, and the court decided on the appropriate punishment to fit the crime....
>
> In Fay's case, the court decided to mete out the punishment of caning, jail and a fine after he had pleaded guilty to five charges.... The Ministry of Foreign Affairs has ... informed the US Embassy that the law in Singapore must take its course, and that Fay would be given every opportunity to defend himself with representation by counsel of his choice, and this was what happened. The US embassy has also been told that Singaporeans and foreigners are subject to the same laws in Singapore.[132]

The Ministry statement claims a mode of legitimacy for Singapore that is consistent with a Westminster model of the separation of powers, the model upon which the Singapore state has repeatedly said it is based. The Ministry (as an organ of the political-administrative arm of the state) had refrained from commenting on the case until it had been heard and sentence passed. In staying silent until sentence had been passed, the state was institutionally performing the separation of powers. Consistent with the assumption of an institutionally independent judiciary, the Ministry presents the 'law' as autonomous, such that "the court decided" on the punishment and "the law in Singapore must take its course". The Ministry's claims obscure the minimal discretion of statist courts enforcing a 'law' in which an extreme punishment has been mandated by Parliament. And when the Ministry says the same laws apply to all in

132 "The Law Must Run Its Course", *Straits Times* (4 March 1993) 25.

Singapore, it invokes the humanist 'rule of law' ideal of the impartiality and incorruptibility of 'law'.

This claim signifies an ironic inversion of values, an inversion facilitated by the density of the category 'law'. Humanist 'law' in a 'common law' system, 'law' captured by a Diceyan and liberal ideal for the 'rule of law', strives for impartiality and incorruptibility, but also seeks to see the individual who stands before the 'law', to recognise the particularities of each case and to render the rules of 'law' transparent to a public which must observe the 'law'.[133] In the Fay case, however (as shown later), the courts, the police and the state refused to see the individual. The 'law' that was enforced was never transparent, never entirely accessible to the public because the legislative text concealed a history of coded meanings and politically motivated enforcement related to the opposition Barisan. The 'rule of law' principle that punishment should be proportionate, and not cruel and degrading, was violated by the *Vandalism Act*'s history of being, in part, enacted to "humiliate" those who dared paint slogans challenging the government.[134]

THE IMPORTANCE OF BEING SERIOUS

Fay pleaded guilty and so his case did not go to trial. There was, however, a sentencing hearing at which Fay's counsel called for probation, pointing out that Fay was a remorseful first offender who had co-operated with the police, made full restitution and assisted the police in their investigations. Acknowledging the general rule that young offenders would generally be considered for probation, the court turned to the logic of exception, rejected the mitigation plea and refused to consider probation because this was a case in which

> the offence is serious. In such cases, the courts cannot ignore the needs of the general public and must do whatever is necessary for the

[133] Kleinfeld, *supra* note 107 at 69, note 46 therein.

[134] Sing., *Parliamentary Debates*, vol. 25, col. 297 (26 August 1966) (Lee Kuan Yew).

> protection of the public. Accordingly when a young offender commits an offence which would make right thinking members of the public feel that justice cannot be done except by the passing of a custodial sentence, it would not be right that any sentence other than a custodial one should be imposed.
>
> I am of the view that the deliberate and wilful vandalising of 18 motor vehicles within a period of 10 days are very serious offences and that the only appropriate sentence is a custodial sentence.[135]

The excessiveness of the court's language in its repeated characterisation of spraying cars with paint as "serious" and "very serious offences", and its reference to the court's obligation to protect the public and respond to the expectation of "justice" from "right thinking members of the public", are alarming for the lexical consistency with the press reports.[136] That a court should adopt and apply the category "very serious offence" to the spraying of cars with paint, and further characterise Fay as someone who endangered the public, demonstrates two things. The first is the extraordinary consistency in the discursive construction of the Fay episode within Singapore, with mainstream media, police and courts simplistically and repeatedly characterising the episode as extreme and therefore justifiably requiring an extreme punishment.

The second is the adoption, by the judiciary, of the interpretations placed upon events by the political-administrative arm of state, through the device of adopting and replicating the state's characterisations and categories. In the process, the court adopted a key feature of the state's rhetorical strategy: exceptionalism. The court refused to apply to Fay the general rule of regarding a young, remorseful first offender as a suitable candidate for the rehabilitative prospects of probation rather than the retributive consequences of penal incarceration and caning.

Fay appealed against the sentence.[137] At the High Court, the Chief Justice substantially replicated the Subordinate Court's implicit characterisation

[135] *Fay v. PP*, *supra* note 102 at 8–9.

[136] Tan, *supra* note 127.

[137] *Fay v. Public Prosecutor* [1994] 2 Sing.L.R. 154 (H.C.).

of Fay as a danger to the public when rejecting the appeal that Fay be considered for probation:

> [A]ll the acts of vandalism were committed relentlessly and wilfully ... and amounted to a calculated course of criminal conduct.... [T]aking into account the need to secure the interests of the general public, [the district judge] was fully justified in imposing a custodial sentence and the mandatory minimum of three strokes of the cane in respect of each charge of vandalism.[138]

The High Court's dismissal of Fay's appeal reinscribes the pattern of coherence and continuity between public discourse and judicial statism manifested by the hearing at first instance. Similar discursive patterns were evident in the trial of Shiu Chi Ho.

JOINT TRIAL: NARRATIVE OF POLICE ABUSE

The prosecution sought, and the court granted, the joint trial of Shiu, Fay and a fifteen-year-old Malaysian boy, Harun Sharudin Bin Sufian Saufi (Harun). Counsel for Fay and Shiu objected to the joining on the basis that the evidence of one defendant might implicate the other, but the court, granting the prosecution's application, said "the accused persons" would not be prejudiced in their defence.[139]

All three boys had originally pleaded 'not guilty' when faced with fifty-three charges (Fay) and forty-five charges (Shiu).[140] But in what appears to have been a plea bargain that involved playing the boys off against each other, Fay and Harun pleaded guilty to a reduced number of charges, and the Deputy Public Prosecutor told the court that the two boys would be used as prosecution witnesses in the state's case against Shiu, who continued to plead not guilty.[141]

[138] Ibid. at 159.

[139] "Youths on Vandalism Charges: Judge Orders Joint Trial", *Straits Times* (3 February 1994) 24.

[140] "Teens Vandalism Trial Postponed", *Straits Times* (24 February 1994) 17.

[141] "Two Teenagers 'to Plead Guilty'", *Straits Times* (26 February 1994) 30; "Two Foreign Students Admit Vandalism, Mischief", *Straits Times* (1 March 1994) 3.

When Shiu's trial opened, he was tried on four vandalism charges.[142] His counsel challenged the admissibility of Shiu's statements to the police, alleging that Shiu had been assaulted by the police and forced to admit to vandalism while in police custody,[143] charges the police denied. Shiu, in his evidence, said that police had punched him in the chest, slapped his face and hit his calf with a ruler when he denied committing vandalism.[144] Shiu also said that the police had told him that he would be allowed to return home sooner if he admitted guilt, that the charges of vandalism would be dropped in favour of charges of mischief and that the police could "make his father lose his job".[145] Shiu's father testified that his son had told him that he had been assaulted by a police officer[146] and that his son had had "a red patch on his left leg" after having been in police custody. Shiu's father said a police officer had asked him to persuade his son to plead guilty.[147] In order to explain why he had not filed a complaint against the police, Shiu's father quoted a Chinese proverb by which he implied that he hoped to appease the police by not filing a complaint about the treatment of his son.[148]

In the course of his trial, when Shiu denied participating in the vandalism with Fay and others, Harun testified that Shiu and Fay had been with him when they went to vandalise cars.[149] Harun denied Shiu's

[142] *Shiu v. PP*, *supra* note 104; "Police Officers Hit Me, Says Hongkong Student"' *Straits Times* (17 March 1994) 25.

[143] *Shiu v. PP*, *supra* note 104 at 7, 10–16; "HK Boy 'Gave Names of Others' ", *supra* note 113 at 2.

[144] *Shiu v. PP*, *supra* note 104 at 13; "Police Officers Hit Me", *supra* note 142.

[145] *Shiu v. PP*, *supra* note 104 at 12–14; "Police Officers Hit Me", *supra* note 142 at 25. Shiu Chi Ho's father was employed by a statutory board, the Singapore Broadcasting Corporation, as the head of the drama division. Essentially, this meant that he was a government employee.

[146] *Shiu v. PP*, *supra* note 104 at 13.

[147] Ibid. at 15; "Police Asked Me to Persuade Son to Plead Guilty: Witness", *Straits Times* (18 March 1994) 31.

[148] This was reported in the press but is not reflected in the judgment. The judgment shows that the court asked Shiu senior if he had taken his son to see a doctor. The father answered that he had not, because his son had said he did not want to see a doctor, and that he had given his son Chinese medicine instead: *Shiu v. PP*, *supra* note 104 at 15.

[149] Ibid. at 28; "HK Youth Denies Charges and Claims He Was Elsewhere", *Straits Times* (23 March 1994) 24.

counsel's proposition that he was implicating Shiu in order to avoid being sentenced to caning himself.

Shiu produced alibis who testified that at the times stated in the charges, he had been elsewhere and in other company. He also said that while he had at a certain point been friendly with Fay, they had had a falling out, after which he had not spent time in Fay's company. At the end of a nine-day trial, however, citing contradictions between the written statements and oral testimony, and pointing to details of Shiu's parents' evidence the court found unbelievable, the court found that the defence "had not raised any doubts whatsoever as to the truth of the prosecution's case or as to the guilt of the accused" and held that the prosecution had proved its case beyond a reasonable doubt.[150]

The trial of Shiu Chi Ho reveals the manner in which 'rule by law' unfolds in the Singapore court setting. The court was careful to observe 'rule of law' procedures, conducting a trial within a trial to decide upon the admissibility of the written statements that Shiu made while in police custody, statements Shiu alleged he had made because he had been assaulted, threatened and induced.[151] Shiu and his witnesses – his friends and parents – gave evidence, were examined and cross-examined. The testimony of the police was weighed against that of Shiu, his young alibis and his parents in a manner that produced a reasoned judgment identifying flaws, contradictions and improbabilities in the evidence of the non-state actors. But in assessing the evidence, at no point did the court allow these contradictions and flaws to add up to a reasonable doubt.

The 'rule by law' prosecutorial advantage arising from procedural rules which permit the police to hold and question suspects for forty-eight hours without access to counsel[152] was not acknowledged by the court. The court had the 'rule of law' capacity to counter this imbalance in power by acknowledging its existence. The individual, as a sixteen-year-old

[150] *Shiu v. PP*, *supra* note 104 at 47.

[151] Ibid. at 12.

[152] *Criminal Procedure Code* (Cap. 68, 1985 Rev. Ed. Sing.) s. 36 (2).

boy, could have been rendered more visible, more of an individual, through the court's recognition of the situational intimidation inherent to the conditions in which Shiu made his written statement and testified in court. Like their encounter with the police, taking the witness box in court would have been an anxiety-ridden experience for Shiu's friends and parents. But the court did not perceive or respond to Shiu as a particularly vulnerable "accused person."

The court also replicated state discourse in refusing to see 'vandalism' as anything but a "serious offence."[153] Rejecting defence counsel's mitigation plea that probation rather than prison was called for, the court held that while, in general, the court would consider probation for young offenders, this case was an exception to the rule:

> The interests of the young offender however must be balanced against the interests of society and the courts must do whatever is necessary for the protection of the public. Accordingly, when serious offences are involved especially when as in this case they are committed wilfully and deliberately I was of the view that the only appropriate sentence was a custodial one.[154]

The court rejected the defence, producing a judgment observant of the 'common law' expectation that a court must engage with argument and counter-argument, assessing and evaluating the case made by both prosecution and defence. But in refusing to acknowledge the pressures underpinning the production of Shiu's written statements, the court was statist rather than liberal.[155] In brief, Shiu's trial illustrates the discursive practices of a statist court employing 'rule by law' strategies while performing 'rule of law' procedures such that the standing, visibility and very individuation of Shiu were erased and the "seriousness" of 'vandalism' was reiterated.

153 *Shiu v. PP*, *supra* note 104 at 46.

154 Ibid. at 47.

155 This pattern of coherence and continuity between court and state is also evident in the Chief Justice's dismissal of Fay's appeal against his sentence: *Fay v. Public Prosecutor* [1994] 2 Sing.L.R. 154 (H.C.).

In addition to these judicial discourses, in a governmentalist appropriation of the Fay and Shiu prosecutions, the Singapore state selected features of the cases to launch an 'Asian values' account of 'law' and punishment in the perpetually vulnerable 'nation'.

EAST VERSUS WEST: SOCIAL ORDER AND PUNISHMENT

The reformulation of the Fay episode via the category 'Asian values' was, significantly, launched by Lee Kuan Yew. Lee, then Senior Minister in the cabinet of his successor, Goh Chok Tong, had been Prime Minister of Singapore for thirty-one years. We have seen the centrality of Lee to the enactment of the 1966 *Punishment for Vandalism Act*. Lee's authoring of the 1994 revitalisation of the *Vandalism Act* through 'Asian values' illustrates how, almost thirty years later, Lee remained central to Singapore's 'rule by law' reconfigurations of the 'rule of law'.

Because of Lee's enduring, powerful and transformative leadership of Singapore[156] and his highly charismatic personality,[157] anything he says carries especial weight in the Singapore public domain. Two weeks after Fay's appeal had been dismissed, Lee spoke on a current affairs television programme. The following extract is from the *Straits Times* report on the programme:

> The Senior Minister noted that the US government, Senate and media had used the Fay incident to ridicule Singapore, saying that the punishment was too severe. "The country dares not restrain or punish the individuals, forgiving them for whatever they've done.... That's why the whole country is in chaos. Drugs, violence, unemployment and homelessness, all sorts of problems in its society". Thus, while America is the world's richest and most prosperous country, "it is hardly safe and peaceful".... [H]e said Singapore's stand was that the government must protect society. If not, there would be chaos.... Most

[156] Ho Khai Leong, *Shared Responsibilities, Unshared Power: The Politics of Policy-Making in Singapore* (Singapore: Marshall Cavendish, 2003) at 92–128.

[157] Ho asserts that Lee's charisma "has made him a Singapore cultural icon": ibid. at 96.

> Singaporeans also believed group interest must prevail. This was the right thing to do, for if they listened to the Americans, they would go downhill, he said.... Commenting on the difference between the West and the East on human rights issues, Mr Lee said the former regarded society as serving individual interests, while the latter placed importance on the group.[158]

Lee denies the validity of the US critique by characterising it as "ridicule". His deprecation of US penal technologies ("The country *dares not* restrain or punish the individuals", emphasis mine) implies that it is a weak and ineffectual country that "forgives", resulting in "drugs, violence, unemployment and homelessness" – a weakness he contrasts to the strength and determination of Singapore encoded in punitive state violence. Lee frames his assertions in a manner that conflates state and citizen ("Singapore's stand was that the government must protect society. If not, there would be chaos.... Most Singaporeans also believed group interest must prevail"), assuming popular consent for 'law' as coercion and for violent punishment. Human rights are explained away in crudely reductive terms: 'East' prioritises 'the group' and 'West' prioritises the individual.

Lee expressed this analysis of American social decline in April. Four months later, in the crucial month of August, the state repeated Lee's account of 'Asian values' and punishment. The state presented the sentencing of Fay and Shiu as a cautionary tale about 'East' and 'West', featuring the theme of the desirable disciplinary power of shame, through an essentialising presentation of the two boys. August is a month of heightened patriotism in Singapore because National Day, the anniversary of Singapore's becoming an independent, sovereign republic, is on 9 August.

On 1 August 1994, the press reported that Senior Minister Lee had written to Shiu's parents:

> SM Lee has assured the boy's parents that the government and SBC[159] have not lost their regard for him because of the conviction of his

[158] "US Reaction to Fay Case Shows It Dare Not Punish Criminals", *Straits Times* (13 April 1994) 3.

[159] "SBC" stands for Singapore Broadcasting Corporation. See also note 145.

> son ... and was sorry to hear the couple had been put into a "difficult and embarrassing position" by the publicity. A statement from SM's office said Mr Shiu's reticence about his son's difficulties "were those of a Confucianist who was ashamed that his son should have been involved in such an incident".[160]

Lee's letter, and the statement from his office, invoke and revitalise the "middle sort of knowledge"[161] from combining the discourses of 'Asian' (in this instance, more narrowly, "Confucian") in expressing approval of Shiu's father's sense of shame. Lee's characterisation erases the significance of the young Shiu's plea of 'not guilty' and the resulting publicity of a trial – a trial at which Shiu alleged police brutality and recounted how the police had threatened that they had the power to ensure his father would lose his job. Shiu senior took the stand at this trial to attest to his son's account of his time in police custody and the presence of a bruise on his son's thigh.[162] The trial contradicts this neat characterisation of an appropriate Confucian reticence, a desirable shame-shaped silence. Lee deals with the contradiction by simply leaving the trial out of his account.

Six days after Lee's letter to Shiu senior had been publicised, on Sunday, 7 August, two days before National Day, the *Sunday Times* ran a long interview with the reticent Shiu senior: "Biggest Crisis Has Brought Family Even Closer".[163] At this point I should note that Michael Fay's parents were divorced. He lived in Singapore with his mother and stepfather. Shiu Chi Ho's parents were not divorced. This difference between the family situations of the boys became amplified when, on 21 August, Prime

[160] "SM Urges SBC Drama Head to Stay Despite Son's Vandal Conviction", *Business Times [of Singapore]* (1 August 1994).

[161] Colin Gordon, "Introduction", in James D. Faubion, ed., *Michel Foucault: Power* (London: Penguin, 1994) xviii.

[162] *Shiu v. PP*, *supra* note 104; "Police Officers Hit Me", *supra* note 142 at 25; "HK Boy 'Gave Names of Others'", *supra* note 113 at 2.

[163] Leong Weng Kam, "Biggest Crisis Has Brought Family Even Closer", *Straits Times* (7 August 1994) 4.

Minister Goh Chok Tong gave a National Day Rally speech[164] entitled "Moral Values: The Foundation of a Vibrant State".[165] In his speech, Goh reiterated the stance introduced by Lee's 'Asian values' account of how penal violence protects the 'nation'. Reiterating Lee's themes, Goh too presented contemporary Singapore as a 'nation' at risk. In 1994 it was no longer "Communists and Communalists" who threatened Singapore.[166] Instead, "broken families", indulgence and indiscipline had become the sources of danger, and the parental imposition of corporal punishment was the point at which moral decay might be arrested and prevented.

In his speech, Goh first set out a description of a range of economic policies by which the government had secured and maintained the value of the people's assets. He then warned that while the economic future of Singapore was promising, continued economic success would be possible only with

> the right values ... a sense of community and nationhood, a disciplined and hardworking people, strong moral values and family ties.... Singaporeans have the right values to progress. Our Asian culture puts group interest above individual.[167]

Goh linked economic prosperity to a certain morality:

> You may think decline is unimaginable. But societies can go wrong quickly. US and British societies have changed profoundly in the last 30 years. Up to the early 60s, they were disciplined, conservative, with the family very much the pillar of their societies.

[164] The Prime Minister's National Day Rally speech is the Singapore equivalent of the US President's state of the union address. See also Kenneth Paul Tan, "Singapore's National Day Rally Speech: A Site of Ideological Negotiation" (2007) 37:3 *Journal of Contemporary Asia* 292.

[165] "National Day Rally Address by Prime Minister Goh Chok Tong, Speech in English, August", online: Speech-Text Archival and Retrieval System <http://stars.nhb.gov.sg/stars/public>.

[166] Sing., *Parliamentary Debates*, vol. 24, col. 5 (8 December 1965); discussed in Chapter 1.

[167] Goh, *supra* note 165.

> Since then both the US and Britain have seen a sharp rise in broken families, teenage mothers, illegitimate children, juvenile delinquency, vandalism and violent crime.[168]

This chain of decline that Goh presents begins, significantly, with broken families and ends in violent crime. This domino effect is presented as virtually inevitable again and again throughout his speech. It is noteworthy that he dates the decline of the United States and Britain from the early 1960s, as if to imply that all things 'Western' in the structures of the Singapore 'nation' (a 'nation' that dates from 1965) derive from a time of 'Western' strength and social vitality, and are therefore morally valid. The post-1960s decline of the United States and Britain becomes a cautionary tale for Singapore. He warns that Singapore society is changing in ways that show the risk of Singapore going into similar decline:

> Singapore society is also changing. Singaporeans are more preoccupied with materialism and individual rewards. Divorce rates are rising slightly. There are some single parents, and some increases in drug addiction and juvenile delinquency.
>
> Recently ST [the *Straits Times*] carried an advertisement showing a boy saying: "Come on, Dad. If you can play golf five times a week, I can have Sustagen once a day." I found the language and the way the boy speaks most objectionable. Why put an American boy's way of speaking to a father into a Singaporean boy's mouth? ... These advertisements will encourage children to be insolent to their parents. Many American children call their fathers by their first names, and treat them with casual familiarity. We must not unthinkingly drift into attitudes and manners which undermine the traditional politeness and deference Asian children have for their parents and elders. It will destroy the way our children have grown up – respectful and polite to their elders.
>
> Lesson 1: Do not indulge yourselves and your family, especially young children and teenagers.[169]

[168] Ibid.

[169] Ibid.

Goh's reasoning, rhetoric and instructive stance are perfect examples of the governmentality Foucault associated with economic neo-liberalism, "a kind of pedagogical ascendancy and a claim to lead, confronting ... citizens with the realities and disciplines of the market and tutoring them in the duties of economic enterprise".[170]

Goh presents the parental imposition of corporal punishment as the antidote to social decay:

> In America, indulgent upbringing of children has brought sorry consequences. If you slap your child for unruly behaviour you risk going to jail. At a grocery store in Georgia, a nine-year-old boy picked on his sister and was rude to his mother. The mother slapped him. A police officer saw red marks on the boy's face and asked if he had been slapped before. "I get smacked when I am bad," the boy said. The mother was handcuffed and hauled to jail for child abuse. She was released on S$33,000 bail. The charges were later dropped, not because the police felt that were wrong, but because they feared they could not prove to the court that the mother's slapping had caused excessive pain to her son.
>
> British justice also seems to have gone liberal and soft.... The American and British peoples are fed up with rising crime rates, and want to get tough on crime. This is why Michael Fay's vandalism aroused such interest.[171]

In a nutshell, Goh's argument is that parental indulgence of 'bad' behaviour is the possible dark side of affluence – a dark side best contained by parents empowered to discipline through corporal punishment. Through juxtaposition and repetition (rather than a discernible logic), the 'Asian value' of subordinating individual interests to group interests becomes the partner to economic prosperity and social order constituted by disciplined, hierarchical, intact families in which parents punish with an appropriate act of violence. Goh's speech suggests that the mother in Georgia

[170] Gordon, *supra* note 161 at xxiii.
[171] Goh, *supra* note 165.

who slapped her young son was behaving appropriately; it was the police who inappropriately undermined this mother.

Goh brought the focus of his argument sharply back to 'Asian values' when he continued:

> Compare the attitudes of Michael Fay's parents and Shiu Chi Ho's parents. Fay's parents were outraged instead of being ashamed. They went on TV, talk-shows, blaming everyone but themselves. Shiu's parents showed pain, avoided publicity and considered leaving Singapore because of a sense of shame. On the other hand, Michael Fay, back in America, got drunk and when his father protested, he tackled the father and wrestled him to the ground. I cannot imagine a Chinese son, or any other Asian son, physically tackling his father. But that may happen when sons call their fathers by their first names and treat them as equals.... In Confucian society, a child who goes wrong knows he has brought shame upon the whole family. In America, he may win instant stardom.[172]

Embedded in Goh's speech were two messages: first, that the mechanism for maintaining control – in the family, in society – must be corporal punishment; and second, that the citizen is to the state as the child is to the father. Without corporal punishment and hierarchical deference to authority, Singapore's economic prosperity and social order would necessarily, predictably decline into the morass of US and British social decay. State violence and tough 'law' become one inextricably entwined such that the precarious Singapore 'nation' is held together by an all-seeing, all-knowing state.

STATIST COURTS

The extraordinary dominance of state discourse in Singapore and the impact of this public discourse upon the operation of 'law' are captured by a 2007 judgment on 'vandalism', *Wong Shan Shan v. PP*.[173] In this case,

[172] Ibid.

[173] *Wong Shan Shan v. Public Prosecutor* [2007] SGDC 314 (Sing. Dist. Ct.) [*Wong*].

a nineteen-year-old woman pleaded guilty to two counts of vandalism. She had sprayed paint on the door and gate of a flat, and had written with a marker on the external walls of the flat. She was sentenced to two months' imprisonment. Forty-one years after the *Vandalism Act* had been passed, the District Court echoed the language and sentiments of the Minister who, in 1966, had argued:

> Damaging or destroying public property which is provided for the benefit of the people must be considered extremely serious, for it is the people themselves who ultimately pay for the services and amenities provided by the Government. However, there are, regrettably, certain irresponsible persons in the community who find a cruel joy in destroying and damaging public property. In the interests of the nation, it is therefore necessary that the minority who cause damage should be dealt with severely.[174]

In 2007 the District Court that sentenced Wong explained in its judgment:

> [T]hese acts of vandalism on public property were committed using either spray colour paints or marker pens.... The menace caused and the difficulty to remove such paints and marker stains need no elaboration. To underscore the gravity of such offences, Parliament has prescribed mandatory minimum caning of three strokes where the act of vandalism involved the use of paint, tar and other indelible substances. However, in the present case, no caning was imposed given the accused's gender.[175]

Echoing the state's 1966 arguments in *PP v. Liu Tong Ban*,[176] the Court held up the severity of the punishment as the indicia of the gravity of the offence. The Court in *Wong* noted that the accused had been diagnosed with early paranoid psychosis but found that she was "not of unsound mind" at the time of the offences and decided to exercise its discretion by sentencing her to two months imprisonment, to be served concurrently, on each charge of vandalism.

174 Sing. *Parliamentary Debates*, vol. 25, col. 291 (26 August 1966) (Wee Toon Boon).

175 *Wong, supra* note 173 at paras. 18–19.

176 "Reasons Behind the Vandalism Bill ...," *supra* note 37.

The 2007 District Court characterised the markings made by Wong as a "menace", an offence Parliament had determined to be "grave", recalling the statist discourse of the courts in the Fay and Shiu cases. The ahistorical texture of legislation, its susceptibility to uncritical interpretation within a regime of statist legalism, along with a state dominance of the public domain, has meant that in a post–Cold War world in which pro-Vietcong slogans are no longer an issue, 'vandalism' continues to occupy the category of 'serious offence'. Indeed, the "seriousness" of 'vandalism' has been reinscribed for the twenty-first century, not just through cases such as *Wong*, but also through the *Corruption, Drug Trafficking and Other Serious Crimes (Confiscation of Benefits) Act*[177] and the Association of Southeast Asian Nations (ASEAN) 2002 Treaty on Mutual Legal Assistance in Criminal Matters. In this ASEAN treaty, Singapore has listed vandalism, along with drug trafficking and the trafficking of girls and women, as a "serious" crime.

The paucity of judicial interrogation of legislative text so evident in the jurisprudence of 'vandalism' raises the question as to why Singapore courts, so able to deal with sophisticated and complex argument in the domain of commercial law,[178] produce such essentialising unreason in judgments to do with 'vandalism'. The answer, I think, lies in reading the *Vandalism Act* as an exercise of state power, in the state's power to command discourse. With the 1966 *Punishment for Vandalism Act*, the state generated a discourse of vandalism that no non-state actor, except perhaps the judiciary, was placed to contest. But the judiciary, chided by the Prime Minister in Parliament in 1966 for deciding according to legal principles rather than Singapore 'realities', became obedient to Parliament's command, reading into legislative text the sub-text it had been instructed to see.

[177] Cap. 65A, 2000 Rev. Ed. Sing.

[178] See, for example, Yong C.J.'s decision on the doctrine of clogs, or impediments, on the equity of redemption, which, in addition to reviewing and evaluating the doctrine, assesses the impact of innovations in financial instruments: *Citicorp Investment Bank (Singapore) Ltd v. Wee Ah Kee* [1997] 2 Sing.L.R.759. The complexities of the decision have been discussed in Kelvin Low & Tang Hung Wu, eds., *Principles of Singapore Land Law* (LexisNexis, 2009) at 530.

Discursive continuity between judgments and state discourse on 'vandalism' works in tandem with the absence of judicial interrogation of the Act's definitions and categories to produce a reductionist reading of legislative text. This constraint empties the adversarial system of its potential to produce narratives that counter the state's homogenising account of 'vandalism'. Vandalism is a "serious" offence because the state says it is.[179] The point at which reason ends is, perhaps, the state's authoritative pronouncement.

THE PANOPTICON 'NATION'

In 1994, with the Cold War over, the anti-Communist sub-text that was used to legitimate the violence of caning in 1966 was dropped. Communism was no longer the threat to the 'nation' that it had once been.

While the detail of the 1966 sub-text of Communism no longer applied in 1994, the theme of national vulnerability, necessitating a strong state prepared to act through strong 'law', was retained and reinscripted. In the 1994 discourse, the threat to the 'nation' was not the ideological and military might of Communism, but the laxity of 'Western' values – a laxity symbolised by the absence of corporal punishment in contemporary 'Western' states, accounting for the indiscipline and moral degeneracy of the once invincible 'West'. This new moral threat to the 'nation' was, according to the 1994 discourse on the Fay case, countered by the desirable and deterrent severity of corporal punishment. Thus, even after the

[179] It is interesting to note that, in comparison, the English legal system addresses 'vandalism' (without using this term) under the *Anti-Social Behaviour Act 2003* (UK), 2003, c.38, s. 43, through a system of fines specified in "penalty notices" issued by local authority officers or police support community officials. The UK Home Office website suggests that graffiti is not considered a serious offence; online: <http://www.homeoffice.gov.uk/anti-social-behaviour/penalties/penalty-notices/>. The *Anti-Social Behaviour Act* does not appear to have repealed the *Criminal Damage Act 1971* (UK) 1971, c. 48, under which the maximum penalty for acts understood as vandalism is imprisonment for ten years, but imprisonment is infrequently meted out as a sentence: Allen Cross, "Vandalism: An Anglo-American Perspective" (1979) 2 *Police Studies* 31.

Cold War, the violence of 'law' was needed to police the borders of the vulnerable 'nation', even if those borders were now notional and moral, pertaining to the disciplinary territory of the values of the 'nation'.

The interpretive susceptibility of legal text permitted 'vandalism', a category emptied of its 1966 sub-text of anti-Communism, to become available to other sub-texts in 1994: the 'nation's vulnerability to moral pollution and social decay, sovereign autonomy, Asian values. In both 1966 and 1994, this range of sub-texts related to a state construction of the 'nation'. As a category, 'vandalism' became impenetrable when coupled with "the conditions of effective domination"[180] of this exceptionally hegemonic state. It was surely these conditions that enabled a legal text enacted for one masked purpose – criminalising leftist 'politics' – to be interpreted by all organs of state so consistently that a different masked purpose – a display of sovereign autonomy through 'law' as pedagogy – was served in the caning of Michael Fay.

I close this case study with one last question: Why did the Singapore state need to repeatedly, excessively insist upon the validity of its 'law', going to such lengths, nationally and internationally, to explain its conduct in the Fay case in a manner that insisted upon the state's 'lawful', rational identity? Singapore, I would argue, is, as a state, akin to the panopticon prison. Bentham's design for a circular prison – cells arranged around a central surveillance tower from which all cells are visible – uses light and space, as Foucault points out, "to induce in the inmate a state of conscious and permanent visibility that assures the automatic functioning of power".[181] The prisoner cannot know whether or not the central tower is occupied, but the prisoner is always aware of being visible:

> Bentham laid down the principle that power should be visible and unverifiable. Visible: the inmate will constantly have before his eyes the tall outline of the central tower from which he is spied upon.

[180] Cover, *supra* note 49 at 1616.

[181] Michel Foucault, *Discipline and Punish: The Birth of the Prison*, 2nd ed., trans. by Alan Sheridan (New York: Vintage, 1995) 201.

> Unverifiable: the inmate must never know whether he is being looked at at any one moment; but he must be sure that he may always be so.[182]

Singapore is like a panopticon prison because it is especially small, the state is especially hegemonic and there are constant reminders in the public domain that state surveillance is pervasive. If the Singapore 'nation' is akin to the panopticon prison, then the supervisory space of the central tower must remain darkened. The state with uncertainty about the levels to which its legitimacy is grounded in consent cannot risk the light of questioning being shone upon the supervisory, disciplinary governance of the 'law' by which it manages the 'nation'. The US critique of the caning of Michael Fay as a violent, disproportionate, rights-violating penal excess shone a questioning light upon the Singapore state's legality, modernity and rationality – facets of state identity that are crucial to the Singapore state's assertions of legitimacy.[183] The Singapore state's reformulation of the event as an 'East' versus 'West' episode allowed the state to deflect the human rights critique and invalidate the 'West' as the source of the questioning light. By reformulating the Fay case, the state reclaimed itself as the source of morality, restating (in a way that was not challenged within the public domain of the 'nation') that, by punishing bodies, it was securing the 'nation'.

[182] Ibid.

[183] The argument about the role of rational modernity in the construction of state legitimacy was made in Chapter 1.

4 POLICING THE PRESS

Newspaper and Printing Presses Act

THIS CHAPTER PRESENTS A SECOND CASE study: the 1974 *Newspaper and Printing Presses Act* (or *Press Act*).[1] This case study demonstrates the manner in which the enactment of legislation has undermined and reconfigured a freedom closely connected to the freedom of expression and the pluralism of political liberalism: the freedom of the press. If the *Vandalism Act* has been a 'law' through which the visible, public space of 'nation' has been rendered ideologically homogenous, then the *Press Act* is the tool through which the discursive space of 'nation' has been homogenised. The technologies of press management entrenched by the *Press Act* have resulted in a highly policed discursive space in the 'nation', leading to an ever greater legal and discursive conflation between 'nation' and the PAP-state.

The 1974 enactment of the *Press Act* is inextricably linked to events in 1971, when three Singapore newspapers were subject to a series of repressive government measures that resulted in the closing down of two newspapers and a change of ownership and control of a third.[2] The state

[1] *Newspaper and Printing Presses Act* (Cap. 206, 2002 Rev. Ed.) [*Press Act*].

[2] Francis Seow, *The Media Enthralled: Singapore Revisited* (Boulder: Lynne Rienner, 1998) 38 – 105; Sing., *Parliamentary Debates*, vol. 31, cols. 5–10 at 9 (21 July 1971) (Dr Benjamin Henry Sheares); Lee Kuan Yew, *From Third World to First: The Singapore Story: 1965–2000* (Singapore: Singapore Times Editions, 2000) 212–18 [*From Third World to First*]; Simon Cassady, "Lee Kuan Yew & the Singapore Media: Purging

accused all three papers of undermining national security. According to the state, the papers had advocated divisive Communalist agendas, overtly or covertly furthered the cause of Communism or had undermined the 'nation' by being proxies for foreign interests. Three years after these events, the 1974 *Press Act* was brought into being.[3] Before proceeding to an analysis of the *Press Act*, this chapter traces texts and events that operated as a proto-enactment of sorts: Lee Kuan Yew's 1971 address to the International Press Institute (IPI) justifying the detention without trial of the four newspaper executives.[4] These detentions and the state's discourse at the time demonstrate how, in 1971, the state strategically used the public domain as a performative space, presenting its discursive legitimisations for 'rule by law' in a manner that lent dramatic urgency to its narratives of national vulnerability.

The *Press Act* is a 'law' which enables state surveillance and control of the ownership, management and funding of newspapers.[5] The 1971 state discourse of an undermined national security was invoked yet again fifteen years later, in 1986, when the state sought to justify measures to control the 'foreign press'.[6] This chapter traces the discursive and legal continuities between the events of 1971, the 1974 enactment of the *Press Act* and the 1986 'foreign press' amendment, as part of this project's larger concern with the ways in which legislation has constructed a state discourse of legitimacy through a strategic management of the ambivalences between 'rule of law' and 'rule by law'.

the Press" (1975) 4:3 *Index on Censorship* 3–6; Cherian George, "History Spiked: Hegemony and the Denial of Media Diversity", in Michael D. Barr & Carl A. Trocki, eds., *Paths Not Taken: Political Pluralism in Post-War Singapore* (Singapore: NUS Press, 2008) 264–80 [*History Spiked*].

[3] The debates on the second reading of the Bill were conducted in March 1974: Sing., *Parliamentary Debates*, vol. 33, cols. 913–32 (27 March 1974).

[4] Lee Kuan Yew, "The Mass Media and New Countries", paper presented at the General Assembly of the International Press Institute, 9 June 1971 [*Mass Media*].

[5] *Press Act*, s. 7 to s. 16.

[6] Sing., *Parliamentary Debates*, vol. 48, cols. 369–74 (31 July 1986) (Mr Wong Kan Seng).

SIGNIFICANCE OF THE *PRESS ACT*

The *Press Act* is an important legal text, for three main reasons. First, it marks an early moment in the nation-state's history in which the state extended the legal exceptionalism of the Emergency (1948–60) into the post-Emergency civic domain. This extension of Emergency exceptionalism is evident in the concentration of power in the hands of the executive, the ousting of the courts and the invocation of internal security to justify undermining the freedom of the press through state control and scrutiny of the management, ownership and finances of newspaper companies.

Second, the *Press Act* marks a development in 'law' as governance in that it combines colonial licensing technologies[7] (requiring the registration of, and issuing of licences for, all printing presses and newspapers) with corporatist technologies which appear to be modelled on the colonial *Straits Times* memorandum and articles of association.[8] Another 'law' as governance feature of the *Press Act* is its use of these corporatist technologies to effect co-option in that all newspapers must be companies with a two-tiered share structure: management shares and ordinary shares.[9] The significance of this structure is that while ordinary shares carry one vote per share, management shares carry two hundred votes per share when it comes to the appointment and dismissal of staff.[10] Additionally, management shares can be held only by state-approved individuals and corporations.[11] Effectively, therefore, newspaper companies are managed by state appointees, if not state proxies.[12] As a result, the public domain

[7] The *Press Act* retains the content of the colonial 1920 *Printing Presses Ordinance*, which can be traced to an Indian act applicable to the Straits Settlements, the 1835 Act XI, *Printers and Publishers*.

[8] Sing., "Report of the Select Committee on the Newspaper and Printing Presses Bill", Parliament 3 of 1974 (17 August 1974) [*Report on the Press Bill*] B12 at col. 24.

[9] *Press Act*, s. 8 and s. 10.

[10] *Press Act*, s. 10(11).

[11] *Press Act*, s. 10(1)(c).

[12] All but one of Singapore's dailies is published by Singapore Press Holdings, a government-linked company. The other daily, *Today*, is published by MediaCorp, another

has become inaccessible to any newspaper that is not ideologically compliant to the state.[13]

Third, if the *Punishment for Vandalism Act* was designed to contain a certain sort of expression of political opposition in the public domain, the *Press Act*, arguably, was (and is) designed to contain the public expression of critique and dissent through newspapers. Specifically, the *Press Act* appears to have been initiated by the state's desire to silence the public expression of critique by a newspaper that advocated on behalf of a certain section of the 'Chinese-educated' within Singapore.[14] This paper, the *Nanyang Siang Pau* (or *Nanyang*), became a platform for a section

government-linked company. Through "government-linked companies and private holding companies with close ties to the government", the state has "a near monopoly of the media": Dianne K. Mauzy & Robert Stephen Milne, *Singapore Politics Under the People's Action Party* (London: Routledge, 2002) at 137.

13 For wider scholarship on the Singapore state's management of media, in addition to the references cited at *supra* note 2, see Cherian George, *Singapore the Air-Conditioned Nation: Essays on the Politics of Comfort and Control, 1990–2000* (Singapore: Landmark, 2000); Cherian George, "Singapore: Media at the Mainstream and the Margins", in Russel Heng, ed., *Media Fortunes, Changing Times: ASEAN States in Transition* (Singapore: Institute of South East Asian Studies, 2002) [*Media at the Mainstream*]; Cherian George, "Consolidating Authoritarian Rule: Calibrated Coercion in Singapore" (2007) 20:2 *Pacific Review* 127 [*Consolidating Authoritarian Rule*]; Wendy Borkhorst-Heng, "Newspapers in Singapore: A Mass Ceremony in the Imagining of the Nation" (2002) 24 *Media, Culture & Society* 559; Soek-Fang Sim, "Obliterating the Political: One-Party Ideological Dominance and the Personalization of News in Singapore 21" (2006) 7:4 *Journalism Studies* 575; Jonathan Woodier, "Securing Singapore/Managing Perceptions: From Shooting the Messenger to Dodging the Question" (2006) 23 *Copenhagen Journal of Asian Studies* 57.

14 Seow, *supra* note 2; Carl Trocki, "David Marshall and the Struggle for Civil Rights in Singapore", in Michael D. Barr & Carl A. Trocki, eds., *Paths Not Taken: Political Pluralism in Post-War Singapore* (Singapore: NUS Press, 2008) 124. Hong & Huang write of the "language fault-lines" in Singapore politics: Hong Lysa & Huang Jianli, *The Scripting of a National History: Singapore and Its Pasts* (Singapore: NUS Press, 2008) at 109. The essentialist and reductive use of the categories 'English-educated' and 'Chinese-educated' with reference to Singaporeans bearing the 'race' name 'Chinese' is a feature of Singapore discourse highlighted in Chapter 5's discussion of the so-called Marxist Conspiracy. See also Huang Jianli, "The Young Pathfinders: Portrayal of Student Activism", in Michael D. Barr & Carl A. Trocki, eds., *Paths Not Taken: Political Pluralism in Post-War Singapore* (Singapore: NUS Press, 2008) at 188.

of the population that opposed the state's policies pertaining to 'Chinese' language, culture and education. The state denied that its actions against the *Nanyang* were motivated by the *Nanyang*'s criticism. Instead, the state said its actions against the paper were necessitated by the "step-by-step campaign that accused the Government of trying to destroy Chinese culture".[15]

In Chapter 3's discussion of the *Punishment for Vandalism Act*, I described Singapore's 1966 context. Key features of that 1966 social and political environment continued to feature in the early 1970s. The PAP-state, although dominant and the only party present in Parliament, had yet to secure the levels of hegemony and popular compliance that marked its rule from the late 1970s onwards. Popular discontent and agitation centred on issues of 'Chinese' education, the valuing of 'Chinese' language and culture and the economic and social place within the 'nation' of 'Chinese-educated' Singaporeans.[16]

The 'Chinese'-language university, Nantah, had become something of a rallying point for these issues,[17] crystallising around the lack of government funding for Nantah and the lack of government recognition of Nantah degrees when it came to employment in the civil service.[18] Indeed, Nantah and 'Chinese' medium education were issues at the forefront of the September 1963 general elections,[19] with key Nantah players aligning themselves with the Barisan,[20] a party whose leaders were 'Chinese-educated',[21] unlike the 'English-educated' leaders of the PAP.[22]

15 Leslie Fong, "Three Newsmen Held", *Straits Times* (3 May 1971) 1; Lee, *From Third World to First*, *supra* note 2.

16 Hong & Huang, *supra* note 14; Huang, *supra* note 14.

17 Hong & Huang, *supra* note 14 at 111.

18 Ibid. at 109–62.

19 Sai Siew Min & Huang Jianli, "The 'Chinese-Educated' Political Vanguards: Ong Pang Boon, Lee Khoon Choy & Jek Yeun Thong", in Lam Peng Er & Kevin Y. L. Tan, eds., *Lee's Lieutenants: Singapore's Old Guard* (St Leonards: Allen & Unwin, 1999) 132 at 145–48.

20 Ibid.

21 Ibid.

22 Ibid.

The "language fault lines"[23] among Singapore's 'Chinese' were a highly charged, highly political issue.

Nantah had an early history of association with the opposition Barisan, both at the level of university elite, in the form of its founding father, and at the level of its student body.[24] Additionally, the PAP-state characterised Nantah student activism as "pro-communist" and "communist managed".[25] The student perception that the PAP-state was attempting to "destroy Chinese education"[26] erupted into large-scale student protests in September 1965, when the university's administration (put in place by the PAP in 1964)[27] accepted the recommendations of a review committee report. Nantah students perceived the report as an attempt to dismantle the autonomy of Nantah and "destroy Chinese education" in favour of the English language.[28]

The *Nanyang* was the largest of Singapore's four 'Chinese'-language dailies.[29] As a newspaper, the *Nanyang* was sympathetic to the cause of 'Chinese' education.[30] Its coverage gave voice to students' grievances, and its editorials argued for the relevance of 'Chinese'-language education in the new nation.[31] The *Nanyang* accused the PAP's leaders of being deracinated and against 'Chinese' education.[32] With an all-PAP Parliament and

[23] Hong & Huang, *supra* note 14 at 109.

[24] Ibid. at 91, 112; Sai & Huang, *supra* note 19 at 147, 148.

[25] Yao Souchou, "All Quiet on the Jurong Road: Nanyang University and Radical Vision in Singapore", in Michael D. Barr & Carl A. Trocki, eds., *Paths Not Taken: Political Pluralism in Post-War Singapore* (Singapore: NUS Press, 2008) at 170.

[26] Hong & Huang, *supra* note 14 at 117.

[27] Sai & Huang, *supra* note 19.

[28] Ibid.

[29] C. M. Turnbull, *Dateline Singapore: 150 Years of "The Straits Times"* (Singapore: Times Editions, 1995) 287, 226.

[30] The state was at pains to disclaim that the detentions of the *Nanyang* executives were designed to suppress "criticism on Chinese education or culture either by *Nanyang* or any other newspaper in Singapore": Hong & Huang, *supra* note 14 at 98.

[31] Seow, *supra* note 2 at 47, quotes Lee Eu Seng (elder brother of one of the detained pressmen and also a member of the family who owned the newspaper) at a press conference saying that "being a Chinese-language paper, we naturally would encourage the study of the Chinese-language".

[32] *Supra* note 15.

the shutting down, through the *Vandalism Act*, of public space for the expression of dissent, newspapers with a degree of autonomy from the state must have become an important non-state voice in an increasingly constrained public domain. Apart from the autonomous newspapers, there was little public articulation of non-state voices with the capacity to reach the 'nation'.

The events of 1971 involving these three newspapers have been documented in detail in Francis Seow's *The Media Enthralled*.[33] The context I set out here is drawn largely from his monograph. Seow argues that although the government acted against three newspapers (the 'Chinese'-language *Nanyang* and two English-language papers, the *Singapore Herald* and the *Eastern Sun*), its primary target was the popular *Nanyang*.[34] But because of a political climate in which the 'Chinese-educated' felt a great deal of hostility towards and suspicion of the PAP, the state could not been seen to be targeting a popular 'Chinese'-language newspaper that had accused the state of marginalising the 'Chinese'-educated in the new economy of the nation-state.[35] Thus, the state identified two English-language papers that could be included in what the state presented as a security operation.[36] The state alleged that all three newspapers were fronts for hostile foreign interests intent on undermining the 'nation'[37] – allegations that rested on the state's surveillance apparatus rather than on evidence. In keeping with the framing of the issue as one of national security, the state's first major public move against the papers involved the detentions, under the *Internal Security Act*, of four executives from the *Nanyang*,[38] alleging

[33] Seow, *supra* note 2.

[34] George, *History Spiked*, *supra* note 2 at 269.

[35] Ibid.

[36] Seow, *supra* note 2.

[37] Lee Kuan Yew, "Address by the Prime Minister at the Seminar on Communism and Democracy", 28 April 1971. Lee's speeches are available at the Singapore–Malaysia collection of the Central Library, National University of Singapore. See also Seow, *supra* note 2 at 39.

[38] Seow, *supra* note 2, at 40.

that the *Nanyang* had launched a deliberate campaign to "stir up Chinese racial feelings".[39]

Both the *Singapore Herald* and the *Eastern Sun* were relatively young newspapers, dependent on lines of credit from banks to fund their fledgling operations.[40] The state alleged, inter alia, that because these two newspapers were not yet profitable, the 'foreign' individuals and banks that had invested in, or extended credit to, the papers could not possibly be bona fides.[41] For the state, the lines of credit were evidence of foreign "black operations" designed to use the papers as a vehicle to sow discontent and disaffection, leading to the destabilisation of the 'nation'.[42]

Editorial content in the *Singapore Herald* critical of certain government policies was cited by the state as evidence of that paper's anti-national political agenda.[43] The absence of critique in the *Eastern Sun*, on the other hand, was explained as a sinister waiting game on the part of hidden Communist backers who wanted to entrench the paper before using it as a tool to destabilise the 'nation'.[44] Pressure was put on the *Singapore Herald*'s bank, Chase Manhattan, to foreclose on the loan it had made.[45] The *Eastern Sun*'s operations were brought to an end by the collective resignation of the key staff members of that paper, all of whom were foreign nationals.[46] Upon resigning, the *Eastern Sun*'s staff made a statement declaring its belief that the paper was anti-Communist, but the pall of government suspicion made their positions as journalists untenable.[47]

The more established *Nanyang* was owned and operated by a wealthy family and so was not susceptible to the kind of financial pressures that

[39] Ibid. at 38–47; Turnbull, *supra* note 29 at 291.
[40] Seow, *supra* note 2 at 52–60.
[41] Ibid. at 56–102.
[42] Ibid. at 52–88.
[43] Ibid. at 40.
[44] Ibid.
[45] Ibid. at 56–100.
[46] Ibid. at 52–54.
[47] Ibid.

were placed on the other two papers. Perhaps this is why the *Nanyang* received the most coercive of state attentions: Four of its executives were detained without trial. With the enactment of the *Press Act*, the paper was forced to undergo a change of ownership and control, which would necessarily have altered the character of the newspaper.[48]

Seow's account of the state's management of the three newspapers emphasises the degree to which the state staged and performed its version of accounts, bewildering and intimidating the non-state actors into a tongue-tied acquiescence where possible[49] and resorting to outright coercion where it was not.[50] Seow emphasises the dominance of Lee Kuan Yew in these public moments, describing his management of a crucial press conference on the *Singapore Herald* thus:

> Lee almost invariably dominates the press conference, during which he keeps the dramatis personae on a tight leash, cutting them off whenever they show signs of balking or straying from the agreed text or script.[51]

The state's use of the public domain to stage its legitimacy through the simple but effective strategy of discursive dominance is a remarkably consistent feature of state responses to contestation on 'law'. This 1971 press conference that Seow presents in detail is one such instance.[52] Lee's address to the IPI Helsinki assembly (discussed later) is another. Chapter 5 presents accounts of such moments involving lawyers, and Chapter 7 argues that the new *Public Order Act* is designed to ensure that the state remains the lead actor on the stage of 'nation', not just marginalising, but almost obliterating, those it considers fools and jesters.

When, in 1971, the Singapore state began to act against the three newspapers it characterised as threats to the 'nation', the state produced

[48] See also George's assessment of these events, *History Spiked*, *supra* note 2 at 270–73.
[49] Seow, *supra* note 2 at 66–71.
[50] Ibid. at 51.
[51] Ibid. at 66.
[52] Ibid. at 66–70.

many statements and repeated explanations as to how and why these papers were "anti-national". In a diversity of accounts unimaginable in a post-1971 Singapore, the state's accusations and interpretations were subject to a lively challenge from the newspapers involved, particularly from the *Nanyang*.[53] Readership of the targeted papers shot up.[54] Led by the Singapore National Union of Journalists, supporters of the *Singapore Herald* launched a campaign to keep their paper financially afloat.[55] The three newspapers denied that they were "anti-national", "Communist" or fronts for sinister enemies.[56] The papers pointed out that the state had no proof with which to back its accusations and invited the state to make its case in court, should it have a case to make.[57] The owner of the *Nanyang* issued a personal statement saying that in a country without an opposition in Parliament, the *Nanyang* was filling a crucial void by expressing the citizens' frustrations and concerns and that questioning the state was an expression of loyalty and patriotism.[58]

International press organisations also questioned the state's version of events, expressing their abhorrence of the detentions without trial of the Nanyang pressmen and calling for an evidentiary establishment of facts and guilt.[59] This international critique appears to have been assessed as significant enough to warrant the personal attention of Prime Minister Lee Kuan Yew, reflecting the need for states to generate legitimacy both with citizens and by obtaining the recognition of other states.[60] Barely five weeks after detaining the *Nanyang* executives, Lee vigorously defended

[53] Ibid. at 42–48.

[54] Ibid. at 46, 59.

[55] Ibid. at 74.

[56] Seow, *supra* note 2.

[57] Ibid.

[58] Ibid. at 44.

[59] Ibid. at 50; "Transcript of the Question-and Answer Session Following the Address to the 20th General Assembly of the International Press Institute at Helsinki by the Prime Minister" (9 June 1971) 7–10.

[60] J. Borneman, "State: Anthropological Aspects", in Neil J. Smelser & Paul B. Baltes, eds., *International Encyclopedia of the Social & Behavioural Sciences* (Amsterdam: Elsevier, 2004) 14968.

his government's actions at the June 1971 IPI Annual Assembly in Helsinki, denying that the state was motivated by the desire to oppress and silence its critics.[61]

STAGING LEGITIMACY: THE HELSINKI PLATFORM

Lee's Helsinki speech is a text richly revealing of the Singapore state's constructions of the roles of the press, the citizen and the state. If 'law' as governance involves the state's selection of objects for policing and the construction of state knowledge about those objects,[62] then this speech is the precursor to the 1974 *Press Act* and establishes a legal-administrative template for state–press relations that has endured to this day.

In summary, Lee argued at the Helsinki assembly that Singapore newspapers had periodically become fronts for hostile foreign interests and that the Singapore government, as a responsible government, must act to prevent this 'anti-national' subversion. Lee's argument involved a lengthy criticism of 'the West', a description of Singapore's particular vulnerabilities arising from 'race', 'religion' and susceptibility to 'Communism' and a construction of 'Western' culture as a security threat equivalent to the dangers of 'Communism' and 'Communalism'.[63]

Lee argued at Helsinki that because the press had been either an 'anti-national' local proxy for foreign black operations or 'anti-national' in its portrayals of 'Western' "permissiveness in sex, drugs and dress-styles", the state acted legitimately and in the interests of the 'nation' when it extended its policing of the press. In making this argument, Lee authoritatively asserted his knowledge about a range of subjects: 'the press',

[61] Lee, *Mass Media, supra* note 4.

[62] Michel Foucault, "Governmentality", in James D. Faubion, ed., *Michel Foucault: Power, Essential Works of Foucault, 1954–1984* (London: Penguin, 2002) vol. 3 at 208–10.

[63] The speech made by the Head of State on the occasion of the opening of the first Parliament of the Republic of Singapore in December 1965 is discussed in Chapter 1; in this speech "Communism and Communalism" were set out as the twin dangers to the 'nation'.

foreign black operations, Singapore's 'people', the 'West'. This assertion of knowledge facilitated his reclassification of 'the press' such that it was made into an object of control in a far more totalising manner than by the colonial state. With the Helsinki reclassification, the role of 'the press' was (and remains) altered so that 'the press' becomes not a public, institutional voice of 'the people' with the capacity to investigate and critique the manner in which a state exercises power, but the partner of the state in the project of 'nation' – instructing 'the people', selecting appropriate material from the 'West' (science and technology, facets of culture that are aesthetic and uplifting), while protecting 'the people' from moral corruption. Consequently, rather than Singapore's press keeping a watchful eye on the state's exercise of power, the role of the state is to protect the 'nation' from the power of the press.[64] Implicit to the *Press Act* is the assumption that the state itself could never threaten the 'nation'. It is this rescripting of 'press' as a category inherently tied to the security of the 'nation' that is at the heart of the manner in which the Singapore state extended Emergency legal exceptionalism to the 1974 *Press Act*.

Relying on a series of assumptions and constructing a series of binary relationships, Lee argues in this speech that media content from outside the 'nation' (whether from the 'West' or the rest of Asia) represents a risk to Singapore's capacity to achieve "progress". Media output from the 'West' is a danger because its portrayals of violent demonstrations and free love are confusing for 'the people'. Media output from Asia is a threat because it is irredentist, ideologically divisive or exports factionalism and tensions from countries of origin into Singapore's immigrant communities. With these dangers, it is the 'nation' that is at stake: in terms of territory, the morality of 'the people' and the economic impetus towards development. If the "art of government is the correct manner of managing individuals, goods and wealth",[65] then Lee's speech justifies the

[64] Lee, *Mass Media*, *supra* note 4.

[65] Foucault, *supra* note 62 at 207.

state's management of 'the press' as part of the management of a series of threats against the especially vulnerable Singapore 'nation'.

Lee makes his argument by Othering both 'the people' and 'the West' and uses his speech as a platform from which, as the personification and voice of the 'nation', he instructs both the press and 'the people' on their respective roles. I have organised the analysis of this important speech through a discussion of Lee's main themes. Lee opened his speech by likening news reporting to advertising[66]:

> The sustained repeated "sell" through all mass media ... undoubtedly helps to shape attitudes to fashions in clothes, foods and consumer durables.... It is therefore not improbable that the sustained plugging of a line can also mould public opinion on political issues and policies.[67]

Lee's recognition of the power of repetition in shaping beliefs is recognition of the role of media discourse and of the power represented by discursive dominance in the public domain. His analogy to advertising suggests that the commodity being sought is the consent, if not the compliance, of 'the people' to the project of 'nation', a project which gives primacy to economic development. Alternative conceptions of, and goals for, the 'nation' are excluded by his framework. His seemingly speculative musing upon the "not improbable" relationship between "the sustained plugging of a line" and public opinion takes on a more sinister cast in view of the state dominance of the public domain that was engineered by the *Press Act*. Following from the *Press Act*, Singapore has been characterised by a media environment in which all domestic newspapers, radio

[66] After Herman and Chomsky's seminal *Manufacturing Consent*, thinking of news as a process by which power and business elites manage and commodify readers has almost become standard, but Lee's speech was made in 1971, a good seventeen years before *Manufacturing Consent* was published: Edward S. Herman & Noam Chomsky, *Manufacturing Consent: The Political Economy of the Mass Media* (New York: Pantheon, 1988).

[67] Lee, *Mass Media*, *supra* note 4.

and television have been produced by state-controlled (and later, state-owned) agencies.[68]

His Othering of 'the people' is in striking continuity with colonial constructions of 'natives' as people of inferior ability. For Lee, 'the people', in particular the young among 'the people', are limited in intelligence and in their capacity for critical thinking. Lee conveys this subordinating assessment most frequently by his description of 'the people' as easily confused, invoking their confusion four times in his speech. For example:

> At a time when new nations require their peoples to work hard and be disciplined to make progress, their peoples are confused by watching and reading of the happenings in the West. They read in newspapers and see on T.V. violent demonstrations in support of peace, urban guerillas, drugs, free love and hippieism. Many people are uncritically imitative.[69]

Lee sets himself and his audience apart from the uncritically imitative 'people'. It is 'the people' who need media presentations of Singapore's problems that are simple and clear. It is 'the people' who need consistency between the values and attitudes taught at school and media content. In other words, 'the people' cannot deal with complexity, nor can they be trusted to engage in the process of making their own assessments. Lee arrogates to himself the power to determine what is and is not relevant for 'the people'. He issues to 'the people' the instruction to "work hard and be disciplined to make progress",[70] a didacticism that simultaneously infantalises 'the people' and elevates the state by placing Lee in the position of pedagogue.

[68] The Internet introduced a new, less controllable player to the scene. Nonetheless, the state has demonstrated its capacity and intent to police the Internet. See Cherian George, *Contentious Journalism and the Internet: Towards Democratic Discourse in Malaysia and Singapore* (Singapore: Singapore University Press, 2006) [*Contentious Journalism*].

[69] Lee, *Mass Media, supra* note 4.

[70] Ibid.

While his elitism invites parallels to colonial 'race' and power hierarchies, his construction of 'the people' as requiring a simple, consistent and instructive newspaper content is also consistent with the modernist state's disciplinary project of governmentality – a project he furthers with his pedagogic stance and pastoral concern:

> The mass media can help to present Singapore's problems simply and clearly and then explain how if they support certain programmes and policies these problems can be solved.
>
> More important, we want the mass media to reinforce, not to undermine, the cultural values and social attitudes being inculcated in our schools and universities. The mass media can create a mood in which people become keen to acquire the knowledge, skills and disciplines of advanced countries. Without these, we can never hope to raise the standards of living of our people.
>
> If they are to develop, people in new countries cannot afford to imitate the fads and fetishes of the contemporary West.[71]

The binary between 'foreign' and 'nation' that informs Lee's speech casts the state as a protective force nurturing a susceptible 'people'. The sources of danger, in one way or another, are 'foreign'. This rhetoric and the stance of pastoral, pedagogic concern for 'the people' mask the fact that it is the state that threatens selected members of 'the people'. Those individuals who experienced the most coercive of state actions – detention without trial – suffered at the hands of the state, not at the hands of 'foreigners'. The "foreign agencies" remained shadowy and hidden, beyond the scope of the state to produce as proof positive, beyond the scope of punishment. In this state strategy of selecting ideologically autonomous or oppositional sections of the population as targets for state coercion, the state perpetuates the *Punishment for Vandalism Act*'s sub-textual determination that 'anti-PAP' is equivalent to 'anti-national'.

The neo-colonial elitism that informs Lee's derogatory characterisations of 'the people' accompanies a conflicted Othering of 'the West': 'The

[71] Ibid.

West' is the site of an undesirable social and moral "malaise" exemplified by "violent demonstrations in support of peace, urban guerrillas, drugs, free love and hippieism". And yet 'the West' is also the site of desirable "scientific and technological triumphs". The 'problem' which Singapore faces is that

> [t]o take in Western science, technology and industry, we find that we cannot completely exclude the undesirable ethos of the contemporary West.... So we must educate Singaporeans not to imitate the more erratic behaviour of the West.[72]

By refusing to recognise the social and political contexts for his list of 'Western' ills (violent demonstrations, urban guerrillas, free love), by characterising these behaviours as "erratic", "strange", "undesirable" and by employing an extended metaphor of 'the West' as diseased ("malaise", "maladies", "ills", which the Singapore government must "inoculate" its people from), Lee portrays the 'West' as degenerate and in decline. Lee cites these social ills as if they originate in 'the West'. By characterising 'the West' as the site of violence and sexual excess, Lee implies these behaviours and phenomena are alien to, and absent from, Singapore. This is richly ironic given Singapore's history as a centre of the colonial opium trade[73] and the colonial legal characterisation of 'the Chinese' as a polygamous 'race'.[74]

Lee offers two explanations for undesirable phenomena in the 'West': first, the discounting of "the puritan ethics of hard work, thrift and discipline"; and second, the dehumanising effects of science and technology. His explanations imply that the West can only continue to

[72] Ibid.

[73] Carl A. Trocki, *Opium and Empire: Chinese Society in Colonial Singapore, 1800–1910* (Ithaca, NY: Cornell University Press, 1990).

[74] See, for example, *Re Loh Toh Met, Decd Kong Lai Fong & Ors v. Loh Peng Heng* [1961] 1 M.L.J. 234, in which the Johore Bahru Court of Appeal usefully summarises the jurisprudence on 'Chinese' polygamous marriages. Up to the enactment of the 1961 *Women's Charter* (Cap. 353, 1997 Rev. Ed. Sing.), which (generally) defined "marriage" in Singapore as monogamous, this body of jurisprudence was relevant to Singapore.

descend deeper into decline. For Lee, 'the West' is the site of an inexorable, unreasoned degeneration. In contrast, his examples of Singapore violence are all explained in clear cause-and-effect terms. The 1950 "jungle girl" riots[75] were caused by a Malay newspaper's publication of a certain photograph; the 1964 'race' riots were caused by a sustained campaign conducted by a Malay newspaper falsely alleging 'Chinese' oppression of 'Malay' rights; the "outbursts of violence by young Chinese workers and students" were precipitated by "calculated campaigns" conducted by newspapers. Thus, according to Lee, two features consistently mark moments of violence that beset Singapore. First, violence is always linked to 'race', 'religion' or 'Communism'; and second, violence arises only because the mass media has misled 'the people'. By presenting violence and disorder in Singapore as explicitly cause and effect in nature, Lee constructs a profoundly legitimising role for state coercion undertaken in order to pre-empt wider public violence.

Bearing in mind that this speech was delivered by Lee to the world's media representatives, his presence at the Helsinki assembly points to the importance he accords to the standing of the PAP-state in the eyes of the 'West'. As a "new nation" dependent on 'Western' investments, the PAP-state wants to be perceived as legitimate; it needs to differentiate itself from other "new nations" characterised by corruption and despotic uses of power. The state's legitimacy depends upon Lee's being able to convince his audience, an audience comprising the very individuals who make 'the press' the influential opinion-maker that Lee is so wary of. And while the world's journalists can validly demand evidence of "foreign subventions" and "foreign black operations", Lee's account of Singapore's peculiarities of 'race' and 'religion' are less easily challenged. The chronology of violence that he presents as precipitated by the press is a history that, as Prime Minister of a multi-racial post-colonial nation-state, he is

[75] Lee's reference was to the riots, which, in the dominant national narrative, were precipitated by the colonial court's decision in favour of 'Dutch' biological parents and against the 'Malay' adoptive mother in a custody battle: *In Re Maria Huberdina Hertogh; Inche Mansor Abadi v. Adrianus Petrus Hertogh and Anor.* [1951] 1 M.L.J. 164 (Sing. C.A.).

able to authoritatively expound to an international audience without an equivalent expertise.

The binaries Lee sets up, locating virtue in the 'East' and vice in the 'West', were not new to Singapore public discourse, and as discussed in Chapter 3's analysis of the 1994 Fay case, these binaries have continued to play an instrumental role in Singapore state discourse. What *is* new and significant about Lee's cataloguing of 'Western' faults, however, is his coupling of civil activism – demonstrations – with the decline of sexual morality. This coupling is highly significant because it enables him to discipline Singapore's population at multiple levels. In the context of 1971, "violent demonstrations in support of peace" and "strange behaviour of demonstration and violent-prone young men and women in wealthy America" are almost certainly references to the US civil movement against the Vietnam War. Lee ignores the *non-violent* anti-war activism that was such a strong feature of the time, repeatedly conflating demonstrations with violence, thereby delegitimising collective civilian activity against states.

Eliminating public and associational expressions of dissent has been a cornerstone of the PAP-state's management of the public domain since it took power in 1959.[76] The US anti-war demonstrations, rendered vivid and visible through the media, were images and instances of citizens mobilising to express opposition to their government's policies. Lee's certainty of the irrelevance of such news to Singapore is consistent with the pedagogical project of 'nation'. Lee constructs 'the people' as apolitical digits in the all-important project of economic progress:

> The strange behaviour of demonstration and violence-prone young men and women in wealthy America, seen on T.V. and the newspapers, are not relevant to the social and economic circumstances of new under-developed countries. The importance of education, the

[76] Much has been written on state repression and management of public activity. For a sampling, see generally references in Chapter 1 in the discussion on 'law', political liberalism and the moderate state.

> need for stability and work discipline, the acquisition of skills and expertise, sufficient men trained in the sciences and technology, and their ability to adapt this knowledge and techniques to fit the conditions of their country, these are vital factors for progress.[77]

'The people', as constructed by Lee, are so apolitical and so ignorant that media representations of demonstrations in "wealthy America" would "confuse" them. The 'people' must not be "confused" into taking positions on political issues or into expressing their views. Lee's insistence that this "strange behaviour" is irrelevant to "new under-developed countries" is at odds with Singapore's geographical proximity to Vietnam and with the history of opposition, within Singapore, to the PAP government's support for the US war in Vietnam.[78] In this light, an opening moment of his speech takes on a particular resonance:

> The recent bitter rows over T.V. and newspaper coverage of the war in Vietnam was a sad admission that even in highly developed countries, objectivity was the subjective views of the owners and commentators of the mass media as against those of the Nixon administration.[79]

Lee attributes a desirable "objectivity" to the Nixon administration while deprecating the mass media's owners and commentators. Perhaps the media's coverage of anti-war activity in "wealthy America" threatens the PAP-state precisely because of the resonance with, and relevance to, Singapore. Significantly, Lee's selection of characterisations ignores the massive demonstrations that marked, for example, China's Cultural Revolution or the Quit India movement. Violence and disorder are thus framed as belonging to an alien space of the 'West', marked by social practices and values that are morally corrupt, irrelevant to and undesirable for Singapore.

[77] Lee, *Mass Media*, *supra* note 4.

[78] Chapter 3's discussion of the events precipitating the *Vandalism Act* reflects this history.

[79] Lee, *Mass Media*, *supra* note 4.

LEE THE PASTORAL PEDAGOGUE

Lee's speech is, in many ways, akin to a curriculum which addresses three actors in the project of 'nation': 'the people', the press and the state. 'The people' must "work hard and be disciplined to make progress"; "become keen to acquire the knowledge, skills and disciplines of advanced countries ... to raise the standards of living"; recognise the "importance of education, the need for stability and work discipline, the acquisition of skills and expertise"; train in "the sciences and technology ... [with the] ability to adapt this knowledge and techniques to fit the conditions of their country." The people must not "imitate the fads and fetishes of the contemporary West." The press must

> present Singapore's problems simply and clearly and then explain how if they support certain programmes and policies these problems can be solved.
>
> More important, we want the mass media to reinforce, not to undermine, the cultural values and social attitudes being inculcated in our schools and universities. The mass media can create a mood in which people become keen to acquire the knowledge, skills and disciplines of advanced countries ... to raise the standards of living of our people.[80]

The state must "educate Singaporeans not to imitate the more erratic behaviour of the West"; "inoculate" parts of the population from "Western ills"; use censorship to eradicate the influences of the Kuomintang and Maoist China; ensure that Singapore's domestic media is not "surreptitiously captured by their proxies"; "neutralise the intentions" of "foreign agencies that use local proxies to set up or buy into newspapers ... to make political gains by shaping opinions and attitudes."

Lee's most emphatic formulation of the role of the state is delivered as his conclusion. When "foreign agencies" seek to use local proxies to shape opinions and attitudes,

[80] Ibid.

> [m]y colleagues and I have the responsibility to neutralise their intentions. In such a situation, freedom of the press, freedom of the news media, must be subordinated to the overriding needs of the integrity of Singapore, and to the primacy of purpose of an elected government. The government has taken, and will from time to time have to take, firm measures to ensure that, despite divisive forces of different cultural values and life styles, there is enough unity of purpose to carry the people of Singapore forward to higher standards of life, without which the mass media cannot thrive.

His assertion that subversion through proxies is what "foreign agencies from time to time" do is in keeping with the climate of suspicion of the Cold War context of 1971. What is confusing about Lee's concluding argument, however, is the manner in which he combines two apparently separate categories of threats to Singapore into a compound internal security framework justifying exceptions to the principle of freedom of the press: Threats arising from the empire building of "foreign agencies" are bracketed with the hardly comparable threat of contemporary 'Western' culture.

This bracketing of hostile foreign powers and 'Western' culture, and the slightly ludicrous solemnity of Lee's hope that "the pill plus the traditional importance of the Asian family unit, where paternity is seldom in doubt"[81] will morally protect Singapore, make strategic sense in terms of how his argument adds up to a justification of the silencing of the three newspapers. Morality, by his argument, is a core internal security issue. It is 'the nation' that is at stake, and it is the state that guards the 'nation' by policing morality. This categorisation of morality as an internal security issue legitimates preventive state action that watchfully pre-empts the violence and disorder that enemies of the 'nation' seek to unleash. Emergency legal exceptionalism is, after all, characterised by the exercise of state power against those who have yet to commit crimes – a power justified as preventing and pre-empting acute social disorder.

[81] Ibid.

All in all, Lee is at pains to convince his Helsinki audience that, in detaining the *Nanyang* executives and closing down newspapers, the state acted not from the petty despotism of wanting to silence critics, but from the unimpeachable high-mindedness of responsibly securing the 'nation' from sinister 'foreign' enemies, ideological and cultural. Lee reconfigures the contours of state legitimacy through slightly oblique invocations of the 'rule of law', employing one modernist category associated with the 'rule of law' – 'nation' – to legitimise his demotion of another modernist category associated with the 'rule of law' – 'free press'. The almost missing element in Lee's concluding formulation, 'the people', is imported through his reference to the "primacy of purpose of an elected government". In other words, in keeping with 'rule of law' ideals for 'nation', Lee claims his ultimate legitimacy from 'the people'; a rich irony given that so much of his speech has delegitimised 'the people' by infantalising them.

Lee invokes "elected government" in a manner that implies 'the people' had been offered viable alternatives to the PAP. A strong Barisan had indeed represented such an alternative before the 1963 Operation Coldstore,[82] but the combination of repressive state actions and the failure of the Barisan to consolidate its position against the monolithic force of the PAP-state has meant that, since 1963, the Singapore electorate cannot be said to have been offered a viable alternative to the PAP at the ballot box.[83] How much authority could 'the people' vest in an elected government when the opposition had been systematically and irreparably undermined by the state's use of policing, surveillance and detention without trial?

When the *Press Bill* was debated in an all-PAP Parliament,[84] no substantive challenges to the Bill were raised, none were expressed in the

[82] Operation Coldstore (which I discussed briefly in Chapters 1 and 3 in order to contextualise the manner in which the PAP came into power) was the security operation in which the state detained about 112 left-wing opponents in February 1963.

[83] Garry Rodan, "Westminster in Singapore: Now You See It, Now You Don't", in Haig Patapan, John Wanna & Patrick Weller, eds., *Westminster Legacies: Democracy and Responsible Government in Asia and the Pacific* (Sydney: UNSW Press, 2005) 109.

[84] Sing., *Parliamentary Debates*, vol. 33, cols. 913–32 (27 March 1974).

press and, as the following discussion shows, the limited contestation expressed in the Select Committee Hearings on the Bill were also carefully managed. The text of the *Press Act* thus becomes the ultimate legitimising reduction of the Helsinki template.

PERFORMING LEGITIMACY THROUGH SELECT COMMITTEES

Three of the four enactments examined in this volume went to Select Committees as part of the process by which they were brought into being. Part of the Westminster parliamentary apparatus, Select Committees are constituted to scrutinise proposed legislation.[85] Select Committees also typically invite submissions from the public, creating opportunities for 'law' to be produced in as considered and informed a manner as possible.[86]

The Singapore state's management of the Select Committee Hearings on the *Newspaper and Printing Presses Bill* suggests a heightened state awareness of the need for the Select Committee to perform the state's 'lawfulness'. The state had initially stipulated the minimum period for written representations from the public,[87] an interval of just fourteen

[85] Select Committees are constituted pursuant to Singapore's *Parliament (Privileges, Immunities and Powers) Act* (Cap. 217, 2000 Rev. Ed. Sing.) [*Parliament Act*] and Standing Orders made pursuant to the *Parliament Act*. The *Parliament Act* states that the privileges, immunities and powers of Parliament, the Speaker, members and committees of Parliament shall be the same as in the UK House of Commons: s. 3.

[86] Standing Order 78 states the general rule that bills committed to a Select Committee should publicly invite written representations and that those who write such representations should indicate their readiness to appear before the Committee. Standing Order 101(1) excepts Select Committees on bills from the general rule that the Committee should be constituted "in such a manner as shall ensure that, as far as is possible, the balance between the Government benches and the Opposition benches in Parliament is reflected in the Committee". In any event, given the absence of opposition members in Parliament until early 1982 and the current two opposition members, the partisan nature of Select Committees in Singapore is inevitable.

[87] The Standing Orders of Parliament require that the public be given "not less than fifteen days" to submit written representations to a Select Committee. Clear days are defined as excluding Saturdays, Sundays, public holidays and the days on which the events happened. The public notice inviting submission appeared on Saturday,

days. This brief window for public submissions suggests the state sought to perform its compliance with a procedural requirement, which, in its substantive detail, obstructed rather than facilitated the submission of written representations by non-state actors.[88]

Significantly, the closing date for representations was then extended by five weeks. The state did not explain why it extended the period, but the covering letter from the only 'Chinese'-language newspaper to make representations, the *Shin Min Daily News* (or *Shin Min*) suggests the reason: In the initial fourteen days, no representations had been made to the Select Committee by any of the 'Chinese'-language newspapers. If the 'Chinese' press did indeed perceive the state's 1971 crackdown as directed at the *Nanyang* in particular, and at the 'Chinese' press in general, perhaps the absence of submissions was akin to a boycott of sorts. On 9 May 1974, some eighteen days after the first closing date, the Select Committee wrote to the directors of the *Shin Min* asking them to submit representations on the Bill.[89]

The *Shin Min*'s representations read like a defensively scripted protestation of virtue and innocence, and reveal that the state had selected for co-option one rather apprehensive section of the 'Chinese'-language press[90]:

> The agreement for the setting up of Shin Min Daily News ... provides that the Shin Min Daily News would uphold the interest of the people and of the Republic of Singapore as its highest policy, support

30 March 1974, announcing that the closing date for submissions was 20 April, another Saturday. 12 April was Good Friday and thus a public holiday. By my count this left exactly fifteen clear days: Standing Orders of Parliament, SO 78 (Advertisement when bill committed to a Select Committee) read with SO 1(2) (Interpretation); *Report on the Press Bill, supra* note 8 at i.

[88] In the course of the Select Committee Hearings, the Chairman of the *Straits Times* pointed to the Board's difficulties in preparing its submissions within the brief time allotted: Sing., "Report of the Select Committee on the Newspaper and Printing Presses Bill", August 1974, 3rd Parliament at B2.

[89] Ibid. at A10.

[90] Ibid. at A10–A12.

> fully all the policies of the Government of our Republic and maintain social order and good traditions, and should not be subject to any influence by any foreign government, political party, organisation or individual....
>
> After the "Black Newspaper incidents" that took place here in the middle of June 1971, the International Press Institute held a meeting at Helsinki, capital of Finland. Prime Minister Lee Kuan Yew attended the meeting and elucidated our social conditions at the meetings, and had heated debates with participants from various countries who all held an opposing attitude. I also spoke at the meeting saying that there was adequate press freedom in the Republic of Singapore and the Shin Min Daily news had never been subjected to any coercion or interference by the Government. That talk had had quite a convincing effect on the meeting, the Reuters news agency of Great Britain had also cabled it to all the world, beneficial to the good reputation of our country.
>
> Prime Minister Lee held a press conference at Helsinki, I was present testifying that the Government of Singapore had dealt with every newspaper in a fair and reasonable manner.[91]

There is a slightly ludicrous quality to the anxiety with which the *Shin Min* sets out the purposes of the newspaper, in that these purposes seem to have been scripted to counter precisely those accusations levelled by the state against the three newspapers in 1971. The *Shin Min* conjoins upholding "the interest of the people" with fully supporting government policies in a manner that conflates government policy with patriotism. In doing so, the *Shin Min* adopts the state's definition of the single actor that, to the exclusion of all others, is permitted to determine the best interests of the 'nation': the state. The *Shin Min*'s emphatic declaration that it is not subject to any "foreign" influences, and that it maintains "social order and good traditions" along with its acquiescence to the state's appropriation of 'nation', constructs a pre-emptive defence against the three main accusations the state made against three other papers in 1971.

[91] Ibid.

The man who is named as author of the submissions, Louis Cha, was both the head of the *Shin Min Daily News* and Vice-Chairman of the Board of Directors. Cha seems to have been particularly concerned that permanent residents, such as himself, should not be excluded from directorships or from holding management shares. In setting out the ways in which he has been a 'good citizen' – attending the Helsinki assembly in order to attest to the presence of press freedom in Singapore and affirm that the state had dealt with all newspapers fairly and reasonably – Cha reveals the extent to which the state was conscious of the need to use Helsinki, and later the Select Committee, as platforms upon which to perform its legitimacy in the national and international public domains. Cha also reveals the extent to which he has been co-opted.

This fragment of the *Select Committee Report* is a revealing 'rule by law' fault-line in this apparently 'rule of law' moment. It is a fragment that betrays not just the extent to which the state has scripted its performances with respect to these events, but also the extent to which the state is aware of the fragility of its reputation for 'lawfulness'. The state's attempts to closely control and manage presentations and performances of its legitimacy speak of its anxiety to be seen as legitimately 'rule of law'. And yet the *Press Bill* was debated in a one-party Parliament and reported upon in a public domain in which the press had been disciplined into acquiescence. When the 'Chinese' press ignored the processes by which the *Press Bill* was being made into 'law', the state revised its time lines so as to ensure that a voice from the 'Chinese' press would be seen to be part of the 'law'-making process. The Select Committee Hearings were thus, in part, about 'law' as public theatre. This keen state awareness of the need to present and repeatedly perform its observance of 'law' emerges as a consistent feature of the legislative moments examined by this project.

THE 1974 *PRESS ACT*: GOVERNANCE, IDEOLOGY AND INVESTMENT

The most significant alteration to press regulation effected by the *Press Act* involves a two-tiered shareholding structure that includes a category of shares called 'management shares'.[92] Each management share carries two hundred votes (as opposed to one vote per ordinary share) when it comes to the appointment and dismissal of the directors, journalists and staff of newspaper companies.[93] Crucially, management shares can be held only by those who possess the written approval of the state.[94] The state can also withdraw that approval and direct newspaper companies to transfer management shares to another party.[95] Because management shares can be held only by those approved by the state, this seemingly bureaucratic pre-requisite effects a powerful, but quiet state control of newspapers.

The state's discretion to withdraw approval and direct transfers of management shares means that management shares are a powerful tool for citizen self-censorship. Surely the necessity for state approval points to the co-option tethered to management share ownership. The management shareholder has to conduct the shareholding and its immense voting power in a manner that sustains the state's pleasure, deriving power and commercial benefit from a discretionary approval that might be withdrawn at any time.[96] Ownership of management shares is thus not a simple matter of a contract between the newspaper company and the shareholder. The state is a ghostly third party to that contract.

Management share ownership under the *Press Act*, although shaped as a rights-bearing commercial instrument, is in substance more akin to a gift, a dispensation bestowed by the state. This dispensation involves a discretionary exercise of state power which cannot be questioned or challenged in court.[97] The newspaper company's avenue of appeal against state determinations of which parties might hold management shares is

[92] *Press Act*, *supra* note 1, s. 10.

[93] Ibid.

[94] Ibid.

[95] Ibid.

[96] See also George's argument about the monopoly profitability represented by the possession of annual permits that newspapers are required to obtain: George, *Consolidating Authoritarian Rule*, *supra* note 13 at 147.

[97] *Press Act*, *supra* note 1, s. 20.

limited to an appeal to the state[98] – judge in its own cause. With the *Press Act*, rights, power and privileges are held by the state, not by shareholders and not by newspaper companies. Thus, through the vehicle of the *Press Act*, the state appropriates the power to control newspaper operations employing the mechanism of state approval for shareholders who posses determining votes. In this way, the compliance and subordination of newspapers to the state are facilitated by the efficient governmentality of selecting certain citizens or corporations to positions of power in newspapers.[99] As a consequence of the *Press Act*, only newspapers that are ideologically compliant with the state can be produced for the domestic market. In this way, censorship and ideological compliance become institutionalised, normalised and legitimised while retaining the commercial structures that allow the injection of market capital into newspapers.

THE *PRESS ACT* AFTER 1974

The 1974 *Press Act* has been amended eight times.[100] The 1977 amendment prevents ownership and control by families and small groups of individuals by limiting the shareholdings of any party to 3% of the ordinary shares.[101] The 1977 amendment was probably directed at the two main Chinese newspapers, the *Nanyang* and the *Sin Chew Jit Poh*, both of which were owned and operated by wealthy families.[102] The most

[98] *Press Act*, *supra* note 1, s. 10, s. 13, s. 15, s. 16, s. 20.

[99] Another 'law' as governmentality feature of the *Press Act* is the state surveillance and control of the funding of newspapers. The *Press Act* facilitates state efficiency in that it obliges newspapers to report financial details to the state (s. 19). In particular, "funds from foreign sources" require the approval of the Minister (s. 19). Non-disclosure is a criminal offence (s. 17). In 1974 the penalty was imprisonment for up to three years or a fine of up to S$10,000 or both. Under the current Act, the fine could go up to S $50,000 (s. 17). The possible prison term of up to three years remains.

[100] The version of the *Press Act* available on the website run by the Attorney General's Chambers sets out the legislative history of the Act; online: <http://statutes.agc.gov.sg/>.

[101] Sing., *Parliamentary Debates*, vol. 37, cols. 66–68 (29 June 1977) (Mr Jek Yeun Thong).

[102] In his memoirs, Lee Kuan Yew refers to the 1977 amendment, saying, "I do not subscribe to the Western practice that allows a wealthy press baron to decide what voters should read day after day": Lee, *From Third World to First*, *supra* note 2 at 218.

significant of all the amendments, however, is the 1986 amendment empowering the state to circumscribe the sale and circulation of "foreign publications ... declared as having engaged in the domestic politics of Singapore".[103] Before discussing the 'foreign press' amendment, it is useful to contextualise the 1986 amendment with reference to one of the most significant political developments of the 1980s: the election to Parliament of the first opposition Member of Parliament to enter the parliamentary chamber in the history of the nation-state, J. B. Jeyaretnam.

When Jeyaretnam won his parliamentary seat in November 1981, he was the first opposition member Singaporeans watched enter Parliament.[104] A lawyer, Jeyaretnam tended to frame issues in 'rule of law' terms, calling for transparency, accountability, justice and championing the rights of citizens.[105] His (and, from 1984, Chiam See Tong's)

[103] Sing., *Parliamentary Debates*, vol. 48, col. 369 (31 July 1986) (Mr Wong Kan Seng).

[104] In August 1965, when Singapore became independent, the eight Barisan Members of Parliament who either were not detained under Operation Coldstore or had not fled the country in fear of being detained protested against the Singapore government's complicit relationship with the British, and the detentions without trial of Coldstore, by boycotting Parliament. On J. B. Jeyaretnam's political career, see Chris Lydgate, *Lee's Law: How Singapore Crushes Dissent* (Melbourne: Scribe, 2003); Michael D. Barr, "J. B. Jeyaretnam: Three Decades as Lee Kuan Yew's Bete Noir" (2003) 33:3 *Journal of Contemporary Asia* 299. Ho argues that Jeyaretnam's 1981 electoral victory marked a resumption of the democratisation process: Ho Khai Leong, *Shared Responsibilities, Unshared Power* (Singapore: Times Media Private, 2003) 30–31. Sadly, Jeyaretnam died of a heart attack in September 2008.

[105] See, generally, parliamentary debates between January 1982 and December 1986. To supply just two examples of Jeyaretnam's 'rule of law' discourse: in the debate on the *Criminal Law (Temporary Provisions) (Amendment) Bill* ("But this Act, Sir, has provisions in it which depart from the rule of law. The rule of law is that no person may be deprived of his liberty, be incarcerated in prison unless he has been tried before a court or a tribunal and has been found guilty") (Sing., *Parliamentary Debates*, vol. 44, col. 1885 [26 July 1984]); and in the debate on parliamentary opposition ("Are we going to set our face towards a constitutional orderly progress, development towards a parliamentary democracy, a democratic State where every citizen knows his rights, and every citizen knows where he can get his remedies for those rights ... and he is allowed maximum participation in the governing of this country?") (Sing., *Parliamentary Debates*, vol. 46, col. 167 [15 May 1985]). See also Kevin Y. L. Tan, "Lawyers in Singapore Politics, 1945–1990", Paper presented at *Paths Not Taken: Political Pluralism in Postwar Singapore* (2005) (unpublished). Tan assesses Jeyaretnam as "by far, the most active

"aggressive use of question time",[106] along with the March 1985 introduction of the televising of Parliament,[107] have been credited with fostering political literacy in Singapore.[108] Until Jeyaretnam entered Parliament, democracy had been constructed by the state as the delivery of efficient and corruption-free government, improved living conditions and a benevolent paternalism.[109] Through Jeyaretnam, a recalibrated understanding of democracy as including checks on absolute power was disseminated.[110] The political legitimacy of the state, in addition to dealing with this new discursive challenge, was undermined by Singapore's first major post-independence recession. Because political legitimacy in Singapore is built so much on the achievement of material well-being,[111] the recession was especially critical for the credibility of the ruling party.

Jeyaretnam won his seat in November 1981. Starting in January 1982, a sequence of state-initiated events unfolded which involved the considerable weight of the state's legal-administrative apparatus bearing down upon this single opposition Member of Parliament (there were seventy-four PAP members)[112] in two ways: court proceedings and disciplinary hearings for breach of parliamentary privilege.[113] Singapore media did

voice in Parliament" and describes him as "probably one of the most important opposition leaders in the post-independence period" who "saw the role of lawyers as watchdogs of government. His speeches in Parliament revealed a clear slant towards legal and constitutional issues".

106 Chan Heng Chee, "Internal Developments in Singapore", in Verinder Grover, ed., *Singapore: Government and Politics* (New Delhi: Deep & Deep, 2000) 128 at 129.

107 Ibid. at 130.

108 Ibid.

109 Ibid. at 129.

110 Ibid.

111 See the discussion of prosperity, and the references therein, in Chapter 1.

112 Chan, *supra* note 106 at 129.

113 In 1972 and 1973, the Workers' Party commenced defamation proceedings against Tay, a ruling party Member of Parliament and the Attorney General: *Workers' Party v. Tay Boon Too & Anor* [1975–1977] 1 Sing.L.R. 124. The Workers' Party lost the suit and in 1975 was ordered to pay costs of S$17,101. The Workers' Party was unable to pay this sum. The matter was left from July 1975 until 3 February 1982, some three months after Jeyaretnam's electoral victory, when Tay applied to the court for leave to levy execution for the unpaid costs. Tay's application precipitated a series of events which resulted in

not suggest that the court and parliamentary proceedings were unwarranted, unjust or politically motivated. 'Foreign' media, on the other hand, did suggest these things,[114] which became highly relevant for the parameters of interpretation of the 1986 'foreign press' amendment to the *Press Act.*

At the 1984 general elections, Jeyaretnam's constituency returned him to Parliament with a stronger margin of victory, a second opposition member was voted in and the ruling party's support dropped 12.6% from the previous general election.[115] The state's position hardened.[116] It was now dealing with a "repoliticised, articulate and better educated population who had enjoyed a continuous period of stability and affluence".[117] In May 1986, the government introduced the *Newspaper Printing Presses (Amendment) Act* (1986 amendments).

the Workers' Party going into receivership and, in 1983, charges relating to the accounts of the Workers' Party being brought against Wong Hong Toy and J. B. Jeyaretnam, who were Chairman and Secretary-General of the Workers' Party. See *Public Prosecutor v. Wong Hong Toy & Anor* [1984–1985] I Sing. L.R. (H.C.), *Wong Hong Toy & Anor v. Public Prosecutor* [1986] I Sing.L.R. (H.C.) 469.

On the breach of parliamentary privilege proceedings in 1982, see Sing., *Parliamentary Debates*, vol. 41, cols. 1305–12 (22 March 1982); vol. 42, cols. 119–25 (31 August 1982). Although Jeyaretnam was found guilty of breaching privilege, penalties were waived. See also Christopher Tremewan, *The Political Economy of Social Control* (Hampshire: St Martin's Press, 1999) at 206–209. In 1986 Jeyaretnam was again found to be in breach of parliamentary privilege and was disqualified from Parliament: *Jeyaretnam J B v. Attorney General* [1988] 1 Sing.L.R. 170 (CA). Sing., "Report of Commission of Inquiry into Allegations of Executive Interference in the Subordinate Courts" (July 1986) Paper Cmd. 12 of 1986; Sing., Committee of Privileges – First Report (Parl. Paper 3 of 1987); Second Report (Parl. Paper 4 of 1987); Third Report (Parl. Paper 6 of 1987); Fourth Report (Parl. Paper 7 of 1987); Fifth Report (Parl. Paper 9 of 1987).

114 See, for example, M. Kirkpatrick, "Jeyaretnam's Challenge", *Asian Wall Street Journal*, 17 October 1985.

115 Jon S. T. Quah, "The 1980s: A Review of Significant Political Developments", in Ernest Chew & Edwin Lee, eds., *A History of Singapore* (Singapore: Oxford University Press, 1991) 385–400 at 386. Chan evaluates the strong voting for poorly educated, hardly known candidates as widespread protest votes against unpopular policies; *supra* note 106 at 129.

116 Gary Rodan, "Asia and the International Press: The Political Significance of Expanding Markets" (1998) 5:2 *Democratization* 125 [*International Press*].

117 Chan, *supra* note 106, 130.

NEW DANGERS: FOREIGN PUBLICATIONS

The 1986 amendments allowed the government to restrict the sale or circulation of selected foreign publications that had been "engaging in the domestic politics of Singapore".[118] This amendment, and the others that followed in order to consolidate its efficacy, extended the state's control of press representations of the state[119] beyond the borders of Singapore into the 'foreign press'. One leading Southeast Asian scholar has described the 1986 amendments as "a move away from simply exerting direct pressure on journalists and editors in favour of broader legal and financial penalties on the publisher and other parties to the production of a publication".[120]

The *Press Bill* followed upon a series of articles in the *Far Eastern Economic Review* and the *Asian Wall Street Journal* that had been critical of the Singapore government.[121] In October 1985, the state brought proceedings against the *Asian Wall Street Journal* (*AWSJ*) with reference to an article on the state's actions against Jeyaretnam.[122] The Attorney General cited the *AWSJ* for criminal contempt of court for implying in this article that Singapore's judiciary was "compliant".[123] The *AWSJ* pleaded guilty and apologised.

[118] *Press Act*, *supra* note 1, s. 24.

[119] The practice of the state exerting direct pressure upon domestic journalists is revealed in the minutes of the Select Committee Hearings on the 1974 *Press Act* (*supra* note 8 at B9, col. 17) and in the quotations from press personnel quoted in George, *Consolidating Authoritarian Rule*, *supra* note 13.

[120] Rodan, *International Press*, *supra* note 116.

[121] Seow, *supra* note 2, 142–45.

[122] Kirkpatrick, *supra* note 114.

[123] *Attorney General v. Zimmerman & Ors* [1984–1985] 1 Sing.L.R. 814. The state successfully obtained orders of contempt against the Singapore correspondent, the editor, publishers, proprietors, printers and distributors of the *Asian Wall Street Journal* for an article which suggested that the conviction of opposition parliamentarian J. B. Jeyaretnam had outraged many Singaporeans who believed that the government was trying to wipe out the opposition leader and his party, and the demotion of the magistrate who found Jeyaretnam innocent at first instance buttressed the case of these Singaporeans. The court found that the article was calculated to bring the judiciary of Singapore into contempt and to diminish its authority.

When, nine months after the prosecution of the *AWSJ*, the 1986 amendments were introduced to Parliament,[124] the framework of the speech delivered by the Minister tabling the Bill replicated key features of Lee Kuan Yew's 1971 Helsinki speech. Like Prime Minister Lee in 1971 and Minister for Culture Jek in 1974, the Minister asserted that 'the press' was influential in determining public opinion; that the 'domestic press' understood the need to be the state's partner in 'nation'-building; and that 'race', 'religion' and geo-politics made Singapore an especially vulnerable 'nation':

> Newspapers and news magazines are an influential tool for shaping public opinion.... A responsible press is crucial to nation building. Our local newspapers know that Singapore's multi-racial and multi-religious society is small and vulnerable. They are extremely careful about not causing any offence to any racial, religious or linguistic group. They need to have a keen sense of our security and economic circumstances in the Southeast Asian and global context. They know what would undermine Singapore's prosperity and long-term survival. Their ownership, management and editorial control therefore have to be in the hands of Singaporeans.[125]

This excerpt shows how the formula of Lee's 1971 argument has been rehearsed and reproduced to become a Singapore 'truth' fixture. In 1971, 1974, 1986 and beyond,[126] the state's argument has been that because newspapers have the capacity to influence opinion, it is incumbent on the state to police the press in order to protect Singapore from sinister and hidden foreign enemies. The state has also insisted that "freedom of the press" must be subordinated to "the overriding needs of

[124] Sing., *Parliamentary Debates*, vol. 48, col. 396 (31 July 1986) (Mr Wong Kan Seng).

[125] Ibid.

[126] For a 2010 instance substantially replicating the substance of Lee's Helsinki arguments, see "Political Context Important When Considering Media's Role: Shanmugam", *ChannelNewsAsia* (5 November 2010), reporting on a speech delivered by the Minister for Law at the inaugural *Free Press for a Global Society* forum at Columbia University, New York. The full text of the Minister's speech is available at http://app2.mlaw.gov.sg/News/tabid/204/Default.aspx?ItemId=515.

the integrity of Singapore".[127] Lee's 1971 argument, an argument that was countered and challenged in its time, has been consolidated into a legitimising rationale for legislative restrictions on the press alongside increased state control of press management and content, all of which is underpinned by the state's discourse of national vulnerability. Legislation, in tandem with the state's command of the public domain, has enabled a 'rule by law' reworking of 'rule of law' understandings of press–state relations.

Just as in 1971 and 1974, the 1986 discourse on the 'press' rehearses the need for an exception to the principle of the freedom of information, an exception necessitated by urgent concern for the very existence of the 'nation'. The legal exceptionalism predicated on constructing the 'foreign press' as a security threat is amplified by the state's appropriation of the discourse of rights, pointing to a significant development in state discursive strategies. In 1971 Lee did not dismiss or discount "freedom of the press"; he subordinated it to the extremity of national security. At the time, Lee was at pains to convince his audience that the state acted in the interests of the 'nation' to protect a vulnerable Singapore from sinister "foreign" enemies. In 1986, however, the state no longer (explicitly) acknowledged its erosion of basic legal freedoms, relying instead on its capacity to discursively set new parameters for the meaning of "freedom of information". In 1986 the discourse of rights had been appropriated by the state:

> [W]hat is at issue here is not freedom of information or free flow of ideas. There is no intention to curb the flow of information or ideas by banning the publications. A ban will be misrepresented by such publications and opportunists as fear of exposing our people to their reporting. We have no such fears.... We know that it is not possible to seal Singapore off completely.... So the issue is not freedom of information or free flow of ideas.... The issue before us is: how do we stop such publications from profiting financially by consistently attempting

[127] Lee, *Mass Media*, *supra* note 4.

> to manipulate local opinion and interfering in our domestic politics under the guise of freedom of the press. The Bill is the answer.... If absolute freedom is exercised by the foreign press in Singapore and if they are allowed to interfere with our domestic political process, manipulate local opinion by slanted and divisive reporting, then the price we pay will be chaos and confusion and this will lead to instability and strife. No investor will then want to put his money in Singapore.[128]

The state's insistence that its technologies of controlling sale and circulation do not amount to a ban recalls Lee Kuan Yew's 1966 determination not to make martyrs of the "Aid Vietnam" activists. In 1966 the use of the category 'vandalism' to criminalise public disobedience detracted from the political contestation represented by the posters and banners. The state redefined the content and meaning of anti-American slogans as anti-national 'vandalism' in order to justify a punishment specifically designed to humiliate: mandatory caning. Both the punishment and the categorisation were intended to deny the activists the moral status of political prisoners.

Similarly, in 1986 the power of the state to restrict the sale and circulation of 'foreign press' that "interferes in domestic politics" denies the moral status of a conscionable 'free press' to the 'foreign press'. At the same time, the state's methods set in place structures through which the 'foreign press' might be coerced, punished and co-opted through bottom-line concerns for profitability and market share. Indeed, the 1986 amendments to the *Press Act*, along with the high quantum of damages awarded by Singapore courts to the state for defamation and contempt of court, have by and large resulted in the state's extracting compliance from the 'foreign press', thereby extending the state's management of constructions of its legitimacy in public discourse.[129]

[128] Sing., *Parliamentary Debates*, vol. 48, cols. 372–73 (31 July 1986) (Mr Wong Kan Seng).

[129] Seow tracks the history of how, within three years of the 1986 amendments, the following 'foreign publications' had their circulations cut: *Time*, *Asian Wall Street Journal*,

THE SUSCEPTIBLE SINGAPOREAN

Just as in the 1971 and 1974 constructions of confused and infantalised 'citizens', in 1986 the partner to state authority is citizen susceptibility. The state's argument simultaneously structures a distance between the policing, knowledgeable state and its susceptible, silent citizens. Singaporeans are constructed as beings without agency – as acted upon and therefore needing the authoritative protection of the state. The state speaks of "reporting which seeks to ... arouse the feelings of our people"[130] and foreign publications which "try to influence our people",[131] of how these ill intentions add up to "campaigns to influence local public opinion".[132] There is no expectation, on the part of the state, that Singaporeans have the capacity to make assessments in an ideologically plural public domain, to discern suspect motives or to perceive reporting as slanted. The state's role of policing 'foreign publications' and exposing their mala fides is necessitated by the vulnerability of its citizens and justifies the 'punishment' of undermining the profit motive of 'foreign publications'.

Asiaweek and *Far East Economic Review*. In the early 1990s, the *Economist* and the *International Herald Tribune* had their circulations restricted: Seow, *supra* note 2 at 148–78. The 1986 'foreign press' amendment and the state's highly visible use of this power has resulted in an "extensive self-censorship [that] characterizes international press reporting on Singapore": Rodan, *International Press supra* note 116 at 129. In recent years, the 'foreign press' has taken to placating the Singapore state. For example, Bloomberg LP apologised in 2002 (Terrence Lee, "Internet Use in Singapore: Politics and Policy Implications" [2003] 107 *Media International Australian incorporating Culture and Policy* 75, 81); the *Economist* apologised in 2006 ("The Economist Apologises to Lee Kuan Yew", *Bangkok Post* [21 January 2006]; the *Financial Times* apologised in 2007 ("Malaysia Applauds Lee Kuan Yew's Defamation Win: Report", *Malaysiakini* (19 October 2007). The expansion of self-censorship from the domestic to the international media through "pressure, intimidation and litigation" is noted also in Shanthi Kalathil & Taylor C. Boas, *Open Networks; Closed Regimes: The Impact of the Internet on Authoritarian Regimes* (Washington, DC: Carnegie Endowment for International Peace, 2003) at 76.

[130] *Supra* note 123.

[131] Sing., *Parliamentary Debates*, vol. 48, cols. 372–373 (31 July 1986) (Mr Wong Kan Seng).

[132] Ibid.

As noted in the discussion of 'rule of law' and 'rule by law' (Chapter 1), one of the key markers of 'rule of law' structures is institutional safeguards against the concentration of power in the hands of too few. The power of governments, in particular, is ideally moderated by institutional practices designed to ensure transparency, accountability and review. In violation of these 'rule of law' principles, the operational procedures of the *Press Bill* place power squarely in the hands of the executive. The Minister explained the workings of the *Press Bill* thus:

> [T]he Minister will be empowered, by order published in the Gazette, to declare a foreign publication as engaging in the domestic politics of Singapore. The Minister will exercise this power reasonably and in good faith and on proper grounds. The declaration of a foreign publication is not a matter to be entered into lightly. There need not be any fear that the Minister is given such a discretion to act.[133]

Significantly, 'rule of law' concerns are addressed – that power be exercised reasonably, in good faith and on proper grounds. But the way in which 'rule of law' is conventionally expected to ensure bona fides in the exercise of administrative power is not built into the 1986 amendments. There is no provision for review of administrative discretion, no justiciability, no recourse to a non-state agency for a party that feels aggrieved by the executive's decision. Instead, the state asserts its bona fides and expects that this should suffice. It is not the institution of 'law' or the structures of governance that protect 'the people'. Instead, the public is asked to trust the individuals who hold power. Through discourse and legislation, the substance of 'law' is reconfigured in a manner that attenuates rights and consolidates the state's power.

Newspapers have a particular reach into the public domain that in many ways matches the reach of the state. In 1971 the targeted newspapers countered the state's accusations and allegations with verve, reaching into national and international networks for support, such that the state's actions against the papers received attention in the international

133 Ibid. at col. 374.

as well as the national public domain. Lee's IPI address shows that it was clearly important to the state to present itself as acting legitimately in its dealings with the press. All in all, the state's 1971 dealings with the three newspapers were noisy, vibrant and contentious; and they dominated the Singapore public domain for about five months.[134] It is a testimony to the efficacy of the *Press Act* that the state has never since had to act repressively against a domestic newspaper.

With regard to domestic newspapers, since the *Press Act* became 'law', state–press relations have been marked by an absence of the kind of concerted counter-narrative that marked 1971. The policing of the press has become institutionalised in a manner which depoliticises the dismantling of the press as a non-state public voice. The *Press Act*'s technologies of licensing, shareholdings and executive approval remove state policing of the press from the scrutiny of the national and international public domain. These technologies shift press management into an un-newsworthy tedium of regulation and procedural hurdles marked by an absence of transparency as to which parties do and do not apply for, or receive, state approval for ownership of management shares. The state has never again been seen, in the public domain, to be attacking the institutional or associational identity of a (domestic) newspaper – probably because it has never again needed to. Instead, when the state chastises the press, it targets individual journalists and faults particular articles.[135] Typically,

[134] Seow, *supra* note 2.

[135] Some notable examples are, first, the state's critique of the columns produced by Catherine Lim (Catherine Lim, "The PAP and the People: A Great Affective Divide", *Straits Times* (10 September 1994); Catherine Lim, "One Government, Two Styles", *Straits Times* [20 November 1994)]); Chan Heng Weng, "PM Goh Remains Committed to Consultation and Consensus Politics", *Straits Times* (4 December 1994); Chan Heng Weng, "There Are Limits to Openness", *Straits Times* (29 December 1994); Chua Mui Hong, "PM: No Erosion of My Authority Allowed", *Straits Times* (5 December 1994). See also Kenneth Paul Tan, "Who's Afraid of Catherine Lim? The State in Patriarchal Singapore" (2009) 33 *Asian Studies Review* 43; K. S. Rajah, "Negotiating Boundaries: OB Markers and the Law", in Bridget Welsh et al., eds., *Impressions of the Goh Chok Tong Years in Singapore* (Singapore: NUS Press, 2009) 107; Kevin Y. L. Tan, "Understanding and Harnessing Ground Energies in Civil Society", in Gillian Koh & Ooi Giok Ling, eds.,

the state's chastisement receives far more press space than the original offending article ever did,[136] and the newspaper that has run the article does not ally with the individual journalist in an assertion of collective identity or responsibility. In the unequal contest of power and resources, the individual is left without institutional support and without a space in the public domain to counter the state's accusations and imputations of mala fides.[137]

This pattern of occasionally reprimanding individual journalists, and the absence of a collective, institutional identity in the way newspapers respond, speaks of the success of the disciplinary project of the *Press Act*: Neither the public nor domestic newspapers rally around the ideal of press freedom any more. The press no longer sees itself as the necessary fourth estate,[138] as it did in 1971. Consequently, while individuals within the institution might require corrective public instruction, newspapers themselves no longer need to be reigned in by state action.

The 'rule by law' provisions of the 1974 *Press Act*, underpinned by the social memory of state coercion of journalists,[139] has endured such that

State–Society Relations in Singapore (Singapore: Oxford University Press, 2000) 98); and second, the state's critique of the columnist "mr brown": "S'poreans Are Fed, Up with Progress!" *Today* (30 June 2006); K. Bhavani, "Distorting the Truth, Mr Brown?" *Today* (3 July 2006). "*Today* Paper Suspends Blogger's Column", *Straits Times* (7 July 2006); Tang Hsiang-yi, "Surviving on the Edge in Singapore: Mr Brown's Satirical Podcasting Finds a Way Out", Paper presented at *Convergence, Citizen Journalism & Social Change: Building Capacity*, University of Queensland, March 2008.

[136] The examples listed at *supra* note 135 illustrate this.

[137] *Supra* note 135.

[138] Tey Tsun Hung, "Confining the Freedom of the Press in Singapore: A 'Pragmatic' Press for 'Nation-Building'?" (2008) 30 *Human Rights Quarterly* 876; Birch discusses the reworking of the notion of the Fourth Estate in Singapore: David Birch, *Singapore Media: Communication Strategies and Practices* (Melbourne: Longman, 1993) at 25–27.

[139] In addition to the detentions without trial of the *Nanyang* executives in 1971, in early 1977 Singapore nationals who were correspondents for 'foreign' publications were on the receiving end of state coercion. *Far Eastern Economic Review* correspondent Ho Kwong Ping was arrested and charged with disseminating protected information: Seow, *supra* note 2 at 112; Derek Davies, "The Press", in Michael Haas, ed., *The Singapore Puzzle* (Westport, CT: Praeger, 1999) 77 at 91–94. And a correspondent for the *Financial Times* and the *Economist*, Arun Senkuttuvan, was detained without trial (Seow, *supra*

'rule of law' rhetoric, co-option and corporatist technologies foster 'rule by law' legitimacy for the state's management of the press, even as individual and institutional freedoms are attenuated and rendered subject to state determinations of national security. The state's use of legislation to effect press control has had far-reaching and enduring consequences for the Singapore public domain and has played a significant role in the construction of legitimacy for the state's 'rule by law'.

THE INTERNET AND PUBLIC DISCOURSE

This case study has focused on the silencing impact of the *Press Act* and the state's discursive template for both Singapore newspapers and the 'foreign press'. At this juncture, the question that arises is, what impact has been made by the Internet? Singapore's information and communication technology sector has been described as "one of the world's most dynamic ... [with] sky-high Internet penetration rates, with an estimated 2.1 million citizens online out of a total population of 4.5 million".[140] Kalathil and Boas note that while the general expectation has been that the Internet will enhance democratisation in Singapore,

> its government's achievement [is] of what many believed impossible: extensive ICT [information and communications technology] development with a negligible erosion of political control.... [O]ther authoritarian regimes, most notably China, have taken an active interest in learning from Singapore's example.[141]

This canny management of information and communications technology, such that the Internet serves rather than undermines authoritarianism,

note 2 at 113). British newspaper reporting on these detentions were the subject of a parliamentary debate on the role of foreign correspondents: Sing., *Parliamentary Debates*, vol. 36, cols. 1521–29 (23 March 1977). Birch notes that in the 1970s the four *Nanyang* executives, two editors of the Malay newspaper, the *Berita Harian*, and the Singapore correspondent of the *Far Eastern Economic Review* were all detained without trial: Birch, *supra* note 138 at 18.

140 Shanthi Kalathil, "Dot.Com for Dictators" (2003) 135 *Foreign Policy* 41.

141 Kalathil & Boas, *supra* note 129 at 73.

might be seen as a logical extension of dual state legality. Just as 'law' has been disaggregated to serve state goals related to the economy and social control, so too has the Internet been used to enhance governance even as its political impact has been neutered. Significantly, this governance strategy operates within an environment of "generalised self-censorship as users anticipate and avoid government backlash".[142]

The body of scholarship on Singapore 'law' pertaining to the Internet[143] finds that Singapore's legal, social, economic and political conditions have

[142] Ibid. at 79.

[143] For a sampling, see Thio Li-ann, "The Virtual and the Real: Article 14, Political Speech and the Calibrated Management of Deliberative Democracy in Singapore" (2008) *S.J.L.S.* 25; Cherian George, "No News Here: Media in Subordination", in Bridget Welsh et al., eds. *Impressions of the Goh Chok Tong Years in Singapore* (Singapore: NUS Press, 2009); Cherian George, "The Internet's Political Impact and the Penetration/Participation Paradox in Malaysia and Singapore" (2005) 27 *Media, Culture & Society* 903; George, *Contentious Journalism*, *supra* note 68; George, *Media at the Mainstream*, *supra* note 13 at 173; Randolph Kluver & Carol Soon, "The Internet and Online Political Communities in Singapore" (2007) 17:3 *Asian Journal of Communication* 246; Randolph Kluver, "Political Culture and Information Technology in the 2001 Singapore General Election" (2004) 21 *Political Communication* 435; James Gomez, "Online Opposition in Singapore: Communications Outreach without Electoral Gain" (2008) 38:4 *Journal of Contemporary Asia* 591; James Gomez, *Internet Politics: Surveillance and Intimidation in Singapore* (Bangkok: Think Centre, 2002); Terence Lee, "Emulating Singapore: Towards a Model for Internet Regulation in Asia", in Steven Gan, James Gomez & Uwe Johannen, eds., *Asian Cyberactivism: Freedom of Expression and Media Censorship* (Singapore: Friedrich Naumann Foundation, 2004) 162; Terence Lee, "Internet Control and Auto-regulation in Singapore (2005) 3:1 *Surveillance & Society* 74; Terence Lee & David Birch, "Internet Regulation in Singapore: A Policy/ing Discourse" (2000) 95 *Media International Australia Incorporating Culture and Policy* 147; Garry Rodan, "The Internet and Political Control in Singapore" (1998) 113 *Political Science Quarterly* 63; Yao Su Cho, "The Internet: State Power and Techno-Triumphalism in Singapore" (1996) 82 *Media International Australia* 73; Kalathil & Boas, *supra* note 129; Woo Yen Yen Joyceln & Colin Goh, "Caging the Bird: TalkingCock.com and the Pigeonholing of Singaporean Citizenship", in Kenneth Paul Tan, ed., *Renaissance Singapore? Economy, Culture, and Politics* (Singapore: NUS Press, 2007); Tan Chong Kee, "The Canary and the Crow: Sintercom and the State Tolerability Index", in Kenneth Paul Tan, ed., *Renaissance Singapore? Economy, Culture, and Politics* (Singapore: NUS Press, 2007); Garry Rodan, "Embracing Electronic Media but Suppressing Civil Society: Authoritarian Consolidation in Singapore" (2003) 16:4 *Pacific Review* 503; Tang Hang Wu, "The Networked Electorate: The Internet and the Quiet Democratic Revolution in Malaysia and Singapore", (2009) 2 *Journal of Information Law and Technology*.

limited the liberalising impact of the Internet.[144] Four factors have been identified as constraints upon the potential of the Internet in Singapore: first, the dominance of the state's conceptions of applicable norms for free speech[145]; second, a highly policed public domain; third, wide-ranging legal restraints on Internet activity[146]; and fourth, the perception of surveillance of cyber space.[147] Much of the scholarship stresses the context of generalised self-censorship in which these strategies operate, such that the government is able to extend its methods of controlling print and broadcast media to the Internet by relying "less on technical censorship than on the underlying infrastructure of social control.... [U]sers anticipate and avoid government backlash".[148]

In keeping with the instructive performances of 'law' evidenced by this project, the state has periodically conducted highly public prosecutions[149]

[144] See references *supra* note 139. Reporters Without Borders has also consistently found that both print media and the Internet are strongly controlled by the state. Their reports on Singapore from 2002 to 2008 are online: <http://www.unhcr.org/refworld/publisher,RSF,SGP,0.html>. The state (unsurprisingly) discounts the assessments of press freedom produced by Reporters Without Borders and Freedom House: "Divorced from Reality" *Today* (27 October 2009).

[145] Of particular interest is the role of the 'Asian values' discourse in constructing "a willingness to accept economic benefits in place of political rights [and] in justifying the maintenance of information controls and authoritarian rule": Kalathil & Boas, *supra* note 129 at 72.

[146] Relevant instruments include the *Sedition Act*, the *Internal Security Act*, the *Official Secrets Act*, the *Public Entertainments and Meetings Act*, the *Penal Code*, the *Religious Harmony Act*, the *Broadcasting Act*, defamation law, laws relating to contempt of court and contempt of Parliament, and the quasi-legal Internet Code of Practice administered by the Media Development Authority: Ang Peng Hwa & Yeo Tiong Min, *Mass Media Laws and Regulations in Singapore* (Singapore: Asian Media Information and Communication Centre, 1998).

[147] See references *supra* note 13.

[148] Kalathil & Boas, *supra* note 129 at 77–79.

[149] The *Sedition Act*, which appears not to have been invoked by the state since the 1966 sedition charges made against Barisan leaders (Chapter 3), was used in 2005 to prosecute evangelist Christians for distributing pamphlets that were offensive to people of other faiths: *Public Prosecutor v. Ong Kian Cheong and Another* [2009] SGDC 163; and to charge and warn bloggers: *Public Prosecutor v. Koh Song Huat Benjamin and Anor.* [2005] SGDC 272; Zakir Hussain, "Blogger Who Posted Cartoons of Christ Online Being Investigated", *Straits Times* (14 June 2006); "Warning for Blogger Who Posted Cartoon of Christ", *Straits Times* (21 July 2006).

or chastisements[150] of bloggers. Civil society groups that organise primarily through the Internet, such as the gay rights group, People Like Us, have repeatedly found that when they gather in material space (as opposed to cyber space), even for 'leisure activities',[151] the police are present to prevent the planned activities from taking place, insisting that the event is 'political' and therefore requires police permits.[152]

An emerging trend is the heightened policing of the Internet in anticipation of general elections. In 2001, 2006 and 2011, legal control over blogs and podcasts was stepped up just before general elections.[153] In these moments, the state's discourse reiterated that 'politics' is the discursive terrain that citizens may not, as citizens, enter.[154] The passport, so to speak, to engage in "explicit political content", "espouse a political line" or "persistently propagate, promote or circulate political issues relating to Singapore" is registration as a political site with the Media Development Authority.[155] As with the *Press Act*, the state has managed the regulation of new media through bureaucratic technologies originating in the colonial state's desire to police newspaper content.

[150] The blogger with a fortnightly column in *Today*, "mr brown", was publicly chastised for his satirical column on the inequitable distribution of resources in Singapore (see references *supra* note 135). Although he was questioned, no charges were brought against him, but *Today* stopped running the column by "mr brown" from the moment the state chastised him.

[151] With reference to the events of August 2007, Zakir Hussain, "No Go for Gay Picnic, Run at Botanic Gardens", *Straits Times* (8 August 2007); "Police Declare Joggers an "Illegal Assembly", online: <http://www.yawningbread.org/>.

[152] Ibid. Singapore's "first outdoor gay event" drew a thousand people in May 2009: Nur Dianah Suhaimi, "Pink Event Draws 1,000", *Sunday Times* (17 May 2009).

[153] Kalathil & Boas, supra note 129 at 77–79; "Political Podcasts, Videocasts Not Allowed During Election", *Straits Times* (4 April 2006); Sue-Ann Chia, "New Media, Same Rules", *Straits Times* (15 April 2006); Jeremy Au, "The Online Citizen to Be Listed as Political Association", *Straits Times* (12 January 2011).

[154] Ibid.

[155] Ibid. It must be noted, however, that despite this regulatory climate, political satire, in the form of the "Persistently Non-Political Podcast", generated a scathing representation of the state's intimidating and heavy-handed response to an opposition candidate's mis-steps in the filing of his Elections Department paperwork: Tang Hsiang-yi, *supra* note 135.

The consensus is that the Internet "has only exerted a modest pressure" on the "chilled" digital speech of Singapore, in contrast to the democratising it has enabled in Malaysia.[156] The political culture that created the *Press Act* at the height of the Cold War and revitalised it in the mid-1980s has been able to renew its 'law' and its discursive abhorrence of 'politics', to constrain and contain new media in a new century. Even if a new set of regulations has been drawn up to manage new media, the pervasive and entrenched culture of state suspicion of media[157] and the state's capacity to conduct surveillance and intimidate its citizens[158] have emasculated the potential of new forms of media to be potent players in public discourse.

156 See generally references *supra* note 143.

157 George, *Consolidating Authoritarian Rule*, *supra* note 96; Kalathil & Boas, supra note 129; S. Ramesh, "Gazetting TOC Will Not Impede Its Freedom of Expression: Shanmugam", *Today* (15 February 2011).

158 Ibid.

5 POLICING LAWYERS, CONSTRAINING CITIZENSHIP

Legal Profession (Amendment) Act, *1986*

THIS CHAPTER PRESENTS THE THIRD CASE study of this project: the 1986 amendments to the *Legal Profession Act*[1] (*LPA*). Together with the study of the *Religious Harmony Act* (Chapter 6), the analysis of the *Public Order Act* (Chapter 7) and the discussion of the 'foreign press' amendment to the *Press Act* (Chapter 4), this case study demonstrates how, after achieving a spectacular level of economic prosperity,[2] as well as social and political stability,[3] the state clung to the construct of the perpetually vulnerable 'nation' when enacting 'laws' designed to constrain citizenship and civil society.

A liberal concept of citizenship and the capacity for civil society to counter the state are major constituents of political liberalism,[4] a mode of 'politics' which, in turn, informs the 'rule of law'.[5] The studies of the

[1] *Legal Profession Act* (Cap. 161, 2001 Rev. Ed. Sing.).

[2] Linda Low, *The Political Economy of a City-State: Government-Made Singapore* (Singapore: Oxford University Press, 1998) 45–50.

[3] Ibid.

[4] Terence C. Halliday, Lucien Karpik & Malcolm Feeley, "Introduction: The Legal Complex in Struggles for Political Liberalism", in Terence C. Halliday, Lucien Karpik & Malcolm Feeley, eds., *Fighting for Political Freedom: Comparative Studies of the Legal Complex for Political Change* (Oxford: Hart, 2007) 1 at 10–11. See also Terence C. Halliday & Lucien Karpik, "Politics Matter: A New Framework for the Comparative and Historical Study of Legal Professions", in Terence C. Halliday & Lucien Karpik, eds., *Lawyers and the Rise of Western Political Liberalism* (Oxford: Clarendon Press, 1997) 15.

[5] See the discussion of a genealogy for 'rule of law' in Singapore in Chapter 1.

Vandalism Act and the *Press Act* are part of a larger picture of how, by the late 1970s, opposition parties, trade unions, civil society and the press had been silenced, emasculated or co-opted.[6] The PAP had consolidated its rule in such a way that the state was inextricably an extension of the party.[7] If the voices targeted by the *Vandalism Act* and the *Press Act* belonged to working-class, 'Chinese'-educated sections of the population who supported the opposition Barisan, then the voices targeted by the *LPA*, the *Religious Harmony Act*, and the *Public Order Act* might be seen as directed at a more middle-class, 'English'-educated section of the

[6] The containment of the press is addressed in Chapter 4. On opposition parties, trade unions and civil society, in addition to Chapter 4, see generally, Christopher Tremewan, *The Political Economy of Social Control* (Hampshire: Macmillan Press, 1994); Hong Lysa & Huang Jianli, *The Scripting of a National History: Singapore and Its Pasts* (Singapore: NUS Press, 2008); Carl A. Trocki & Michael D. Barr, eds., *Paths Not Taken: Political Pluralism in Post-War Singapore* (Singapore: NUS Press, 2008); Kay Gillis, *Singapore Civil Society and British Power* (Singapore: Talisman, 2005); Terence Chong, *Civil Society in Singapore: Reviewing Concepts in the Literature* (Singapore: Institute of Southeast Asian Studies, 2005); Terence Lee, "The Politics of Civil Society in Singapore" (2002) 26:1 *Asian Studies Review* 97; Garry Rodan, "Civil Society and Other Political Possibilities in Southeast Asia" (1997) 27:2 *Journal of Contemporary Asia* 14; James Gomez, "Restricting Free Speech: The Impact on Opposition Parties in Singapore" (2006) 23 *Copenhagen Journal of Asian Studies* 105; Kevin Hewison & Garry Rodan, "The Decline of the Left in Southeast Asia" (1994) *Socialist Register* 235; Hussin Mutalib, "Illiberal Democracy and the Future of Opposition in Singapore" (2000) 21 *Third World Quarterly* 313; Frederic C. Deyo, "The Emergence of Bureaucratic-Authoritarian Corporatism in Labour Relations", in Ong Jin Hwee, Tong Chee Kiong & Tan Ern Ser, eds., *Understanding Singapore Society* (Singapore: Times Academic Press, 1997) 353; Noeleen Heyzer, "International Production and Social Change: An Analysis of the State, Employment and Trade Unions in Singapore", in Ong Jin Hwee, Tong Chee Kiong & Tan Ern Ser, eds., *Understanding Singapore Society* (Singapore: Times Academic Press, 1997) 374.

[7] Rodan argues that the merger of state and party in Singapore accounts for the longevity of the PAP regime: Garry Rodan, "Singapore 'Exceptionalism'? Authoritarian Rule and State Transformation", in Edward Friedman & Joseph Wong, eds., *Political Transitions in Dominant Party Systems: Learning to Lose* (London: Routledge, 2008) 231. Chan's 1975 argument that 'politics' in Singapore had become so diluted that it was visible primarily in bureaucratic arenas has been very influential in scholarship on Singapore: Chan Heng Chee, "Politics in an Administrative State: Where Has the Politics Gone?" in Ong Jin Hwee, Tong Chee Kiong & Tan Ern Ser, eds., *Understanding Singapore Society* (Singapore: Times Academic Press, 1997) 294.

population that was beginning to ask the state to honour the promised liberalism of 'nation'.

This chapter focuses on two key moments at which the Law Society of Singapore entered the public domain to advocate for the 'rule of law'. In considering the roles of individual lawyers[8] as well as the Law Society, this chapter also offers a genealogy accounting for absent human rights counsel in Singapore. The chapter first contextualises the place of Singapore lawyers as advocates for the 'rule of law', tracing events from the 1960s through to the present to account for the conditions of possibility for a (mostly) quiescent legal profession. The fissures in this quiescence reveal much about the impossibility of cordoning Singapore 'law' off from the political liberalism inherent to the modes of 'law' informing Singapore. The second half of the chapter presents a close reading of the 1986 Select Committee Hearings on the *LPA*, demonstrating how the state used public discourse to dismantle three crucial rights informing civil society: the right of non-state actors to organise, the right of non-state actors to enter the public domain and the right of non-state actors to publicly engage the state in a relationship of parity. In short, this case study illustrates how, in the prosperity and stability of the 1980s,[9] the state renewed its hierarchical relationship with 'the people', subordinating citizens to the state's discursive and coercive dominance while crippling the capacity of lawyers to become spokespersons[10] for counter-narratives of 'law'.

LAWYERS IN A QUANDARY

In examining lawyers' advocacy for the 'rule of law', this case study reveals how Singapore lawyers, like lawyers in many other jurisdictions and at

[8] Kevin Y. L. Tan, "Lawyers in Politics, 1945–1990", in Kevin Y. L. Tan & Michael Hor, eds., *Encounters with Singapore Legal History* (Singapore: Singapore Law Journal Society, 2009) 529.

[9] Low, *supra* note 2.

[10] Lucien Karpik, *French Lawyers: A Study in Collective Action, 1274 to 1994*, trans. by Nora Scott (Oxford: Clarendon Press, 1999).

many other points in history, have taken it upon themselves to speak for political liberalism.[11] However, in terms of the 'rule of law'/ 'rule by law' duality of Singapore, Singapore lawyers are caught in something of a quandary. Lawyers who are Singapore citizens are placed in a polity in which, despite the Westminster-model state structure and valorisation of basic legal freedoms via the *Constitution*, there is a low level of rights awareness[12] and a high level of state dominance of the public sphere.[13] Additionally, state discourse has constructed 'citizenship' in terms of citizens' duties and subordination to the knowing and authoritative state rather than in terms of citizens' rights and capacity to make demands of the state.[14]

However, because of their professional training, lawyer-citizens access meanings of 'law' derived from a wider 'common law' discourse, a discourse that necessarily extends beyond the borders of the 'nation'. This wider 'common law' discourse exalts individual rights and the roles of 'law'[15] and of lawyers[16] in articulating and protecting such rights. Singapore's lawyer-citizens might be seen as being in an especially

[11] Halliday, Karpik & Feeley, *supra* note 4. See also Halliday & Karpik, *supra* note 4 at 15.

[12] Li-ann Thio, "Lex Rex or Rex Lex? Competing Conceptions of the Rule of Law in Singapore" (2002) 20:1 *Pacific Basin Law Journal* 22 at 39.

[13] Cherian George, "Consolidating Authoritarian Rule: Calibrated Coercion in Singapore" (2007) 20:2 *Pacific Review* 127.

[14] Terence Lee, "Gestural Politics: Civil Society in 'New' Singapore" (2005) 20:2 *Journal of Social Issues in Southeast Asia* 132.

[15] Michael Rutter, *The Applicable Law in Singapore and Malaysia* (Singapore: Malayan Law Journal, 1989) 574–606.

[16] There is an extensive scholarship on the role of lawyers in battles for rights. See, in particular, Halliday & Karpik, *supra* note 4; Halliday, Karpik & Feeley, *supra* note 4; Austin Sarat & Stuart A. Schiengold, eds., *Cause Lawyers and Social Movements* (Stanford, CA: Stanford University Press, 2006); Stuart A. Schiengold, *The Politics of Rights: Lawyers, Public Policy and Political Change*, 2nd ed. (Ann Arbor: University of Michigan Press, 2004); Chidi Oguamanam & W. Wesley Pue, "Lawyers' Professionalism, Colonialism, State Formation and National Life in Nigeria, 1900–1960: (2007) 13:6 *Social Identities* 769; Stanley D. Ross, "The Rule of Law and Lawyers in Kenya" (1992) 30:3 *Journal of Modern African Studies* 421; Terence C. Halliday, *Beyond Monopoly: Lawyers, State Crises and Professional Empowerment* (Chicago: University of Chicago Press, 1987).

conflicted position: caught between their everyday knowledge as citizens of the peculiarly Singaporean limits of 'law' and their professional knowledge as 'common law' lawyers of the 'rule of law' ideals that underpin the nation-state.

When, in 1986, the Law Society stepped into the public domain, it was taking upon itself the role of what Karpik has called spokesperson for publics.[17] Karpik points to ways in which publics are imagined as well as real – constructed by lawyers in order to constitute themselves as validly speaking on behalf of something larger than themselves.[18] In 1986 it was, I would argue, the 'rule of law' strand of Singapore 'law' that prompted the Law Society to take upon itself the role of spokesperson, issuing a press statement critiquing the proposed 'foreign press' amendment to the *Press Act*.[19] By articulating a critique propelled by the principle that state power should be accountable and transparent in its operations,[20] the Law Society was surely imagining its public as the collective citizen of political liberalism: rights-bearing and empowered, vis-à-vis the state. At the time of these events, the Law Society was Singapore's primary legal professional association. Significantly, it was the first time the Law Society had successfully entered the public domain to contest the state's formulation of 'law'.

SILENCED LAWYERS: A GENEALOGY

Before the Law Society's 1986 statement is analysed, it is necessary to ask the question: Why had the Law Society been absent from the public domain up to this point? In other words, if legal professions typically fight for political liberalism,[21] what had kept Singapore's legal professions

[17] Karpik, *supra* note 10.

[18] Ibid.

[19] Paul Jacob, "Existing Laws Adequate, Says Law Society", *Straits Times* (22 May 1986) 28.

[20] The Law Society's critique is detailed later in the chapter.

[21] Halliday, Karpik & Feeley, *supra* note 4.

silent in the face of an illiberal regime's many violations of the 'rule of law'? This question has a two-part answer, the first factual and the second speculative. First, the Law Society had once before, in 1969, attempted to enter the public domain but had failed to do so, as I explain later. Second, members of the profession, having witnessed the state's coercion of certain lawyers, probably chose silence, complicity and collusion as safer modes of professional conduct. I will first briefly set out the 1969 attempt of the Law Society to render public its opposition to the state's removal of juries from Singapore's legal system.

In 1969 the Law Society of Singapore[22] was foiled in its attempts to enter the public domain to create public awareness of the issues at stake in the state's proposal to abolish jury trials.[23] Singapore had already partially abolished jury trials in 1959, limiting juries to capital cases. In 1969, when the state wanted to abolish jury trials altogether, David Marshall, a prominent lawyer and Singapore's first Chief Minister, galvanised the Law Society into taking a collective stand against the total abolition of juries.[24] Marshall, already a leading member of the profession,[25] had been a "major public figure"[26] in Singapore politics from at least 1954.[27]

A public notice inviting written representations to the Select Committee on the *Criminal Procedure (Amendment) Bill*, the Bill that would effect the removal of juries, was issued on 16 June 1969.[28] The

[22] In 1969 the association was known as the Singapore Advocates and Solicitors Society. For convenience, I use the name "Law Society" when referring to the Society in both 1969 and 1986.

[23] Francis T. Seow, *The Media Enthralled: Singapore Revisited* (Boulder: Lynne Reinner, 1998) at 38–39.

[24] Marshall was Chief Minister for just fourteen months, from April 1955: Kevin Y. L. Tan, *Marshall of Singapore: A Biography* (Singapore: Institute of Southeast Asian Studies, 2008) 490–94 [*Marshall of Singapore*].

[25] In 1972 Chief Justice Wee described Marshall as "generally acknowledged by the members of the legal profession to be one of its leaders": *Re David Marshall; Law Society v. Marshall David Saul* [1972–1974] Sing.L.R. 132 [*Re David Marshall*] at 133.

[26] Tan, *Marshall of Singapore*, *supra* note 24 at 226.

[27] Ibid. at 222.

[28] Sing., "Report of the Select Committee on the Criminal Procedure Code (Amendment) Bill," December 1969, 2nd Parliament [*CPC Report*] at i.

Law Society, in addition to responding to this notice,[29] sent copies of the Society's resolution opposing the proposed abolition to domestic newspapers, but the newspapers did not publish the Society's statement,[30] nor did the press run articles on the issue until December,[31] when the Bill was before Parliament for its second and third readings, and passed into 'law'.[32] In June and July, when the press refused to publish the Law Society's statement, broadcast media also refused Marshall's appeals to give publicity to the Law Society's concerns.[33] Francis Seow asserts that the state used the *Essential Information (Control of Publications and Safeguarding of Information) Regulations* to prevent media from publicising the Law Society's resolution.[34] These *Regulations* were originally constituted pursuant to the *Emergency (Essential Powers) Act of 1964*. Their deployment in this instance reveals the extent to which Emergency legal instruments were utilised by the state post-Emergency to police public discourse. This one incident is a telling reflection of the extent to which, even in 1969 (before the coercion of the 1971 detentions discussed in Chapter 4), the media lacked independence from the state.

While in 1969 the Law Society was unable to enter the public domain to express its concern that legal processes would become vulnerable to executive power through the elimination of juries,[35] it was subject to a somewhat bullying encounter with the state over its opposition to the state's proposals.[36] This encounter took the shape of the Council's

[29] Council of the Singapore Advocates and Solicitors Society, "Memorandum on the Criminal Procedure Code (Amendment) Bill", *CPC Report*, *supra* note 28 at A27–A34.

[30] Seow, *supra* note 23 at 38.

[31] "Other Branches of Law Need Reform", *Straits Times* (16 December 1969); "Singapore Judges Its Juries", *Straits Times* (20 December 1969); "End of Jury Trials in S'pore", *Straits Times* (23 December 1969); "Our Case Proved Beyond All Doubt – Minister", *Straits Times* (23 December 1969).

[32] Seow, *supra* note 23 at 38–39.

[33] Ibid.

[34] Ibid.

[35] *CPC Report*, *supra* note 28 at A27–A34.

[36] Ibid.; Tan, *Marshall of Singapore*, *supra* note 24 at 493–94.

appearance before a Select Committee on the *Criminal Procedure Code (Amendment) Bill*.[37]

Select Committees in Singapore have generally been constituted to examine draft legislation, often inviting submissions from the public and conducting hearings so as to take into account the responses of non-state actors.[38] The process increases the opportunities for informed and inclusive legislation. Select Committee Hearings are generally conducted in a courteous, collegiate manner. The Committee is generally appreciative of those invited to appear before the Committee as bearing a certain expertise or representing certain views that may be taken into account.

In general, Select Committee Hearings in Singapore have proceeded along the lines of the model I have described.[39] Lee Kuan Yew's questioning of the Law Society Council in 1969, and in particular his interrogative and accusatory questioning of Marshall, stand out as exceptions to this general practice. The Select Committee Hearings became a platform for Lee Kuan Yew to repeatedly accuse the Council, and Marshall, of "politicking" through the Law Society.[40] Lee dominated the hearings,

[37] *CPC Report, supra* note 28 at B33–B58, B68–B84.

[38] Select Committees are constituted pursuant to Singapore's *Parliament (Privileges, Immunities and Powers) Act* (Cap. 217, 2000 Rev. Ed. Sing.) [*Parliament Act*] and parliamentary Standing Orders. Section 3 of the *Parliament Act* states that the privileges, immunities and powers of Parliament, the Speaker, members and committees shall be the same as those of the Commons House of Parliament of the United Kingdom at the establishment of Singapore.

[39] I have reviewed all seventy-one of the Select Committee reports dating from 1965 to the present. Select Committees have generally conducted questioning in a courteous and collegiate manner. When questioning representatives of opposition political parties, the questioning has sometimes been rather aggressive (for example, the questioning of the Singapore National Front in Sing., "Report of the Select Committee on the Maintenance of Parents Bill", October 1995, 8th Parliament, and the questioning of the Singapore Democratic Party in Sing., "Report of the Select Committee on Land Transportation Policy", January 1990, 7th Parliament). I would evaluate the level of aggression and antagonism displayed toward the Law Society Council in 1986 as unmatched by the conduct of any Select Committee Hearings, either before or after the 1986 Hearing on the *LPA*.

[40] *CPC Report, supra* note 28, paras. 532–33, 543, 544, 550, 551, 632–37, 639–40, 654, 657, 659, 660, 667, 671, 672, 687.

asking some 73% of the questions.[41] Lee's discursive dominance was augmented by a highly adversarial manner. While the rest of the Select Committee questioned the Council with civility, Lee's questioning proceeded as if he were conducting cross-examination.[42]

Lee's questions were framed in a manner that signalled his refusal to recognise the Law Society's submissions as a joint effort.[43] Lee split the associational identity of the Society and the Council in three ways. First, he repeatedly referred to the Society's submissions as originating from, and authored by, Marshall.[44] Second, Lee questioned the capacity of the Council to represent the Singapore Bar and the Law Society.[45] Third, Lee repeatedly asked Council members to speak as individuals, from their personal convictions, rather than as members of the Council.[46] Lee's questioning and disparagement of Marshall revealed such a high level of personal animosity[47] that the Chairman of the Hearings sought to mitigate the attack.[48] Lee also repeatedly characterised the list of submissions as a political document (calling it, by turns, a political essay, political treatise, political submissions or political dissertation)[49] and selectively deployed its arguments and choice of language to attack the Council, such that the substance of the Council's concerns was never actually addressed.

In short, the state involved the Council of the Law Society in the Select Committee Hearings in order to attack and delegitimise the Council. The state did not address the arguments of the Law Society concerning the implications and consequences of abolishing juries. The accusatory nature of the questioning, together with the pressure on media to keep the Law

41 Of the 350 questions the Select Committee asked the Council, 257 were asked by Lee.

42 *CPC Report*, *supra* note 28 at B33–B58, B68–B84; Tan, *Marshall of Singapore*, *supra* note 24 at 493–94.

43 *CPC Report*, *supra* note 28, paras. 545, 883.

44 Ibid., paras. 550, 552, 573, 610, 628, 660, 686, 883.

45 Ibid., paras. 519–24, 529–32, 573–80, 601–604, 902, 944.

46 Ibid., paras. 567, 568, 571, 572, 620–21, 637, 684–85, 689, 903, 931–57.

47 Ibid., paras. 550, 551, 632–37, 663–66, 668, 884, 888, 924–30.

48 Ibid., paras. 637, 660, 691.

49 Ibid., paras. 533, 543, 551, 552, 679.

Society's arguments out of the public domain, constitutes a crucial chapter in the story of Singapore's silenced legal profession. It is also noteworthy that at the time of the Hearings, there was absolutely no reporting in the Singapore press on the proceedings.[50] The matter entered the public domain through the press, quite briefly, only in December 1969, when the Select Committee presented its report to Parliament,[51] revealing yet again the level of state management of the public domain.

DISCIPLINING DETAINEES' LAWYERS

A second category of state responses to lawyers is relevant to the issue of the quiescence of Singapore's legal profession. Briefly, lawyers who have represented individuals the state considers enemies have themselves been treated as enemies or become targets of coercive measures. In 1971, for example, when David Marshall acted for the detained *Nanyang* executives[52] in the *Lee Mau Seng* habeas corpus proceedings,[53] it precipitated much professional and personal hardship for Marshall.

The judgment delivered out of the *Lee Mau Seng*[54] habeas corpus proceedings has become a landmark decision in the corpus of Singapore law,[55] with the High Court delivering a statist judgment affirming the power of the state to script detention orders in terms that lack the clarity of specificity and upholding the state's power to delay a detainee's access to counsel.[56] This case has had far-reaching consequences for Singapore

[50] I make this assertion on the basis of a search of the *Straits Times* from June to December 1969.

[51] *Supra* note 31.

[52] Lee Mau Seng was the younger son of the Lee family that owned the *Nanyang*: Seow, *supra* note 23 at 42. He had been the general manager of the paper. See also Tan, *Marshall of Singapore*, *supra* note 24 at 453.

[53] *Lee Mau Seng v. Minister for Home Affairs, Singapore & Anor.* [1969–1971] Sing.L.R. 508 [*Lee Mau Seng*]. See also Rowena Daw, "Preventive Detention in Singapore: A Comment on the Case of Lee Mau Seng" (1972) 14 *Mal. L.R.* 276.

[54] Ibid.

[55] Tan, *Marshall of Singapore*, *supra* note 24 at 452.

[56] Ibid.; *Lee Mau Seng*, *supra* note 53.

'law'[57] and Singapore's lawyers, in part because of disciplinary proceedings brought against Marshall in relation to this case.[58] These proceedings are relevant not just to a genealogy of silenced lawyers, but also to this project's larger concern with the Singapore state's management of public discourse, as explained later.

Lee Mau Seng and the three other *Nanyang* executives were detained in the early hours of the morning of 2 May 1971.[59] Between 2 May and 22 May, the detainees were not granted access to counsel.[60] A hearing in open court for the habeas corpus application in *Lee Mau Seng* took place on 26 May 1971.[61] The hearing was adjourned in order that Marshall might take instructions from his clients.[62] The adjournment extended to 7 June 1971,[63] the same date, ironically, that the International Press Institute General Assembly in Helsinki was to commence.[64]

After the hearing of 26 May, the Attorney General (representing the state in the habeas corpus proceedings), speaking to the Chief Justice and Marshall in the Chief Justice's outer chambers, expressed his concern that the affidavits of the *Nanyang* executives (Marshall's clients) not be published, or their contents leaked, before 7 June.[65] This anxiety to keep the affidavits out of the public domain was probably an attempt to

[57] Li-ann Thio, "Rule of Law Within a Non-Liberal 'Communitarian' Democracy: The Singapore Experience", in Randall Peerenboom, ed., *Asian Discourses of Rule of Law* (London: Routledge, 2004) 183 at 206–208.

[58] *Re David Marshall, supra* note 25; Tan, *Marshall of Singapore, supra* note 24 at 499.

[59] *Lee Mau Seng, supra* note 53 at 510.

[60] Ibid.

[61] *Re David Marshall, supra* note 25 at 134.

[62] Seow writes that the adjournment was granted in order to allow Marshall to take instructions: *supra* note 23 at 48. In his judgment on the disciplinary proceedings against Marshall, the Chief Justice says the reasons for the adjournment "are immaterial for present purposes" but notes that when the court sat on 26 May, representatives of both the domestic and the international media were present to report on the proceedings: *Re David Marshall, supra* note 25 at 134–35.

[63] *Re David Marshall, supra* note 25 at 134–35.

[64] Ibid. at 135.

[65] *Re David Marshall, supra* note 25 at 135; Tan, *Marshall of Singapore, supra* note 24 at 499.

manage the international opprobrium generated by the detentions of the *Nanyang* executives.[66] Marshall told the Attorney General and the Chief Justice that his office never gave any pleadings to the press before trial and that neither he nor his office would give these affidavits to the press for publication.[67]

What Marshall did do, however, was to send slightly modified versions of his clients' affidavits to certain carefully chosen parties.[68] The recipients included the Secretary General of Amnesty International and the editor of London's *Sunday Times*, Harold Evans.[69] The documents were amended by deleting the identifying markers of an affidavit.[70] They were labelled as client's instructions to counsel instead.[71] On 1 June, Marshall went to see the Attorney General to inform him that he had sent the affidavits by post, as instructions rather than affidavits, to contacts in London.[72] The Attorney General replied that the state would be making an application to strike out sections of the affidavits.[73] Later that day, the Attorney General sent a letter to Marshall saying that he considered Marshall to have breached the undertaking given in the Chief Justice's outer chambers on 26 May and asking that Marshall contact the individuals he had posted the affidavits to, by telegram, to make sure the contents of the affidavits were not published.[74] Marshall agreed to send the telegram if the Attorney General withdrew his letter.[75]

[66] The IPI's monthly bulletin following the Helsinki General Assembly attributes the record turnout and "heightened drama" of that meeting to Lee Kuan Yew, while the Director of the IPI, in his message, describes Lee as having "overshadowed" the other speakers in that session: "Lee Kuan Yew: Record Assembly Felt Unusual Pressures" and Ernest Meyer, "Vigour in Disagreement Is Democracy"; *IPI Report*, June/July 1971, 1–2.

[67] *Re David Marshall, supra* note 25 at 135.

[68] Ibid.

[69] Ibid. As an interesting aside, after Lee delivered his Helsinki address on 9 June, when the floor was opened, Evans was the first to question Lee.

[70] Ibid.

[71] Tan, *Marshall of Singapore, supra* note 24 at 499–500; *Re David Marshall, supra* note 25 at 135.

[72] *Re David Marshall, supra* note 25 at 135.

[73] Ibid. at 136.

[74] Ibid.

[75] Ibid.

The next day, 2 June, Marshall gave copies of the affidavits (in their original form as filed on 26 May) to Derek Round, a member of the IPI Secretariat who had been sent to Singapore by the IPI to conduct research on the detentions of the *Nanyang* executives in order to report to the Helsinki assembly.[76] Derek Round, contravening Marshall's explicit instructions about the date upon which the document might be made public, distributed copies to press agency representatives on 6 June at an IPI briefing on the Singapore situation.[77]

On 4 June, the Attorney General applied for certain portions of the affidavits to be struck out as "scandalous, irrelevant or otherwise oppressive".[78] The affidavits of the four *Nanyang* executives would have been a powerful and public repudiation of the state's condemnatory characterisations of these four men as 'Communists' and 'Communalists'.[79] This application was heard and granted by the Chief Justice in chambers.[80] The significance of this application being heard in chambers is that only the judge and the lawyers involved would have been present. Media could not have been present, and the censoring consequences of the Attorney General's successful application for the striking out may not have become known. However, because of Marshall's contact with Round, the original affidavits, as filed on 26 May, did enter the public domain and were disseminated at the IPI Helsinki assembly on 6 June. It was this conduct that led to Marshall's being subject to disciplinary proceedings.

If the Attorney General was furious at the limited dissemination of the affidavits,[81] this state actor must have been even more enraged at the media's access to full texts of the affidavits as originally filed on 26 May (rather than the affidavits modified by the Attorney General's successful

[76] Ibid. at 136–37.

[77] Ibid.; Tan, *Marshall of Singapore*, *supra* note 24 at 500.

[78] *Re David Marshall*, *supra* note 25 at 136.

[79] The allegations that form the basis of detention are replicated in the judgment: *Lee Mau Seng*, *supra* note 53 at 510–13.

[80] *Re David Marshall*, *supra* note 25 at 136.

[81] The judgment describes a "heated argument" between Marshall and the Attorney General on 1 June: *Re David Marshall*, *supra* note 25 at 136.

application to strike out certain portions). It is tempting to speculate that the distribution of the affidavits by Round on 6 June contributed to Lee's being on the receiving end of some particularly challenging questions on 9 June.[82]

The Attorney General lodged a complaint against Marshall with the Law Society for professional misconduct.[83] Disciplinary proceedings were instituted.[84] Marshall was found guilty of "grossly improper conduct in the discharge of his professional duties"[85] and suspended from practice for six months.[86] The "problematic" judgment[87] delivering this disciplinary penalty failed to clarify exactly how Marshall had been improper in his professional conduct, and the penalty shocked the legal profession.[88] Perhaps the gaps and problems in the judgment delivered from the disciplinary proceedings[89] point to a sub-textual outcome the judgment was unable to spell out: state retribution against Marshall's having facilitated the dissemination of narratives countering the state's version of events at the IPI Helsinki assembly. Marshall's suspension shocked the legal profession[90] and must have operated as exemplary punishment, instructing lawyers on the ways in which the state might express its displeasure against counsel for those detained without trial.

There is a second, more alarming aspect to this sub-textual public instruction: the possibility that the state's intention was to warn lawyers that the state would conflate counsel and client in construing risks to the 'nation'. This possibility is raised by two further state actions against lawyers in the 1970s.

[82] *IPI Report, supra* note 66. Louis Cha, the anxious Shin Min member of Lee's delegation to the IPI, had also described the debates as "heated" and Lee's audience as holding opposing views: 1974 Report on the Press Bill at A10–A12.

[83] Tan, *Marshall of Singapore, supra* note 24 at 500.

[84] *Re David Marshall, supra* note 25 at 132–33.

[85] Ibid. at 138.

[86] Ibid.

[87] Tan, *Marshall of Singapore, supra* note 24 at 501.

[88] Ibid.

[89] Ibid.

[90] Ibid.

Marshall was suspended in October 1972. In 1974 and 1977, the state took even more coercive action against two lawyers, T. T. Rajah and G. Raman. Both men were detained without trial.[91] One of them, T. T. Rajah, has already been an unnamed actor in this study. He was the counsel who brought the appeal against the caning of the fifteen-year-old boy, Ang Chin Sang, who in 1966 was convicted of 'vandalism' for putting up posters urging "Yankees" to go home.[92] Rajah also defended the Barisan leaders charged with sedition[93] and acted for many Barisan members and activists.[94]

Rajah appears to have been fearless in his dealings with the state, bringing orders of contempt against high-ranking state actors for prejudicing his clients' chances of a fair trail by making public statements before their cases had been heard,[95] and deploying administrative law to bring orders of mandamus against state actors who had tortured and force-fed his imprisoned clients who were on a hunger strike.[96] Rajah also represented political detainees who had been held without trial under the *Internal Security Act* in bringing habeas corpus applications.[97] In other words, Rajah engaged in legal processes to draw attention to

[91] Lawyer T. T. Rajah was detained for eighteen months from January 1974 to 12 December 1975, while lawyer G. Raman was detained in February 1977: Seow, *supra* note 23 at 113; Amnesty International, *Report of an Amnesty International Mission to Singapore, 30 November to 5 December 1978* (London: Amnesty International, 1980) [*1978 Amnesty Report*].

[92] *Ang Chin Sang v. Public Prosecutor*, [1970] 2 M.L.J. 6 (Sing.H.C.); discussed in Chapter 3.

[93] "Two Barisan Leaders Arrested on Sedition Charge", *Straits Times* (16 April 1966) 1; "The Barisan Sedition Case Takes New Turn", *Straits Times* (26 April 1966) 1.

[94] "Counsel, DPP Clash over 'Inspiration Day'", *Straits Times* (8 October 1967) 9; "96 Barisans Get 4 Months for Contempt" *Straits Times* (21 December 1967) 4.

[95] *Re Application of Lau Swee Soong; Lau Swee Soong v. Goh Keng Swee & Anor* [1965–1968] 1 Sing.L.R. 661 (Sing.H.C.); *Re Application of Foong Jam Keong* [1967] 2 M.L.J. 202.

[96] *Re Rajah TT; Law Society v. Thampoe T Rajah* [1972–1974] 1 Sing.L.R. 423 [*Re T. T. Rajah*]. On the hunger strikes and forced feeding, see also Said Zahari, *The Long Nightmare: My 17 Years as a Political Prisoner* (Kuala Lumpur: Utusan, 2007) 55–68.

[97] *Lau Lek Eng & Ors v. Minister for Home Affairs & Anor* [1972–1974] 1 Sing.L.R. 300 (H.C.); *Wee Toon Lip & Ors v Minister for Home Affairs & Anor* [1972–1974] 1 Sing.L.R. 303 (H.C.).

the manner in which a statist legal system was bearing down upon the PAP's political opponents. In 1972, investigating a complaint made by the Attorney General against the manner in which Rajah had conducted summonses he brought for political detainees, the Law Society initiated disciplinary proceedings that resulted in Rajah being found guilty of professional misconduct.[98] He was suspended from practice for two years from February 1973.[99] About a year after this suspension commenced, Rajah was himself detained without trial.[100] He was held from January 1974 to December 1975.[101]

Marshall's suspension from practice, along with the suspension and detentions of Rajah and later Raman, suggests a pattern of state retribution towards lawyers who have contested the state in the public domain when acting in their professional capacities. When state-initiated disciplinary actions culminate in penalties that prevent primary breadwinners from making their living, the hardship that is experienced by the lawyer and his loved ones extracts a deeply personal price from lawyers ready to represent the state's antagonists. This punishment of lawyers who act for those the state categorises as enemies might explain the sixteen-year gap between habeas corpus applications that have been brought in Singapore by detainees.[102] Between 1972, when T. T. Rajah acted for the Barisan activists, and 1988,[103] despite a total of 210 individuals having been detained without trial,[104] detainees no longer challenged the legitimacy of their detentions in court.

[98] *Re T. T. Rajah*, *supra* note 96.

[99] Ibid. at 428.

[100] *1978 Amnesty Report*, *supra* note 91.

[101] Ibid.

[102] The digital database Lexis holds Singapore decisions. A search on Lexis shows that between 1972 and 1988, no habeas corpus applications were brought by *ISA* detainees.

[103] The so-called Marxist conspirators, many of them lawyers, brought habeas corpus applications from 1988 to 1990. These are discussed later.

[104] The figures for detentions under the *ISA* were supplied in response to a question in Parliament: Sing., *Parliamentary Debates*, vol. 69, col. 1991 (Mr Wong Kan Seng).

In short, by the late 1970s, the state had established and consolidated a discursive monopoly on the subject of 'law'. This monopoly might be seen as having been broken by the entry into Parliament of the man who has become Singapore's iconic opposition figure, J. B. Jeyaretnam.[105] With Jeyaretnam's electoral victory, not only was the state's public discourse monopoly on 'law' broken, but the staged, performative facet of Singapore 'law' became like a series of concentric circles.

If the centre of the series is the category 'law', then the circles embrace lawyer-Prime Minister Lee Kuan Yew and two other lawyers who were approximately Lee's age: opposition politician J. B. Jeyaretnam and the 1986 President of the Law Society, Francis Seow.[106] Not only were all three men lawyers of roughly the same age, all three had received their legal education in England and had been called to the English Bar as part of their legal professional qualifications. In other words, all three lawyers had been inducted into 'law' at the source, so to speak, of the 'common law'. And if Lee was (and is) the voice of 'rule by law', then Jeyaretnam and Seow were voices of 'rule of law'. In 1986, when the 'foreign press' and *LPA* amendments were presented on the stage of the Singapore 'nation', 'law' was no longer a one-person show.

In Chapter 4 I described how J. B. Jeyaretnam's entry into Parliament precipitated an upsurge in the discourses and performances of both 'rule of law' and 'rule by law'. The Singapore state found a multitude of ways to make regulation, procedure, as well as parliamentary and legal processes its weapons in undermining Jeyaretnam's political and legal careers.[107] I also argued that the 'foreign press' amendment appears to have been prompted by somewhat scathing reportage in publications such as the *Asian Wall Street Journal* and the *Far Eastern Economic Review* on the state's legal proceedings against Jeyaretnam.[108]

[105] See the discussion on the relationship between Jeyaretnam's electoral victory and the 'foreign press' amendment in Chapter 4.

[106] Lee was born in 1923, Jeyaretnam in 1926 and Seow in 1928.

[107] See Chapter 4.

[108] See Chapter 4.

While Jeyaretnam's electoral victory precipitated an alarming spike in instrumentalist applications of 'law', this period also saw more advocacy for a liberal account of 'law' from non-state actors. Jeyaretnam's presence in Parliament facilitated media exposure for his critique of the state.[109] In addition to this resilient 'rule of law' stalwart, a rather more unexpected voice for a liberal 'rule of law' that emerged was that of the 1986 President of the Singapore Law Society, Francis Seow.

In January 1986, Francis Seow was elected to the presidency of the Law Society. Seow – who, like Marshall, is reputed to have great personal charm and presence – was a well-known member of the Bar. He had been Solicitor General from 1967 to 1970.[110] After he left the Legal Service, he had had a rather chequered professional career in the private sector.[111] In 1973 Seow was suspended from practice for professional misconduct,[112] and in 1984 he was suspended again following a conviction for making a false declaration.[113] At the time of his election to the presidency of the Law Society, Seow had already been a member of the Council in 1976 and 1977,[114] but 1986 was the first time he had been elected to the office of President.

Under Seow, the Law Society did something it had not attempted since the thwarted efforts of the 1969 Council. It issued a press statement on proposed legislation by questioning the terms of the *Press Bill.* Specifically, the Law Society found the phrase "engaging in domestic politics" troubling:

> There are ambiguities in the Bill. For example, the terms "engaging in" and "domestic politics" are not defined although these terms form the

[109] Chan Heng Chee, "Internal Developments in Singapore", in Verinder Grover, ed., *Singapore: Government and Politics* (New Delhi: Deep & Deep, 2000) 128 at 130.

[110] Paul Jacob, "The Man at the Centre of the Controversy", *Straits Times* (9 October 1986) 16 [*Man at the Centre*].

[111] Tan, *Marshall of Singapore*, *supra* note 24.

[112] Jacob, *Man at the Centre*, supra note 110.

[113] Ibid.

[114] Sing., "Report of the Select Committee on the Legal Profession (Amendment) Bill", October 1986, 6th Parliament, [*SC Report on LPA*] at B66, para. 422.

> basis of the Bill. Since this Bill is aimed at foreign publications, which – in the words which have been attributed to the Minister – "have been commenting frequently on local issues and distorting the truth", these terms should have been defined. The omission to define them will result in subjective interpretation and implementation of the Bill.[115]

This criticism is entirely consistent with 'rule of law' principles about the need for 'law' to be clear and accessible[116] and with the 'common law' expectation that legislation, in particular, should exhibit clarity by defining key terms.[117] The Law Society's press statement is informed by another 'rule of law' assumption, that the operation of 'law' should be predictable, 'objective' and transparent.[118]

Apart from being consonant with 'rule of law' assumptions, the press statement was in keeping with the *LPA*. Under the *LPA*, as it was then framed, the Council of the Law Society's functions included examining and reporting upon current or proposed legislation should it think fit[119] and protecting and assisting the public in all matters to do with law.[120] When making the press statement, the Law Society was, on the face of it, acting in accordance with its powers and duties as framed by the 'law' of the *LPA* and the constitutional rights of freedom of speech and of association.[121] Despite these conceptual and textual entitlements to question proposed 'laws', the state insisted that the Law Society had, by making a public statement, breached state–Law Society relations. The state's extreme vigilance of public discourse on 'law' is conveyed by the extraordinary rapidity with which it responded to the Law Society's press statement.

[115] Ibid. at B82–84.

[116] These parameters and principles for the 'rule of law' might be traced to Dicey's definitions and Hayek's later elaborations: Brian Z. Tamanaha, *On the Rule of Law: History, Politics, Theory* (Cambridge: Cambridge University Press, 2004) 63–70.

[117] *SC Report on LPA supra* note 114.

[118] Ibid.

[119] *Legal Profession Act* (Cap. 161, 1985 Rev. Ed. Sing.) s. 39(1)(c).

[120] Ibid. at s. 39(1)(f).

[121] *Constitution*, Art. 14.

ACCELERATED STATE RESPONSES

The state's legal-administrative machinery was highly efficient in addressing the counter-narrative on 'law' generated by the Law Society's press statement. The Law Society made its press statement on 21 May 1986.[122] A little more than three months later, on 25 August 1986, the *Legal Profession (Amendment) Bill* was introduced to Parliament. In the meantime, the 'foreign press' amendment to the *Press Act* had been debated and passed in Parliament at the end of July. Again, the Law Society made a press statement,[123] and because the *Legal Profession (Amendment) Bill* was to go before a Select Committee and the public had been invited to make its submissions for consideration, the Law Society made written submissions to the Committee. The closing date for submissions was 8 October 1986. The Committee began its hearings on the very next day, 9 October.

The 'rule of law' / 'rule by law' ambivalence of the Singapore state is reflected in the way the state carefully adhered to 'rule of law' *procedures* while scripting a 'law' (ironically, concerning the legal profession) that undermines 'rule of law' *principles*. With three readings in Parliament, invitations to the public to make submissions and Select Committee Hearings, the state was visibly engaging in a 'rule of law' process, apparently engaging the public and its representatives in a consultative democratic process in the public domain. But with only two opposition members in a seventy-seven-seat Parliament[124] (one of whom was besieged by a series of legal actions),[125] two days of 'debate', just two weeks for the public to make submissions, media under the direct or indirect control of the

[122] Jacob, *Man at the Centre*, supra note 110.

[123] "Lawyers Want Govt to Hear Their Views Before Passing Bill", *Straits Times* (25 September 1986) 18.

[124] Jon S. T. Quah, "The 1980s: A Review of Significant Political Developments", in Ernest C. T. Chew & Edwin Lee, eds., *A History of Singapore* (Singapore: Oxford University Press, 1991) 385 at 386.

[125] See Chapter 4, "The Press Act After 1974."

state, and commencing Select Committee Hearings the day after submissions closed, the implication was that the state was refusing to substantively engage with the legal profession in negotiating 'law'.

The immediacy of the state's responses suggests that the state was very concerned to maintain its discursive monopoly on 'law'. One powerful and powerfully performative way in which the state asserted its discursive command was its appropriation of the Select Committee Hearings on the *LPA*. These Hearings were ostensibly set up to study the proposed amendments to the *LPA*. However, the state used them to effect a different end: the interrogation-cum-instruction of the Council of the Law Society.

SELECTIVE HEARING: INTERROGATION AND STATE AUTHORITY

If Lee Kuan Yew's questioning of the Law Society Council in 1969 departed from general practice in terms of Lee's antagonistic questioning, then the Hearings on the 1986 amendments to the *LPA* were set up to be even more adversarial. The 1986 Hearings proceeded as if they were an interrogation rather than Select Committee Hearings.[126]

In 1986 an especially adversarial framework was established by the state in three ways. First, it issued subpoenas to the Council requiring its members to attend the Hearings.[127] In doing so, the state ignored the courteous readiness of the Council to appear before the Committee.[128] Arguably, in subpoenaing the Council, the state was treating its members as hostile and untrustworthy individuals. Second, the state took evidence from the Council under oath[129] instead of engaging in a conversation

[126] With two exceptions: The questioning of Chelva Rajah (B214–19) and Warren Khoo (B204–13) was courteous: *SC Report on LPA*, *supra* note 114. Khoo was a state appointee to the Council. Rajah was later appointed as a judicial commissioner.

[127] *SC Report on LPA*, *supra* note 114 at B110, para. 799.

[128] Ibid. at A3.

[129] Perhaps because it was so unusual for Select Committees to subpoena and to examine witnesses under oath, the Chairman highlighted the fact of the oath not to the Attorney-General but to the Council; *SC Report*, *supra* note 114 at B23.

with the Council, as is usually the case at Select Committee Hearings.[130] Administering the oaths enabled the state to periodically remind Council members that they were under oath, thus punctuating the proceedings with the state questioning the veracity of Council members.[131] Third, with two exceptions,[132] the manner in which the questions were put to the Council was akin to extremely accusatory and intimidating cross-examination. The Prime Minister himself used the word "cross-examination" in referring to his questioning of Council member Teo Soh Lung.[133]

In the process, state actors often spoke more than the Council members, such that the narrative that was permitted to emerge was one managed and controlled by the state. Indeed, at one point, when the first Council member to be questioned attempted to resist the Prime Minister's reformulation of his answers, a reformulation which involved a characterisation that the Council member had not proposed, the Prime Minister explicitly refused to allow that member to choose his own words. By insisting on certain words, the Prime Minister ensured his command of the very building blocks of discourse:

> *PM:* You did not know of public disquiet, or you had no public disquiet?
> *ELIAS:* Disquiet of the public is not the words I would choose. Let me use my own, if I may, Mr Prime Minister.
> *PM:* No. My question to you was ...[134]

Only the Attorney General, the main state actor to appear before the Committee, was allowed to generate a continuous and self-directed narrative.[135] As demonstrated later in the chapter, despite the structure

[130] None of the Select Committee Hearings conducted before or after these on the *LPA* appears to have administered oaths.

[131] *SC Report on LPA supra* note 114 at B43, para. 246; B46, para. 274; B70, paras. 465–66; B101, para. 728; B122, para. 871; B167, para. 1197A.

[132] *Supra* note 126 above.

[133] *SC Report, on LPA supra* note 114 at B181, para. 1311.

[134] Ibid. at B36, paras. 166–67.

[135] Ibid. at B1–B16.

of an encounter between state and non-state actors, the state managed to shape discursive outcomes – exerting its authority to insist on the use of certain words, strategically repeating its characterisations of events and motives, so as to render irrelevant the text actually produced by certain Council members.

THE ROLE OF LEE KUAN YEW

The Select Committee constituted by Parliament to examine and report on the 1986 amendments included the Prime Minister, Lee Kuan Yew. In 1986, when the Hearings took place, Lee had been Prime Minister for twenty-seven years, and most ordinary Singaporeans were very much in awe of him and of the power he wielded.[136]

At the Hearings, of the 1,609 questions asked, 1,139 were asked by Lee. This amounts to more than 70% of the questions. In the process, Lee reiterated (either overtly or by implication) the exercise of surveillance by the state[137]; the nature and validity of his own authority and knowledge arising from his role in the Republic's foundational years[138]; his enhanced authority arising from his membership in the legal

[136] One scholar has described Lee in these terms: "The grandeur of his presence – mystical, physical, psychological and political – is still very much felt, accepted and embraced by the Singapore public.... Lee's charisma has ... been associated with traits of ruthlessness, toughness, determination and pragmatism ... qualities that complement his autocratic personality": Ho Khai Leong, *Shared Responsibilities, Unshared Power: The Politics of Policy-Making in Singapore* (Singapore: Marshall Cavendish, 2003) 91, 95.

[137] *SC Report on LPA*, *supra* note 114 at B21, B31, B47–52, B61–71, B83–84, B89, B105–16, B110–16, B127, B 141, B195–200, B203.

[138] Ibid. at B23 (Lee on his role in the decision to abolish juries), B42 (Lee on his participation in the Constitutional Commission), B60 (Lee recounting Francis Seow's performance as Deputy Public Prosecutor), B88 (Lee asserting that "no President of the Law Society or the Bar, the old committee of the Bar, has ever gone public and criticized Government legislation"), B133–34, B146, B151 (Lee on the historical roots of the Legal Service Commission and three constitutional conferences, all of which he attended), B135 (Lee on the "sewing up" of the Singapore Constitution from the Federal Constitution of Malaysia upon Singapore's sudden independence), B38 (Lee on the history of the *LPA*).

profession[139]; and his centrality to the discretionary exercise of power by the government.[140]

The Hearings demonstrate how Lee took a commanding role, leading most of the questioning, refusing to heed the Chairman's instructions to change his line of questioning[141] and demonstrating an extraordinary grasp of 'facts' and 'figures'[142] that helped to convey his sure hand in the ruling of Singapore, as well as the centrality of his person to the government. The deference of the Chairman to Lee and the relative passivity of the rest of the Select Committee during the Hearings facilitated Lee's dominance of the discourse generated by the event.

This discursive dominance encapsulates a mode of leadership which necessitates citizen subordination – an instruction that was vividly conveyed to the 'nation' when the 1986 Hearings became the first Select Committee Hearings to be televised in Singapore.[143] Clearly, the state intended the Hearings to be as visible an exercise as possible. In televising and rendering public this contest between lawyers and the state on the parameters of 'law' (following the limited and far less public encounter of 1969), the state used its power to unilaterally determine the content and meaning of this crucial category, accounting in part, I would argue, for the passivity of lawyers in today's public domain. This role of subordination,

[139] Ibid. at B132, para. 952; B134, para. 959; B89, para 638.

[140] Ibid. at B38, para. 186; B65–66, paras. 419–20; B79–80, paras. 556–57; B82, para. 573; B136, para. 971; B196, para. 1438; B198, para. 1472; B199, para. 1478.

[141] Ibid. at B66, para. 425–26.

[142] Ibid. at B28 ("of 1,300 members of the Bar, some 800 members or more have been graduates of the University of Singapore or the National University of Singapore"), B 29 ("1,300 members, growing at the rate of 200 graduates a year), B87 ("activity on behalf of 1,335 members").

[143] At the time these Select Committee Hearings were televised, I had just graduated from the National University of Singapore and was obtaining my professional qualifications. The departure from past practice in televising Select Committee Hearings was widely commented upon. I have recently confirmed with senior members of the legal profession in Singapore that these were the first hearings ever to be televised. Unfortunately, the state broadcasting corporation, MediaCorp, has ignored both letters and emails asking for confirmation.

necessitating obedience from citizens, has had far-reaching consequences for civil society in Singapore.

The term 'civil society' is notoriously difficult to pin down,[144] but in the continuum of meanings, civil society is generally acknowledged to involve voluntary group activity that is independent of the state and other hegemonic forces.[145] I rely on Walzer's definition of civil society as "the space of uncoerced human association"[146] and, in this chapter, use 'civil society' to indicate individuals coming together because of shared interests and concerns, and acting as a group, in a manner that is autonomous, in order to better represent and articulate those concerns. The bundle of meanings tied to 'civil society' is generally taken to derive from notions of informed, participatory and rights-bearing citizenship that are inherent to 'democracy' and political liberalism. Thus, if civil society is about the autonomous associational activity of citizens, which activity is sometimes directed at influencing policy, then citizens must be able, first, to form and act in groups; second, to engage with policy issues and express their views in the public domain; and third, to be independent of the state.

The Hearings recalibrated notions of state–citizen encounters while depicting a central feature of the state's duality in that the state diligently adhered to 'rule of law' requirements procedurally while substantively

[144] Gershon Shafir, "The Evolving Tradition of Citizenship", in Gershon Shafir, ed., *The Citizenship Debates: A Reader* (Minneapolis: University of Minnesota Press, 1998) 1.

[145] For example, "the space of uncoerced human association and also the set of relational networks – formed for the sake of family, faith, interest and ideology – that fill this space": Michael Walzer, "The Civil Society Argument", in Gershon Shafir ed., *The Citizenship Debates: A Reader* (Minneapolis: University of Minnesota Press, 1998) at 291–92; and "a competitive political space, structurally located between official public life and private life, in which a range of voluntary, autonomous organisations have asserted the right to influence public policy": Michael Bernhard, "Civil Society and Democratic Transition in East Central Europe" (1993) 108:2 *Political Science Quarterly* 309; "Civil society is one form of political space … [an] avenue for contesting and shaping public policy [requiring] greater independence from the state": Gary Rodan, "Civil Society and Other Political Possibilities in Southeast Asia" (1997) 27:2 *Journal of Contemporary Asia* 14.

[146] Walzer, *supra* note 145.

effecting a 'rule by law' erosion of individual rights. The Hearings illustrate this dual state feature as well as the state's use of coercion, public discourse and legislation to effect three ends: first, the silencing of the lawyers involved; second, the dismantling of potential civil society leadership attaching to the Law Society; and third, the instruction, not just of lawyers but of all citizens, on the state's determinations of the limits of 'law' and civil society. More specifically, the Hearings launched a state-scripted demarcation of 'law' as a category of knowledge and activity distinct from 'politics', such that any comment made by lawyers in the public domain on a matter deemed by the state to be 'political' would be a violation of the permissible. Most crucially, the Hearings instructed all citizens that a 'rule of law' questioning of the state's 'rule by law' practices would be treated as a political challenge warranting extreme state coercion. In short, the Hearings became a platform for the very public performance of state power – a performance that (explicitly and implicitly) focused on state formulations of the permissible limits of civil society engagement by lawyers.

The setting for this performance was akin to a courtroom, with the members of the Select Committee arrayed, like a full bench of the judiciary, on an imposing and raised dais.[147] The spatial composition of the room was such that the Council members were seated on a lower level, in a position of subordination to the state. If the stage, so to speak, simulated a courtroom, the Hearings unfolded as if Council members were on trial. And if the Council members were on trial, the state was both judge and prosecutor. In the process, the President of the Law Society, Francis Seow (FS in the following extracts), and two other Council members were discredited,[148] with the state asserting that Seow was unfit to be President because he was, inter alia, in debt. Council member Teo Soh Lung was accused of using the Law Society as a covert operation

[147] This description is based on photographs of the Hearings I purchased from the *Straits Times*.

[148] *SC Report on LPA supra* note 114, paras. 277–651. The excerpts I present have been modified in that I have introduced dashes when the minutes suggest the speaker has been interrupted.

to further the ends of the opposition Workers' Party.[149] Teo denied this, but it was Lee (PM in the extracts) who spoke more, whose dominance allowed his narrative to drown hers. It was Lee's assertions that became 'fact' in the public domain.[150]

As part of the pedagogical exercise, the state used the Hearings to question the professional competence of the Council in two ways: first, for not recognising the difference between justiciable and non-justiciable issues; and second, for not recognising the *Press Bill* as a 'law' outside the expertise of the Law Society because it was about advertising revenues or inflicting punishment on the press:

> *PM*: Mr Seow, read page two of your statement, "Ambiguous and subjective"...
> *FS*: For example, the terms "engaging in" and "domestic politics" are not defined although these terms form the basis of the Bill. Since this Bill is aimed at foreign publications, which – in the words which have been attributed to the Minister – "have been commenting frequently on local issues and distorting the truth" these terms should have been defined. The omission to define them will result in subjective interpretation and implementation of the Bill.
> *PM*: Mr Seow, you served in the AG's Chambers as Solicitor-General?
> *FS*: I did.
> *PM*: Is this legislation which decides a justiciable issue or is it legislation which gives administrative discretion?
> *FS*: Administrative discretion?
> *PM*: Yes. You know the difference. A newspaper banned is not able to go to court to determine whether it is right or wrong. The newspaper stays banned. Why are you feigning ignorance? Why

[149] *SC Report*, *on LPA supra* note 114 paras. 670–833.

[150] "Government Must Act if Law Society Used for Political Ends: PM", *Straits Times* (10 October 1986) 18; 'PM: It's My Job to Stop Politicking in Professional Bodies', *Straits Times* (10 October 1986) 14.

did you sign this document? Miss Teo may be ignorant but you are not. The legislation is enabling administrative legislation, like powers to detain, are you ...?

FS: Yes, I accept that.

PM: So this was a misrepresentation that it was a justiciable issue?

FS: No, I would not accept what you say in that context. What we are trying to say here, what the Sub-Committee is trying to say here is that this should have been defined. The expression should have been defined.

PM: Why should it be defined?

FS: All right, if that is the way the legislature of parliament feels, then so be it. But we are only doing our honest best.

PM: It is enabling legislation to allow the Minister to exercise administrative powers, not for the Courts to decide whether or not the Minister acted within the judicial definition of those words, "domestic politics". You have appeared for the State against political detainees?

FS: Yes I have.

PM: Yes. We don't argue about whether or not they are a threat to the security of the State. The Minister certifies that they are, and they remain a threat. Right?

FS: Yes, I agree.

PM: Now, read punishments, next page –

PM: [interrupting] Stop there. Is this a matter within the professional competence of the Law Society Council – whether a newspaper earns its revenue by advertising or by sales? How do lawyers become experts, develop expertise on these matters, to advise the Government, to assist the Government in these matters?

FS: Correct.

PM: How?

FS: If you were to isolate it in the way you have done, then of course it looks a bit incongruous. Certainly.

PM: It is absurd, isn't it?

(*SC Report*, B82–84, paras. 593–96)

This excerpt shows how, with no trace of irony, the Prime Minister likened the operation of the *Press Bill* to that prime example of legal exceptionalism: detention without trial. The Prime Minister's analogy, along with his accusatory characterisation of the Law Society's critique as "a misrepresentation that it was a justiciable issue", builds up to his assertion that the parameters of 'law' are set by Parliament, not the courts. Sadly, Seow seems to lack the 'rule of law' language with which to counter the Prime Minister's disparaging dismissal of the Law Society's critique.

The Prime Minister's cross-examination mode of questioning focuses on undermining the Council's professional ability – accusing Teo of "ignorance" and Seow of "feigning ignorance", and declaring as "absurd" the idea that "lawyers become experts" or have "professional competence" to speak on the substance of the *Press Bill*. The Prime Minister's delineation of the *Press Bill* as a 'law' outside the expertise of the Law Society because its concerns are advertising revenues or inflicting punishment on the press recasts the *Press Bill* as an instrument of bureaucracy, requiring expertise of a different kind. By denying the *Press Bill*'s necessarily 'legal' nature, the ways in which it erodes access to news and information and the role of lawyers in facilitating its operations, the Prime Minister rejects the validity of the Law Society's critique. The public was not to think that the Council, as lawyers, had the requisite professional knowledge or expertise:

> *PM*: How does your Council become experts as to how to control or inflict punishment on the press? What particular experience have you got with the press that makes you say that the Bill does not achieve this purpose? Have you had experience working with the press or defending them or whatever?
> *FS*: No, I don't have.
> *PM*: This is a statement of opinion?
> *FS*: Yes, an opinion.
> *PM*: Unconnected with your position as lawyers?
> *FS*: Well, I wouldn't say so. I wouldn't say so.
> *PM*: Put it in a different way. Who would know more about revenue of newspapers – an advertising agency, a survey agency, or lawyers?
> *FS*: Of course, the advertising agency, naturally.

PM: Then why do you want to blunder into a terrain which is not yours? You are not experts in this. The Government has taken expert advice from people who do know.

(*SC Report*, B85, paras. 601–605)

The Hearings, beamed into the homes of watching citizens, rendered those citizens a silent, passive audience. The narrative space granted to the Council was minimised by the state's style of questioning. In addition to the frequent interruptions, the Council was silenced by the already authoritative state's especially authoritative insistence on its own characterisations and interpretations. The state frequently ignored and denied the answers actually given by the Council to questions that were often a vehicle of complex and damning assumptions. The Hearings became a pedagogical exercise, discursively instructing all citizens, but in particular lawyers, on the way in which the state would manage the ambivalent spaces between 'rule of law' and 'rule by law'.

ASSOCIATIONAL ACTIVITY AND INDIVIDUAL CULPABILITY

Civil society rests, in part, on the capacity for individuals to organise themselves into groups and engage in associational activity. The 'rule of law' grounding of associational activity as a 'right' is reflected in Article 14 of the *Constitution*[151]:

Freedom of speech, assembly and association
14(1) Subject to clauses (2) and (3) –
(a) every citizen of Singapore has the right to freedom of speech and expression;
(b) all citizens of Singapore have the right to assemble peaceably and without arms; and
(c) all citizens of Singapore have the right to form associations.

[151] The restrictions on these rights spelled out in Article 14 are, generally, restrictions Parliament may confer in the interests of security, international relations, public order or morality and, specifically, attention to the associational activity of student unions and trade unions.

In the Hearings, the state questioned the Council in a manner which constructed accountability for the Law Society's statements as individual rather than associational. The associational and collective nature of activity and responsibility was not recognised by the state, as reflected in these extracts from the questioning of Francis Seow, first, by the Minister for Law, then by the Prime Minister:

> *MINISTER*: "With regard to the Newspaper and Printing Presses (Amendment) Bill and the Law Society's press statement which was issued in your name, do you recall that there was one paragraph in your press statement which said that even if the Bill –
> *FS*: [interrupting] May I correct you there, Mr Minister? That statement admittedly went out under my hand. But it was deliberated, voted by the entire Council, and therefore of course I assume full responsibility, therefore, as President.
>
> (*SC Report*, B55, para. 333)

> *PM*: Mr Seow, you issued this statement on the Newspaper and Printing Presses (Amendment) Bill?
> *FS*: I did under my hand in circumstances which I have already told you.
> *PM*: You drafted it?
> *FS*: No.
> *PM*: Who did?
> *FS*: I think it was our Sub-Committee. After which it was gone over by members of the Council. I cannot really recall that. But the draft was prepared by the Sub-Committee.
> *PM*: And the Sub-Committee is headed by Miss Teo Soh Lung?
> *FS*: I believe she is one of the Committee members.
> *PM*: She heads the Sub-Committee?
> *FS*: If you say so, I am prepared to accept that.
>
> (*SC Report*, B82, paras. 576–80)

> *FS*: Yes, certainly. I will seek the decision of the Council because I don't act alone, and we will certainly bear what the –

PM: [interrupting] But if they act contrary to your interests, which would be the case if they refused to accede after this meeting, there must be something damning to hide, isn't it?
FS: I am not quite sure I understand you. Could you please repeat your question?
PM: You are suggesting that you are quite prepared to act in accordance with the way the Minister has suggested?
FS: Yes, speaking personally for myself. Yes, certainly.
PM: But the Council may not agree and therefore you may be thwarted in the attempt?
FS: I doubt whether they will disagree. But anyway, I will certainly use all the persuasive powers at my command –
PM: That is exactly what I suggested. And I doubt whether they will disagree because if they disagree they will put you –
FS: in an awkward position as it were.
PM: Yes?
FS: I am prepared to accept that.

(*SC Report*, B57–58, paras. 354–58)

As can be seen from these exchanges, the state refused to accept the collective nature of Council decisions. In this last exchange, the Prime Minister made clear, first, that the individual, Seow, would be held responsible for the actions and decisions emanating from the collective leadership of the Council; and second, that a refusal to disclose the information asked for could only mean "there must be something damning to hide", making it clear that Seow would not be relieved of culpability as an individual because of a decision made by the collective.

The Prime Minister's sub-textual warning was that the state would operate on the assumption of mala fides on the part of the Council and, by extension, of Seow. Additionally, the Prime Minister's line of questioning set up a shifting of issues. Instead of the focus being on the confidentiality of sources, the issue became one of the loyalties of the Council to Seow. When the Prime Minister said, "But if they act contrary to your interests, which would be the case if they refused to accede after this meeting"; not only was the leader made responsible for his followers, the followers were made responsible for their leader. The Prime Minister's reference to the watching Council members implies the Prime Minister's awareness of the sub-text of threat that underpinned his questions to Seow.

The state's insistence on individual culpability, on refusing to recognise associational responsibility, was at the fore in the Minister for Law's questioning of Council member Teo Soh Lung (TSL in the following extracts), Teo had already been separated from the associational grouping of the Council and selected for individual attention by the Prime Minister's questioning of Seow set out earlier.

> *MINISTER*: You also drafted the article which later became a press release?
> *TSL*: Mr Chairman, can I clarify here? I did not draft the report. It was my Committee which drafted it.
> *MINISTER*: Yes. You are the Chairman of the Committee?
> *TSL*: I am the Chairman.
> *MINISTER*: You played a leading role in that? Let's not be modest. If you did, let us know.
> *TSL*: I don't see the question here because as Chairman –
> *MINISTER [INTERRUPTING]*: Who drafted it? Who put out the first draft?
> *TSL*: All of us did.
> *MINISTER*: All of you put out the first draft?
> *TSL*: Everyone in the Sub-Committee put out the first draft. We did it in parts.
> *MINISTER*: But how is that possible?
> *TSL*: It is possible.
> *MINISTER*: Miss Teo, when a draft is put to a Committee, somebody has to put up the initial outline, the initial sketch of the draft, isn't it? Who did it?

At this point, Teo Soh Lung asked the Chairman to rule on the permissibility of questioning focused not on the *Legal Profession (Amendment) Bill* (which was what the Select Committee had ostensibly convened for) but on the *Newspapers and Printing Presses (Amendment) Bill.* The Prime Minister intervened to instruct the Chairman to rule, and the Chairman told her she had to "answer all questions asked". The Minister for Law resumed his questioning.

> *MINISTER*: Who put up the first draft?
> *TSL*: All of us sat down and worked on it. We worked in parts. Some members worked the first part and the others worked the second and third parts. Then it was a collective effort, put them together. Then we presented it to the Council.
> *MINISTER*: Who put them together?
> *TSL*: All of us had a hand in it.
> *MINISTER*: You played the leading role in that draft, did you not?
> *TSL*: I wouldn't say I played a leading role. I mean, we all played our roles.
> *MINISTER*: What about the article, the press release, which was later issued? Did you have a hand in drafting that?
> *TSL*: I had no hand in the press release. What we did was that we did an article meant to be published in the papers for the laymen.
> *MINISTER*: Who drafted it?
> *TSL*: My Committee did.
> *MINISTER*: What was your role in it?
> *TSL*: As a Chairperson. In fact, I did very little on the article itself. It was a joint effort.
>
> (*SC Report*, B 99–100, paras. 710–23)

The Minister's persistent questions, designed to elicit an acknowledgement of individual culpability, signal the state's refusal to accept Teo's consistent position of associational responsibility. A few moments later, the Prime Minister intervened again, this time to take over the questioning of Teo on the Law Society press statement which had described the

Newspaper and Printing Presses (Amendment) Bill as ambiguous and subjective because the terms "engaging in" and "domestic politics" had not been defined.

> *PM*: You are suggesting that, because this is a submission made by a group of lawyers to the Law Council and has been issued in the name of the President, that it is defective law not to define it?
> *TSL*: In order to do away with the ambiguities that we should define these terms.
> *PM*: What is there ambiguous? The Minister has decided that a magazine or a newspaper has engaged in domestic politics and gazettes it under section 18 (A) (1) of the Act as amended. That's the end of the matter. Have you not learned that in the law school?
> *TSL*: Yes, I learned that in law school. But in order to –
> *PM*: [interrupting] But you are being difficult?
> *TSL*: I am not being difficult, Mr Lee.
> *PM*: Read page three on Punishments. What does it say? This is your handwork? Read it aloud....
>
> (*SC Report*, B 108, paras. 779–82)

This extract demonstrates that the Prime Minister's questioning proceeded on the assumption of Teo's personal responsibility. The Prime Minister's questions became a platform for accusations ("This is your handwork") that ignored Teo's insistence on group responsibility. When her answers displeased him, he accused her of not cooperating with the Committee ("you are being difficult"). As the next excerpt demonstrates, the Prime Minister's questions became more and more intimidating and accusatory, all the time targeting Teo for culpability as an individual:

> *PM:* Now you are telling us in the statement that the penalties were not appropriate for the offences created. What do you suggest are the appropriate penalties, because your duty is to assist us? If you say these penalties are not appropriate, what penalties

would be appropriate? Your duty under the Act is to assist, not to oppose. How do you assist us? Tell us, because we would be obliged to you.

TSL: Mr Chairman, I must say that I have forgotten most of the things about this Newspaper and Printing Presses Act. And if Mr Lee wants me to enlighten him or to clarify things –

PM: [interrupting] No. Miss Teo, I am asking you about the document you drafted with your Committee a bare three months ago. And if you withhold information and refuse to answer relevant questions, you know there are penalties. So let us not be difficult?

TSL: I am aware –

PM: [interrupting] I want to know from you now, since you say that these penalties were not appropriate, what would be appropriate?

TSL: Mr Chairman, I am aware that there would be consequences if I do not answer the questions here. But what I am saying is that if Mr Lee wants me to check on that, what is the appropriate punishment, then I need to refer back to the Bill, to the Act itself and to the papers that I have. I just need time. It's not that I want to avoid answering his question.

PM: You need time to look up papers which have the answer or you need time to think up a plausible reply?

TSL: Perhaps if you could furnish me with the Act itself. I –

PM: [interrupting] No. You are the drafter of this document?

TSL: Yes, but I need to know what was the penalty that –

PM: [interrupting].

(*SC Report*, B109, paras. 785–90)

The Prime Minister disbelieved Teo's answers. He cast her replies as attempts to "withhold information" or refusals to answer "relevant questions". When Teo spoke of her need to refer to documents in order to answer his questions, the Prime Minister immediately indicated his distrust and suspicion ("You need time to look up papers which have the answer or you need time to think up a plausible reply?"). The Prime Minister's questions and statements reflected a strong assumption, on the part of the state, of Teo's mala fides. This mala fides is hard to perceive in her answers, suggesting that the state had characterised Teo in certain ways before the Hearings even commenced.

Consistently, throughout the Hearings, associational identity and responsibility were denied by the state. The accusing and intimidating manner in which individual members of the Council were held responsible might arguably be perceived by non-state actors as a 'rule by law' recasting of the 'rule of law' right to associational activity. The constitutional guarantee of the freedom of speech, assembly and association was moulded into a range of illiberal constraints when the state, in its conduct of the Hearings, discursively constructed an atomisation of associational identity.

DEBATE IN THE PUBLIC DOMAIN

One of the criticisms levelled at the government by the Law Society was that the government had not consulted the Law Society on the *Legal Profession (Amendment) Bill*.[152] In general, a consultative process involves two-way communication between government and people. Embedded in this expectation of a communicative exchange is the notion of the right to expression, of the participatory and engaged citizen having a voice and being heard. The assumption is of a listening, concerned government, a representative government that wants to, and must, converse with citizens.

In the Hearings, however, the Singapore state constructed "consultation" rather differently, to mean moments of engagement between the President of the Law Society and the Minister for Law, with the Minister properly discharging his obligation to "consult", first, if the Minister for

152 "Lawyers Want Govt to Hear Their Views Before Passing Bill", *supra* note 123.

Law had been accessible to the President of the Law Society,[153] or second, if copies of bills "affecting the legal profession or affecting other matters which may be of concern to the legal profession" were sent to the President of the Law Society in advance of publication[154] or on the day of their first reading in Parliament.[155] Perhaps most crucially in terms of the civil society ideal of the public domain as a space for the exchange and expression of ideas, the state insisted that by making public statements critical of the *Press Bill*, the Law Society had opposed rather than assisted the government. This state abhorrence of public critique emerged in the Prime Minister's questioning of Harry Elias (HE in the following excerpts), a Council member who had been the immediate past President of the Law Society:

> *PM*: Would you say that the Bar has a unique role to play in the social affairs of Singapore?
> *HE*: I think we have a role to play, a very positive and a contributory role to play, in the social affairs of Singapore. I would give you an illustration.
> *PM*: That it should engage in a public debate with the Government over the Newspaper and Printing Presses (Amendment) Bill?
> *HE*: In a debate, yes, but not public.
> *PM*: And once it became public because the President issued a statement, it must lead to a join-in of issues?
> *HE*: That was not my style, Mr Prime Minister.
> *PM*: Has it been done by any other President?
> *HE*: I don't think it's fair to say that Mr Francis T Seow was the man that joined issue. I think Mr Francis Seow –
> *PM*: [interrupting] No. Mr Elias, before I press you harder, let me remind you that we are here to elucidate issues so that we can come to the right conclusions. And if you take a defensive position

[153] *SC Report on LPA*, *supra* note 114 at paras. 69–70; B24, paras. 320–32; B53 –B54.
[154] Ibid. at B24, para. 70.
[155] Ibid. at B58, para. 359.

or if you feel you have got to defend the Council, and you more and more get into a join-in of issues position, the end-result must be an amendment which is much less sympathetic than what you would have got, wouldn't it? If I felt confidence in the profession and the way it is run by the Council, I would repose a great deal of responsibility on it, wouldn't I? Because I moved from the old Advocate and Solicitors Ordinance to the Legal Profession Act in 1967 when Mr Punch Coomaraswamy was the Speaker and he persuaded me to constitute the Law Society. If I had come to the conclusion that it was wrong, that the Society is incapable of rising up to its responsibilities, I would go back to the old Advocates and Solicitors Ordinance or Act. Right?

HE: That would be from your point of view. Yes, Mr Prime Minister.
PM: Yes. Therefore let me ask again: has any previous President taken on the Government on amending legislation publicly, or have they made their representations as lawyers?
HE: Publicly?
PM: Yes, as lawyers, to the Minister to improve the law?
HE: Publicly. The emphasis is that word.
PM: Yes.
HE: No.
PM: And when the Council takes it on publicly, the Government must reply publicly? Yes?
HE: The meeting of minds, Mr Prime Minister.

(*SC Report*, B37–38, paras. 182–90)

The significance of the Prime Minister's references to the colonial *Advocates and Solicitors' Ordinance* is discussed later. For now, I retain the focus on the state's displeasure with the public nature of the statement, with a further excerpt from the Prime Minister's questioning of Seow. This excerpt shows the Prime Minister again insisting that a public critique was an expression of opposition to the government:

> *PM:* Yes. How does your statement assist the Government and the courts on matters affecting legislation and the administration and practise of law in Singapore?
> *FS:* Well, for one thing it will open your eyes to the error of your ways, if you agree with us. If you don't –
> *PM:* [interrupting] By coming out in a statement in public and not telling the Minister, "Look, if this is what you are going to do, it is not effective. We suggest you consider alternatives." But you went public. How did that assist the Government?
> *FS:* We did write in.
> *PM:* It doesn't say "to oppose the Government". It says "to assist the Government".
> *FS:* Naturally. By publishing this, we had no intention of opposing the Government.
>
> (*SC Report*, B88, paras. 628–30)

The Prime Minister makes it clear that he regards the public expression of a critique as adversarial. He insists that it is *because* the Law Society made a public statement that the Hearings are being conducted in a public and adversarial manner ("when the Council takes it on publicly, the Government must reply publicly"). If the primary breach of the Law Society lies in the public articulation of criticism, the implications for the scope of associational activity and civil society are bleak. When the state's position is that an exchange of views conducted behind closed doors between the Law Society President and the Minister for Law is an acceptable form of "consultation", the state appears to be more concerned about being perceived and presented, in the public domain, as unquestionably and unfailingly "right". There is no public space for the citizenry at large to be part of this "consultation" even when 'law' impacts upon all.[156]

[156] I should, however, note that since 2008 the state has initiated some public consultation on legislation, as is reflected by the Ministry of Law website: http://app2.mlaw.gov.sg/PublicConsultation/ClosedConsultations/tabid/247/Default.aspx. See also note 200 *infra*.

The Prime Minister does not give reasons for his displeasure with the Law Society's efforts to engage in a public 'debate'. The rhetorical framing of the Prime Minister's statements makes them appear to be explanations, but he does not actually present reasons. When the Prime Minister refers to the Law Society's statement as taking the government on, he offers no explanation as to how the statement amounts to a challenge to the government rather than being just a critique of the terms and import of the *Press Bill*.

This cause-and-effect framing of the Prime Minister's assertions can be confusing. When, for example, he says, "[O]nce it became public because the President issued a statement, it must lead to a join-in of issues", the Prime Minister denies the already public nature of debate on the *Press Bill*. In a Westminster-model 'rule of law' system, 'law' is necessarily in the public domain. Parliamentary debates, with the two opposition members in the seventy-seven-seat house criticising the *Press Bill*, were already public. Contrary to the Prime Minister's assertion, the debate did not become public *because* the Law Society President issued a statement. The sense of outrage that informed the Prime Minister's assertions of the Law Society having breached some kind of unwritten code of conduct ("has any previous President taken on the Government on amending legislation publicly?") appears to be outrage at criticism having been expressed in the public domain.

It is stating the obvious to point out that if lawyers are to lead publics towards political liberalism,[157] they must have access to the public domain. But if, in the eyes of the state, critique of a facet of governance is understood as opposition warranting a highly adversarial state response, then lawyers can no longer assume the 'law' of political liberalism[158] in which engaged citizens access the public sphere. It is tempting to disparage the disproportionate and distorting nature of the state's

[157] Karpik, *supra* note 10; Halliday, Karpik & Feeley, *supra* note 4 at at 10–11.

[158] Ibid.

response to public critique from lawyers as brutish authoritarianism, but the Singapore state is not simplistically authoritarian.[159] Instead, I would see the state's fury as symptomatic of its anxiety to protect and perpetuate its reputation as a 'lawful' state. The 'rule of law' assumptions of the Law Society's critique pointed to the impoverishment at the heart of the state's construction of 'law'. It was, I would argue, the basic legal freedoms that the Law Society spoke for that so threatened the Singapore state's legitimacy.

NEO-COLONIALISM IN THE POST-COLONIAL LEADER

In the earlier excerpt of the exchange between the Prime Minister and Elias, the Prime Minister's references to the *Legal Profession Act* and the colonial *Advocates and Solicitors Ordinance*[160] highlight a strong current of neo-colonialism informing the state's attitude towards lawyers. Under British colonial rule, the profession could examine and report upon current or proposed legislation only when such legislation was submitted to it for consideration by the colonial administration. In 1966, a year after Singapore became an independent republic, the *LPA* replaced the colonial *Advocates and Solicitors Ordinance*. Modelled, in part, upon the colonial Ordinance, the national Act empowered the profession to comment on legislation without the need for any initiating reference by the state. It is this crucial difference between the colonial and the national legislative instruments that the Prime Minister appears to be referring to.

[159] See generally references cited in Chapter 1, in the section entitled " 'Rule of Law': Thick, Thin, Dual and Dicey."

[160] Ordinance (No. 32) of 1934. The *Advocates and Solicitors Ordinance* was the result of a rationalisation exercise conducted in 1934 and was derived from the 1907 Courts Ordinance. A. de Mello, "Eastern Colonies: Review of Legislation, 1934, Straits Settlements" (1936) 18:3 3rd Ser. *Journal of Comparative Legislation and International Law* 156.

The *LPA* frames the Law Society's standing to comment on 'law' as one of the "powers and purposes" of the Society. But the Prime Minister recasts this not as a power and purpose but as a privilege that he, as the Prime Minister, has granted and thus might validly revoke:

> PM: [interrupting] No. Mr Elias, before I press you harder, let me remind you that we are here to elucidate issues so that we can come to the right conclusions. And if you take a defensive position or if you feel you have got to defend the Council, and you more and more get into a join-in of issues position, the end-result must be an amendment which is much less sympathetic than what you would have got, wouldn't it? If I felt confidence in the profession and the way it is run by the Council, I would repose a great deal of responsibility on it, wouldn't I? Because I moved from the old Advocate and Solicitors Ordinance to the Legal Profession Act in 1967 when Mr Punch Coomaraswamy was the Speaker and he persuaded me to constitute the Law Society. If I had come to the conclusion that it was wrong, that the Society is incapable of rising up to its responsibilities, I would go back to the old Advocates and Solicitors Ordinance or Act. Right?

In asserting his power to amend the *LPA*, the Prime Minister's stance is that of a knowing leader who makes decisions on the basis of his "confidence" in lawyers, a "confidence" that has to be earned and deserved. The privilege of "responsibilities", responsibilities that were enabled not by the colonial *Advocates and Solicitors Ordinance* but by the national *LPA*, might be revoked by the Prime Minister should he feel the constituting of the Law Society was "wrong" because lawyers were incapable of "rising up" to their responsibilities. (The state's continuing insistence on this restraint upon the Law Society is discussed later). Inherent to the Prime Minister's stance is an assertion of his ascendancy. From his elevated position as the leader who grants privileges, he is positioned to determine whether or not the Law Society has been deserving.

It is striking that the Prime Minister uses 'I' in speaking of the power to decide upon the terms of the *LPA*. It is the 'rule by law' domain of personal relationships, personal discretion, rather than the 'rule of law' space of institutional capacities that is foregrounded when he formulates the history of the *LPA* and the Law Society in terms of his having been persuaded by the then Speaker to constitute the Law Society. The Prime Minister's placing of himself at the centre of the institutions at stake reflects a widely held perception that it is Lee Kuan Yew the individual, with his towering and forceful personality, that *is* the government of Singapore.[161] After all, very few leaders of very few governments can claim to have been in power in both 1963 and 1986 and thus position themselves as central to the process of 'law'-making. And surely, it is this very centrality, this very continuity, that fosters the Singapore model of a consolidated 'rule by law' instrumentalism.

Adding to the authority that already accords to Lee by virtue of his office, his successes, his long leadership and his personality[162] is the augmenting factor of his own membership in the legal profession. Lee explicitly refers to himself either as a lawyer[163] or as an advocate and solicitor,[164] on one occasion saying, "In my knowledge, first, as an advocate and solicitor and second, as Prime Minister".[165]

Lee reminds the Council of his personal path to the profession when his questions and statements convey a confident comparison of the English Bar and the Singapore Bar, on one occasion celebrating the pedigree of his legal education: "Mr Lim, you are not like Miss Teo. You were trained in a very reputable school of law"[166] (and a few moments later), "Let's be honest as one graduate of the Cambridge

161 Ho, *supra* note 136 at 53–54.
162 Ibid. at 92–99.
163 *SC Report on LPA*, *supra* note 114 at B132, para. 952.
164 Ibid. at B134, para. 959.
165 Ibid. at B89, para. 638.
166 Ibid. at B146, para. 1032.

Law School to another".[167] The disparaging of Teo's National University of Singapore legal education and the exalting of his and Lim's Cambridge degrees encapsulate an interesting conflict that marks different moments of Lee's assertions in the Hearings. At different points, and to different ends, Lee alternates between nationalist expressions of necessary distinctions from British legal practices, and yet, as in this moment of disparagement of a National University of Singapore legal education, there is a persistent admiration for British institutions and ideologies.

MODES OF SILENCING: DETENTION WITHOUT TRIAL

I opened this case study by arguing that lawyers in Singapore are caught between their everyday knowledge, as citizens, of a certain susceptibility of 'law' to power and their professional knowledge of the 'rule of law' ideals that inform the declared structures of the nation-state. In the course of the Hearings, it was perhaps Council member Teo Soh Lung who most embodied this conflicted position. She argued for the supremacy of the *Constitution*;[168] resolutely addressed the Chair of the Hearings, invoking the intended and expected powers the Chair was meant to be wielding that Lee had usurped and violated; and highlighted the breach manifested by state surveillance:

> *PM*: I just want to take you through your speech at this EGM ... [T]hese are not legal arguments, this is agitprop. Read your first paragraph ...
> *TSL*: Mr Chairman, can I ask a question? This speech appears to have been a transcript of what I said at the EGM. And I would like to know how this managed to get into the hands of Mr Lee.

[167] Ibid. at B148, para. 1041.
[168] Ibid. at B127–34, paras. 906–60.

PM: In the age of the tape recorder, you want to know how I am able to get a transcript of what you said?
TSL: But how did the tape recorder get into the EGM room?
PM: I am not interested, Miss Teo. I am interested in taking you through what you said. I didn't make the speech. You did. If you didn't make the speech – ?
TSL: I am not denying making the speech.
PM: Let's go through it.
TSL: But I would like to know how that ...
PM: How was I given the speech? By the Ministry of Law.
TSL: So the Minister for Law had set a tape recorder in the room?
PM: Yes please. I assume that.[169]

The Hearings were consistently marked by a sub-text of state surveillance, in, for example, the state's command of the details of Seow's personal financial affairs, and yet Teo, alert to the assumptions of rights discourse and the 'rule of law', was equipped (perhaps by her National University of Singapore Law degree), despite the extremely intimidating and aggressive questioning she was subjected to, to highlight the violation represented by the transcript in her hands. Teo's faith in the operation of the 'rule of law' in Singapore was perhaps most poignantly captured by the habeas corpus proceedings to which she was party.

Eight months after the Hearings, in May 1987, Teo found herself among sixteen individuals who were rounded up and detained without trial under the *Internal Security Act*.[170] The sixteen were accused of being part of a Marxist conspiracy to overthrow the state. During 1987 and 1988, a total of twenty-two people were accused of being part of this "Marxist conspiracy" and were detained without trial. In brief, the state's position was that the individuals it arrested and detained had been part of an international conspiracy, based in London, to overthrow the government and establish a Communist state.

[169] Ibid. at B154, paras. 1087–92.
[170] Tan Jing Quee, Teo Soh Lung & Koh Kay Yew, eds., *Our Thoughts Are Free: Poems and Prose on Imprisonment and Exile* (Singapore: Ethos, 2009) 140.

At the time, media coverage of the event, a major event on the Singapore political scene, did not reflect the general disbelief with which the announcements of the "conspiracy" were met. With the passage of time, however, a muted rejection of the state's version of events began to surface in the media,[171] and in a July 2007 feature article marking twenty years since the first round of arrests, the major English-language daily, the *Straits Times*, a newspaper whose output is generally viewed as conservative, wrote:

> Although the Government described its swoop as anti-Marxist, many critics read it as a much broader clampdown on political activism – and therefore as relevant today as it was 20 years ago.... [Some] portray the Marxist spectre as a 'bogyman' conjured up to justify crushing any potential political challenge.... Since many civil society types saw the detainees as fired-up do-gooders ... the arrests were interpreted by critics as a warning against activism of any kind.[172]

Apart from Teo, who was detained in May 1987, another Council member, Tang Fong Har, was among those rounded up in June 1987. They were conditionally released in April 1988 after having made televised confessions confirming the state's version of events. Shortly after this conditional release, some of them, including Teo and Tang, made a joint press statement, denying their participation in a "Marxist conspiracy", asserting that what they had been doing was "advocat[ing] more democracy, less elitism, protection of individual freedoms and civil rights, greater concern

[171] See "A Giant of Singapore's Legal History", *Straits Times* (6 June 2005), which refers to "the so-called Marxist conspiracy". See also Cherian George, "The Cause Celebre of the Chattering Classes", *Straits Times* (29 December 1999), in which the reference is to the "Marxist conspiracy". Most significantly, though, is the 2001 report of an interview with Tharman Shanmugaratnam. Shanmugaratnam is, at present, a Singapore cabinet minister. In 1987 he was among those under suspicion and questioned by the Internal Security Department. In an interview given to the Singapore press, he is described as still disagreeing publicly with the arrests of some friends at the time, saying, "Although I had no access to state intelligence, from what I knew of them, most were social activists but not out to subvert the system"; Susan Long, 'Been There, Done That, and Thrived', *Straits Times* (14 December 2001).

[172] Lydia Lim, "20 Years On: Impact of Marxist Plot on S'pore", *Straits Times* (7 July 2007).

for the poor and the less privileged and less interference in the private lives of citizens".[173] They were re-detained almost immediately after making this statement.

Tang was out of the country and so escaped re-arrest. Teo was among those re-arrested. Patrick Seong had acted as counsel for some of the detainees who made the press statement. He had also been a sub-committee member of the Law Society 1986 Council. He was detained in April 1988 because "surveillance showed that he had egged on and brought about the publication of the joint statement".[174]

Seow, by then no longer President of the Law Society,[175] was detained in May 1988 after appearing before the High Court for two of the detainees in habeas corpus proceedings. The government said Seow had been collaborating with an American Embassy official to facilitate US interference in Singapore's domestic politics.[176] With Seow's detention, a total of four Law Society Council members had been detained without trial in the eighteen months or so following the pedagogical exercise of the Hearings. Perhaps the detentions were designed to further instruct lawyers, and all citizens, on how completely the state might silence voices that questioned its formulations of 'law'. Read together with the history of state actions

173 Ibid.

174 Sing., *Parliamentary Debates*, vol. 51, col. 326 (1 June 1988) (Prime Minister Lee Kuan Yew).

175 Seow was disqualified from the presidency in November 1986 when the 1986 amendments to the *LPA*, disqualifying advocates and solicitors who had been suspended for six months or more from holding office in the Council, came into effect. It is hard not to see that amendment as targeting Seow. Indeed, in the course of the Hearings, Lee Kuan Yew intimated that this new disqualification had been formulated specifically to prevent Seow from holding office. *SC Report on LPA*, *supra* note 114 at A4 (for the Law Society's memorandum on the amendments) and B65 (for Lee's statements).

176 See, generally, Sing., *Parliamentary Debates*, vol. 51, cols. 307–53 (1 June 1988). Seow had declared his intention to contest the 1988 general elections and was released in July, after having been detained almost four months, in order to participate in the elections. On 17 August, a week before Nomination Day and nine days before Polling Day, the press reported that Seow was to be charged with six counts of tax evasion. He lost the seat in a very close contest. Seow left Singapore before the tax evasions were tried and placed himself in exile, writing from his position as a Fellow at Harvard.

against lawyers in the 1970s, it is as if a new generation of lawyers needed to be instructed through the exemplary punishment of a few on the state's sub-textual determinations of 'law' and public discourse.

If lawyers constitute themselves as spokespersons by, in part, constructing the 'publics' they speak for,[177] the 'rule of law' assumptions of the Law Society's critique suggests that they imagined their 'publics' as empowered and rights-bearing citizens of a 'rule of law' nation. But a very different state–citizen relationship is suggested by two features of the Hearings: first, the state's outrage at the Law Society's having made a public statement; and second, the fact that this was the first public statement ever made by the Law Society.[178] By making a press statement critiquing a proposed 'law', the Law Society breached the everyday practice of citizen acquiescence inherent in the state's dominance of the public domain. State dominance, after all, requires citizen subordination.

As a form of public pedagogy, the Hearings serve to repair the Law Society's infringement of the unwritten rules of state–citizen engagement. The state's hostile and intimidating dominance, established through the Hearings, rendered the Law Society Council necessarily and inherently subordinate to the Select Committee. The assumption underpinning the Law Society's critique of the 'foreign press' amendment was of a participative and engaged citizenry entitled to articulate views in the public domain. This assumption was inconsistent with the state's sometimes explicit, sometimes sub-textual script of a hierarchy in which the citizen is always subordinate and silent, in a decorous acquiescence to state authority.

A LOST MOMENT FOR THE LEGAL COMPLEX

In the Halliday, Karpik and Feeley studies on the relationship between legal professions and political liberalism,[179] alliances between different

[177] Karpik, *supra* note 10.

[178] As noted earlier, in 1969 the Law Society was thwarted in its attempt to make a public statement.

[179] Halliday, Karpik & Feeley, *supra* note 10.

branches of the legal professions have been shown to be particularly powerful in effecting the defence of basic legal freedoms against the executive.[180] Their concept of the legal complex captures this network of legal professions, such that lawyers and the judiciary, for example, might come together when mobilising on behalf of rights.[181] This chapter has already shown how the early 1970s featured an atomised legal complex in the moments when courts aligned with the state in punishing, so to speak, lawyers who represented political prisoners. In the late 1980s, the habeas corpus applications made by Teo and others showed a momentary promise of Singapore's Bench and Bar coming together to protect basic rights.

Teo had consistently denied any involvement in a Marxist plot. In her written representations to the advisory board constituted to review detention orders, she asserted her innocence and claimed that she had been legitimately exercising her civil and political rights, saying that she believed her arrest and detention might have been intended to prevent her from participating in politics.[182] Habeas corpus proceedings brought by Teo and some others[183] were unsuccessful until the landmark decision[184] of *Chng*,[185] by which the Court of Appeal delivered its decision jointly on four appeals, including Teo's. The Court of Appeal quashed the detention orders speaking for the 'rule of law':

[180] Ibid.

[181] Ibid.

[182] *Teo Soh Lung v. Minister of Home Affairs & Ors* [1988] I Sing. L. R. 679 (H.C.).

[183] *De Souza Kevin Desmond & Ors. v. Minister of Home Affairs & Ors.* [1988] 1 Sing. L.R. 517.

[184] Li-ann Thio, "Trends in Constitutional Interpretation: Oppugning Ong, Awakening Arumugam?" (1997) *S.J.L.S.* 240–90 [*Trends in Constitutional Interpretation*]. Michael Hor has described *Chng* as "perhaps the single most important constitutional decision in the history of the nation"; Michael Hor, "Law and Terror: Singapore Stories and Malaysian Dilemmas", in Michael Hor, Victor Ramraj & Kent Roach eds., *Global Anti-Terrorism Law and Policy* (Cambridge: Cambridge University Press, 2005) 273, 281.

[185] *Chng Suan Tze v. Minister of Home Affairs & Ors. and Other Appeals* [1988] 1 Sing. L. R. 132 (C.A.) [*Chng*]; *Teo Soh Lung v. Minister For Home Affairs & Ors.* [1989] 1 Sing. L. R. 499 (H.C.); *Teo Soh Lung v. Minister For Home Affairs* [1990] 2 M.L.J. 129 (Sing. C.A).

> In our view, the notion of a subjective or unfettered discretion is contrary to the rule of law. All power has legal limits and the rule of law demands that the courts should be able to examine the exercise of discretionary power.[186]

The Court's words hold the promise of a collaborative legal complex mobilisation, of judges uniting with lawyers to assert the 'rule of law' in the face of 'rule by law' state practices. Unfortunately, despite a robust judgment, the Court found the detention order flawed in a manner that was easily remedied administratively. Teo found herself presented with a new detention order even as she was being driven out of the detention centre.

Teo's release and re-detention occurred on 8 December 1988. Teo commenced fresh proceedings for a writ of habeas corpus on 13 December 1988. On 16 December, two amendment bills were presented to Parliament – one to amend the *Constitution*, another to amend the *Internal Security Act*. The bills were speedily passed on 25 January 1989 and gazetted into effect by 28 January.[187] These two amendments barred judicial review of internal security detentions on substantive grounds, limited review to the very narrow issue of procedural compliance and barred appeals to the Privy Council.[188]

When Teo initiated a new round of habeas corpus proceedings, her counsel argued that the amendments had the effect of depriving Teo of the right to effective judicial review of the legality, rationality and constitutionality of her detention and were therefore void because contrary to the supreme law of the *Constitution* and (given the time frame within which they were passed) in violation of the constitutional guarantee of equality before the law. The court rejected this argument.

[186] *Chng*, *supra* note 187 at para. 156.

[187] *Teo Soh Lung v. Minister For Home Affairs* [1990] 2 M.L.J. 129 (Sing. C.A) para. 3 [*Teo Soh Lung 1990*].

[188] This was the first step in removing the Privy Council from the hierarchy of Singapore courts.

Instead, it "adopted an anaemic, positivist conception of the rule of law",[189] holding:

> It is erroneous to contend that the rule of law has been abolished by legislation and that Parliament has stated its absolute and conclusive judgment in applications for judicial review or other actions. Parliament has done no more that to enact the rule of law relating to the law applicable to judicial review.[190]

The decision has been described as conceiving of 'law' as entirely within Parliament's hands and denying the role of the courts in policing, so to speak, the content of 'law' – thereby rendering irrelevant the status of the *Constitution* as the legal text that sets substantive standards.[191] Teo's application failed, both at the High Court and at the Court of Appeal.[192]

If the Hearings were one mode of silencing advocacy for the 'rule of law', the detentions were undoubtedly an even more effective imposition of silence. Detaining Teo and others under the *Internal Security Act* removed the possibility of the public advocacy of a trial. Without a trial, a counter-narrative could not emerge. The hurried amendments to the *Constitution* and the *Internal Security Act* removed substantive judicial review, thereby silencing the one remaining forum for a challenge to the state's narrative of events. A counter-narrative had become almost completely impossible.

HISTORY REPEATS ITSELF: ALARMING CONTINUITIES, REVEALING DIFFERENCES

There are three firsts attendant upon the events this case study describes: the first public critique of the state by lawyers in their associational

[189] Thio, *Trends in Constitutional Interpretation*, *supra* note 186, 244.
[190] *Teo Soh Lung 1990*, *supra* note 189.
[191] Thio, *Trends in Constitutional Interpretation*, *supra* note 186, 244.
[192] *Teo Soh Lung 1990*, *supra* note 189.

identity; the first transformation of Select Committee Hearings into a quasi-courtroom; and the first televising of Select Committee Hearings. But there are also important ways in which these events reprise an earlier history relating to the 1969 Select Committee hearings on the amendments to the *Criminal Procedure Code* to abolish jury trials.

Just as we have seen with the 1986 Hearings, the 1969 sessions between the Select Committee and the Council were dominated by Lee Kuan Yew. In the process, Lee generated most of the text, using questions as platforms to express opinions and accusations. At both times, the associational identity of the Law Society's Council was not recognised. At both times, Lee's adversarial style of questioning involved the rhetorical strategies of frequent interruption and the posing of questions that compounded assumptions and accusations. Just as Lee accused Teo of "politicking" in 1986, in 1969 he repeatedly accused Marshall of "politicking". Just as Lee disparaged Teo, Seow and others in 1986, in 1969 he disparaged Marshall. Just as Lee threatened the 1986 Council with a loss of powers to review proposed legislation, in 1969 Lee too referred to reservations he had about powers granted to the Council, by implication threatening their removal – a removal he ironically effected in 1986. Lee's 1969 questions also conveyed a level of surveillance over Marshall. In 1986 surveillance was an even stronger feature of the Hearings. Just as in 1969 Lee appropriated the Hearings on the *Criminal Procedure Code* to question the Council on a range of other matters, so too in 1986 Lee did not limit himself to the bill before the Committee.

The differences that emerge between the two hearings are also significant. In 1969 the Council was less intimidated by Lee, more capable of holding its ground and articulating its 'rule of law' views and responses. In 1969 the Chairman of the proceedings reined Lee in, asking that he limit his questions to the Bill before the Committee.[193] And in 1969, when Lee persisted in presenting the 'administration of justice' as a field of activity apart from 'politics', the Council was able to assert the essentially political

[193] *CPC Report*, *supra* note 28 para 660.

nature of the administration of justice.[194] In short, the 1969 Council was less intimidated and more fluent in its rights discourse. It is as if, in the course of the seventeen years between the two hearings, Singapore lawyers lost some of their capacity to speak to their Prime Minister without fear and to constitute themselves as spokespersons for the 'rule of law'. The Council of 1969 was less intimidated, more articulate, more versed in the 'rule of law'. In 1969 detentions without trial of lawyers had yet to take place. In 1969 the disciplinary suspensions of lawyers acting for political opponents of the state had yet to take place. In contrast to the situation in 1969, in 1986 'rule by law' had become more entrenched.

Chapter 4 has described how, in 1971, three newspapers that had in different ways articulated critiques of the state were shut down by the state. At the time, the state conveyed the legitimacy of its dealings with these three newspapers through a range of performative and staged declarations of its bona fides. For example, the state "staged"[195] a press conference at which a much younger Prime Minister Lee Kuan Yew interrogated the bankers, editor and managing director of a newspaper he accused of being fronts for hostile foreign interests.[196] The state's narrative then, as it was fifteen years later when dealing with the Council, was that it was acting to protect the 'nation'. The significant continuity between the 1971 silencing of a feisty press and the 1986 silencing of lawyers is that the state used the public domain to enact the state's capacity to impose its interpretations upon non-state actors. At both times, the state insisted that the contesting voices belonged to 'fronts' for hidden 'Communist' (1971) or 'Marxist' (1986) threats. The further important commonality between the two moments is that the state's discursive dominance was underpinned by its turn to coercion. At both times, the spokespersons (for different 'politics' and different publics) were detained without trial.

[194] Ibid. *at* paras. 671–72.

[195] Seow, *supra* note 23 at 66.

[196] Ibid.

LAWYERS IN A DUAL STATE: NO 'PUBLICS', NO 'POLITICS'

The events described in this case study illustrate an instrumentalist appropriation of legal proceedings and the subject of 'law' to effect public instruction designed to prevent lawyers from becoming spokespersons for political liberalism. The manipulation of 'law' by power made it possible for the Hearings, an ostensibly 'rule of law' event, to become a pedagogical exercise. The state used prosecutorial techniques and procedures – oaths, subpoenas, cross-examination – in tandem with strategies of narrative dominance – interruption, repetition, characterisations – to transform the Hearings into an instruction on the state's definitions of the limits of 'law' and of lawyers' public advocacy. In the process, the Singapore state enacted its paternalism, forcefully asserting its superior knowledge and insights. And in selectively celebrating things English while selectively disparaging things Singaporean, the ambivalent post-colonialism of the state was revealed. All in all, 'law' was redefined during the Hearings as a positivist expression of the state's will that was not to be questioned.

If lawyers educated in the traditions and ideals of the 'common law' have the rights-literacy and the professional imperative to become spokespersons for the 'rule of law', then the events of 1986 demonstrate how a hegemonic dual state effects three outcomes: first, the dismantling of legal professional autonomy; second, the unilateral designation of 'politics' as a subject outside the valid concern of lawyers; and third, the demarcation of the public domain as a space for state dominance that mutes lawyers' critique of state formulations of 'law'. If the state became instructor, it was not just the Council that was meant to be re-educated. The discrediting and disempowerment of the Council instructed all citizens (but perhaps especially citizen-lawyers) on the way in which the ambivalent spaces of 'law' were available to the state to define and demarcate. The Hearings reinforced the lawfulness of the state without granting legitimising space to the Law Society's criticism. In other words, the Hearings demonstrated that the limits of 'law' were contained not within the text and underlying ideals of the *Legal Profession Act* and the *Constitution*, but in discourse: in the state's power to characterise, interpret and insist.

For almost twenty years after the Hearings, the Law Society of Singapore stayed out of the public domain. It made no public statements on legislation formulated in opaque language and, publicly at least, questioned no *Internal Security Act* detentions. The Law Society's recent statements on the mandatory death penalty and the decriminalisation of homosexuality[197] might be read as carefully calibrated to maintain the Society's liminal and uncertain space.[198] If the Hearings were, in part, an instruction, then its lessons had surely been learnt.

In October 2007, the International Bar Association held its annual conference in Singapore, as I noted in Chapter 1. Lee gave a keynote address at the conference, citing Singapore's high rankings in rule of law and governance indicators as proof of the existence of the rule of law in Singapore. The state capitalised upon the IBA's selection of Singapore as a conference venue to assert that even the IBA acknowledged Singapore's 'rule of law' legitimacy.[199] In July 2008, however, the IBA's Human Rights Institute (Ibahri) released a report (referred to here as the Ibahri Report) on Singapore critiquing the Singapore state's continued repression of individual rights, lamenting the passivity of the Law Society when it came to issues of law reform and recommending that the government immediately repeal the prohibition of the Law Society's commenting on legislation.[200] What is most striking about the exchange between the state

197 K. C. Vijayan, "Law Society Call for Decriminalisation of Homosexuality", *Straits Times* (5 April 2007).

198 These statements were made before the Ministry of Law instituted a public consultation process. The official public consultation process appears to have been initiated in 2008 and is a welcome development, but it does not seem to have altered the unspoken understanding that the Law Society must not critique the state.

199 Lee Kuan Yew, "Why Singapore Is What It Is", *Straits Times* (15 October 2007); Rachel Evans, "Singapore Leader Rejects Amnesty", *International Financial Law Review* (18 October 2007), online: <http://www.iflr.com/Article/1983342/Singapore-leader-rejects-Amnesty.html>.

200 Ibahri, "Prosperity Versus Individual Rights? Human Rights, Democracy and the Rule of Law in Singapore" July 2008 [*Ibahri Report*].

and the Law Society that followed is that the Law Society, like a child that had learnt its lesson, asked for the prohibition to be lifted, then indicated its acquiescence to the state's stern refusal.[201] This compliance suggests that the Law Society had reconfigured its own understanding of 'law' such that the rights-bearing citizen had become suitably subordinate.

Responding to the Ibahri Report, both the state and the Law Society disclosed that the state had engaged the Society on issues related to 'law' and legislation, but quietly, outside the public domain,[202] indicating another way in which the Law Society had learnt its lesson, so to speak. However, in tandem with its performance of obedient, citizen subordination, the Law Society has nonetheless incrementally pushed the boundaries excluding it from the public sphere. In 2008, for example, it launched a public lecture series on public law, urging Singapore lawyers to become less apathetic about human rights.[203] The Society has also deplored the lack of a principled and transparent penal policy and called for a review of policy on crime and punishment in Singapore.[204] And in September 2009, more than a year after the Ibahri Report was released, the President of the Law Society revived the issue of the Society's role in speaking for 'law' reform.[205] Again it was rebuffed, and again it acquiesced. But crucially, the performance of permission-seeking and of an unyielding state refusal[206] revitalises the issue of the Singapore Law Society's emasculation and

[201] "We Don't Tango with the Govt: Michael Hwang", *Straits Times* (25 July 2008); Clarissa Oon, "Law Society Head Revives Issue of Role in Reform", *Straits Times* (13 September 2009).

[202] Zakir Hussain, "No Change to Act Governing Law Society", *Straits Times* (14 July 2008). The Ministry of Home Affairs had indicated some months earlier that it had accommodated the Law Society's requests for extensions on deadlines for feedback on proposed amendments to the *Penal Code*: Natalie Soh, "Big Changes to Penal Code to Reflect Crime's Changing Nature", *Straits Times* (18 September 2007).

[203] "The Law Society President Says Lawyers Apathetic About Public Law", *Straits Times* (18 March 2008). A series of three public lectures on International Law and Human Rights were delivered by Professor Li-ann Thio in December 2008.

[204] Aaron Low, "Penal System Works", *Straits Times* (19 January 2009).

[205] Oon, *supra* note 203.

[206] Ibid.

returns to the public domain the issue of how Singapore's Law Society is constrained in ways its counterparts in other jurisdictions are not.[207]

To retain my metaphor of a parent–child dynamic in the state–Law Society interactions, the public law series of public lectures, the call for penal policy review and the periodic references to Ibahri's critique suggest that the Law Society's apparent compliance is punctuated by moments of adolescent-like subversion and rebellion. Inherent to this strategy of a piecemeal and tentative testing of boundaries, however, is the Society's acceptance of the state's appropriation of the role of exclusive spokesperson for Singapore 'law'. If the Law Society, a social actor with the authority and the capacity to speak on 'law' in the public domain, remains (mostly) silent, then the state has managed to make complicit a major social actor with the rights-literacy and authority to challenge the state's 'rule by law' formulations. The opportunities for 'rule of law' interpretations to emerge in the public domain, interpretations that might lead other citizens to grasp their 'rule of law' status and rights, have thus diminished. As a result, the state has consolidated its management of the ambivalence of 'law' to its advantage, maintaining its discursive claims to legitimacy through the silence of complicit citizens. Until it receives permission to do so, the Law Society of Singapore therefore seems unlikely to autonomously, publically and consistently speak for the political liberalism inherent to the 'rule of law'.

[207] A telling comparison was made in January 2009 by Philip Jeyaretnam once he had stepped down from the presidency of the Law Society. Addressing Singapore's Institute of Policy Studies at its annual flagship conference, Jeyaretnam spoke on the problematic perception of the legal profession's lack of independence from the state. He called for the removal of restrictions on the Law Society's power to comment on law and noted that while China had abolished the practice of placing state-appointed lawyers on committees leading the Bar, the Singapore government still appointed officeholders to the Singapore Law Society's Executive Committee; online: http://theonlinecitizen.com/2009/01/philip-jeyaretnam-remove-perception-of-government-intervention-in-legal-profession/.

6 POLICING RELIGION

Maintenance of Religious Harmony Act

THIS CHAPTER PRESENTS A STUDY OF THE *Maintenance of Religious Harmony Act* (or *Religious Harmony Act*).[1] The *Religious Harmony Act*, formulated as part of the state's response to the so-called Marxist conspiracy, became a platform for the state's discursive construction of 'religion' as a national security issue, such that 'religion' (like 'vandalism', the press and lawyers speaking on 'law') became a category of threatening activity requiring anticipatory and preventative action by the state. Just as the state's response to lawyers in 1986 might be seen as an effort to dismantle an embryonic civil society leadership attaching to lawyers, so too the *Religious Harmony Act* might be seen as repressing another potential civil society leader: the Catholic Church. This was, after all, the period of the late 1980s, when the Catholic Church had already played a prominent role in the 'people's power' movement that forced Marcos to step down in the Philippines.

In Singapore, the 1980s saw activists from the Catholic Church critiquing the state in terms of its failure to deliver rights and prosperity to an underclass unable to advocate for itself. The state responded to this critique as it had to the Barisan in 1966, the Chinese press in 1971 and the 'foreign press' and the Law Society in 1986: It characterised the critics as threats to national security, silenced them and passed a 'law' legitimising

[1] Cap. 167A, 2001 Rev. Ed. Sing. [*Religious Harmony Act*].

the state's positions. The 1991[2] *Religious Harmony Act* became the silencing 'law' that built upon the coercion of detaining certain Catholic social activists under the *Internal Security Act*[3] between 1987 and 1990. Before presenting an analysis of the terms of the *Religious Harmony Act*, the question that must be addressed is, what are the conditions that make a 'law' on religious harmony possible in the first place?

LINEAR CHRONOLOGIES AND RECURSIVE DISCOURSE

In Chapter 1, I discussed an excerpt from the 1965 address of Singapore's first Head of State on the occasion of the opening of the first Parliament of the new Republic of Singapore. In this speech, the state highlighted the vulnerability of the 'nation' to 'Communism' and 'Communalism' and presented the secular, rational nation-state as the antidote to dangerous irrationalities of 'race' and 'religion'.[4] Many of the themes of this 1965 text on the precarious nature of Singapore's existence have remained central to the state's self-description. For example, in 1971 the detained executives of the 'Chinese'-medium newspaper, the *Nanyang Siang Pau* were accused of "glamourising communism and stirring up communal and chauvinistic sentiments over Chinese language",[5] thereby threatening the 'nation'. The 1987–88 detentions of lawyers accused of being "Marxist

[2] While the possibility of legislation along the lines of the *Religious Harmony Act* was raised by Lee Kuan Yew as early 1987 (Joseph B. Tamney, *The Struggle over Singapore's Soul: Western Modernization and Asian Culture* [Berlin: Walter de Gruyter, 1996] at 32) with the presidential speech at the opening of Parliament in 1989, and a 1989 parliamentary White Paper echoeing Lee's 1987 statements, the Bill was not introduced to Parliament until 1990 and the Act was not brought into effect until 1991. It is tempting to speculate that, in the interim, the state was securing the co-operation of religious groups and organisations so as to minimise opposition at the time of the parliamentary debates.

[3] Cap. 143, 1985 Rev. Ed. Sing. [*ISA*].

[4] Sing., *Parliamentary Debates*, vol. 24, cols. 5–14 (8 December 1965) (Yang Di-Pertuan Negara Encik Yusof Ishak) [1965 Presidential Address].

[5] *Lee Mau Seng v. Minister for Home Affairs, Singapore & Anor.* [1969–1971] Sing.L.R. 508 at 511.

conspirators" illustrates how the term 'Communist' became revitalised in a world on the cusp of the fall of the Berlin Wall. The legitimising rationales for the *Press Act* (both in 1974 and 1986) and the 1994 state account of the Michael Fay case have also illustrated the way 'nation' as a category has been enmeshed with 'race' in constructing the 'West' as endangering Singapore. When it comes to the category 'religion', however, it is the *Religious Harmony Act* which illustrates the state's legislative and discursive formulations of how these twin threats ('Communalism' and 'Communism') endanger the 'nation'.

Thirty-four years after the 1965 presidential address, in 1989, again on the occasion of the opening of Parliament, a different Head of State delivered a different address. Significantly, the Prime Minister leading the 1989 government, Lee Kuan Yew, was the same Prime Minister who had led the government of 1965. This 1989 address upon the opening of Parliament echoed the 1965 formulations of 'nation' and religion under the heading "A Multi-Religious Society":

> *Religious Tolerance and Moderation.* Religious harmony is as important to us as racial harmony. Singapore is a secular state, and the supreme source of political authority is the *Constitution*. The *Constitution* guarantees freedom of religion. However, in Singapore racial distinctions accentuate religious ones. Religious polarisation will cause sectarian strife. We can only enjoy harmonious and easy racial relationships if we practise religious tolerance and moderation.
>
> *Religion and Politics.* Religious organisations have always done educational, social and charitable work. In doing so, they have contributed much to our society and nation. However, they must not stray beyond these bounds, for example by venturing into radical social action. Religion must be kept rigorously separate from politics.
>
> Religious groups must not get themselves involved in the political process. Conversely, no group can be allowed to exploit religious issues or manipulate religious organisations, whether to excite disaffection or to win political support. It does not matter if the purpose of these actions is to achieve religious ideals or to promote secular objectives. In a multi-religious society, if one group violates this taboo, others will follow suit, and the outcome will be militancy and conflict.

> We will spell out these ground-rules clearly and unequivocally. All political and religious groups must understand these ground-rules, and abide by them scrupulously. If we violate them, even with the best intentions, our political stability will be imperilled.[6]

In 1989, as in 1965, the state explicitly presents itself as "secular". The groundwork for the *Religious Harmony Act* is laid, in part, by invoking the rationality and modernity of a secularism that enables the solution to a national problem (religious intolerance) in a national law (the *Religious Harmony Act*). In this assertion that religious harmony is as important as racial harmony, 'race' and 'religion' are explicitly constructed as entwined. In the state's construction of these social categories, 'religion' and 'race' are always about potential "polarisation", which is the definite cause of "sectarian strife". Embedded in the bundle of meanings carried by 'religion' is the way in which 'religion' is about the security of the 'nation'. Contextually, therefore, Singapore has been consistently and recursively primed for a certain sort of attention to 'religion'. 'Religion' has been repeatedly associated with the potential to generate violence that imperils political stability, a potential violence that only the secular, rational state can hold at bay.[7]

The state's use of discourse to construct its authoritative ascendancy has already been noted through an analysis of state discourse in the first three case studies of this project. This 1989 excerpt from the President's

[6] Sing., *Parliamentary Debates*, vol. 52. cols. 16–20 (9 January 1989) (President Wee Kim Wee) [1989 Presidential Address].

[7] See Tong Chee Kiong, *Rationalising Religion: Religious Conversion, Revivalism and Competition in Singapore Society* (Leiden: Brill, 2007). Also of interest is the sudden increase in state-commissioned scholarly work on 'religion' in the period 1988–89: Eddie Kuo, Jon Quah & Tong Chee Kiong, *Religion and Religious Revivalism in Singapore* (Singapore: Ministry of Community Development, 1989); Eddie Kuo, *Religion in Singapore: An Analysis of the 1980 Census Data* (Singapore: Ministry of Community Development, 1989); Eddie Kuo, Jon Quah & Tong Chee Kiong, *Religion in Singapore: Report of a National Survey* (Singapore: Ministry of Community Development, 1989); Jon Quah, *Religion and Religious Conversion in Singapore: A Review of the Literature* (Singapore: Ministry of Community Development, 1989). This surge in state-commissioned literature has been highlighted by Tamney, *supra* note 2.

address illustrates some of the ways in which the state reiterates its authority. There is, for example, the frequent use of imperatives ("[T]hey *must not* stray beyond these bounds; Religion *must* be kept rigorously separate from politics; Religious groups *must not* get themselves involved in the political process") and confident assertions of the future that allow no room for uncertain outcomes or the questioning of state power ("[I]f one group violates this taboo, others will follow suit, and the outcome will be militancy and conflict; If we violate them ... our political stability will be imperilled"). These textual strategies cast the state-author as almost omniscient. The future is not acknowledged as unknowable. Instead, the state's expert knowledge from handling the 'nation' in the past is written into the state's certainty in predicting future outcomes. These outcomes are almost always constructed as destructive to the 'nation' unless the state exercises its authority in preventative action.

Perhaps the most significant way in which this excerpt constructs authority, however, lies in the state's construction of itself as secular, rational and modern. 'Religion' is framed as a counter-national, counter-modern force, requiring the containment of the secular rationality represented by 'law'. In the 1989 reference to the *Constitution* as "the supreme source of political authority", the secularism of the state is anchored and the role of 'law' is elevated. The crucial qualification to the constitutional guarantee of the freedom of religion is supplied by the contrast marker 'however' ("The *Constitution* guarantees freedom of religion. *However*, in Singapore racial distinctions accentuate religious ones"). This contrast marker indicates that freedom of religion must be curtailed because of Singapore's peculiarities of 'race' and 'religion'.[8] The imperative 'must'

[8] The extent to which 'race' and 'religion' remain features of the discourse of Singapore exceptionalism was signalled in November 2010 when the Minister for Law invoked these markers of difference to justify constraining press freedom. When the moderator pointed out that the United States, Canada, the United Kingdom, New Zealand, France, Ireland, Spain and much of Eastern Europe are also racially and ethnically plural, the Minister's response was to reiterate that Singapore's survival was precarious and differences of 'race' and 'religion' lent themselves to violence: Inaugural Forum, "A Free Press for a Global Society", at Columbia University, New York, Question and Answer

that frames the permissible ("[T]hey *must not* stray beyond these bounds, for example by venturing into radical social action") delineates a boundary of the acceptable ("educational, social and charitable work") and the unacceptable ("radical social action"). There is no explanation of how and when the acceptable, nation-building "educational, social and charitable work" becomes the unacceptable, nation-destabilising "radical social action"; but the very assured and authoritative way in which this assertion is made communicates the state's authority to unilaterally demarcate these boundaries.

THE AUTHORITY TO DETERMINE INTENTION

Just as the exceptional vulnerability of the 'nation' is used to explain Singaporean limits on the freedom of religion, so exception, framed as a response to the pragmatics of a plural population, is used to explain the irrelevance of intention:

> [N]o group can be allowed to exploit religious issues or manipulate religious organisations. It does not matter if the purpose of these actions is to achieve religious ideals or to promote secular objectives. In a multi-religious society, if one group violates this taboo, others will follow suit, and the outcome will be militancy and conflict.

In other words, intention cannot be relevant when the security of the state is at risk, when it is the violence inherent to 'religion-race' that must be contained. In this project's excavation of legislative retractions of 'rule of law' rights, this seeming reason for the obliteration of intention is more significant than the presidential address acknowledges. Embedded in this declaration, "It does not matter if the purpose of these actions is to achieve religious ideals or to promote secular objectives" lies the

Session with Minister for Home Affairs and Minister for Law, Mr K. Shanmugam and Moderator Prof. Frederick Schauer, Distinguished Professor of Law, University of Virginia Law School; transcript available at http://app2.mlaw.gov.sg/News/tabid/204/Default.aspx?ctgy=Transcripts [Transcript from Free Press Session].

contradiction of a fundamental principle of criminal law[9] requiring that both action and intention be proven in order to find guilt. Giving relevance to the intention of a social actor involves giving voice to that actor. By erasing individual intention as legally meaningful, the space for a non-state voice is closed off. The state becomes the sole actor empowered to define 'guilt' and determine meaning.

Just as Lee Kuan Yew's 1971 address to the International Press Institute set the template for the 1974 *Press Act*, so too does this 1989 presidential address set the template for the *Religious Harmony Act*. Indeed, in the final text of the *Religious Harmony Act*, 'intention' is not explicitly referred to, and in the absence of recognition of 'intention' as a factor with legal significance, 'intention' is implicitly erased. An ouster clause prevents judicial review,[10] there is no provision for a trial or legal representation and the Minister's obligation to take into account the representations of non-state actors upon whom the state imposes repressive orders[11] is not something that can be reviewed. Effectively, the judicial determination of 'intention' as an elemental factor of guilt is appropriated by the state as executive prerogative.

This brief consideration of state discourse unpacks, yet again, some of the ways in which the state's ideological argument is more complex than the language of its texts might suggest. The accessible simplicity of the language, the clarity of the short sentences, the construction of a logical sequence ('if not *x*, then *y*') in the argument all serve to elide the complexities that are reduced to essentialist simplifications in the state's position. The apparent simplicity is a telling reflection of the state's command of

[9] In the corpus of Singapore law, the departure from the principle of the prosecutor's need to prove guilty intention is perhaps most dramatically manifested by the *Misuse of Drugs Act* (Cap. 185, 2001 Rev. Ed. Sing.), which reverses the presumption of innocence into a presumption of guilt, so that if a person is found in possession of banned substances, the onus of proving innocence lies upon the accused person.

[10] The Act provides for restraining orders which give the state wide-ranging powers of control over the speech, movement, employment, communications and activities of individuals: *Religious Harmony Act*, *supra* note 1, s. 8 and s. 9.

[11] Ibid., s. 8(5).

ideological power, such that its positions might be presented as common sense,[12] concealing the manufacture of consent[13] – a consent underpinned by the coercive power of 'law'. This coercive underpinning is conveyed by the detentions without trial of the so-called Marxist conspirators.

THE 'MARXIST CONSPIRACY': WHEN HIDDEN DANGERS ARE VISIBLE ONLY TO THE STATE

In May 1987, a group of young, English-educated professionals,[14] including four Law Society Council members, were accused of being part of a Marxist conspiracy to overthrow the state. Over 1987 and 1988, a total of twenty-two people were accused of involvement in this 'conspiracy' and were consequently detained without trial. In brief, the state's position was that the individuals it arrested and detained had been part of an international conspiracy, based in London, to overthrow the government and establish a Communist state. Because the arrests took place in stages, the 'Marxist conspiracy' was in the public domain and received a great deal of media coverage for an extended period. About ten of the detained people were associated with the Catholic Church and were actively involved with the social-work arm of the Church.[15] Among the

[12] Norman Fairclough, *Language and Power* (London: Longman, 1989) 33.

[13] Manuel Castells, "The Developmental City-State in an Open World Economy: The Singapore Experience" (Berkeley: University of California, 1988), online: <http://brie.berkeley.edu/publications/working_papers.html>; see Herman and Chomsky's study of the links between political power and media concerns: Edward S. Herman & Noam Chomsky, *Manufacturing Consent: The Political Economy of the Mass Media* (New York: Pantheon, 1988).

[14] In the parliamentary debates on the detentions, there was repeated reference to the need to abandon the stereotype of 'Communist', for example: "As against the old communist/Marxist who could be identified by his Chinese education background, hiding in the jungles, the modern day Marxist is primarily English-educated with impeccable behaviour". See Sing., *Parliamentary Debates*, vol. 49, col. 1452 (29 July 1987) (Bernard Chen).

[15] Michael D. Barr, "Singapore's Catholic Social Activists: Alleged 'Marxist Conspirators'", in Michael D. Barr & Carl Trocki, eds., *Paths Not Taken: Political Pluralism in Post-War Singapore* (Singapore: NUS Press, 2008) 228.

Catholic social workers were a number of lawyers.[16] A great deal of state and media attention was focused on this group of Catholic social workers and the institution of the Catholic Church. Overseas networks for the Catholic Church brought the issue a fairly high level of media attention internationally.[17] The 'Marxist conspiracy' was almost certainly the event that precipitated the *Religious Harmony Act*.[18]

In December 1989, some eighteen months after the first round of detentions, a White Paper was tabled in Parliament setting out the government's reasons for wanting a law on 'religious harmony'.[19] Appended to the White Paper was an Internal Security Department (ISD) report

16 Lawyers among those detained included Patrick Seong, Francis Seow, Tang Lay Lee, Teo Soh Lung and Kevin de Souza. In 2009 and 2010, in a remarkable development for the Singapore public domain, three books were published containing the recollections and poems of many of the so-called Marxist conspirators on the topic of their detentions: Fong Hoe Fang, ed., *That We May Dream Again* (Singapore: Ethos, 2009), and Tan Jing Quee, Teo Soh Lung & Koh Kay Yew, eds., *Our Thoughts Are Free: Poems and Prose on Imprisonment and Exile* (Singapore: Ethos, 2009); Teo Soh Lung, *Beyond the Blue Gate: Recollections of a Political Prisoner* (Petaling Jaya: Strategic Information and Research Development Centre, 2010). In these books, the alleged conspirators detail their motives for social justice work and their experiences under detention, including experiences of torture. Their extremely moving accounts are striking for the consistency with which they speak of the search for 'justice' and their concern for the underprivileged.

17 See the account of Cathrine Whewall in the foreword to *That We May Dream Again*, *supra* note 16 at 6.

18 See Li-ann Thio, "Control, Co-optation and Co-operation: Managing Religious Harmony in Singapore's Multi-Ethnic, Quasi-Secular State" (2006) 33 *Hastings Constitutional Law Quarterly* 197 [*Control, Co-optation and Co-operation*]; Tamney, *supra* note 2; Christopher Tremewan, *The Political Economy of Social Control in Singapore* (Hampshire: St Martin's Press, 1994) 145; Barr, *supra* note 15; Michael Hill, "Conversion and Subversion: Religion and the Management of Moral Panics in Singapore" (Asian Studies Institute, Working Paper No. 8), online: <http://www.victoria.ac.nz/asiastudies/publications/working/08ConversionandSubversion.pdf>. Hill arrives at a conclusion similar to some of those made in this paper, but conducts his analysis through the lens of moral panic. For a reading of the 'Marxist conspiracy' and the *Religious Harmony Act* that is uncritical of state discourse, see Khun Eng Kuah, "Maintaining Ethno-Religious Harmony in Singapore" (1998) 28:1 *Journal of Contemporary Asia* 103.

19 Sing., "Maintenance of Religious Harmony", Cmd. 21 of 1989 [White Paper].

entitled "Religious Trends: A Security Perspective". This report details ways in which three forms of behaviour threatened public order and religious and racial harmony in Singapore: "Aggressive and Insensitive Proselytisation"; "Mixing Religion and Politics" (under this heading, the conduct of certain Catholic priests is detailed); and "Religion and Subversion" (under this heading, the conduct of certain 'Marxist conspirators' is detailed).[20] When the bill was debated in Parliament, members addressed the popular perception that the proposed bill was a reaction to the 'conspiracy'.[21]

Significantly, the state's account of the 'conspiracy' was rarely clear about the precise nature of the activities of the Catholics it detained. Instead, the focus was on the threat to the 'nation' that had been averted and the need for citizens to submit themselves to the state's authority. In this way, a 'rule of law' scrutiny of the state's exercise of power in effecting this most egregious of 'rule by law' technologies – detention without trial – was resisted and rejected without an explicit acknowledgement that issues of 'law' and individual rights were at stake. One example of the state's discursive dwelling upon the importance of trusting, submissive citizens can be seen in a speech made to Parliament in July 1987 by Goh Chok Tong,[22] then First Deputy Prime Minister and poised to become Prime Minister in November 1990. Goh's speech was long and an apparent defence of the state's decision to order the arrests, but at no point in the speech did Goh address the basic question of what the 'conspirators' actually *did* that so imperilled the 'nation'.

In his speech, Goh did not offer facts to the public. Rather than disclosing 'facts', Goh assured the public that hard questions had been put to the ISD by the "Prime Minister and me"[23] and the "younger leadership",[24]

[20] Ibid. at 19.

[21] Sing., *Parliamentary Debates*, vol. 54, col. 1076 (22 February 1990) (Aline Wong).

[22] Sing., *Parliamentary Debates*, vol. 49, cols. 1484–89 (29 July 1987) (Goh Chok Tong, First Deputy Prime Minister).

[23] Ibid. at col. 1484.

[24] Ibid. at col. 1485.

and the ISD convinced them of the seriousness of the threat. In other words, Goh argued for the necessary sufficiency of discretionary state authority, instructing 'the people' to trust in their leaders' assessments – assessments made on the basis of surveillance. To legitimise this demand, Goh resuscitated that Cold War phantom – 'Communism'.

The logic of Goh's speech presents a trusting, submissive citizenry as necessary because of the disguised, sinister and secret nature of 'Communists': "[I]t is difficult to uncover Communist conspiracies because they work in cells, secretly, furtively".[25] The furtive, hidden 'Communists', visible only to the state (via surveillance), supply an ostensible reason for the ordinary citizen's inability to know what the state knows. Goh's claims build a narrative of danger, of fearful consequences should the state fail to act:

> [I]f we do not destroy them now, they will destroy us later.... [I]n the future ... these plotters could press the button and destabilise the whole place. Our decision was not to take chances with the lives of Singaporeans. Do not risk the prosperity.[26]

The enormity of the consequences (with the extraordinary allusion to nuclear annihilation in the phrase "press the button") is presented as an argument justifying the detentions. Lives, prosperity, the 'nation' – everything is at stake.

As part of this narrative of the danger held at bay by the ever-watchful state, Goh criminalises 'Communists' and the detainees through lexical juxtaposition: "Every society has its share of criminals, anti-social elements, child molesters, rapists, communists or communist-types. Singapore is no exception".[27] His narrative of danger extends beyond the borders of Singapore with shadowy international connections: "These people do not work by themselves.... [T]here is a larger scheme of things involving others outside Singapore",[28] a level of danger clearly beyond the capacity of

[25] Ibid.
[26] Ibid. at col. 1487.
[27] Ibid. at col. 1485.
[28] Ibid. at col. 1486.

ordinary citizens to grasp or to protect themselves from. The condemnation of 'Communists' and the impossibility of detecting their dangerous natures in their appearance further emerged through a radicalising comparison of the detainees with Ieng Sary: "I have met Ieng Sary twice.... He looked gentle, chubby, cherubic ... yet he is an inner member of Pol Pot's clique".[29]

Goh uses future danger as justification for present action: "[D]o we regard them as posing an immediate threat to Singapore? ... To be frank, the answer is no".[30] He then positions himself as a member of the ruling elite and presents the state's good faith in responsibly arriving at the decision to order the ISD action: "We asked many questions. We wanted to be very sure that the conspiratorial activities ... were indeed prejudicial to the security of Singapore.... All of us were satisfied".[31] Significantly, though, he avoids addressing the substance of the "conspiratorial" and "nefarious activities", implying that if the ruling elite is satisfied, then the citizen should be too. This same avoidance of crucial detail is replicated when Goh says that "the longer term threat to our security was obvious and real and I do not have to belabour this point",[32] firmly removing the focus from 'fact' to an assertion of state authority. The operations of 'law' thus become increasingly hidden. Freedoms are violated and lives trampled upon on the basis of conversations conducted behind closed doors between different state actors. The 'rule by law' governance of the process is obscured by the demand for trust.

In rounding off his argument, Goh re-presents the narrative of Singapore's perpetual vulnerability (to enemies both within and without):

> Singapore is an open country.... We are therefore vulnerable to security threats and to manipulation by people outside Singapore. We are a small country. If we are destabilised, it will be very difficult to right the ship so that it can sail on even keel.[33]

[29] Ibid. at col. 1485.

[30] Ibid.

[31] Ibid.

[32] Ibid. at col. 1486.

[33] Ibid. at col. 1488.

The sub-text of this argument appears to be that general principles to do with individual rights and freedoms cannot apply to Singapore because of these exceptional vulnerabilities.[34] The legal exceptionalism that must follow from Singapore's exceptional vulnerabilities justifies the decision to order the detentions on the grounds of national interests: "[T]he Government cannot avoid unpleasant decisions if these are in the overall interest of the state".[35] By calling the decision to order the detentions "unpleasant", Goh minimises the nature and the impact of detentions. There is no acknowledgement in this description that issues of 'law', of fundamental liberties guaranteed by the *Constitution*, are at stake. The detainees are constructed by this discourse not as individuals but as members of the category 'Communists', a category that in Singapore is replete with social meanings of sinister dangers.

This strongly authoritative and authoring state inscribes yet again the binary that state discourse has put in place since (at least) the 1966 parliamentary debates on the *Vandalism Act*: subordinate citizens/ascendant state. In this 1989 moment, 'citizens' are constructed by Goh as social beings receptive to the authority of the state, needing to be informed and instructed by the all-seeing state. If the state is authoritative and permits the citizen to relate to the state only in submission and subordination, then the conduct of the Catholic social workers was a violation of this dynamic. Arguably, these individuals breached the state's 'rule by law' hierarchy in two ways: First, the Catholic social workers were not passive citizens (this point is discussed later); and second, the activities they were engaged in dislodged the submerged social category 'class'.

'CLASS' AND ACTIVISM IN THE 'MARXIST CONSPIRACY'

'Class' is almost an absent category in public discourse in Singapore. The state's construction of nationhood tends to assume that material

[34] For a 2010 rehearsal of this argument, see Transcript from Free Press Session, *supra* note 8.

[35] Ibid.

prosperity has been delivered to all via meritocracy. As Goh put it (in the same speech), if Singaporeans "learn hard, study hard, work hard, they can climb up the ladder in Singapore". The implication of this declaration is that there are no obstacles to social and economic mobility in Singapore – no class barriers that impede diligence and determination and no manner in which citizens are not placed upon a level playing field.[36]

Many of the activities of the Catholic social workers centred on supporting economically disadvantaged groups in Singapore. It might fairly be said, then, that their activities brought 'class' to the forefront of public discourse in a way that state-generated discourse did not. In his study of the 'conspiracy', Michael Barr describes the activities of the Catholic social workers as "not overtly ideological, being directed predominantly at helping particular groups and individuals".[37] Barr relates how, for example, the Catholic social workers assisted "foreign workers",[38] advising on processes by which they could exercise their rights, teaching them English, helping individual workers represent themselves to the Ministry of Labour when they had a grievance, providing advice and refuge to abused and frightened foreign maids and acting as liaison with the Ministry of Labour for the maids.[39]

The Catholic social activists also conducted a campaign against the government's introduction of the twelve-hour shift. A report was written

[36] On the dereliction of the ideal of multi-racial meritocracy, see Lily Zubaidah Rahim, *The Singapore Dilemma: The Political and Educational Marginality of the Malay Community* (Shah Alam: Oxford University Press, 1998). On the growing income divide, see Ishita Dhamani, "Income Inequality in Singapore: Causes, Consequences and Policy Options" (May 2008) http://www.mas.gov.sg/resource/eco_research/eco_education/Esss2007/uni_%201st_%20Ishita.pdf.

[37] Barr, *supra* note 15.

[38] Barr uses the term 'migrant workers', but in Singapore the term commonly used is 'foreign workers'. 'Foreign workers' are typically people who engage in manual labour and are often employed to work in Singapore under terms which prevent their remaining in Singapore or becoming citizens or migrant workers. See also the *Employment of Foreign Workers Act* (Cap. 91A, 1997 Rev. Ed. Sing.).

[39] A significant proportion of the foreign domestic workers in Singapore are Filipinas, who are usually Catholic.

and the issue given prominent coverage in the *Catholic News*. A government Member of Parliament, who was also Catholic and a senior official of the National Trade Union Congress, engaged the authors of the report in a debate in the letters page of the *Catholic News*. This debate was picked up by the press. In this way, the debate crossed from Catholic community space into 'national' space. The Catholic activists also led a campaign to raise awareness of the consequences of retrenchment so as to pressure employers, trade unions, the government and society to treat the retrenched with a sense of justice and compassion.[40] A 1985 statement on retrenchment was published in the *Catholic News*. A booklet on the results of a survey of retrenched workers was also published but was marked "for private circulation".

The Catholic social workers also initiated awareness-raising measures on industrial rights such as minimum wages and workplace health and safety, and supplied leadership training to workers who wanted improvements in work conditions. They initiated another campaign against the elitism of the Graduate Mothers Priority Scheme, which gave the children of graduate mothers priority in enrolling their children in schools of choice. They also published a critique of other elitist features of the education system, such as the Gifted Education Programme.

If this was the limit of the activities of the Catholics, they could easily have been labelled "young idealists out to improve society" rather than "sinister Communists out to wreck Singapore".[41] But the state's interpretation of these actions was very different and is best captured by the ISD's report appended to the White Paper:

> In the mid-80s, a number of Catholic priests ventured into 'social action' and acted as a political pressure group. A few of them formed the Church and Society Study Group which published political booklets criticising the Government on various secular issues....

[40] See also Fong, *supra* note 16 and Tan, Teo & Koh, *supra* note 16.

[41] Goh, *supra* note 22 at col. 1484.

> [It] accused the Government of emasculating the trade unions and enacting labour laws which curtailed the rights of workers....
>
> *The Catholic News* ... also began publishing articles and editorials on economic and political issues. It criticised multi-national corporations, the amendments to citizenship laws and the *Newspaper & Printing Presses Act*, and Government policies on TV3 and foreign workers.
>
> Vincent Cheng ... embarked on a systematic plan to infiltrate, subvert and control various Catholic and student organisations, including the Justice & Peace Commission of the Catholic Church, and Catholic student societies in the NUS and Singapore Polytechnic. He planned to build a united front of pressure groups for confrontation with the Government.... Some of the articles adopted familiar Communist arguments to denounce the existing system as 'exploitative', 'unjust' and 'repressive'.[42]

In the state's construction of events, labour rights and regulation, the economy and 'political issues' are secular and are thus outside the domain of what individuals and institutions linked to 'religion' might be permitted to participate in or express an opinion on. The ISD report does not define 'politics', but it does supply the probable boundaries marking this problematic territory from which the state so urgently seeks to exclude citizens.

RELIGION: THE NEW COMMUNISM?

At the time of the 'Marxist conspiracy', it was the 'Communist' identity of the detainees that was discursively presented and insisted upon. However, given the essentially atheist ideology of 'Communism', the Catholic identity of some of the detainees made 'Communist' a particularly unconvincing label. Three months after the first detentions, in August 1987, Singapore's then Prime Minister, Lee Kuan Yew, spoke

[42] White Paper, *supra* note 19 at 15–18.

of creating a new state body that would make sure 'religion' was not used for subversive purposes. 'Religion', Lee said, must not get mixed up with 'politics'. The proper role of religious groups, he said, was charity and community work, such as the setting up of childcare centres.[43] These same sentiments were expressed in the President's speech delivered at the 1989 opening of Parliament,[44] and the very same paragraphs from the President's speech were repeated in the opening to the White Paper.[45] Lee's remarks and the President's speech presage the core content of the eventual text of the *Religious Harmony Act*. It is stating the obvious to point out that the rhetorical strategy of repetition can be a powerful tool in public discourse. In Singapore, the 1965 discursive characterisation of 'religion' as a security issue was renewed by the 1987 and 1989 state imperative that 'religion' stay out of 'politics'. What began as a state-scripted account of the ways in which Singapore is an exceptionally vulnerable nation became entrenched as 'law' in the *Religious Harmony Act*.

After the President's speech in January 1989, the danger that the 'conspiracy' represented was reframed in a way that extracted and highlighted the religious identity of the Catholics among the detainees. The Cold War had all but petered out, and the end of that year was marked by the fall of the Berlin Wall. The ISD report appended to the White Paper indicates that the 'Marxist conspirators' were still officially 'Communist', but the 'Communist' identity was now framed by the primacy of 'religion'.[46] This shift laid the groundwork for a discursive construction of an endangered 'religious harmony' requiring 'maintenance' via a new 'law'.

The words "Maintenance of Religious Harmony" in the title of the Act present a highly ideological position as an uncontested, objective

[43] Tamney, *supra* note 2 at 32.
[44] 1989 Presidential Address, *supra* note 6.
[45] White Paper, *supra* note 19 at 1.
[46] Ibid. at 13.

'truth'. 'Religious harmony' is framed as an existing state of affairs that must be 'maintained'. There are complex possibilities in and around 'religious harmony' – what does it mean? Does 'religious harmony' exist? Who determines the presence and parameters of 'religious harmony'? In this compound title, however, all other possibilities are obscured and excluded. Additionally, the Act fails to define key terms. For example, the Act cites this conduct as endangering 'religious harmony': "carrying out activities to promote a political cause, or a cause of any political party while, or under the guise of, propagating or practising any religious belief."[47] "Political cause" is not defined, nor is "religious belief". By not defining key terms, the *Religious Harmony Act* requires citizens to adopt the same ideological positions as the state, interpreting the language of the *Religious Harmony Act* in a manner consistent with the state's definitions because no others are available.

In keeping with these implied definitions, the offence created by the *Religious Harmony Act* is in a strange class of its own. The offence is not the actual or potential conduct of promoting a political cause (for example). Instead, the offence consists of breaching the terms of a restraining order. Restraining orders are an administrative device created by the *Religious Harmony Act* and have probably been modelled on the orders the state can make under the *Internal Security Act*.[48] Under the *ISA*, when detainees are released, the state can make orders specifying conditions of release, orders which typically restrict the activities of detainees. Similarly, the *Religious Harmony Act* empowers the state to restrain the activities and communications of individuals and institutions connected to 'religion'.[49] Under the *Religious Harmony Act*, a restrained person goes before the courts only if that person breaches the terms of the restraining order.[50] Until the restraining order has been breached, an offence has not been committed. The

[47] *Religious Harmony Act*, *supra* note 1, s. 8(1)(b).
[48] *ISA*, *supra* note 3, s. 10.
[49] *Religious Harmony Act*, *supra* note 1, s. 8(2).
[50] Ibid., s. 16.

restrained person in breach of an order goes before the courts in order to be convicted.[51] The court does not have the power to call into question the orders and decisions made by the Minister.[52] The court's function is only to decide on the sentence from the range of specified fines and prison terms set out by the *Religious Harmony Act*.[53] The only mechanism to check the exercise of state power built into the *Religious Harmony Act* is the Presidential Council for Religious Harmony (discussed later).[54]

This two-tiered operation for restraining orders means that the conduct that results in the imposition of a restraining order is in a strange class of its own – the conduct is not, in itself, illegal. That conduct is, instead, in the assessment of the state actually or potentially a threat to 'religious harmony', a term which (when read in the context of state discourse on 'religious harmony') might well mean a challenge to state policy and hegemony.

A restraining order may be made if, in the Minister's assessment, a person is causing or attempting to cause enmity, ill-will or hostility between different religious groups, conducting politics in the guise of religion, undertaking subversion in the guise of religion or exciting disaffection in the guise of religion.[55] So even though the Act is called the *Maintenance of Religious Harmony Act*, three of the four limbs focus on 'crimes' against the state – conducting politics, engaging in subversion or exciting disaffection, all under the guise of 'religion'. Indeed, similarities in language suggest that the *Religious Harmony Act* has been modelled on the *Sedition Act*. The *Religious Harmony Act* adopts the *Sedition*

[51] Ibid.

[52] Ibid., s. 18.

[53] Ibid., s. 16.

[54] The members of this Council are state appointees: ibid. s. 3. It has been argued that "in the composition of ... the Council, the government has co-opted leaders of the main religions, rendering them accountable both for their own conduct as leaders and for that of their followers": Li-ann Thio, "Working out the Presidency: The Rites of Passage" (1995) *S.J.L.S.* 500 [*Working out the Presidency*].

[55] *Religious Harmony Act*, *supra* note 1, s. 8(1).

Act's definition and parameters for "seditious tendency" and replicates "seditious tendency" as the trigger for restraining orders:

Religious Harmony Act	Sedition Act
The Minister may make a restraining order against any person who has committed, or is attempting to commit, the act of "exciting disaffection against the President or the Government": s. 8(1)(d)	The *Sedition Act* defines a "seditious tendency" as including "a tendency to ... excite disaffection against the Government": s. 3(1)(a).
The Minister may make a restraining order against any person who has committed, or is attempting to commit, the act of "causing feelings of enmity, hatred, ill-will or hostility between different religious groups": s. 8(1)(a).	The *Sedition Act* defines a "seditious tendency" as including "a tendency to promote feelings of ill-will and hostility between different races or classes of the population": s. 3(1)(e).

If the parameters for conduct endangering 'religious harmony' are a cipher for sedition (which, in turn, may well be a cipher for dissent), then the technologies for dealing with this conduct are clearly derived from the *ISA*. The *ISA* empowers the state, in sweeping terms, to make orders restricting a person in terms of activities, places of residence, and employment.[56] The *ISA* also permits the state to prohibit an individual from addressing public meetings and from holding office in, or participating in the activities of, or acting as advisor to, any organisation or association.[57] The Minister's powers to constrain activity and communication under the *Religious Harmony Act*'s restraining orders[58] are remarkably similar to the restrictions and constraints listed under the *ISA*, with a particular focus on restraining communication to 'religious' audiences and to holding office in editorial boards and publication committees of 'religious' audiences.[59]

[56] *ISA*, *supra* note 3, s. 8(1)(b).

[57] Ibid.

[58] *Religious Harmony Act*, *supra* note 1, s. 8.

[59] Ibid.

Significantly, the *Sedition Act* and the *ISA* were brought into being by the colonial authorities during the Emergency, when British control had met with the greatest resistance. In replicating the language of the *Sedition Act* and the *ISA*, the state has scripted the *Religious Harmony Act*, a 'law' purportedly concerned with 'religious harmony', by modelling it on laws explicitly designed to protect the state. Clearly, despite the state's insistence on a discursive separation between 'religion' and 'politics', 'religion' in Singapore is already and inherently about 'politics'.

RESTRAINING ORDERS: DEVELOPING STATE KNOWLEDGE OF 'RELIGION'

Restraining orders might be made against two classes of people: officials or members of religious groups or institutions[60] or "any person".[61] The orders restrain those who, in the state's assessment, have acted, or attempted to act, in any of the ways listed in the preceding table. The individual may be restrained from speaking or writing to any congregation, parish or group of worshippers on any theme specified in the restraining order. The sweep of this power to selectively control communication implies the state's detailed knowledge of the themes (already and potentially) addressed by the restrained individual. Once an order has been issued, the prior permission of the Minister is needed to speak or write on the prohibited topics. An individual may also be restrained from being involved in any way with the printed material of any religious group.

In the detail of this attention to the restrained person's communications – the content of what is said, the constituency of the reading or listening audience – the *Religious Harmony Act* brings into being a new way in which the state polices 'religion' by policing discourse. In effect, a restraining order operates to silence an individual. Communication, oral and written, is restrained in two ways: in terms of content and in terms

[60] Ibid., s. 8(1).
[61] Ibid., s. 9(1).

of audience. It is groups of people identifiably associated with 'religion' that the state does not permit the restrained person to communicate with on the forbidden topics. Under the terms of the *Religious Harmony Act*, a restrained person might conceivably speak or write on the forbidden topics to individuals and to groups of people who are not a congregation, parish, worshippers or members of a religious group or institution.[62] And, quite specifically, the prohibition is on addressing listeners or readers on "any subject, topic or theme as may be specified in the order, without the prior permission of the Minister".[63]

The *Religious Harmony Act* pays a significant level of attention to the participation of the restrained person in the processes of production around print material. She or he may not print, publish, edit, distribute or in any way assist or contribute to any publication produced by any religious group without the Minister's prior permission.[64] The restrained person may also be restrained from holding office in an editorial board or a publications committee of any religious group.[65] Again, just as with the provisions on addressing a 'religious' group, the aim appears to be to silence the restrained person on particular topics, with reference to particular audiences. The restraints with regard to participation in print material are broader than the restraints on addressing a religious group. Perhaps, in this sweeping exclusion from editorial boards and distribution committees, the possibility of the restrained person's views being expressed by another, or slipping through the net of state surveillance, is taken care of. Through these prohibitions, the state diligently maps new terrains of knowledge for 'religion' that must be policed.

[62] The Select Committee points out that the limited scope of restraining orders means that the Minister "cannot stop the person from talking about the very same subject to a non-religious group, such as a political rally": Sing., "Report of the Select Committee on the Maintenance of Religious Harmony Bill", October 1990, Parliament 7 of 1990, para. 20 [*SC Report on Religious Harmony*].

[63] *Religious Harmony Act*, *supra* note 1, s. 8.

[64] Ibid., s. 8(2)(b).

[65] Ibid., s. 8(2)(b) and s. 8 (2)(c).

In summary, although restraining orders mimic the constraints the state places upon detainees released from detention without trial, a restraining order does not involve detention or imprisonment. Instead, the terms of the *Religious Harmony Act* require state policing and surveillance upon a restrained person's communications. More important, a restraining order places the obligation on restrained people to police themselves.

RESTRAINING ORDERS, RESTRAINING SELF

In the way restraining orders work, it is as if specific events relating to the 'Marxist conspiracy' are being addressed. For example, the Church publication, the *Catholic News*, was a print vehicle for the campaigns and concerns of the social-work arm of the Church.[66] At the time of the arrests, priests led masses for the detained individuals.[67] As a result of state pressure on the Church, both the publication and the masses were stopped.[68] At the time of the arrests, a great deal of publicity was raised for the detainees by friends and contacts overseas.[69] In a catch-all provision, even this sort of communication is silenced[70]: The Minister may issue a restraining order against any person making any statement or causing any statement to be made concerning the relations between a religious institution and the government.[71]

When it comes to communicating with a 'religious' audience, the space given to the state to permit some topics but not others necessitates a vigilant self-surveillance on the part of the restrained individual. The individual will need to script and censor her or his own texts before engaging in communication in order to ensure continued compliance

[66] Barr, *supra* note 15.
[67] Ibid. See also Fong, *supra* note 16 at 61.
[68] Ibid.
[69] Ibid.
[70] *Religious Harmony Act*, *supra* note 1, s. 9.
[71] Ibid.

with the terms of any restraining order. The parameters of the *Religious Harmony Act*'s prohibitions conjure (at least in my mind) an image of the state's agents sitting among worshippers, congregations and believers across Singapore, monitoring spoken and written communication, ensuring compliance with existing restraining orders and identifying other people who should be subject to new restraining orders. In the sub-text of the *Religious Harmony Act* there is a script for an omniscient, omnipresent state – a state engaging in policing citizens and punishing transgressors, all for the good of the 'nation'.

Of all the silences the *Religious Harmony Act* empowers the state to impose, perhaps the most deafening silence follows from the ouster clause: All orders, decisions and recommendations under the *Religious Harmony Act* are final and shall not be called into question in any court.[72] The White Paper (a document written by the government and presenting the government's rationale for the law to Parliament) supplies the state's reasons for the ouster clause:

> Prompt action may be necessary to stop a person from repeating harmful, provocative acts. A Court trial may mean considerable delay before judgment is pronounced, and the judicial proceedings may themselves stoke passions further if the defendant turns them into political propaganda.[73]

In the state's objection to a defendant turning a trial into "political propaganda" is the imputation that the legal process is open to abuse in terms of the platform and publicity it might afford a defendant.[74] The sub-text of this imputation is that "political propaganda" is not something the state generates. The state, with its greater knowledge, generates 'truth', not 'propaganda'.

[72] Ibid., s. 18.

[73] White Paper, *supra* note 19 at 8.

[74] When detentions are made under the *ISA*, it is primarily the state's version of events that is publicly disseminated. For example, in the most recent detentions of men alleged to be Jemaah Islamiah activists, all the media coverage has presented the state's account. The detainees have had no voice.

In the range of ways the *Religious Harmony Act* works to silence individuals as a means of maintaining 'religious harmony', it is as if the unstated purpose of the *Religious Harmony Act* is to maintain the state's dominance of public discourse. Without a trial, a counter-narrative cannot emerge in the public domain, ensuring the unchallenged dominance of the state in the discourse of 'law', 'nation' and 'religion'. The *Religious Harmony Act* provides for speedy, discreet (perhaps even secretive) action.

'LAW' AS PERFORMANCE

In producing the *Religious Harmony Act*, the Singapore state engaged in a highly visible process by which it demonstrated its rational, 'rule of law' identity.[75] This process involved moments of consultation and engagement with non-state players on the terms of the *Maintenance of Religious Harmony Bill*, in the following ways.

The "Maintenance of Religious Harmony" was the subject of a White Paper.[76] After the Bill was introduced in Parliament, it was the subject of parliamentary debates and of extensive media coverage. A Select Committee was appointed. This Committee invited public submissions on the Bill, held hearings (most of which were public) and issued a detailed report.[77] The final text of the *Religious Harmony Act*, the product of these somewhat protracted processes, showed little substantive departure from the state's original formulation.[78] In other words, the

[75] The procedural practice required of the Westminster-model process of 'law'-making is set out in Standing Orders of the Parliament of Singapore, online: <http://www.parliament.gov.sg/Publications/standingOrder.htm>. See also the *Parliament (Privileges, Immunities and Powers) Act* (Cap. 217, 2001 Rev. Ed. Sing.); M. Stanley Ryan, *Parliamentary Procedure: Essential Principles* (New York: Cornwall, 1985).

[76] White Paper, *supra* note 19.

[77] *SC Report on Religious Harmony*, *supra* note 62.

[78] The final page of the White Paper (*supra* note 19) lists the five amendments made to the Bill in response to this process: the clarification that the proposed legislation is consistent with constitutional provisions on religion (paras. 7–9); the emphasis on respecting common values and the right of each individual to accept or not accept a religion (paras. 18a, 18b); the suggestion that the Council for Religious Harmony be made a

consultative process was demonstrably engaged in by the state without in any way compromising its hegemony. Throughout this process, the state came closest to grappling with the problematic terms 'religion' and 'politics' in the Select Committee report's discussion of the role of the courts.[79] In this report, the Select Committee noted the concern of "a number of representors" that

> the Bill ... concentrated too much authority in the hands of the Executive ... [and] these powers could be arbitrarily misused to suppress legitimate expression of dissenting views. Several representors argued strongly for the safeguard to be a judicial one, i.e. to empower the courts, instead of the Executive, to decide what constituted causing ill-will among religious groups, or mixing of religion and politics in unacceptable ways.[80]

The Committee agreed that additional safeguards were desirable but argued vigorously against a judicial role, preferring instead to vest discretionary power to assess the Minister's decision in the President.[81] The first of its stated reasons was (repeating the White Paper's rationale and adopting the same rhetoric) that prompt action might be needed, and a trial might have the effect of creating delays and of stoking passions further.[82] The Committee's second "strong argument against vesting power in the courts" was that

> the division between religion and politics is not a well-defined one. The area of overlap is considerable. It is not possible to draw the line so clearly that the courts can determine on the basis of facts and law whether an action falls on one side of the line or the other.[83]

Presidential Council (para. 35); the inclusion of lay as well as clerical representatives on the Presidential Council (para. 36); and the proposal to inform the Council that the Minister intends to issue a prohibition order at the same time that the affected person is notified (para. 40). None of these amendments goes to the heart of the proposed Act.

[79] *SC Report on Religious Harmony*, *supra* note 62 at v–ix.

[80] Ibid. at v.

[81] Ibid. at viii.

[82] Ibid. at vi.

[83] Ibid.

In stating this 'reason' for judicial exclusion, the Committee implicitly acknowledges the contradiction inherent in the terms and the purpose of the *Religious Harmony Act.* If legislation directed at ensuring that 'religion' and 'politics' do not mix is understood (by the state that constructs the distinction) to be seeking to demarcate categories that exist on a continuum rather than in isolation, how can that 'law' be effected or effective?

The Committee's solution to this unexpressed conundrum is to assert the validity of decisions made by those who hold political power in the state – a repetition of the theme of the necessary authority of the state. In this instance, however, the expertise of the state is not being asserted as against the citizen but the courts:

> [E]ven if a clear line could be drawn, it would not be the duty of the courts to decide where this line should be. For example, should abortion be a legitimate matter for religious groups to discuss? Should national service be considered a purely secular issue? These are questions of public policy. Their answers depend on what is necessary to maintain religious harmony and what is in the overall interests of society. They are not questions of law to be settled on the basis of legal arguments and precedents.
>
> The issue is what is wise for the Government to allow, not what is lawful for a person to carry out. These public policy decisions are properly the responsibility of the Executive and Parliament. Leaving them to the courts merely forces the judiciary to make political decisions. In a highly charged situation, a controversial and difficult decision is unlikely to be more acceptable to the public simply because it was made by the courts.[84]

The rhetorical questions used here are confusing for the answers they suggest: that abortion is not a legitimate matter for religious groups to discuss and that national service is not a purely secular issue.[85] Even

[84] Ibid. at vii.

[85] For a discussion of the ways in which issues of 'race' and 'religion' have been dealt with by state discourse and the courts when it comes to compulsory military service (known as national service), see Thio, *Control, Co-optation and Co-operation*, *supra* note 18.

more confusing is the assertion that public policy is outside the domain of the courts because of an incompatibility between 'wisdom' and 'law'. In attempting to set out a reasoned argument for excluding the courts, the Committee raises more questions than it answers. The most problematic question raised (possibly unintentionally) concerns the function of 'law' in the 'nation' if legal arguments and precedents cannot address an issue delineated by a legislative instrument.

In particular, the distinction the Committee draws between what is "lawful for a person to carry out" and what is "wise for the Government to allow" points to a risk-ridden gap between legal conduct and conduct that, while legal, might threaten the "overall interests of society" – a gap that only Parliament and the executive might be trusted to close. If the judiciary needs to be rescued from the invidious task of making "political decisions", is the Committee implicitly acknowledging that any application of the *Religious Harmony Act* must intrinsically be 'political'? The Committee points to limits in what 'law' can achieve without any apparent awareness of the irony of defending the need for a new 'law'. Implicit in the Committee's arguments is a measure of recognition of the ways in which the *Religious Harmony Act* departs from principles of the rule of law:

> [T]he purpose of the Bill is preventative, not punitive. It is to enable the Government to act before damage is done, not primarily to punish a person after he has committed a crime.... [A]n order restraining a person from saying or doing certain things is in effect a formal warning to him to desist or else face more serious consequences. If a person had unintentionally caused feelings of ill-will by his words, it may be necessary to restrain him from repeating them, but we should not convict him of a crime, at least not yet. By issuing such an order, we avoid criminalising the issue immediately.... This is far less draconian than charging a person in court immediately and attempting to convict him.[86]

In supplying these reasons for ousting the courts, the Committee appears to acknowledge the ways in which the *Religious Harmony Act* departs

[86] *SC Report on Religious Harmony*, *supra* note 62 at vii.

from the general principles that it is actual conduct (rather than potential outcomes from possible future conduct) that constitutes a crime and that intention is a necessary finding in determining a criminal conviction.[87] The departures are justified, however, as being "less draconian"[88] than the alternative, with no acknowledgement that a new form of criminalising communication of certain sorts is, in fact, being created by the *Religious Harmony Act*.

EMPTY PERFORMANCES? THE PRESIDENTIAL COUNCIL FOR RELIGIOUS HARMONY

In rejecting calls for judicial review of ministerial discretion exercised under the *Religious Harmony Act*, the Select Committee recommended that, instead of the courts, power to review ministerial decisions should lie with a Presidential Council for Religious Harmony. The Presidential Council for Religious Harmony[89] is a "consultative council",[90] two-thirds of which is made up of "representatives of the major religions of Singapore".[91] The remaining one-third of the Council members are citizens

[87] In para. 24, ibid., the Committee addresses the suggestion that "intention" be included as a factor in determining an offence under s. 8(1)(a) of the *Religious Harmony Act* and rejects that suggestion, repeating its position that the government must be able to take preventative, not punitive, action and that the state of mind of the person is irrelevant. For a discussion of the centrality of the presumption of innocence to criminal justice and the implications of the ways in which the presumption has been eroded in Singapore, see Michael Hor, "The Presumption of Innocence: A Constitutional Discourse for Singapore" (1995) *S.J.L.S.* 365.

[88] *SC Report on Religious Harmony*, *supra* note 62 at vii.

[89] *Religious Harmony Act*, *supra* note 1, s. 3.

[90] White Paper, *supra* note 19 at para. 35.

[91] *Religious Harmony Act*, *supra* note 1, s. 3. The Singapore Government Directory lists twelve Council members including a representative each for Sikhism, Islam, Hinduism, Taoism, Protestantism and Catholicism, as well as three laypersons. The faith status of the Chairman, a former High Court judge, is not specified. Along with the Chairman, another Council member, the Hindu representative, is a former High Court judge. Only the Secretary of the Council is a woman. All other members, including the three "laypersons" appointed by the state, are men; online: Presidential Council for Religious Harmony <http://app.sgdi.gov.sg/mobile/agency.asp?agency_id=0000000898>.

who, in the opinion of the Presidential Council for Minority Rights, have "distinguished themselves in public service or community relations in Singapore".[92] These distinguished citizens are meant to be "prominent lay persons",[93]

> included to complement the perspectives of religious leaders on the Council, to avoid direct confrontations between leaders of opposing faiths who may have to pass judgment upon each other's errant followers, and to represent the many Singaporeans who do not belong to any organised religious group.[94]

One-third of the members of the Council, then, are by implication representatives of that other great religion – secularism. The state clearly looks to the secular members of the Council to be the rational, modern, moderating presence, diffusing tensions between religious leaders, who by implication will oppose the rationality of secularism in their interests and loyalties.[95] Significantly, at least two members of the current Council are former justices of the Supreme Court.[96] Retired judges might be perceived as embodying the secular, rational modernity and the statism of Singapore courts. Surely the presence of these former justices in the Council facilitates the dilution of 'religion'.[97]

In the context of Singapore, "minority rights" means the rights of 'racial' minorities and not, for example, people with disabilities or the gay and lesbian community. By designing the Presidential Council for Religious Harmony to be partially nominated by the Presidential Council

[92] *Religious Harmony Act*, *supra* note 1, s. 3(1).

[93] White Paper, *supra* note 19 at para. 36.

[94] Ibid.

[95] See Li-ann Thio, "The Secular Trumps the Sacred: Constitutional Issues Arising from *Colin Chan v Public Prosecutor*" (1995) 16 *Sing. L.R.* 98, for a discussion of secularism in Singapore and state suspicions of and around 'religion'.

[96] See text at *supra* note 91.

[97] Kanishka Jayasuriya, "The Exception Becomes the Norm: Law and Regimes of Exception in East Asia" (2001) 2:1 *Asian Pac. L. & Pol'y J.* 108; Kanishka Jayasuriya, "Introduction", in Kanishka Jayasuriya, ed., *Law, Capitalism and Power in Asia: The Rule of Law and Legal Institutions* (London: Routledge, 1999) 1.

for Minority Rights, the categories of 'race' and 'religion' are once more brought together. The role of the state remains central. The members of both councils are appointed by the Head of State, the President, who in turn comes to power through processes involving affiliation to the state.[98]

The Council for Religious Harmony is presented by the state as an institutional check, of sorts, upon the exercise of executive power when it comes to the issuing of restraining orders. However, given state control of the membership of the Council, this may amount to yet another way in which the *Religious Harmony Act* facilitates the policing of 'religion'. In an ideal situation, the Council presents opportunities for the state and religious leaders to engage in a constructive dialogue. However, in a situation of unequal power relations, the Council presents an opportunity for religious leaders to become co-opted into the state's project of managing 'religion'.[99] In the secrecy of the proceedings of the Council,[100] more silences are engendered by the *Religious Harmony Act*, building on the ways in which the Act frames 'religion' as an issue of national security rather than 'harmony'.

Another question to be asked is, how powerful is the Council? The Minister is required to refer restraining orders to the Council only within thirty days after the order has been made. The Council then has thirty days to make its recommendations to the President. The Council may recommend that the order be confirmed, cancelled or varied. In the meantime, the order has taken effect. The order ceases to have effect only if the President does not confirm it within thirty days of receiving the Council's recommendations. The effect of this schedule is such that, conceivably, the Minister might issue a restraining order and wait until day twenty-nine to refer it to the Council, the Council might take twenty-nine days to make its recommendations and the President then has up to thirty days to confirm the order. Should the President confirm the order,

98 Thio, *Working out the Presidency*, *supra* note 54.
99 Thio, *Control, Co-optation and Co-operation*, *supra* note 18.
100 *Religious Harmony Act*, *supra* note 1, s. 7.

it continues to be in effect. Should the President not issue a confirmation, the restraining order ceases, but it could by then have been in effect for almost three months. Basically, a restraining order might be in place for up to three months, without even the limited institutional check on state power that the Council represents.

In deciding whether or not to confirm a restraining order, as a general rule, the President is required to act on the advice of the cabinet.[101] Where, however, the Council and the cabinet disagree, the decision lies within the discretionary exercise of power of the President.[102] All in all, however, given that presidential candidates have to be establishment figures,[103] Thio has argued that

> in the composition of Presidential Council for Religious Harmony, the government has co-opted leaders of the main religions, rendering them accountable both for their own conduct as leaders and for that of their followers.[104]

The Council brings non-state religious actors within the scope of a state institution established by 'law', shifting these actors into part of the policing apparatus of the state.

THE LAW THAT HAS NOT BEEN USED

The question that arises in 2011 (nineteen years after the *Religious Harmony Act* was gazetted into effect)[105] is, what is the significance of this 'law' if it has not, in fact, ever been enforced? In 1998, eight years after the *Maintenance of Religious Harmony Act* had been passed, Lee Kuan Yew explained the need for the *Religious Harmony Act* thus:

[101] Ibid., s. 12(3).

[102] *Constitution*, Art. 22 I, read with *Religious Harmony Act*, *supra* note 1, s. 12(3).

[103] Thio, *Working out the Presidency*, *supra* note 54.

[104] Ibid.

[105] A 'law' comes into effect not on the day it has its third reading and is passed by Parliament, but on the date set by a government gazette notification. The *Religious Harmony Act* was passed in Parliament in November 1990, but was not gazetted into effect until March 1992. This history is appended to the text of the Act.

> But when the Christians became very active and evangelical ... wanting to convert the Muslims, and the Catholics decided to go in for social action, we were headed for trouble! ... We've just got out of one trouble – communism and Chinese chauvinism – and you want to land into another? Religious intolerance? It's just stupid. Stay out of politics. The *Religious Harmony Act* was passed; after that, it subsided.[106]

Significantly, Lee summarises the activities of 'the Catholics' as "social action". There is no effort in this narrative, ten years after the 'Marxist conspiracy', to resuscitate the 'Marxist' label or to recall the shadowy "nefarious activities"[107] that were said to be so "prejudicial to the security of Singapore".[108] Instead, the threat to the ever-precarious 'nation' is now 'religion', and the terrain that 'religion' must stay out of is 'politics'. 'Communalism', a term broad enough to embrace 'race' and 'religion' (in the 'raced' constructions of 'religion' in Singapore), is reframed as "Chinese chauvinism", thus opening the door for 'religion' to be separately addressed as a security issue.

Lee justifies the *Religious Harmony Act* on two grounds, evangelism and social action, without explaining how social action becomes "politics" or "religious intolerance". If we remove the shadowy 'conspiracy' element from the state discourse on the 'Marxist conspiracy' and bear in mind the activities actually engaged in by the Catholic social workers, then the formula the state constructs is marked by the constant repetition of an unexplained sequence:

> Social action = politics = disaster for the nation

106 Fook Kwang Han, Warren Fernandez & Sumiko Tan, *Lee Kuan Yew: The Man and His Ideas* (Singapore: Times Editions, 1998) 190.

107 Goh, *supra* note 22.

108 Ibid. This different framing, articulated by Lee in 1998, is possibly a reflection of post–Cold War dynamics. In his memoirs, however, Lee maintains the narrative of a Communist threat having surfaced from 1985 to 1987 via a "small group of English-educated pro-Marxist activists": Lee Kuan Yew, *From Third World to First: The Singapore Story, 1965–2000* (Singapore: Times Editions, 2000) 137.

This device of repetition, of asserting ideological positions as if they were 'fact' and 'truth', is a device that shapes the *Religious Harmony Act*.

Lee's 1998 comment credits the *Religious Harmony Act* with "subsiding … religious intolerance". This attribution is intriguing given that the state has not actually issued restraining orders under the *Religious Harmony Act*. Instead, in those moments when the *Religious Harmony Act* might have been invoked, the state turned either to the *Internal Security Act* or to the *Sedition Act*. From 2002[109] onwards,[110] men accused either of being members of the militant Islamist group Jemaah Islamiah plotting acts of violence against the state or, in one case, of being a "self-radicalised" militant,[111] have been detained without trial under the *ISA*. In the media, these men have been presented as motivated by their religious beliefs.[112] If they were indeed plotting against the state, then they were "carrying out subversive activities under the guise of propagating or practising any religious belief", conduct that s 8(1)(c) of the *Religious Harmony Act* seeks to restrain. The detention without trial of these men under the *ISA* may signal the severity of the threat against the state and in this way account for the non-utilisation of the *Religious Harmony Act*, but prosecutions that have been brought under the *Sedition Act* are not as neatly explained.

In 2005 bloggers who posted content that was racist and offensive about Islam were charged under s 3(1)(e) of the *Sedition Act*,[113] which states that "[a] seditious tendency is a tendency to promote feelings of ill-will and hostility between different races or classes of the population of Singapore". In 2006 a blogger who had posted offensive cartoons of Christ was also charged under this section of the *Sedition Act*

[109] Dominic Nathan, "15 Nabbed Here for Terror Plans", *Straits Times* (6 January 2002).

[110] Sue-Ann Chia, "'Self-radicalised' Law Grad, 4 JI Militants Held", *Straits Times* (9 June 2007).

[111] Ibid.

[112] Nathan, *supra* note 109; Chia, *supra* note 110. "ISA Detainee Taught MP's Sons", *Straits Times* (3 February 2002).

[113] "Two Bloggers Jailed for Making Seditious Remarks Online", *Channelnews Asia* (7 October 2005).

but was eventually let off with a stern warning.[114] Even "misdirected proselytisation"[115] has been construed as sedition: In 2009, after a trial that lasted eleven days, a married couple characterised by the press as Christian evangelists were found guilty of having distributed seditious and undesirable publications depicting Islam in disparaging ways.[116] The court found that the couple distributed publications that promoted feelings of ill-will and hostility between Christians and Muslims.[117] They were sentenced to eight weeks imprisonment.[118]

This highly public prosecution of those who violate 'religious harmony' through the technology of the *Sedition Act* might be explained as the state turning to 'law' primarily as a mode of public pedagogy, generating a discourse of the endangered 'nation' through the disciplining of those who transgress. In 2010 the pastors of two evangelist churches were summoned to the Internal Security Department for questioning after online postings of video clips revealed these pastors making disparaging comments about other faiths.[119] Within hours of having been called in by ISD, both pastors apologised[120] and withdrew the offending

[114] Zakir Hussain, "Blogger Who Posted Cartoons of Christ Online Being Investigated", *Straits Times* (14 June 2006); see "Warning for Blogger Who Posted Cartoons of Christ", *Straits Times* (21 July 2006).

[115] Lee, *supra* note 108.

[116] *Public Prosecutor v. Ong Kian Cheong & Dorothy Chan Hien Leng*; Elena Chong, "Couple Guilty of Sedition", *Straits Times* (28 May 2009); "Couple Sentenced to 8 Weeks Jail for Distributing Seditious Publications", *Channelnews Asia* (10 June 2009).

[117] Ibid.

[118] Ibid.

[119] Yen Feng, "ISD Looks into Clip of Sermon which Mocked Taoist Beliefs", *Straits Times* (15 June 2010); Yen Feng, "Church Pastor Says Sorry", *Straits Times* (16 June 2010); "ISD Calls up Pastor for Insensitive Comment", *Straits Times* (9 February 2010); "ISD Acts", *Straits Times* (9 February 2010); "Pastor's Comments on Buddhism/ Taoism 'Inappropriate & Unacceptable': MHA", *ChannelNewsAsia* (9 February 2010); "Pastor Apologises Personally to Buddhist & Taoist Federations", *ChannelNewsAsia* (9 February 2010); Leong Wee Keat, "Pastor's Apology", *Straits Times* (10 February 2010); Grace Chua, "Leaders of Buddhist, Taoist Groups Urge Restraint", *Straits Times* (9 February 2010).

[120] Leong, *supra* note 119.

video clips from their church websites.[121] Unlike the previous episodes in which actual[122] or threatened[123] prosecutions for sedition became the platform for disciplining infringements of 'religious harmony', the evangelist pastors became a different expression of state pedagogy. Prime Minister Lee presented the incidents as examples of religious leaders who "got into trouble",[124] then took a moderate stand to help "calm the ground".[125]

In the time since the *Religious Harmony Act* was passed, the state has responded to moments of discourse that offend the ideal of 'harmony' of 'race-religion' through *ISA* detentions, sedition charges and the weighty announcement of ISD questioning. In other words, threats to 'religious harmony' are managed without recourse to the *Religious Harmony Act*. Why then formulate and institutionalise the *Religious Harmony Act*?

LEGISLATION AS POLICY AND POLICING STATEMENT

Perhaps the efficacy of the *Religious Harmony Act* lies not in its application but, as suggested by Lee,[126] in the mere fact of its existence. At least one individual claims to have been told that his conduct has opened him to "three charges of defamation ... prosecution for sedition and contravening Singapore's *Religious Harmony Act*",[127] which suggests to me that the state views the *Religious Harmony Act* as a security 'law', available for use alongside other security laws in maintaining the state's dominance of public *discourse* more than public *order*.

121 Ibid.

122 *Supra* notes 113 and 116.

123 *Supra* note 114.

124 "Religious Leaders Must Take Lead to Safeguard Harmony: PM", *ChannelNewsAsia* (3 December 2010).

125 Ibid. See also "DPM Wong Says 'Glad to Note' Pastor Tan Realised His Mistake", *ChannelNewsAsia* (10 February 2010); "Pastor's Comments on Buddhism/Taoism", *supra* note 119.

126 *Supra* note 106.

127 Michael Dwyer, "Singapore's Accidental Exiles Leave a Damning Vacuum", *South China Morning Post* (2 September 2004).

The individual in question, Zulfikar Mohamad Shariff, came into prominence with his website, Fateha.com, on which he had argued that the sentiments of the detained Jemaah Islamiah activists were understandable, given the Singapore state's close alliances with the United States and Israel. He further argued that state schools should permit Muslim schoolgirls to wear headscarves and that Malay PAP Members of Parliament did not represent the interests of Singapore's Malay-Muslim electorate.[128] Shariff's comments on the Jemaah Islamiah arrests were characterised by the state as having "undermined the fabric of our multi-racial, multi-religious society" by having "cast doubt on the validity of the arrests and express[ed] sympathy for the detainees".[129] In other words, Shariff, like the 'Marxist conspirators', had breached the role of passive acceptance cast for him by the knowing state. In questioning and criticising the state, he had introduced a discursive strand into the public domain that the state was not ready to tolerate. Shariff fled to Melbourne, fearing imprisonment.[130]

While Shariff questioned the state's management of 'religion', the activities of the Catholic detainees, in addition to bringing 'class' to the surface of public discourse, might also be read as questioning the state's management of the economy. It appears to be discursive moments which interrogate particular facets of state ideology that trigger the state's turning to 'law' for its coercive power, prompting the state's rehearsal, yet again, of the narrative of Singapore's exceptional vulnerability. This narrative is used to legitimise law's violence being imposed upon a few before (an unmanifested) violence linked to 'race-religion' – predicted by the state as a certainty – might be visited upon the wider 'nation'.

To return to my question: Why has the state not used the *Religious Harmony Act* when it could have, choosing instead to prosecute

[128] Ahmad Osman, "Ex-Fateha Chief Investigated for Net Comments", *Straits Times* (4 July 2002).

[129] Wong Sher Maine & Chua Min Yi, "Condemn JI Terrorists – Yaacob", *Straits Times* (22 September 2002).

[130] Dwyer, *supra* note 127.

bloggers under the *Sedition Act*? Significantly, the attention of the state was drawn to the offensive blogs and video clips by members of the public. Even the pamphlets distributed by the Christian couple disparaging Islam came to the state's attention through complaints filed with the police.[131] This response from offended citizens suggests that the discursive project of the *Religious Harmony Act* has been successful. Citizens, ideologically consenting to the Singapore model of political pluralism, perceive disparaging comments on faiths and practices as violating the precarious 'harmony' of 'multi-racial, multi-religious' Singapore. It is consistent with acceptance of the state model of control and power in Singapore that these citizens should draw state and public attention to the breach of this 'harmony', seeking a remedy from the state.

In the unwillingness of members of the public to tolerate blog postings (which receive far more attention through police and ISD action than they do from being in cyberspace) there is a consistency with state positions on such matters. When the state turns to the *Sedition Act* and the *Internal Security Act* instead of the *Religious Harmony Act*, the punitive power of the 'law' is powerfully performed in the public domain.[132] All potential violators of 'religious harmony' are more potently instructed by imprisonment for criminal conduct under the *Sedition Act* than by restraining orders under the *Religious Harmony Act*.

The text of the *Religious Harmony Act* has enabled a public process by which the state reiterated and revitalised its version of Singapore's precarious stability. Possibly citizens have understood, not so much from the *Religious Harmony Act* itself as from the larger discourse of 'law', 'nation' and 'religion' facilitated by the formulation of the *Religious Harmony Act*, that the state's notion of 'religious harmony' is central to

[131] *Supra* note 116.

[132] I am grateful to Professor Li-ann Thio, National University of Singapore, for this point.

the security of the 'nation'. The *Religious Harmony Act* has thus served its purpose by functioning as a policy and a policing statement. It does not actually have to be enforced as 'law' in order to be effective.[133] The value of the *Religious Harmony Act* to the state lies primarily in the discourse that it enabled.

[133] The Singapore state said as much when the Minister for Home Affairs, Wong Kan Seng, responded to constitutional lawyer and nominated Member of Parliament Li-ann Thio's query on whether any restraining orders had been issued. The Minister said that the government had come close to "invoking the Act on several occasions" and that the Internal Security Department had issued warnings to certain religious leaders: Sing., *Parliamentary Debates*, vol. 82, col. 1319 (12 February 2007) (Wong Kan Seng).

7 ENTRENCHING ILLIBERALISM

The 2009 Public Order Act

THIS BOOK OPENED WITH A BRIEF ACCOUNT of Lee Kuan Yew's exchange with the IBA – an exchange in which he rehearsed the narratives of exceptionalism, described the duality of the legal system and insisted that Singapore was 'rule of law'.[1] The central role played by this lawyer-leader in the reformulation of the 'rule of law' into an increasingly entrenched 'rule by law' has been demonstrated throughout this project, perhaps most vividly by his conduct during the 1986 Select Committee Hearings on the *Legal Profession Act*. In 2011, with Lee eighty-eight years old, the question arises as to how much of Singapore's strategic management of 'law' is dependent on Lee leading the state, whether as Prime Minister or behind the scenes as Senior Minister and Minister Mentor. In other words, can legitimacy for 'rule by law' continue to be sustained in a Singapore without Lee Kuan Yew? In a tentative explorative of this question, I thread through the chronological logic of the case studies examined in this study with a brief consideration of a new legislative instrument, the 2009 *Public Order Act*.[2] This exploration addresses the question of the sustainability of 'rule by law' legitimacy in a Singapore that has been so dominated, for so long, by one man.

The *Public Order Act* arises from a context of public domain contestation. In this regard, it is 'law' within the same category as the four

[1] Lee Kuan Yew, "Why Singapore Is What It Is", *Straits Times* (15 October 2007).

[2] *Public Order Act 2009* (No. 15 of 2009, Sing.) [*Public Order Act*].

enactments I have studied. While a detailed analysis of the *Public Order Act* is not possible (because the Act was just two years in existence at the time of writing[3] and in this sense had yet to be fully performed), it is instructive to consider the ways in which this (apparently) newly minted legislation rehearses the key strategies, narratives and ideologies evident in the *Vandalism Act*, the *Press Act*, the *Legal Profession Act* and the *Religious Harmony Act*. In other words, the story of the *Public Order Act* suggests that Singapore's 'rule by law' has become an institutional feature of the Singapore state and does not require the personality and presence of Lee Kuan Yew to endure as a mode of legality.

MEGA-EVENTS

The story of the *Public Order Act* begins in September 2006, when Singapore's hosting of the World Bank–International Monetary Fund meetings also drew the international non-governmental organisations and civil society groups opposed to the neo-liberal policies of the World Bank and International Monetary Fund (IMF). A Singapore opposition politician, Chee Soon Juan, seized the moment to bring attention to the unequal contest between himself and the state when a "planned protest march past the convention centre was blocked by a 'human barricade' of police".[4] The barriers put in place by the Singapore state against the (broadly speaking) anti-establishment faction[5] resulted in international

[3] Although debated and passed in Parliament in April 2009, the *Public Order Act* was not gazetted into effect until 9 October 2009.

[4] Tim Brunnel, "Intervention – Extending Hospitality, Offshoring Protest – When the International Monetary Fund and World Bank Came to Singapore" (2007) 26 *Political Geography* 493 at 495.

[5] See, for example, "Barricades to Keep out Trouble at IMF/WB Meet", *Straits Times* (11 September 2006); Liaw Wy-Cin, "S'pore 'Can't Take Chances' with Security", *Straits Times* (11 September 2006); David Boey, "28 Activists Who Pose Security Risk Are Banned", *Straits Times* (12 September 2006); "The Police Stand", *Straits Times* (13 September 2006).

media attention being drawn to the state's repressive management of the public domain.[6]

Just a year after the 2006 World Bank–IMF conference, the November 2007 ASEAN summit also prompted small-scale demonstrations by the same Singapore dissidents. This time, the Singapore opposition party allied with a small group of Myanmar nationals to conduct a protest against the military junta in Myanmar.[7] Some of these Myanmar nationals were later asked to leave Singapore.[8] Both the 2006 World Bank–IMF meetings and the 2007 ASEAN summit introduced a new form of public domain contestation to Singapore: 'Foreigners', positioning themselves as spokespersons for international publics, had entered Singapore's public domain to contest the ideologies of the establishment organisations the Singapore state was playing host to. In doing so, these 'foreigners', establishment and otherwise,[9] critiqued the Singapore state's repressive policies and practices.[10] These events gave Singapore's domestic dissidents

[6] See, for example, Deborah K. Elms, "Let Them Hear the Message of the Masses: IMF/World Bank Meetings", *International Herald Tribune* (30 September 2006); "Govt Takes Issue with IHT Article on Civil Society Groups", *Straits Times* (7 October 2006). For a scholarly analysis, see Alan Collins, "A People-Oriented ASEAN: A Door Ajar or Closed for Civil Society Organisations?" (2008) 30:2 *Contemporary Southeast Asia* 313.

[7] "Singapore Arrests Opposition Members in Myanmar Protest", *Reuters* (8 October 2007), online: Reuters.com <http://www.reuters.com/article/newsOne/idUSSIN30196720071008>. See also Stephanie Pang, "Protest Singapore Style; 3 Marchers, 19 Media, 1,000 Police" *Bloomberg* (19 November 2007), online: Bloomberg.com <http://www.bloomberg.com/apps/news?sid=aHKiTH1 ny.7Q&pid=20601080#>.

[8] Kor Kian Beng, "Myanmar Activists 'Defied Our Laws' ", *Straits Times* (18 September 2008).

[9] Paul Wolfowitz, then President of the World Bank, criticised Singapore as authoritarian when the state refused entry to twenty-seven international civil society activists who had been accredited to attend the World Bank–IMF meetings: Brunnel, *supra* note 4 at 494; "World Bank Accuses S'pore of Breaching Formal Agreement", *Straits Times* (14 September 2006); Tracy Sua & Tanya Fong, "Singapore Stands by Decision to Bar Some Activists", *Straits Times* (9 September 2006).

[10] Jeremy Au Yong, "Singapore Takes Flak for Ban on Protests", *Straits Times* (10 September 2006); Peh Shing Huei & Ken Kwek, "14 Civil Society Groups Call for Event Boycott", *Straits Times* (13 September 2006); Peh Shing Huei, "Activists on S'pore Turnaround: 'Too Little, Too Late'", *Straits Times* (16 September 2006); Brunnel, *supra* note 4.

a platform for a new, international audience as the world's attention was drawn to this anomalous country in which demonstrations cannot happen.

The hosting of both 'mega-events' was presented by the state in terms that fostered legal duality and nationalism. Mega-events have become emblematic of Singapore's organisational capacity.[11] This capacity, in turn, is presented as resulting in a range of economic benefits for the 'nation'.[12] The state's determination to exclude accredited civil society organisations from the World Bank–IMF meetings was justified by Prime Minister Lee Hsien Loong as preventing and pre-empting violence.[13] The state's duality was thus simultaneously performed through its first-world capacity for prosperity-generating efficiency alongside the illiberalism of stability-securing intolerance of contestation.

In January 2009, the Singapore state announced that it was reviewing public order laws and was considering crafting new legislation to deal with civil disobedience,[14] particularly with reference to mega-events such as the ASEAN summit and the World Bank–IMF meetings. In anticipation of the November 2009 APEC summit, the *Public Order Act* was passed in April 2009.[15] Consistent with the dual state's reliance on the national narrative, in presenting the *Public Order Bill* to Parliament the Minister

[11] "S'pore, Through Foreign Eyes", *Straits Times* (16 September 2006); Erica Tay, "PM Thanks S'poreans for Making Meetings a Big Success", *Straits Times* (21 September 2006); Fiona Chan, "Many Thanks and Well Done Singapore, Say Delegates", *Straits Times* (21 September 2006); Krist Boo, "Event Was a Success, Says Lim Hwee Hua", *Straits Times* (21 September 2006); Krist Boo, "Pat on the Back for S'pore as Event Organiser Retires", *Straits Times* (22 September 2006); Li Xueying, "A Well-Oiled Event – Thanks to Team S'pore", *Straits Times* (22 September 2006); Li Xueying, "Meetings Showed Singapore Can Do It", *Straits Times* (22 September 2006); "Thumbs up for S'pore Service Standards", *Straits Times* (29 March 2007).

[12] Sing., *Parliamentary Debates*, vol. 85 (13 April 2009); see also Marcel Lee Pereira, "Many Spin-off Benefits with Mega-Events", *Straits Times* (11 January 2007).

[13] "S'pore 'Right to Blacklist Activists'", *Straits Times* (7 October 2006).

[14] Li Xueying, "Govt Reviewing Public Order Laws", *Straits Times* (17 January 2009).

[15] Sing., *Parliamentary Debates*, vol. 85 (13 April 2009); Loh Chee Kong, "Tough Words for Protestors and Anarchists: DPM Wong", *Today* (16 April 2009).

stressed that, with Singapore's small size, "stability for us is an existential issue – both economically and as a society ... [and a] key competitive advantage".[16] The Minister also highlighted that mega-events had contributed more than 5 billion Singapore dollars to the economy in 2007 and would probably continue to generate significant income for Singapore in the years to come.[17] In brief, just as with the four enactments I have presented, the state turned to 'law' and the narrative of perpetual territorial vulnerability to rationalise and legitimise its management of critique in the public domain, refining existing 'laws'[18] to close the interstitial spaces for public critique exposed by the 2006 and 2007 mega-events.

AUGMENTING PUBLIC ORDER

In essence, the *Public Order Act* might be read as legislation that augments the state's already considerable ideological homogenisation of the public space of 'nation'. It adds to existing legislation on the policing of activities in the public domain[19] by requiring police permits for any gathering or meeting of one or more persons intending to, first, demonstrate support for, or opposition to, the views or actions of any person, group or government; second, publicise a cause or campaign; and third, mark or commemorate any event.[20] I will limit my consideration of the *Public Order Act* to its requirement that police permits be obtained for the publicising of "a cause or campaign".

[16] Sing., *Parliamentary Debates*, vol. 85 (13 April 2009) (K. Shanmugam).

[17] Ibid.

[18] The legislation the state referred to as part of the rationalising exercise of the *Public Order Bill* was the *Miscellaneous Offences (Public Order and Nuisance) Act* (Cap. 184, 1997 Rev. Ed. Sing.), under which any assembly of five or more requires a police permit, and the *Public Entertainments and Meetings Act* (Cap. 257, 2001 Rev. Ed. Sing.), under which certain gatherings of groups of four or more require an entertainment licence.

[19] In addition to the two enactments cited in note 18, the following 'laws' regulate public domain activity: the *Sedition Act*, the *Internal Security Act*, the *Official Secrets Act*, the *Penal Code*, the *Religious Harmony Act*, the *Broadcasting Act* and defamation law.

[20] Sing. *Parliamentary Debates*, vol. 85 (13 April 2009).

It is striking how the terms 'cause' and 'campaign' have come to be invested with accusatory potency, empowering the state to invoke 'law' in securing its hegemonic occupancy of the public domain. In the context of Singapore, to 'campaign' or be part of a 'cause' has come to be understood, in an opaque, inexplicable manner, as a political transgression. The events of 1971 silenced newspapers accused of 'campaigning' for and glorifying a range of 'causes' (Chapter 4). In the 1986 Select Committee Hearings, Lee Kuan Yew shamed and intimidated Teo, accusing her of "campaigning" for the opposition Workers' Party (Chapter 5). The *Religious Harmony Act* was designed to prevent the kind of 'campaigning' and advocacy for 'causes' that the Catholic social workers were accused of engaging in (Chapter 6).

Ironically, as Chapter 3 shows, it was the Barisan's "Aid Vietnam" campaign that precipitated the state's construction of the category 'vandalism' as a masked part of its own counter-campaign. Consistent with the colonial state's practice of using 'law' to secure state control, legislation in the 'nation' has become an extended expression of a state campaign of control. If 'law' is broadly understood as (also) residing within the extra-legal pronouncements of state actors, then the state's discourse (as set out in these case studies) has repeatedly, consistently asserted that the state, and only the state, may legitimately enter the public domain to further 'causes' and conduct 'campaigns'. Crucially, however, this communication has been made sub-textually, through the vehicle of demonising characterisations imposed on non-state actors.

The sub-textual and discursive prohibition on pursuing 'causes' and 'campaigns' acquired a more explicit formulation, in the somewhat hidden shape of subsidiary legislation, from June 1989.[21] (This date is significant because it is a relatively short time after the 'Marxist conspiracy' detentions of 1987–88.) This is when the executive promulgated subsidiary legislation generally requiring official permission for five or more

[21] *Miscellaneous Offences (Public Order and Nuisance) (Assemblies and Processions) Rules* (Cap. 184, R.1, 1997 Rev. Ed. Sing.) [*Miscellaneous Offences Rules*].

people gathering to, first, demonstrate support for, or opposition to, the views or actions of any person, group or government; second, publicise a cause or campaign; or third, mark or commemorate any event. In short, the proscriptions of the *Public Order Act* have existed within the regulatory regime since 1989. The difference is that, under the 1989 subsidiary legislation, the number of five or more people is specified.

In contrast, under the new *Public Order Act*, even *one* person must apply for a police permit so long as the activity is "cause-related".[22] The state could have amended the existing *Miscellaneous Offences Rules* to effect the alteration regarding the number of people rather than enact an entirely "new" 'law'. When so much of the substance of 'law' is so similar, the question that arises is, why has the state seen fit to enact an apparently new 'law'?

As a primary enactment, the *Public Order Act* presents a more performative platform for 'law', delivering a restatement of the state's position on public domain contestation via parliamentary debates and the attendant publicity for state explanations. As with the *Religious Harmony Act*, a policing and policy statement is achieved through the enactment of the *Public Order Act*. In the process of 'law'-making, the state delivers an explicit and expanded statement of its interpretations and expectations. The narrative of national vulnerability, recast through the post-9/11 lens of 'terrorism', is revitalised for a new era. Yet again, legislation becomes the tool constraining the voice of non-state actors in the 'nation'.

Like the four other enactments, the *Public Order Act* gives the executive pre-emptive and preventive power,[23] invoking national security as the legitimising imperative.[24] As in three of the five acts this project studies (the *Vandalism Act* is the exception), the courts are excluded and all appeals against executive decisions must be made to the executive.[25] Like

[22] *Public Order Act*, *supra* note 2.

[23] Ibid. at s. 5.

[24] Sing. *Parliamentary Debates*, vol. 85 cols. 3656–3761 (13 April 2009).

[25] *Public Order Act*, *supra* note 2, s. 11.

the other four acts, the language of the *Public Order Act* is inherently ideological (as the preceding brief discussion of 'cause' and 'campaign' illustrates) and requires compliance with the state's meanings in order to not contravene the Act. As with the other four acts I have studied, the terms of the *Public Order Act*, by requiring even a single "cause or campaign" publicising individual to apply for a police permit, heightens self-surveillance and state surveillance. And like the complicity of the 'West' in the violent repression of the Left in the Cold War climate of the 1966 (Chapter 3) an anxious, post-9/11 'West' lends legitimacy to the Singapore state's 'rule by law' by identifying the dual state as its venue of choice for establishment events.

In brief, the *Public Order Act* is the Singapore state's latest expression of the 'rule by law' reframing of the 'rule of law'. The technologies, discourses and strategies this project has uncovered and outlined through studying the detail of legislation spanning from 1966 to 1991 continue in 2009. Legislation and discourse have become entrenched methods for the state's reconfiguration of 'rule of law'. In a sustained and sustainable manner, an illiberal democracy has secured a hegemonic national legitimacy and a good-enough international legitimacy. Illiberal legislation is thus likely to be a vehicle that sustains continuity past personality, outliving Lee to shape Singapore's 'rule by law' management of the 'rule of law' in the years to come.

8 LEGISLATION, ILLIBERALISM AND LEGITIMACY

THIS PROJECT HAS TRACED THE SINGAPORE state's reconfiguration of the profoundly liberal concept of the 'rule of law' into an illiberal 'rule by law' through the state's manipulation of legislation and public discourse. In tracing this process, I have asked: How does the Singapore state maintain its legitimacy as a 'rule of law' polity despite its 'rule by law' practices? In this concluding chapter, I revisit the specific legislative moments detailed from Chapters 3 to 7 to derive a whole that is greater than its parts: a template for 'law' that facilitates and engenders state legitimacy for 'rule by law'.

The case studies have illustrated how the state tries to make 'law' Singapore-specific through arguments of exceptionalism and the trope of Singapore's perpetual territorial vulnerability. As a preface to the template for 'rule by law' legitimacy offered here and in keeping with the methodological focus on discourse, I first analyse a significant exchange between the International Bar Association Human Rights Institute (Ibahri) and the state. This exchange demonstrates that no matter how much the state's discourse of Singapore exceptionalism has tried to fence off 'law' as 'local', as concept and category, the 'rule of law' is inexorably global. In this global resonance, there is the implication that the remaining challenges to the legitimacy of the PAP state, and possibilities for a resurgence in the 'rule of law' within Singapore, lie externally.

IBAHRI AND THE STATE

I opened this book with a brief account of Lee Kuan Yew's exchange with the IBA – an exchange in which he rehearsed the narratives of exceptionalism, described the duality of the legal system and used tables and rankings to insist that Singapore was 'rule of law'.[1] Eight months after the conference, Ibahri released a report critiquing Singapore's human rights and 'rule of law' record.[2] Ibahri's report was entitled "Prosperity versus Individual Rights? Human Rights, Democracy and Rule of Law in Singapore". Ibahri found that Singapore had limited the freedoms of expression, assembly and the media, in part through the enactment and enforcement of legislation.[3] The report also questioned the capacity of Singapore's judiciary to be independent when determining defamation cases brought by state actors against non-state actors.[4] In other words, Ibahri questioned Singapore's claim to being 'rule of law' and pointed to ways in which it is 'rule by law'.

Ibahri's critique came from a distinctly liberal reading of the 'rule of law', a position indicated by the sub-title of the report: "Human Rights, Democracy and the Rule of Law in Singapore". As I argued in Chapter 1, this liberal conceptualisation of the 'rule of law' informs Singapore's very existence. Singapore's vulnerability to a liberal 'rule of law' critique arises not just from its history but also from the repeated, persistent claim by the state that it is 'rule of law'. The Singapore state responded immediately to Ibahri's critique with press statements.[5] Of more interest, however, is

[1] Lee Kuan Yew, "Why Singapore Is What It Is", *Straits Times* (15 October 2007).

[2] International Bar Association Human Rights Institute, "Prosperity versus Individual Rights? Human Rights, Democracy and the Rule of Law in Singapore" (July 2008), online: <http://www.ibanet.org/Article/Detail.aspx?ArticleUid=0081C460–4B39–4ACB-BB40–8303FCEF DB31> [*Ibahri Report*].

[3] Ibid.

[4] Ibid. at 49–62.

[5] Rosnah Ahmad, "Govt Rebuts Human Rights Accusations", *Today* (10 July 2008); "Govt Rebuts Report Questioning Independence of Singapore Courts", *Channel NewsAsia* (11 July 2008). See also "Judging Singapore's judiciary", *Wall Street Journal*

the state's November 2008 forty-one-page rejoinder to Ibahri (hereafter State Response).[6] The State Response is a text focused upon proving its 'rule of law' standing. In many ways, it reads like a summary of the discourse of 'law' and 'nation' that this project has traced.

In keeping with its inaugural and consistent self-description (Chapter 1), the state opens its discourse on 'law' by aligning itself with 'Western' conceptions of 'law' in a definitive and declaratory manner, describing itself as a "democratic state with a written Constitution which is supreme".[7] Ironically, this claim is immediately qualified by recounting the national narrative. Indeed, in terms of substantive arguments, the state begins and ends its response to Ibahri with the national narrative, a framework it explains as necessary "because your Report has not made an attempt to understand the democratic system in Singapore nor the values which underpin our society".[8] By presenting "democracy" and "values" as situationally specific categories, the state achieves two ends. First, it retains its rhetorical claim to being 'rule of law'. Second, it lays the ground for its argument of exceptionalism without appearing to reframe the 'rule of law'. Instead, it is the liberalism underpinning the 'rule of law' that the state reframes. This strategy suggests that the state does not want to be seen as interfering with the iconic status of the 'rule of law'. In its exchange with Ibahri, the 'rule of law' becomes a symbolic terrain that the state wants to be seen as policing and protecting, in tandem with important international actors such as the IBA.

(15 July 2008), reporting on the Ibahri evaluation, and the Singapore state's response, "Singapore Has an Independent Judiciary", *Wall Street Journal* (24 July 2008).

6 Sing., "Response to the International Bar Association Human Rights Institute's Report on Singapore" (14 November 2008), online: <http://app2.mlaw.gov.sg/LinkClick.aspx?fileticket= gDkKt5ebvTY%3d&tabid=204> [*State Response*].

7 Ibid. at 4, para. 4. In keeping with this line of argument, the state makes similar claims later in its response: "The principle of the Rule of Law is fundamental in Singapore" (8, para. 15); "A strong commitment to the Rule of Law" (11, para. 22(c)); "It would be absurd to believe that such progress would have been possible if Singapore (as you have portrayed) had stamped down on the Rule of Law" (13, para. 27).

8 *State Response*, *supra* note 6 at 4, para. 2.

The state bolsters its claim to comity with 'Western' understandings of the 'rule of law' by rejecting Ibahri's assessment that Singapore has adopted 'Asian values' in its privileging of social and economic rights over civil and political rights.[9] This, the state says, "is quite incorrect".[10] Instead, the state insists:

> The Singapore Government has never asserted the superiority of any particular set of values over others, nor do we believe that cultural differences should be allowed to justify violations of basic human rights.... Singapore shares a strong commitment to the development of human rights.... Our laws and policies protect the freedom, equality and dignity of individuals.[11]

Despite this totalising denial ("never"), as Chapter 3 illustrates, the state most certainly has asserted the superiority of 'Asian values' when it justified the caning of Michael Fay.[12] The jurisprudence of defamation in Singapore also demonstrates how statist courts have entrenched what is, in substance, an 'Asian values' variation with reference to quantifying damages awarded to defamed individuals who are public figures.[13]

Indeed, in the landscape of Singapore 'law', 'Asian values' is just one of the shorthands signifying an underlying constant: the discourse of exceptionalism. Exceptionalism has adopted a range of facades – infantalising characterisations of 'the people' used to justify the 1966 *Punishment for Vandalism Act* and the 1974 *Press Act*; distorted characterisations of public engagement used to constrain the Law Society in 1986; hyperbolic narratives of violence inherent to 'race' and 'religion' used to police the 'foreign press' (1986 amendment to the *Press Act*) and 'religion' (1991

[9] Ibid. at 11, para. 25.

[10] Ibid.

[11] Cover letter appended to ibid. at 2–3, paras. 4(b) and (c).

[12] On the manner in which 'Asian values' arguments shape Singapore's media-controlled policies, see Shanthi Kalathil & Taylor C. Boas, *Open Networks; Closed Regimes: The Impact of the Internet on Authoritarian Rule* (Washington, DC: Carnegie Endowment for International Peace, 2003).

[13] See Chapter 1.

Religious Harmony Act); and alarmist projections of national decline held at bay through corporal punishment and 'Asian values' (the 1994 enforcement of the *Vandalism Act*). In an interesting textual strategy, however, while the state produces concise denials of championing 'Asian values' (denials that read like the inked equivalent of the sound bite), the extended narrative of the report does indeed argue for the necessary privileging of economic certainty and social order over narrow 'Western' understandings of rights.[14] This argument discards the shorthand 'Asian values', while retaining the rejection of a 'Western' critique as irrelevant to,[15] and ignorant of,[16] the specifics of Singapore. In brief, the state reprises its strategy of claiming the legitimising marker – 'rule of law' – then asserts Singapore exceptionalism.

The enduring utility of the discourse of exceptionalism, I would argue, arises from more than the rhetorical habits of a hegemonic state. Singapore's discourse of exceptionalism is strategically focused on two strands of argument: Singapore's exceptional (inaugural[17] and ongoing[18]) vulnerability and Singapore's exceptional (legitimising but

14 *State Response*, *supra* note 6 at 13, para. 28.

15 Ibid. "[Singapore's] leaders knew that no one (not least the various commentators who, after visiting Singapore for a few days, felt able to prescribe the type of governance Singapore should have) owed Singapore a living" (5, para. 6); "What we find, amongst Western commentators, is a focus on one or two aspects (e.g. on a narrow definition of freedom of expression), without a holistic understanding or appreciation of what democracy means; and without bothering to understand how people really live in some of the societies.... If the commentators looked a little more carefully..." (13, para. 28).

16 Ibid.

17 Ibid. "Singapore had independence thrust upon it in 1965. It was (and is) a tiny island in a region that has seen much turbulence, political instability and wars" (5, para. 5; "Singapore started out with an uncertain future" (5, para. 9). This paragraph details a range of ways in which Singapore was vulnerable. "In short, the tiny city state faced a variety of existential threats: economic, social and physical. It faced threats both internally and externally" (6, para. 10).

18 Ibid. "Now, 40 years later, Singapore still continues to face some threats, which arise from its size, location and geopolitical factors" (6, para. 11); "we believe that even long years of absence of open outbreak of communal violence does not mean that the potential for such violence has gone away" (17, para. 37).

also vulnerable) material success.[19] It is the embeddedness of 'law' within modernist governance that enables Singapore's material prosperity to potently undermine a 'rule of law' critique.

LAW *FOR* DEVELOPMENT

In the trajectory of post-colonial nation-states, the 'rule of law' nests within the folds of modernist governance. It thus becomes the vehicle for a range of attributes – efficiency, the absence of corruption, infrastructural and institutional support for capitalist market transactions – that link to development goals.[20] And when it comes to development, Singapore has excelled – "moving with extreme rapidity from colonial outpost ... to one of the world's wealthiest nations".[21] It is a movement in which 'law', specifically 'rule by law', has been a key tool:

> Orchestrated by the government itself in a series of economically, socially and politically premeditated policies involving extensive use of legal techniques and innovations.... No other society ... has made more thorough and successful use of law *for* development.[22]

Consistent with the conflation of 'law', governance and post-colonial development, the state's response to Ibahri details the project of 'nation' under its management: attainments in literacy and education,[23] public

[19] Ibid. "A large number of countries became independent in the post WWII era. Only a very small number of these countries have succeeded in developing and strengthening these institutions, and given their peoples better lives. Singapore is one of those few countries" (5, para. 8); "But as a society and country, [Singapore] is in a far superior position compared to 40 years ago" (6, para. 11); this paragraph details achievements in the fields of literacy and education.

[20] Rachel Kleinfeld, "Competing Definitions of the Rule of Law", in Thomas Carothers, ed., *Promoting the Rule of Law Abroad* (Washington, DC: Carnegie Endowment for International Peace, 2006) 31.

[21] Andrew Harding & Connie Carter, "The Singapore Model of Law and Development: Cutting Through the Complexity", in John Hatchard et al., eds., *Law and Development: Facing Complexity in the 21st Century* (London: Routledge Cavendish, 2003) 191.

[22] Ibid. at 192.

[23] *State Response*, *supra* note 6 at 6, para. 11.

housing and home ownership,[24] low unemployment,[25] infrastructure,[26] health care,[27] foreign direct investment[28] and, most expansively, 'law'. Singapore's attainments in the field of 'law' are disaggregated as the efficiency of the legal system,[29] the competitiveness of enterprises facilitated by legal and regulatory framework,[30] the fair administration of justice,[31] the guaranteed rights of foreign investors,[32] the independence of the judiciary,[33] the supremacy of a 'law' which applies equally to all,[34] the minimal corruption within Singapore[35] and the low crime rate.[36]

This disaggregation, and the juxtaposition of development goals with 'rule of law' goals, offer a valuable functional template for 'rule by law' legitimacy. The vexed question underpinning this project – how does a state that violates rights and freedoms build and sustain its legitimacy? – is, in effect, answered by the state's summary of its success. The apparent proof the state offers – tables, rankings, statistics – epitomises the governmentality inherent to 'nation'. Significantly, the sources of that 'proof' are, overwhelmingly, located within the authoritative 'West'. As I have noted, the state denigrated Ibahri's report as irrelevant to, and ignorant of, Singapore. And yet the state generated a lengthy response engaging with the report. The significance of the triangle of events this study has traced – IBA conference, Ibahri critique, state reply – is that it dramatises the impossibility of a 'rule by law' state unilaterally, univocally, securing its legitimacy in the international public domain. States

24 Ibid. at 7, para.12.
25 Ibid.
26 Ibid.
27 Ibid.
28 Ibid. at 8, para. 14.
29 Ibid. at 7, para. 13.
30 Ibid.
31 Ibid. at 8, para. 13.
32 Ibid. at 8, para. 14.
33 Ibid. at 8, para. 15.
34 Ibid.
35 Ibid. at 8, paras, 15, 16.
36 Ibid. at 9, para. 19.

need the recognition not just of other states[37] but also of international actors with a significant presence on the international stage, such as the IBA. Consequently, when the Ibahri report was released, the Singapore state's quandary was acute. The state had used (indeed, almost flaunted) the IBA's convening in Singapore as a legitimising marker for Singapore 'law'. Yet eight months later, this same legitimising authority had turned around and delegitimised Singapore. This meant that the state could not respond by simplistically demonising the source of the critique, as it does, for example, with Amnesty International reports.[38] The state was compelled to engage with the Ibahri report's content.

Singapore cannot be isolated from a global community of 'nations' if it is to sustain its 'rule of law' standing. Reflecting its notional and temporal location within the post-colonial world, the state's response both deprecates and authorises the 'West'. For example, to support its claim to being 'rule of law', the state cites rankings from two organisations that are based in Switzerland and have been established as 'independent' and not-for-profit:[39] the Lausanne-based IMD World Competitiveness Yearbook 2008[40] and the World Economic Forum Global Competitiveness Report 2007–2008.[41] These rankings are invoked as authority twice in the report.[42] To demonstrate the absence of corruption, the state cites the World Bank

37 J. Borneman, "State: Anthropological Aspects", in Neil J. Smelser & Paul B. Baltes, eds., *International Encyclopedia of the Social & Behavioural Sciences* (Amsterdam: Elsevier, 2004) 14968.

38 Rachel Evans, "Singapore Leader Rejects Amnesty", *International Financial Law Review* (18 October 2007), online: <http://www.iflr.com/Article/1983342/Singapore-leader-rejects-Amnesty. html>.

39 World Economic Forum, online: <http://www.weforum.org/en/about/Our%20 Organization/index.htm>.

40 This yearbook "ranked Singapore 1st out of 55 countries for a legal and regulatory framework that encourages the competitiveness of enterprises, and 6th of 55 countries on the indicator 'Justice is fairly administered'"; *State Response*, *supra* note 6 at 8–9, para. 13.

41 This report "rated Singapore 19th out of 131 countries on the subject of independence of the judiciary from political influence, ahead of Japan, France, Luxemburg and the United States. For the indicator 'Efficiency of Legal Framework', Singapore is ranked 10th out of 131 countries." Ibid. at 8, para. 13.

42 Ibid. at 32, para. 72.

Report on Governance 2007[43] and the 2007 Transparency International Corruption Perception Index.[44]

In the course of its response, the state also refers to rankings of the Times Higher Education Supplement,[45] the Business Environment Risk Intelligence (BERI) Report,[46] the Human Development Index[47] and Mercer Human Resource Consulting.[48] Articles in *Newsweek*,[49] *Business Week*[50] and the *New York Times*[51] praising the state's achievements are also referred to. In other words, the state responds to the critique presented by Ibahri by valorising 'Western' authorities that have assessed it favourably and by ignoring those that have not.

POST-COLONIAL AMBIVALENCE

The need for state recognition must surely be especially conflicted for post-colonial states. Achieving 'rule of law' status involves a hierarchical relationship in which the 'West' appropriates a 'rule of law' ascendancy that qualifies it to assess and evaluate the 'rule of law' status of its former dominions. Post-colonial nation-states such as Singapore that do not have a history of successful anti-colonial independence movements are often placed on a 'rule of law' trajectory at the point of de-colonisation.[52] In a replication and extension of the domination and subordination inherent to the binary of colony/metropole, the Singapore post-colonial state has

43 "The World Bank Report on Governance 2007 ranked Singapore 2nd in the world for Government Effectiveness (after Denmark) and 5th in the world for control of corruption (after Finland, Iceland, Denmark and New Zealand)." Ibid. at 9, para. 16.

44 Ibid.

45 Ibid. at 7, note 3.

46 Ibid. at 7, note 6.

47 Ibid. at 7, note 7; 12, para. 26.

48 Ibid. at 12, para. 26.

49 Ibid. at 7, note 3.

50 Ibid. at 9, note 9.

51 Ibid. at 6, para. 11; 17, para. 36.

52 For post-colonial states with a history of revolutions and rebellions, the criteria of and conditions for legitimacy are probably very different.

chosen to work within the legal-administrative apparatus established by the coloniser. As 'nation', the Singapore state sets out to comply with the standards set by the former imperial master without possessing the West's historical underpinnings for the 'rule of law'.[53] As Clark succinctly notes:

> Though the common law legal systems of England and America pride themselves on having devised the rule of law, in fact it came into being slowly; it was the product of a prolonged political struggle, and in any case was riddled with reversals and exceptions. The west, it should not be forgotten, went through a long period of modernisation, plagued by civil wars, violence, and revolutions.... [T]he idea that not only should the government rule by law, but should also abide by the rules and even be limited by the rules was an idea that took a long time to be actually established. Much of the debate took place in a pre-capitalist economic environment, where political participation was strictly limited to a very small portion of the population. In England, at least, the rule of law, both as an idea and as a constitutional practice pre-dated the industrial revolution and the emergence of democratic politics.[54]

This long and protracted history of the 'rule of law' raises the unanswerable question as to whether an implanted[55] 'rule of law' can take root and flourish. For Singapore, the post-colonial submission to 'Western' determinations of legitimacy took place alongside the project of 'nation'. In tandem with the 'Western' enmeshments of nation-formation, nation-*building* necessarily involved, and continues to involve, the performance

[53] Brian Z. Tamanaha, *On the Rule of Law: History, Politics, Theory* (Cambridge: Cambridge University Press, 2004).

[54] David Clark, "The Many Meanings of the Rule of Law", in Kanishka Jayasuriya, ed., *Law, Capitalism and Power in Asia* (London: Routledge, 1999) 28 at 29–30.

[55] I borrow Rhodes and Weller's characterisation of 'Westminster' systems of government as either "transplanted" (settler colonies such as Australia) or "implanted" (former colonies that "inherited British constitutional arrangements as part of decolonisation"): R. A. W. Rhodes & Patrick Weller, "Westminster Transplanted and Westminster Implanted: Exploring Political Change", in Haig Patapan, John Wanna & Patrick Weller, eds., *Westminster Legacies: Democracy and Responsible Government in Asia and the Pacific* (Sydney: UNSW Press, 2005) 1 at 3.

of separation from the 'West'. At the same time, the economic, defence and developmental ties of the Singapore 'nation' to the 'West' kept (and continues to keep) the new polity "in-dependence".[56] As this study has repeatedly demonstrated, the Singapore state has managed its entanglement by periodically and instrumentally adopting and rejecting selected facets of the 'West'.

THE LEGITIMACY OF 'ENGLISH LAW'

For Singapore specifically, as illustrated by its response to Ibahri, demonstrating its 'rule of law' credentials requires reference to structures put in place by the departing coloniser: constitutionally guaranteed freedoms, Westminster-model parliamentary democracy and modernist bureaucracy. The nation-state cannot step outside the foundations laid by the assessing, ascendant 'West' so long as the nation-state seeks the parity of 'rule of law' arrival. Thus, in its response to Ibahri, the state describes itself in a manner that claims markers of legitimacy consistent with the 'rule of law':

> Singapore is a democratic state with a written Constitution which is supreme. The Government is elected through universal franchise. The Constitution provides for elections to be held regularly. Voting is compulsory and secret.... Singapore has also (unlike so many of the countries in the postcolonial period) built and strengthened the legal system that the British left us instead of debasing and destroying it. Its judiciary is highly ranked and the Courts provide justice in a speedy and efficient manner.... The principle of the Rule of Law is fundamental in Singapore. The Singapore Government exercises its authority through laws that are adopted and enforced by an independent judiciary in accordance with established and accepted procedures. No one is above the law.[57]

[56] Hong Lysa & Huang Jianli, *The Scripting of a National History: Singapore and Its Pasts* (Singapore: NUS Press, 2008) 4–10.

[57] *State Response, supra* note 6 at 4–5, para. 4; 7, para. 13; 8, para. 16.

Just as 'English law' was invoked as a legitimising marker in the 1986 Select Committee Hearings on the *Legal Profession Act*,[58] so too the state refers to colonial governance as if the British governed through the Diceyan ideal. But the project of 'colony' did not promise, nor did it deliver, individual rights and freedoms or restraints on state power. It is 'nation' that has promised these things. To recapitulate an argument made in Chapter 1, it is entirely consistent with goals and beliefs of colonial governance that the Singapore state has subordinated individual rights and crippled the institutional restraints on state power. Rather than strengthening the tenuous 'rule of law' left by the colonial state, the nation-state has augmented the primary tool of colonial governance: 'rule by law'. The irony and slippage in the state's formulaic self-description of Singapore 'law' as derived from what "the British left us"[59] is that the nation-state has indeed built upon and strengthened the duplicitous, bifurcated 'law' left by the British.[60]

CONSTANTLY COLONISED CITIZENS

The enactments I have studied illustrate the repeated enhancement of 'rule by law' in the nation-state – an enhancement that systematically excludes 'rule of law' through legislative text and the discourse of national vulnerability. The *Vandalism Act*, for example, adopts the colonial penal technology

[58] The 1986 amendments to the *Legal Profession Act* (Chapter 5), in addition to restricting the Law Society's power to comment on proposed legislation to those instances when the state invited it to do so, altered the conditions for membership in the Council of the Law Society. The amendments – disqualifying lawyers who had been suspended for six months or more and lawyers who had been convicted of a crime involving fraud or dishonesty – had the immediate effect of disqualifying Francis Seow from the Council. The amendments also increased the state's involvement in disciplinary proceedings against lawyers. At the Hearings, the Attorney General generated a lengthy justification of these amendments by holding up developments in the English legal professions as models worthy of emulation: Sing., "Report of the Select Committee on the Legal Profession (Amendment) Bill", October 1986, 6th Parliament, B1–B23.

[59] *State Response*, *supra* note 6 at 7, para. 13.

[60] Ibid. at 4–5, para. 4.

of caning but severs caning from colonial penal ideologies on the need for proportionality in punishment. Discarding the colonial principle that sanguinary punishment was appropriate only for sanguinary crimes, the nation-state seizes upon the retributive impact of penal caning and the instrumentality of humiliation to enhance its control of the public domain.

Similarly, the *Press Act* adopts the licensing and regulatory regimes of colonial press control but exceeds the colonial state's policing of the press through the two-tiered share structure imposed on newspapers and, later, the gazetting of the 'foreign press'. The 'rule of law' constitutional guarantee of the freedom of expression (a feature of the national, not the colonial, state) is significantly curtailed by the 'rule by law' provisions of the *Press Act*. With the *Legal Profession Act*, the regressive turn is even more overt. The nation-state punishes the Law Society for publically critiquing the state by explicitly scripting the Society's powers in exactly the same manner the colonial state did – limiting the capacity of the Law Society to comment on legislation to those instances in which the state invites it to do so. With the *Religious Harmony Act*, the colonial 'legacy' is evident in the adoption of the text and technologies of two colonial enactments – the *Sedition Act* and the *Emergency Regulations* – while fashioning an apparently new act to address an apparently new problem. In doing so, the *Religious Harmony Act* severely curtails the freedoms of religion, expression and movement.

In short, the nation-state has indeed built upon and strengthened the colonial legal system, but it has done so in a manner that has entrenched the 'rule of law'/ 'rule by law' divide, denied the primacy of individual rights and served the goals of state power. The nation-state has adopted the colonial legal regime in a manner that renders the nation-state a neo-colonising entity, subordinating and infantalising citizen-subjects. This neo-colonial authoritarianism has, importantly, been modified by a national paternalism. The state has achieved social justice by delivering "high economic growth ... [that has] involved and benefited all sections of society, not only a small business and administrative elite".[61]

[61] Harding & Carter, *supra* note 21 at 194.

A TEMPLATE FOR 'RULE BY LAW' LEGITIMACY

The legitimising effect of a widely distributed prosperity has long been cited as the core legitimacy of the Singapore state. I now present a template for 'rule by law' legitimacy in order to demonstrate that if 'law' has been central to development, prosperity and political legitimacy, then there is important detail to Singapore's 'rule by law'. Put differently, authoritarian rule of law has foundations and facades that must be penetrated in order to be analysed.

Extending Exceptionalism Through Legislation

In his argument on Singapore's legal duality, Jayasuriya describes how Singapore has rendered legal exceptionalism (symbolised by the applications of the *Internal Security Act*) something of a norm by never returning to a pre-Emergency legality.[62] Jayasuriya's argument is borne out by the detail and implementation of the *Press Act* and the *Religious Harmony Act*. Both these Acts extend the *ISA*'s exceptionalism into the post-Emergency 'nation'.

Like the *ISA*, these two Acts violate 'rule of law' freedoms (in these instances, press freedom and religious freedom), and they both exclude the courts. Neither of these Acts provides for public accountability or transparency relating to the exercise of ministerial discretion. With both Acts, counter-narratives and non-state assessments and adjudications are excluded. Power converges in the hands of the state, leaving individuals without rights or access to autonomous institutions with the capacity to restrain the state. In this regard, Lee Kuan Yew's 2007 claim to the IBA that Singapore's legal system provides "easy access to justice"[63] can be seen to be problematic in the extreme.

[62] Kanishka Jayasuriya, *Law, Capitalism and Power in Asia: The Rule of Law and Legal Institutions* (London: Routledge, 1999).

[63] Lee, *supra* note 1.

This, then, is the first and most striking feature of 'rule by law' legitimacy: an extension of legal exceptionalism into non-Emergency normalcy, with the executive appropriating judicial functions and preventing the courts from conducting judicial review. The Singapore experience suggests that the instruments and institutions of legal exceptionalism acquire a measure of legitimacy if they pre-exist the regime that adopts and extends them. In Singapore's case, the colonial state's *Emergency Regulations* and the surveillance of Special Branch provide predecessors for the nation-state's *Internal Security Act* and the Internal Security Department.

Legitimising Exceptionalism Through the National Narrative

When it comes to legitimising the nation-state's adoption of the colonial state's instruments of repression, the national narrative plays a significant role. Telling the history of the 'nation' in a manner that celebrates colonial rule (as illustrated by this chapter's discussion of the Ibahri–state exchange), and presenting the colonial legal system as an asset to the 'nation',[64] dulls suspicion and scrutiny of colonial precedent.

Instead of rejecting 'colonial', the nation-state adopts colonial precedents and elevates this adoption in a manner that masks the Othering subordination inherent to colonial legal ideologies.[65] The state's discursive employment of 'English law' as a legitimising marker is rhetorically consistent with the state's claim that Singapore is a 'rule of law' Westminster-model parliamentary democracy. The neo-coloniality of continuities between colonial 'law' and 'national' 'law' is masked through this rhetoric, which is in turn consistent with the national narrative's celebration of colonial rule as the source of modernity, prosperity and the

[64] As Lee did when speaking to the IBA: *supra* note 1.

[65] The subordination of colonial subjects through 'law' has been widely written upon. For a succinct review, see Sally Engle Merry, "Law and Colonialism" (1991) 25:4 *Law & Soc'y Rev.* 889. A thoughtful and more recent piece is Peter Fitzpatrick, " 'Enacted in the Destiny of Sedentary Peoples': Racism, Discovery and the Grounds of Law" (2000) 1:1 *Balayi: Culture, Law and Colonialism* 11.

plural population. The national narrative and legal exceptionalism are mutually constitutive and mutually legitimising.

The Valuing of Colonial Precedent

The national narrative extends its legitimising resonances into the covert legal exceptionalism of non-Emergency legislation when, like colonial legality, legislation in the nation-state encodes the subordination of the individual to the state. In Parliament (the *Vandalism Act* and the *Press Act*) and at Select Committee Hearings (the *Legal Profession Act*), the state has presented national legislation as desirably building upon colonial precedent. In Singapore state discourse, continuity with colonial 'law' is thus presented as a legitimising extension of a valid legal system.

Building on the state's presentation of colonial 'law' as "good" 'law', citizen subordination is seamlessly perpetuated in two ways. First, legislation embeds a disenfranchising hierarchy in a range of ways. For example, the category 'management shares' creates two categories of citizens: those permitted ownership and control of newspapers and those excluded from such ownership (Chapter 4). Another instance of citizen subordination institutionalised through legislation is the amendment to the *Legal Profession Act* designed to replicate the position of the profession under the colonial state, such that the Law Society might comment on legislation only when the state invites it to do so (Chapter 5). In both cases, the nation-state scripts legislation that creates supplicant citizens. Citizens must seek (*Press Act*) or await (*Legal Profession Act*) permission from a state that need not account for its discretionary decisions on the bestowing or withholding of approval.

The *Vandalism Act* creates a violent hierarchical exclusion by criminalising citizens ideologically opposed to the state (Chapter 3), and the *Religious Harmony Act* structures a 'nation' in which all those who believe in or are affiliated with 'religion' must pledge allegiance first, not to God or gods, but to the state (Chapter 6).

The second manner in which subordination is perpetuated is through embedding ideology in legislative text. In his keynote speech to the IBA, Lee characterised Singapore's legal system as having "clear laws".[66] I have argued that the *Vandalism Act*, the *Press Act*, the *Religious Harmony Act*, and the *Public Order Act* all demonstrate a lack of textual clarity. I have shown how the meanings of key terms – 'vandalism', 'interference in domestic politics', 'religious harmony', 'cause or campaign' – are deeply ideological and require a historically specific understanding of Singapore to comprehend the manner in which the state encodes this language.

Citizens are subordinated when the state denies the polysemantic capacity of language and attributes singular meanings to terms it defines, not within legislation, but through public discourse. The case studies illustrate how this process of definition through discourse has unfolded. Put differently, the state employs its hegemonic dominance of the public domain to assign meaning to opaque legislative text. This practice inherently subordinates citizens because it unilaterally excludes other possible meanings. And as shown by my discussion of the Michael Fay case, as well as by scholarship on Singapore's judiciary, Singapore's statist courts accept and enforce the meanings imposed by the state.[67] This subordination encloses citizens in a discursive world in which the state is the only social actor empowered to engage in interpretation, rendering citizens silent, acquiescent receptors of state meaning-making.

Subsequent to the state's coercion against domestic media in 1971 (Chapter 4), counter-narratives rarely enter the public domain. After 1971, when counter-narratives and contestations do surface (as with the efforts of the detained Law Society Council members to repudiate the state's accusations through a press conference), the state responds

[66] Lee, *supra* note 1.

[67] Benedict Sheehey, "Singapore, 'Shared Values' and Law: Non East versus West Constitutional Hermeneutic" (2004) 34 *Hong Kong Law Journal* 67; Ross Worthington, *Governance in Singapore* (London: Routledge Curzon, 2003); Tsun Hung Tey, "Singapore's Jurisprudence of Political Defamation and Its Triple-Whammy Impact on Political Speech" [2008] *Public Law* 452.

coercively. The state's coercion instructs citizens on the interpretive processes attached to language and action. Assigning meaning is understood to be a state prerogative. This effect of commanding meaning is especially potent given that each enactment has been a state response to a moment of contestation, and each enactment has been designed to eliminate a particular source of contestation. There is therefore, through legislation, a successive silencing of non-state actors. Citizens are subordinated to the state in this most fundamental of senses: They have no public domain voice with which to constitute and communicate their understandings of their social realities. In the muting of non-state voices, the state's repeated assertions of its legitimacy gain ascendancy, acquiring the self-evident texture of received knowledge.[68]

In summary, a state ideology of valorising colonial rule underpins the neo-colonial governmentality of legislation such that the 'rule of law' is stripped of its rights content. Through 'rule of law' procedures, legislation is enacted, masking the extent to which the state silences and subordinates citizens. The question that then arises is two-fold: Why is the state so observant of 'rule of law' procedure, and why does it eliminate 'rule of law' content through repressing political contestation in the public domain? In the next section, I argue that Singapore's 'rule by law' legitimacy has been motivated by the paradoxical possibility that, despite its hegemony, the Singapore state's hold on power may be precarious beyond measure.

'RULE BY LAW' AND A TENUOUS GRASP ON POWER

To briefly restate an argument I detailed in Chapter 1, because the PAP-state has come to power without a clear popular mandate[69] and

[68] An example of the uncritical replication of state discourse is evident in this World Bank publication: Waleed Haider Malik, *Judiciary-Led Reforms in Singapore: Frameworks, Strategies, and Lessons* (Washington, DC: World Bank, 2007).

[69] The security operation prior to the 1963 general elections, Operation Coldstore, removed a large swath of the PAP's left-wing opponents from the field, thereby clouding the clarity of the electoral contest.

because it lacks the legitimacy of an ancestral connection to the land, state legitimacy vests very strongly in the delivery of material prosperity and the expression of power through a 'Western' mode of governance attendant upon 'nation'. The 'rule of law', electoral processes and parliamentary proceedings are some examples of the manner in which the Singapore state manifests 'nation'. By performing 'nation', Singapore is constructed as, and proceeds upon the assumption that, in a linear, progressive chronology, 'nation' is the desirable destination of post-colonial independence. This assumption deflects a foundational interrogation as to the shape the post-colonial polity should take. Structures of the 'rule of law' are thus a crucial prop of the performance of 'nation'. In terms of securing national legitimacy, the state maintains forms of the 'rule of law' to prevent the citizen-audience from even considering the possibility of alternative ways of being governed or constituted – alternatives that may point to frailties in the PAP-state's genesis.

Visible, measurable features of the 'rule of law' have thus been unremittingly performed by the Singapore state. This mode of legitimacy not only constructs national legitimacy by holding at bay foundational interrogations as to the grounds for the state's power. It also performs post-colonial nationhood through eliminating corruption, servicing multi-national corporations and building roads and telecommunications that work at first-world levels, thus consolidating national legitimacy and securing international legitimacy. It is consistent with the PAP–British alliance of the Cold War through which the PAP came into power (Chapters 1 and 3) that the state exalts a capitalist order in which foreign investors must be courted and in which 'prosperity' is at the heart of the survival strategy of the vulnerable 'nation'. Perhaps the support of the 'West' for 'rule by law' is assured because the Singapore state's practices and institutions deliver the institutional attributes and values celebrated by 'Western' investors.[70]

It is also consistent with the PAP–Western alliance that in 1966 the Singapore state's turn to corporal punishment (regressive for any crime,

[70] Kleinfeld, *supra* note 20.

let alone a property offence) was met with a complicit silence from the 'West' (Chapter 3). The *Vandalism Act* was, in part, protecting the 'West'. The Act was designed by the Singapore state to eliminate the left wing's protests against the presence in Singapore of US troops on rest and recreation leave from what was then South Vietnam. It was not until almost thirty years later, when a US national, Michael Fay, was at the receiving end of the *Vandalism Act*'s mandatory corporal punishment, that the 'West' critiqued the *Vandalism Act* in 'rule of law' terms. In other words, the 'West' has been selective in the version of the 'rule of law' it has required of Singapore. The Singapore state has been equally selective in terms of the content of 'law', but rather more consistent in terms of the form of 'law'.

The Singapore state's account of the 'rule of law' as a corruption-free delivery of social order and efficiency is so entrenched, so taken for granted and so effective in securing continuing economic and political legitimacy vis-à-vis the citizenry and the 'West' that performances and procedures associated with 'rule of law' continue to supply a legitimising basis for rights-violating legislation in Singapore (as the discussion of the 2009 *Public Order Act* has shown). The state's observance of 'rule of law' procedure is thus a central pillar of its strategies for building legitimacy. Just as 'law' relies on performative facets of procedural legitimacy, elections share this attention to form and help to explain why the Singapore state is so repressive of political contestation in the public domain.[71]

GOVERNMENTALITY, LEGAL EXCEPTIONALISM AND ELECTIONS

To briefly restate the argument I made in Chapters 1 and 3, the PAP's 1963 electoral victory may have been the consequence of a duplicitous alliance with the British designed to eliminate the left wing. In a polarised Cold

[71] Larry Diamond, "Thinking About Hybrid Regimes" (2002) 13:2 *Journal of Democracy* 21; Garry Rodan, "Westminster in Singapore: Now You See It, Now You Don't", in Haig Patapan, John Wanna & Patrick Weller, eds., *Westminster Legacies: Democracy and Responsible Government in Asia and the Pacific* (Sydney: UNSW Press, 2005) 109.

War climate of fear in which 'Communist' was a demonising characterisation, left-wing Socialists who may not have been 'Communist' but who certainly represented a challenge to the PAP's electoral chances were detained without trial in the months prior to the general elections. Thus, rather than coming to power through the unalloyed 'rule of law' legitimacy of the ballot box, the PAP's path to power involved the 'rule by law' flexing of the *Internal Security Act*'s muscular capacity to remove alternative leaders and spokespersons for the disaffected from the public domain.

In keeping with this (admittedly contested) reading of the history, three of the enactments I have studied have been associated with the coercion of detention without trial. While all the enactments studied have been designed to remove sources of critique and opposition from the public domain, the detentions linked to at least three of the acts appear to have been timed in anticipation of electoral impacts:

Legislative Instrument	Related Detentions	Date of General Elections
Press Act,[a] 1974	April 1971	August 1972
Legal Profession Act, 1986	1987 1988	September 1988
Religious Harmony Act, 1991	1987 1988	September 1988 August 1991

[a] There is legal and political brilliance in the timing of the *Press Act*. The 1971 detentions had the effect of silencing critique in all domestic newspapers before the 1972 general elections. The press was informed of the planned changes relating to two-tiered shareholdings from at least January 1973 (Sing., *Parliamentary Debates*, vol. 33, col. 915 [27 March 1974] [Mr Jek Yeun Thong]). By the time the Act was presented to Parliament, "debated" and passed into 'law', the politics and mechanics of press regulation had already been substantively amended. The 1974 *Press Act* was presented to a Parliament and a domestic press that was complicit and compliant such that the Act was unchallenged and served to cement changes for which the ground had already been laid.

Each pre-election exercise of *Internal Security Act* detentions has effected the silencing of a major non-state voice. The 1971 detentions silenced the domestic press; the 1987–88 detentions silenced the Law Society (which extended into a silencing of all civil society)[72]; and the detentions of the Catholic social workers silenced an activist Catholic Church, which appears to have extended into a wider silencing of all actors and institutions associated with 'religion'. The 2009 *Public Order Act* was timed to secure the public domain in anticipation of the November 2009 APEC meetings, signalling the degree to which the state manages its image before the international community.

Possibly, the strategies that supported the PAP's initial electoral victories have become a governance tactic for state longevity: In preparation for each general election, the state relies on the "apparatuses of security"[73] to identify social actors with the capacity to affect electoral success and removes them from the public domain. Adding to the coercive power of detention without trial, the enactments that follow or precede the detentions perform a refinement of 'law' as governance, and represent the management and pursuit of "the perfection and intensification of the processes [government] directs".[74] In short, the state is hyper-vigilant of public discourse because it cannot ever know how much popular support it has and it cannot risk finding out.

Bearing in mind that a key concern of this study is to excavate the complex of factors and conditions that constitute legitimacy for 'rule by law', it is noteworthy that legislation is at the heart of the state's coercive practices. There is, in a narrow sense, legitimacy to coercion that appears to be 'lawfully' conducted. The institutions of surveillance and detention, while secretive, are not secrets beyond the pale of 'law'. Dissenters and critics need not fear a bullet in their backs. With legislation, the state's responses are observably 'lawful' in a manner that walks the line of legitimacy.[75]

[72] Kenneth Paul Tan, *Renaissance Singapore? Economy, Culture and Politics* (Singapore: NUS Press, 2007); Constance Singham et al., eds., *Building Social Space in Singapore* (Singapore: Select, 2002).

[73] Michel Foucault, "Governmentality", in James D. Faubion, ed., *Michel Foucault: Power, Essential Works of Foucault, 1954–1984* (London: Penguin, 2002) vol. 3, 201 at 220.

[74] Ibid. at 211.

[75] I should, however, note that allegations of torture and mistreatment have been made by detainees: Fong Hoe Fang, ed., *That We May Dream Again* (Singapore: Ethos, 2009);

Governmentality, the National Narrative and the Precarious State

The case studies demonstrate that with each act, and with each related *Internal Security Act* detention, the state repeatedly, insistently formulates a particular kind of problem for the particularly vulnerable 'nation':

> A key point arising from Foucault's work is the manner in which the discourses of power engage with that which needs to be governed – the processes of problematisation.... The process of problematisation ... is the formulation of problems, for and by governors ... that cannot have resolution. The maintenance of the problem perpetuates the existence of the government and the forms of governance.... [P]roblematisation ... enables the consideration of any act of regulation/government as a construction, with specific (perhaps unvoiced) objectives ... tackled with particular strategies and techniques.[76]

Although the state consistently presents the problem "that cannot have resolution" as one of 'survival', the case studies suggest that the unvoiced objective of the acts studied is the perpetuation and consolidation of PAP rule. While state discourse presents the state as protecting vulnerable citizens in a vulnerable nation, the pre-electoral timing of detentions and enactments suggests that the irresolvable problem is that of the PAP's mandate. It is the state, not the 'nation', that is at risk.

Legislation is thus instrumentally enacted and the removal of contesting voices strategically timed so as to generate electoral results that

Tan Jing Quee, Teo Soh Lung & Koh Kay Yew, eds., *Our Thoughts Are Free: Poems and Prose on Imprisonment and Exile* (Singapore: Ethos, 2009); Francis Seow, *To Catch a Tartar: A Dissident in Lee Kuan Yew's Prison* (New Haven, CT: Yale Southeast Asian Studies, 1994); Said Zahari, *The Long Nightmare: My 17 Years as a Political Prisoner* (Kuala Lumpur: Utusan, 2007); Teo Soh Lung, *Beyond the Blue Gate: Recollections of a Political Prisoner* (Petaling Jaya: Strategic Information and Research Development Centre, 2010); Tessa Wong, "Former ISA Detainee Wants to Sue the Govt for Damages", *Straits Times* (23 December 2010); Tessa Wong, "Ex-ISA Detainee's Suits Thrown Out", *Straits Times* (19 February 2011).

[76] Chris Dent, "Copyright, Governmentality and Problematisation: An Exploration" (2009) 18:1 *Griffith Law Review* 134.

allow the reiteration of the claim that the PAP possesses a strong popular mandate. Electoral results offer a visible, quantifiable declaration of the popular mandate akin to the tables and rankings that Lee presented to the IBA.[77] Within a paradigm that quantifies the 'rule of law' through figures on court efficiency, electoral percentages amount to proof.

In its wary watchfulness of the existence and extent of a popular mandate, the Singapore state shares a foundational concern with the arbitrariness of its position as ruler that Foucault identified as preceding the development of the governmentality power complex: the Machiavellian prince's concern with "the ability to retain one's principality".[78] Without the post-colonial legitimacy arising from leading an independence movement or bearing an ancestral connection to the land, and without a clear electoral victory traceable to fair and open electoral contests, the Singapore state's connection to its principality seems arbitrary indeed. The apparent clarity of a 'racial' link between the PAP and the majority 'Chinese' population is fractured by the "language fault-lines"[79] between the 'English-educated' and the 'Chinese-educated' 'Chinese' – a "fault-line" linked to split political allegiances, as events related to the *Nanyang Siang Pau* showed (Chapter 4).

All Dangers Are Great Dangers

Foucault summarised *The Prince* as focused upon maintaining the "fragile link" between the ruler and his control of subjects and territory, a focus that required the prince not just to identify dangers but also to rank them into greater and slighter dangers. Significantly, however, while each of the state narratives detailed by my study has identified where the dangers come from and what they consist of, the state has *not* distinguished

[77] Rachel Evans, "Singapore Leader Rejects Amnesty", *International Financial Law Review* (18 October 2007), online: <http://www.iflr.com/Article/1983342/Singapore-leader-rejects-Amnesty. html>.

[78] Foucault, *supra* note 74 at 202–14.

[79] Hong & Huang, *supra* note 56 at 109.

between them in terms of severity. In the eyes of the state, each of these dangers appears to have been extreme. In light of the fundamental instability attaching to the manner in which the PAP came to power (in terms of both 'race' and popular support), perhaps sustaining 'rule by law' legitimacy requires legislation as a tactical response to *any* public domain questioning of the ruler's rule.

I will posit this state response to critique, this perception of all dangers as great dangers, as the corollary of precarious authoritarian rule, with one crucial caveat: The state does not view articulations of critique expressed by citizens without associational identities and authorities as a 'danger'.[80] The case studies suggest that three factors render critique an extreme danger: publics, alliances and transcendences.

ALLIANCES, TRANSCENDENCES AND SPOKESPERSONS FOR PUBLICS

Karpik's concept of spokespersons for 'publics'[81] points to the ways in which social actors who position themselves in the public domain as spokespersons for a cause or an issue construct imagined, as well as real, publics. The case studies suggest that any social actor whose public advocacy or articulation of critique is perceived by the state to constitute the speaker as a spokesperson for publics (whether actual or potential) is dealt with as if constituting a "great danger".

For example, when the 'Chinese'-language newspaper, the *Nanyang Siang Pau*, constituted itself as a spokesperson for the 'Chinese-educated' – faulting the state's education and employment policies, and advocating on behalf of the 'Chinese-educated' (events described in Chapter 4 on the *Press Act*) – the state responded punitively and repressively. Twenty years later, the state constituted itself the spokesperson for

[80] Beng-Huat Chua, *Communitarian Ideology and Democracy in Singapore* (London: Routledge, 1995).

[81] Lucien Karpik, *French Lawyers: A Study in Collective Action, 1274 to 1994*, trans. by Nora Scott (Oxford: Clarendon Press, 1999).

'Chinese' education, but only after it had dismantled all non-state spokespersons for this particular 'public' and after 'Communism' had ceased to be a threat to the state's power and control.[82]

Similarly, the "Aid Vietnam" campaign launched by the opposition Barisan Sosialis precipitated the criminalisation of an encoded crime of 'vandalism' – dispensing harsh and humiliating punishment as a way of decimating support for the opposition party on the ground (Chapter 3). Lawyers who spoke for the 'rule of law' were silenced through public excoriation staged as Select Committee Hearings before being further silenced through detention without trial (Chapter 5). Lawyers in an earlier time who had advocated recognition of the 'rule of law' rights of political prisoners were detained without trial (Chapter 5). And actors associated with 'religion' lost their capacity to critique the state after the *Religious Harmony Act* was passed (Chapter 6).

Just as social actors who present themselves as a spokespersons for publics are a "great danger", so too social actors who possess (actual or potential) alliances with other social actors have, the case studies suggest, been regarded as great dangers. Two factors appear to be at work in the state's response to alliances. First, when the dissenters act or speak associationally, such that a constituency of disaffection is represented by the critique, and second, when that constituency derives support and legitimacy from international networks, the state views the danger as extreme and responds accordingly.

For example, the 1966 instances of 'vandalism' (Chapter 3) represented the collective and organised opposition of left-wing Socialism, as indicated by the Barisan's launching of a campaign to "Aid Vietnam Against American Aggression". Similarly, the activities of the Catholic social workers (Chapter 6) represented the cross-border and institutional might of the Catholic Church as an international entity. In addition, the young Catholic activists represented the threat of transcendent beliefs

[82] Hong & Huang, *supra* note 56 at 4–10.

that subordinated 'nation' to 'God'. Indeed, the socialism of the left-wing Barisan in 1966 might be seen as a parallel to the values of 'religion' that motivated the Catholic social workers to act and advocate on behalf of society's marginalised.

The case studies set out the state's repeated presentation of itself as both the source and the arbiter of the 'nation's values. It is therefore unsurprising that ideologies with networks (whether political or religious) both within and beyond the borders of the 'nation' constitute extreme dangers to a state that constructs itself as the only valid transcendent. Both the 1994 international critique of Singapore's caning of US teen Michael Fay (Chapter 3) and the 1986 Law Society's critique of the 'rule by law' amendment to the *Press Act* (Chapter 5) represent domestic links to a cross-border conception of 'the rule of law' – another source of transcendent values that questioned the state's constructions of legitimacy. The 1986 amendment to the *Press Act* (Chapter 4) revealed the state's wariness of another cross-border alliance, this time between the 'foreign press' and Singapore's besieged opposition politicians. Domestic newspapers, tamed into serving the state by the events of 1971 and the 1974 *Press Act* (Chapter 4), were a threat in 1971 partly because of cross-border alliances represented by the content of reported news, as well as by foreign investment in domestic newspapers.

In summary, the Singapore state has treated public domain critique as a "great danger" when social actors ally with others, speak to transcendent beliefs that subordinate 'nation' and state and constitute themselves as spokespersons for publics. In other words, the Singapore state is not simplistically, brutishly authoritarian. There is a sophistication to the manner in which it excavates the ambivalences between 'rule of law' and 'rule by law' to perform a limited 'rule of law' legitimacy. The state has attended to garnering both national and international legitimacy in a manner that perpetuates colonial strategies and governmentality. It instrumentally employs narratives of history and national vulnerability so as to consolidate the state's reframing of the 'rule of law'.

CONCLUSION

In 2009, in a remarkable development for the Singapore public domain, three new books setting out the accounts of former political detainees were published.[83] These books contain accounts from those detained in 1963's Operation Coldstore and the so-called Marxist conspiracy of 1987–88. These books are remarkable because political detainees are typically released subject to conditions which include restrictions on their communications.[84] Given that from independence in August 1965 to 1988 a total of 210 individuals have been detained without trial[85] (a figure that does not include the estimated 111 individuals detained under Coldstore in 1963), the efficacy of the conditions of release is suggested by the resounding silence maintained (up to 2009) by former detainees living in Singapore.[86]

In these books, alleged conspirators and Communists speak of their moral, political and religious beliefs, countering the state's narratives and

[83] Fong, *supra* note 76 and Tan, Teo & Koh, *supra* note 76; Kor Kian Beng, "Ex-Activists Pen Memoirs for New Book", *Straits Times* (14 November 2009) reports the launch of *The Fajar Generation*, written by former political detainees, many of whom were Barisan leaders. The book was launched on 14 November 2009 and sold out at its launch. Since then, Teo has published another book, *Beyond the Blue Gate*, *supra* note 76.

[84] For example, 'Marxist conspirator' Vincent Cheng was released on condition that he obtain the prior written approval of the Director of the Internal Security Department before leaving Singapore, before associating with or communicating with any previous detainees unless those detainees were members of the Singapore Ex-Political Detainees Association and before associating with or communicating with "any organisation implicated in the Marxist conspiracy". The terms of Cheng's release also prohibit him from participating in organisations and from communicating in a range of ways without the prior written permission of the Internal Security Department: Fong, *supra* note 76 at 69.

[85] The figures for detentions under the ISA were supplied by the state in response to a question asked in Parliament: Sing., *Parliamentary Debates*, vol. 69, col. 1991 (20 January 1991) (Mr Wong Kan Seng).

[86] Before these 2009 publications, only two former detainees living outside Singapore had published accounts of their incarcerations: Francis Seow, *supra* note 76 and Said Zahari, *supra* note 76.

setting out motivations that include the desire for greater social justice. Their extremely moving accounts include details of torture and mistreatment under detention and are striking for the consistency with which they invoke a form of 'law' that serves and protects 'justice'.

In this study, I have argued that liberal norms for the 'rule of law', norms which valorise individual liberties, constitute Singapore's very existence as a post-colonial 'nation'. In detailing the state's failure to uphold crucial aspects of a liberal 'rule of law', I have shown the state's agency in the construction of an instrumentalist 'rule by law'. While state discourse presents 'rule by law' as a necessary feature of Singapore's prosperity and stability, this study has shown the extent to which both the 'rule by law' and its legitimising discourses are constructed by the state[87] so as to augment the state's power and silence its critics. When those critics are actual or potential spokespersons for 'publics', when critics speak to transcendent values and when critics appear to have alliances with other groups, the state appears to regard these discursive moments as "great dangers".

The Singapore state's vigorous repression of voices that question its formulations of 'law' invoke Upendra Baxi's urgent reminder to those of us who deal in 'law' from the stance of scholars:

> A multitude of mass illegalities historically enact forms of citizen understandings and interpretations of the rule of law notion. These divergent insurgencies define forms of popular sovereignty; the rule of law, on this register, is a terrain of struggle of the multitudes against the rule of the miniscule. What space may we provide, and how may 'we' (the 'symbol traders' of the rule of law languages and rhetoric) provide it, for the militant particularisms in our narratives?[88]

[87] As Chouliarki and Fairclough point out, "Social forms that are produced by people and can be changed by people are being seen as if they were part of nature": Lilie Chouliaraki & Norman Fairclough, *Discourse in Late Modernity* (Edinburgh: Edinburgh University Press, 1999) at 4.

[88] Upendra Baxi, "Rule of Law in India: Theory and Practice", in Randall Peerenboom, ed., *Asian Discourses of Rule of Law* (London: Routledge, 2004) 324 at 326.

For those who engage in 'law' as activists, there is no ambivalence. "Systems of law, of rules – actual or projected – demand a sense of justice based on shared ethical foundations, as well as notions of human rights".[89] Through this study, I have become one of the symbol traders in 'rule of law' languages that Baxi addresses. My hope is that demonstrating the constructedness of 'law' in Singapore must, like all critical social science, "contribute to an awareness of what is, how it has come to be, and what it might become, on the basis of which people may be able to make and remake their lives".[90] My desire to adopt a scholarly detachment from the narratives I have uncovered has been thwarted by my growing distress at the violent and repeated amputation of the protective mechanisms of 'rule of law' in the Singapore state's execution of 'rule by law'. Through this project, I have given voice to forms of citizen understandings of 'rule of law' that have been all but erased in the Singapore public domain. The new books produced by former political detainees promise to repair some of that erasure. The national narrative may no longer have such a totalising claim on 'history'.

It is tempting to interpret the presence of books written by former detainees as a shift away from illiberalism in Singapore. But the nuances of illiberal legitimacy are more complex than might be apparent. On the same day that one such book, *The Fajar Generation* was launched, 14 November 2009, President Barak Obama arrived in Singapore for the APEC meetings. The *Public Order Act*, securing the public domain from "mass illegalities", was in place. As APEC unfolded, contemporary detainees held without trial were understood to be 'terrorist', not 'Communist'. Against the visibility of Singapore's orderly prosperity, the illiberalism of a managed press, a silenced civil society and cowed and co-opted religious institutions pale into the barely visible, the very

[89] Bill Bowring, "Whose Rights, What People, Which Community? The Rule of Law as an Instrument of Oppression in the New Latvia", in Peter Fitzpatrick, ed., *Nationalism, Racism and the Rule of Law* (Aldershot: Dartmouth, 1995) 117 at 118. Bowring is described as a "human rights activist" at vii.

[90] Chouliaraki & Fairclough, *supra* note 88 at 6.

marginal. The contextual impossibility of realising the Westminster promise of "[a]n opposition acting as a recognised executive in waiting as part of the regime"[91] is not a newsworthy event, in the way hosting APEC is. In the meantime, Singapore's legal system becomes more and more attractive to more and more regimes.[92]

Although this project has been a study of the Singapore-specific characteristics of a mode of illiberalism that has managed to garner legitimacy, it is important to note that the issue is not limited to Singapore. Enacting legislation that encroaches upon the restraints on state power required by Dicey's 'rule of law'[93] and justifying these encroachments as protective of a vulnerable 'nation' is an issue that crosses many borders.[94] Just as with Singapore, the tool of legislation, and a state's capacity to command a particular presence in the public domain through discourse, empowers other procedurally correct and prosperous states to reconstitute the 'rule of law' into an illiberal and efficient 'rule by law'.

[91] Rhodes & Weller, *supra* note 55 at 7.

[92] "S'pore–Qatar Pact to Study Legal Systems", *Straits Times* (19 November 2009).

[93] Tamanaha, *supra* note 53, at 63–65.

[94] For a sampling of the extensive literature on emergency legislation and the manner in which this violates the 'rule of law', see John Strawson, ed., *Law after Ground Zero* (London: Glasshouse Press, 2002); Giorgio Agamben, *State of Exception*, trans. by Kevin Attell (Chicago: University of Chicago Press, 2005); Michael Hor, Victor Ramraj & Kent Roach, eds., *Global Anti-Terrorism Law and Policy* (Cambridge: Cambridge University Press, 2005); John A. E. Varvaele, "The Anti-Terrorist Legislation in the US: Inter Arma Silent Leges?" (2005) 13 *Eur. J. of Crime, Crim. L. & Crim. Justice.* 201; Joshua D. Zelman, "Recent Developments in International Law: Anti-Terrorism Legislation – Part One: An Overview" (2001–2002) 11 *J. Transnat'l L. & Pol'y* 183; Liz Feket, "Anti-Muslim Racism and the European Security State" (2004) 46:1 *Race & Class* 3; Georgen A. Lyden, "The International Money Laundering Abatement and Anti-Terrorist Financing Act of 2001: Congress Wears a Blindfold While Giving Money Laundering Legislation a Facelift" (2003) 8 *Fordham J. Corp. & Fin. L.* 203.

BIBLIOGRAPHY

CONSTITUTIONAL DOCUMENTS

Constitution of the Republic of Singapore (1999 Rev. Ed.).
Independence of Singapore Agreement 1965 (1985 Rev. Ed.).

LEGISLATION

Administration of Muslim Law Act (Cap. 3, 1999 Rev. Ed. Sing.).
Adoption of Children Act (Cap. 4, 1985 Rev. Ed. Sing.).
Advocates and Solicitors Ordinance (No. 32 of 1934, Sing.).
Anti-Social Behaviour Act 2003 (UK), 2003.
Broadcasting Act (Cap. 28, 2003 Rev. Ed. Sing.).
Children and Young Persons Act (Cap. 38, 2001 Rev. Ed. Sing.).
Children and Young Persons Ordinance (Cap. 128, 1955 Rev. Ed. Sing.).
Civil Law Act (Cap. 43, 1999 Rev. Ed. Sing.).
Corruption, Drug Trafficking and Other Serious Crimes (Confiscation of Benefits) Act (Cap. 65A, 2000 Rev. Ed. Sing.).
Criminal Damage Act 1971 (UK), 1971.
Criminal Procedure Code (Cap. 231, 1955 Rev. Ed. Sing.).
Criminal Procedure Code (Cap. 68, 1985 Rev. Ed. Sing.).
Employment Act (Cap. 91, 2009 Rev. Ed. Sing.).
Employment of Foreign Workers Act (Cap. 91A, 1997 Rev. Ed. Sing.).
Internal Security Act (Cap. 143, 1985 Rev. Ed. Sing.).
Legal Profession Act (Cap. 161, 2001 Rev. Ed. Sing.).
Maintenance of Religious Harmony Act (Cap. 167A, 2001 Rev. Ed. Sing.).
Minor Offences Ordinance (Cap. 117, 1936 Rev. Ed. Sing.).

Miscellaneous Offences (Public Order and Nuisance) Act (Cap. 184, 1997 Rev. Ed. Sing.).

Misuse of Drugs Act (Cap. 185, 2001 Rev. Ed. Sing.).

Muslim and Hindu Endowments Ordinance (Cap. 271, Ordinance XVII of 1905).

Newspaper and Printing Presses Act (Cap. 206, 2002 Rev. Ed. Sing.).

Official Secrets Act (Cap. 213, 1985 Rev. Ed. Sing.).

Parliament (Privileges, Immunities and Powers) Act (Cap. 217, 2001 Rev. Ed. Sing.).

Penal Code (Cap. 224, 1985 Rev. Ed. Sing.).

Public Entertainments and Meetings Act (Cap. 257, 2001 Rev. Ed. Sing.).

Public Order Act 2009 (No. 15 of 2009, Sing.).

Punishment for Vandalism Act (No. 38 of 1966, Sing.).

Sedition Act (Cap. 290, 1985 Rev. Ed. Sing.).

Vandalism Act (Cap. 341, 1985 Rev. Ed. Sing.).

Women's Charter (Cap. 353, 1997 Rev. Ed. Sing.).

"Chronological Table of the Ordinances Enacted From 1st April, 1867 to 30th April, 1955", *The Laws of the Colony of Singapore* (1955 Rev. Ed.), vol. VIII, 206.

SUBSIDIARY LEGISLATION

Miscellaneous Offences (Public Order and Nuisance) (Assemblies and Processions) Rules (Cap. 184, 1997 Rev. Ed. Sing.)

Standing Orders of the Parliament of Singapore, online: <http://www.parliament.gov.sg/Publications/standingOrder.htm>.

JURISPRUDENCE

Re An Advocate (1963), [1964] 1 M.L.J. 1 (Kuching).

Ang Chin Sang v. Public Prosecutor, [1970] 2 M.L.J. 6 (Sing.H.C.).

Re Application of Lau Swee Soong; Lau Swee Soong v. Goh Keng Swee & Anor. [1965–1968] 1 Sing.L.R. 661 (Sing.H.C.).

Re Application of Foong Jam Keong, [1967] 2 M.L.J. 202.

Attorney-General v. Wain and Others (No. 1) [1991] 1 Sing.L.R. 383.

Attorney General v. Zimmerman & Ors. [1984–1985] 1 Sing.L.R. 814.

Bahadur Singh & Anor. v. Bank of India, [1993] 1 Sing.L.R. 634 (Sing.H.C.).

Bank of India v. Bahadur Singh & Anor. [1994] Sing.L.R. 328 (C.A.).

Chng Suan Tze v. Minister of Home Affairs & Ors. and Other Appeals [1988] 1 Sing.L.R. 132 (C.A.).

Citicorp Investment Bank (Singapore) Ltd v. Wee Ah Kee [1997] 2 Sing.L.R.759.

Re David Marshall; Law Society v. Marshall David Saul [1972–1974] Sing. L.R. 132.

De Souza Kevin Desmond & Ors. v. Minister of Home Affairs & Ors. [1988] 1 Sing.L.R. 517.

Michael Peter Fay v. Public Prosecutor [3 March 1994], M/A No. 48/94/01 (Sing. Subordinate Cts).

Fay v. Public Prosecutor, [1994] 2 Sing. L.R. 154 (H.C.).

Goh Chok Tong v. Jeyaretnam Joshua Benjamin [1998] 1 Sing.L.R.

Goh Chok Tong v. Jeyaretnam Joshua Benjamin & Another Action [1998] 3 Sing.L.R. 337 (C.A.).

Goh Chok Tong v. Chee Soon Juan (No. 2) [2005] 1 Sing.L.R. 573.

Jeyaretnam J. B. v. Attorney General [1988] 1 Sing.L.R. 170 (C.A.).

Lau Lek Eng & Ors. v. Minister for Home Affairs & Anor. [1972–1974] 1 Sing.L.R. 300 (H.C.).

Lee Kuan Yew v. J. B. Jeyaretnam [1979] 1 M.L.J. 281.

Lee Kuan Yew v. Seow Khee Leng [1989] 1 M.L.J. 172.

Lee Kuan Yew v. Derek Gwynn Davies & Ors. [1990] 1 M.L.J. 390.

Lee Kuan Yew & Anor. v. Vinocur & Ors. & Another Action [1995] 3 Sing. L.R. 477.

Lee Kuan Yew v. Chee Soon Juan (No. 2) [2005] 1 Sing.L.R. 552.

Lee Mau Seng v. Minister for Home Affairs, Singapore & Anor. [1969–1971] Sing.L.R. 508.

Re Loh Toh Met, Decd. Kong Lai Fong & Ors. v. Loh Peng Heng, [1961] 1 M.L.J. 234.

In Re Maria Huberdina Hertogh; Inche Mansor Abadi v Adrianus Petrus Hertogh and Anor. [1951] 1 M.L.J. 164 (Sing.C.A.).

Mohammed Ismail bin Ibrahim and Another v Mohammed Taha bin Ibrahim [2004] 4 Sing.L.R. 756.

OHC on behalf of TPC v. TTMJ [2002] SGTMP 3.

Public Prosecutor v. Koh Song Huat Benjamin and Anor. [2005] SGDC 272.

Public Prosecutor v. Wong Hong Toy & Anor. [1984–1985] I Sing.L.R. (H.C.).

Public Prosecutor v. Oliver Fricker, Singapore Subordinate Courts DAC0024677/2010.

Re Rajah T.T.; Law Society v. Thampoe T. Rajah [1972–1974] 1 Sing.L.R. 423.

Sonia Chataram Aswani v. Haresh Jaikishin Buxani [1995] 3 Sing.L.R. 627.
Shiu Chi Ho v. Public Prosecutor (25 April 1994), M/A 93/94/01 (Sing. Subordinate Cts.).
Teo Soh Lung v. Minister of Home Affairs & Ors. [1988] 1 Sing.L.R. 679 (H.C.).
Teo Soh Lung v. Minister for Home Affairs & Ors. [1989] 1 Sing.L.R. 499 (H.C.).
Teo Soh Lung v. Minister for Home Affairs [1990] 2 M.L.J. 129 (Sing. C.A).
Wee Toon Lip & Ors. v. Minister for Home Affairs & Anor. [1972–1974] 1 Sing.L.R. 303 (H.C.).
Wong Hong Toy & Anor. v. Public Prosecutor [1986] I Sing.L.R. (H.C.) 469.
Wong Shan Shan v. Public Prosecutor [2007] S.G.D.C. 314 (Sing.Dist.Ct.).
Workers' Party v. Tay Boon Too & Anor. [1975–1977] 1 Sing.L.R. 124.

SINGAPORE GOVERNMENT DOCUMENTS

Parliamentary Debates

Sing., *Parliamentary Debates*, vol. 24, cols. 5–14 (8 December 1965) (Yang Di-Pertuan Negara Encik Yusof Ishak).
Sing., *Parliamentary Debates*, vol. 25, cols. 291–305 (26 August 1966) (Wee Toon Boon).
Sing., *Parliamentary Debates*, vol. 25, col. 298 (26 August 1966) (E. W. Barker).
Sing., *Parliamentary Debates*, vol. 25, cols. 296–97 (26 August 1966) (Lee Kuan Yew).
Sing., *Parliamentary Debates*, vol. 33, cols. 913–32 (27 March 1974).
Sing., *Parliamentary Debates*, vol. 36, cols. 1521–29 (23 March 1977).
Sing., *Parliamentary Debates*, vol. 37, cols. 66–68 (29 June 1977) (Jek Yeun Thong).
Sing., *Parliamentary Debates*, vol. 41, cols. 1305–12 (22 March 1982).
Sing., *Parliamentary Debates*, vol. 42, cols. 119–25 (31 August 1982).
Sing., *Parliamentary Debates*, vol. 44, col. 1885 (26 July 1984).
Sing., *Parliamentary Debates*, vol. 46, col. 167 (15 May 1985).
Sing., *Parliamentary Debates*, vol. 48, col. 369 (31 July 1986) (Wong Kan Seng).
Sing., *Parliamentary Debates*, vol. 48, col. 369 (31 July 1986) (Wong Kan Seng).
Sing., *Parliamentary Debates*, vol. 49, cols. 1484–89 (29 July 1987) (Goh Chok Tong).
Sing., *Parliamentary Debates*, vol. 49, col. 1452 (29 July 1987) (Bernard Chen).

Sing., *Parliamentary Debates*, vol. 51, cols. 307–53 (1 June 1988).
Sing., *Parliamentary Debates*, vol. 51, col. 326 (1 June 1988) (Lee Kuan Yew).
Sing., *Parliamentary Debates*, vol. 52. cols. 16–20 (9 January 1989) (President Wee Kim Wee).
Sing., *Parliamentary Debates*, vol. 54, col. 1076 (22 February 1990) (Aline Wong).
Sing., *Parliamentary Debates*, vol. 69, col. 1991 (20 January 1991) (Wong Kan Seng).
Sing., *Parliamentary Debates*, vol. 82, col. 1319 (12 February 2007) (Wong Kan Seng).
Sing., *Parliamentary Debates*, vol. 86 (19 August 2009) (Lee Kuan Yew).
Sing., *Parliamentary Debates*, vol. 85 col. 3656–3761 (13 April 2009) (K. Shanmugam).

Select Committee Reports and White Papers Presented to Parliament

Sing., Committee of Privileges – First Report (Parl. Paper 3 of 1987); Second Report (Parl. Paper 4 of 1987); Third Report (Parl. Paper 6 of 1987); Fourth Report (Parl. Paper 7 of 1987); Fifth Report (Parl. Paper 9 of 1987).
Sing., "Maintenance of Religious Harmony", Cmd. 21 of 1989.
Sing., "Report of Commission of Inquiry into Allegations of Executive Interference in the Subordinate Courts" (July 1986), Cmd. 12 of 1986.
Sing., "Report of the Select Committee on the Criminal Procedure Code (Amendment) Bill", December 1969, 2nd Parliament.
Sing., "Report of the Select Committee on the Legal Profession (Amendment) Bill", October 1986, 6th Parliament.
Sing., "Report of the Select Committee on the Maintenance of Parents Bill", October 1995, 8th Parliament.
Sing., "Report of the Select Committee on the Maintenance of Religious Harmony Bill", October 1990, Parliament 7 of 1990.
Sing., "Report of the Select Committee on the Newspaper and Printing Presses Bill", August 1974, 3rd Parliament.
Sing., "Report of the Select Committee on Land Transportation Policy", January 1990, 7th Parliament).

Other Government Documents

Government of Singapore, "Singapore in Figures 2009"; online: <http://www.singstat.gov.sg/pubn/reference/sif2009.pdf>.

Sing., "Response to the International Bar Association Human Rights Institute's Report on Singapore" (14 November 2008), online: <http://app2.mlaw.gov.sg/LinkClick.aspx?fileticket=gDkKt5ebvTY%3d&tabid=204>.

Sing., "Singapore: Its History", in *Singapore Year Book 1966*, reprinted in Verinder Grover, ed., *Singapore: Government and Politics* (New Delhi: Deep & Deep, 2000), 33.

Singapore's Initial Report to the UN Committee for the Convention on the Elimination of All Forms of Discrimination Against Women (1999).

SECONDARY MATERIAL: BOOKS

Agamben, Giorgio. *State of Exception*, trans. by Kevin Attell (Chicago: University of Chicago Press, 2005).

Aljunied, Syed Muhd Khairudin. *Colonialism, Violence and Muslims in Southeast Asia* (London: Routledge, 2009).

Ang, Peng Hwa & Yeo, Tiong Min. *Mass Media Laws and Regulations in Singapore* (Singapore: Asian Media Information and Communication Centre, 1998).

Ban, Kah Choon. *Absent History: The Untold Story of Special Branch Operations in Singapore, 1915–1942* (Singapore: Horizon, 2002).

Banakar, Reza & Travers, Max, eds., *Theory and Method in Socio-Legal Research* (Oxford: Hart, 2005).

Barr, Michael D. "Singapore's Catholic Social Activists: Alleged 'Marxist Conspirators' ", in Barr, Michael D. & Trocki, Carl, eds., *Paths Not Taken: Political Pluralism in Post-War Singapore* (Singapore: NUS Press, 2008) 228.

Barr, Michael D. & Trocki, Carl A., eds., *Paths Not Taken: Political Pluralism in Post-War Singapore* (Singapore: NUS Press, 2008).

Bartholomew, Geoffrey. Introduction to *Tables of the Written Laws of the Republic of Singapore, 1819–1971* (Singapore: Malaya Law Review, University of Singapore, 1972).

Barzilai, Gad. "The Ambivalent Language of Lawyers: Between Liberal Politics, Economic Liberalism, Silence and Dissent", in Halliday, Terence C., Karpik, Lucien and Feeley, Malcolm M., eds., *Fighting for Political Freedom: Comparative Studies of the Legal Complex for Political Change* (Oxford: Hart, 2007) 247.

Baxi, Upendra. "Rule of Law in India: Theory and Practice", in Peerenboom, Randall, ed., *Asian Discourses on Rule of Law* (London: Routledge, 2004) 342.

Benjamin, Geoffrey. "The Cultural Logic of Singapore's Multiculturalism", in Hassan, Riaz, ed., *Singapore: Society in Transition* (Kuala Lumpur: Oxford University Press, 1976) 115.

Bhaskaran, Manu. "Transforming the Engines of Growth", in Welsh, Bridget et al., eds., *Impressions of the Goh Chok Tong Years in Singapore* (Singapore: NUS Press, 2009) 201.

Biddulph, Sarah. *Legal Reform and Administrative Detention Powers in China* (Cambridge: Cambridge University Press, 2007).

Birch, David. *Singapore Media: Communication Strategies and Practices* (Melbourne: Longman, 1993).

Borneman, J. "State: Anthropological Aspects", in Smelser, Neil J. & Baltes, Paul B., eds., *International Encyclopedia of the Social & Behavioural Sciences* (Amsterdam: Elsevier, 2004) 14968.

Bowring, Bill. "Whose Rights, What People, Which Community? The Rule of Law as an Instrument of Oppression in the New Latvia", in Peter Fitzpatrick, ed., *Nationalism, Racism and the Rule of Law* (Aldershot: Dartmouth, 1995) 117.

Carothers, Thomas. "The Rule-of-Law Revival", in Carothers, Thomas, ed., *Promoting the Rule of Law Abroad* (Washington, DC: Carnegie Endowment for International Peace, 2006) 3.

Chan, Heng Chee. "Politics in an Administrative State: Where Has the Politics Gone?" in Seah Chee Meow, ed., *Trends in Singapore* (Singapore: Institute of Southeast Asian Studies, 1975) 51.

Chan, Heng Chee. "Political Developments, 1965–1979", in Chew, Ernest & Lee, Edwin, eds., *A History of Singapore* (Singapore: Oxford University Press, 1991) 157.

Chan, Heng Chee. "Internal Developments in Singapore", in Grover, Verinder, ed., *Singapore: Government and Politics* (New Delhi: Deep & Deep, 2000) 128.

Chee, Soon Juan. *Dare to Change: An Alternative Vision for Singapore* (Singapore: Singapore Democratic Party, 1994).

Chia, Doris & Mathiavaranam, Rueben. *Evans on Defamation in Singapore and Malaysia*, 3rd ed. (Singapore: LexisNexis, 2008).

Chin, C. C. "The United Front Strategy of the Malayan Communist Party in Singapore, 1950s–1960s", in Michael D. Barr & Carl A. Trocki, eds., *Paths Not Taken: Political Pluralism in Post-War Singapore* (Singapore: NUS Press, 2008) 58 at 72.

Chin, C. C. & Hack, Karl, eds., *Dialogues with Chin Peng: New Light on the Malayan Communist Party*, 2nd ed. (Singapore: Singapore University Press, 2005).

Chong, Terence. *Civil Society in Singapore: Reviewing Concepts in the Literature* (Singapore: Institute of Southeast Asian Studies, 2005).

Chouliaraki, Lilie & Fairclough, Norman. *Discourse in Late Modernity: Rethinking Critical Discourse Analysis* (Edinburgh: Edinburgh University Press, 1999).

Chua, Beng-Huat. *Communitarian Ideology and Democracy in Singapore* (London: Routledge, 1995).

Chua, Beng-Huat. *Political Legitimacy and Housing: Stakeholding in Singapore* (London: Routledge, 1997).

Clark, David. "The Many Meanings of the Rule of Law", in Jayasuriya, Kanishka, ed., *Law, Capitalism and Power in Asia: The Rule of Law and Legal Institutions* (London: Routledge, 1999) 28.

Conley, Jon M. & O'Barr, William M. *Just Words: Law, Language and Power*, 2nd ed. (Chicago: University of Chicago Press, 2005).

Davies, Derek. "The Press", in Haas, Michael, ed., *The Singapore Puzzle* (Westport, CT: Praeger, 1999) 77.

Davies, Margaret. *Asking the Law Question: The Dissolution of Legal Theory* (Sydney: Lawbook, 2002).

De Konick, Rodolphe, Drolet, Julie & Girard, Marc. *Singapore: An Atlas of Perpetual Territorial Transformation* (Singapore: NUS Press, 2008).

Deyo, Frederic C. "The Emergence of Bureaucratic-Authoritarian Corporatism in Labour Relations", in Ong Jin Hwee, Tong Chee Kiong & Tan Ern Ser, eds., *Understanding Singapore Society* (Singapore: Times Academic Press, 1997) 353.

Doshi, Tilak & Coclanis, Peter. "The Economic Architect: Goh Keng Swee", in Lam Peng Er & Tan, Kevin Y. L., eds., *Lee's Lieutenanants: Singapore's Old Guard* (St. Leonards: Allen & Unwin, 1999) 24.

Fairclough, Norman. *Language and Power* (London: Longman, 1989).

Fairclough, Norman. *Discourse and Social Change* (Cambridge: Polity Press, 1992).

Fairclough, Norman. *Media Discourse* (London: Edward Arnold, 1995).

Fairclough, Norman. *Analyzing Discourse: Textual Analysis for Social Research* (New York: Routledge, 2003).

Fisch, Jörg. *Cheap Lixes and Dear Limbs: The British Transformation of the Bengal Criminal Law, 1769–1817* (Wiesbaden: Franz Steiner Verklag) 1983 .

Fitzpatrick, Peter. *Law and State in Papua New Guinea* (London: Academic Press, 1980).

Fitzpatrick, Peter. "Custom as Imperialism", in Abun-Nasr, Jamil M., Spellenbert, Ulrich & Wanitzek, Ulrich eds., *Law, Society and National Identity in Africa* (Hamburg: Helmut Buske, 1990) 15.

Fitzpatrick, Peter, ed. *Nationalism, Racism and the Rule of Law* (Aldershot: Dartmouth, 1995).

Fong, Hoe Fang, ed. *That We May Dream Again* (Singapore: Ethos, 2009).

Foucault, Michel. *The Archaeology of Knowledge and the Discourse on Language*, trans. by Alan Sheridan (New York: Pantheon, 1972).

Foucault, Michel. *Discipline and Punish: The Birth of the Prison*, 2nd ed., trans. by Alan Sheridan (New York: Vintage, 1995).

Foucault, Michel. "Governmentality", in *Michel Foucault: Power, Essential Works of Foucault, 1954–1984*, ed. by James D. Faubion (London: Penguin, 2002) vol. 3 at 219.

Furnivall, J. S. *Colonial Policy and Practice: A Comparative Study of Burma and Netherlands India* (Cambridge: Cambridge University Press, 1948).

George, Cherian. *Singapore the Air-Conditioned Nation: Essays on the Politics of Comfort and Control* (Singapore: Landmark, 2000).

George, Cherian. "Singapore: Media at the Mainstream and the Margins", in Heng, Russel, ed., *Media Fortunes, Changing Times: ASEAN States in Transition* (Singapore: Institute of South East Asian Studies, 2002).

George, Cherian. *Contentious Journalism and the Internet: Towards Democratic Discourse in Malaysia and Singapore* (Singapore: Singapore University Press, 2006).

George, Cherian. "History Spiked: Hegemony and the Denial of Media Diversity" in Barr, Michael D. & Trocki, Carl A., eds., *Paths Not Taken: Political Pluralism in Post-War Singapore* (Singapore: NUS Press, 2008) 264.

George, Cherian. "No News Here: Media in Subordination", in Welsh, Bridget et al., eds., *Impressions of the Goh Chok Tong Years in Singapore* (Singapore: NUS Press, 2009) 444.

Gillespie, John. *Transplanting Commercial Law Reform: Developing a Rule of Law in Vietnam* (Aldershot: Ashgate, 2006).

Gillespie, John. "Understanding Legality in Vietnam", in Balme, Stephanie & Sidel, Mark, eds., *Vietnam's New Order* (New York: Palgrave Macmillan, 2007) 137.

Gillespie, John & Nicholson, Pip. "The Diversity and Dynamism of Legal Change in Socialist China and Vietnam", in Gillespie, John & Nicholson, Pip, eds., *Asian Socialism and Legal Change* (Canberra: Asia Pacific Press, 2005) 1.

Gillis, Kay. *Singapore Civil Society and British Power* (Singapore: Talisman, 2005).

Ginsburg, Tom & Moustafa, Tamir, eds., *Rule By Law: The Politics of Courts in Authoritarian Regimes* (Cambridge: Cambridge University Press, 2008).

Glenn, H. Patrick. "The Nationalist Heritage", in Legrand, Pierre & Munday, Roderick, eds., *Comparative Legal Studies: Traditions and Transitions* (Cambridge: Cambridge University Press, 2003) 76.

Glenn, H. Patrick. *Legal Traditions of the World: Sustainable Diversity in Law* (Oxford: Oxford University Press, 2004).

Golder, Ben & Fitzpatrick, Peter. *Foucault's Law* (Abingdon: Routledge, 2009).

Gomez, James. *Internet Politics: Surveillance and Intimidation in Singapore* (Bangkok: Think Centre, 2002).

Gordon, Colin. "Introduction", in Faubion, James D., ed., *Michel Foucault: Power* (London: Penguin, 1994) xviii.

Habermas, Jürgen. *Between Facts and Norms: Contributions to a Discourse Theory of Law and Democracy*, trans. by William Rehg (Cambridge, MA: MIT Press, 1995).

Halliday, Terence C. *Beyond Monopoly: Lawyers, State Crises and Professional Empowerment* (Chicago: University of Chicago Press, 1987).

Halliday, Terence C. & Karpik, Lucien. "Politics Matter: A New Framework for the Comparative and Historical Study of Legal Professions", in Halliday, Terence C. & Karpik, Lucien, eds., *Lawyers and the Rise of Western Political Liberalism* (Oxford: Clarendon Press, 1997) 15.

Halliday, Terence C., Karpik, Lucien & Feeley, Malcolm. "Introduction: The Legal Complex in Struggles for Political Liberalism", in Halliday, Terence C., Karpik, Lucien & Feeley, Malcolm, eds., *Fighting for Political Freedom: Comparative Studies of the Legal Complex for Political Change* (Oxford: Hart, 2007) 1.

Han, Fook Kwang, Fernandez, Warren & Tan, Sumiko. *Lee Kuan Yew: The Man and His Ideas* (Singapore: Times Editions, 1998).

Harding, Andrew & Carter, Connie. "The Singapore Model of Law and Development: Cutting through the Complexity", in Hatchard, John & Perry-Kessaris, Amanda, eds., *Law and Development: Facing Complexity in the 21st Century* (London: Routledge Cavendish, 2003) 191.

Harper, Tim. "Lim Chin Siong and the 'Singapore Story' ", in Tan Jing Quee & Jomo, K. S., eds., *Comet in Our Sky: Lim Chin Siong in History* (Kuala Lumpur: Insan, 2001) 3.

Herman, Edward S. & Chomsky, Noam. *Manufacturing Consent: The Political Economy of the Mass Media* (New York: Pantheon, 1988).

Heyzer, Noeleen. "International Production and Social Change: An Analysis of the State, Employment and Trade Unions in Singapore", in Ong Jin Hwee, Tong Chee Kiong & Tan Ern Ser, eds., *Understanding Singapore Society* (Singapore: Times Academic Press, 1997) 374.

Ho, Khai Leong. *Shared Responsibilities, Unshared Power: The Politics of Policy-Making in Singapore* (Singapore: Marshall Cavendish, 2003).

Hong, Lysa. "Making the History of Singapore: S. Rajaratnam and C. V. Devan Nair", in Lam Peng Er & Tan, Kevin Y. L., eds., *Lee's Lieutenants: Singapore's Old Guard* (St. Leonards: Allen & Unwin, 1999) 96.

Hong, Lysa & Huang, Jianli. *The Scripting of a National History: Singapore and Its Pasts* (Singapore, NUS Press, 2008).

Hooker, M. B. *Laws of Southeast Asia* (Singapore: Butterworths, 1986).

Hor, Michael. "Law and Terror: Singapore Stories and Malaysian Dilemmas", in Hor, Michael, Ramraj, Victor & Roach, Kent, eds., *Global Anti-Terrorism Law and Policy* (Cambridge: Cambridge University Press, 2005) 273.

Hor, Michael, Ramraj, Victor and Roach, Kent, eds., *Global Anti-Terrorism Law and Policy* (Cambridge: Cambridge University Press, 2005).

Huang, Jianli. "The Young Pathfinders: Portrayal of Student Activism", in Trocki, Carl A. & Barr, Michael D., eds., *Paths Not Taken: Political Pluralism in Post-War Singapore* (Singapore: NUS Press, 2008).

Huff, W. G. *The Economic Growth of Singapore: Trade and Development in the Twentieth Century* (Cambridge: Cambridge University Press, 1994).

Hunt, Alan & Wickham, Gary. *Foucault and Law: Towards a Sociology of Law as Governance* (London: Pluto Press, 1994).

Jayasuriya, Kanishka. "Corporatism and Judicial Independence Within Statist Legal Institutions in East Asia", in Jayasuriya, Kanishka, ed., *Law, Capitalism and Power in Asia: The Rule of Law and Legal Institutions* (London: Routledge, 1999) 173.

Jayasuriya, Kanishka. ed. *Law, Capitalism and Power in Asia: The Rule of Law and Legal Institutions* (London: Routledge, 1999).

Johnson, Pauline. *Habermas: Rescuing the Public Sphere* (Oxford: Routledge, 2006).

Kalathil, Shanthi, & Boas, Taylor C. *Open Networks; Closed Regimes: The Impact of the Internet on Authoritarian Rule* (Washington, DC : Carnegie Endowment for International Peace, 2003).

Karpik, Lucien. *French Lawyers: A Study in Collective Action, 1274 to 1994*, trans. by Nora Scott (Oxford: Clarendon Press, 1999).

Kleinfeld, Rachel. "Competing Definitions of the Rule of Law", in Carothers, Thomas, ed., *Promoting the Rule of Law Abroad* (Washington, DC: Carnegie Endowment for International Peace, 2006) 31.

Koh, Sharon, Tan, Gillian Koh & Low, Wan Jun Tammy, eds., *Speeches and Judgments of Chief Justice Yong Pung How*, 2nd ed. (Singapore: SNP, 2006) vol. 2 at 18.

Kuo, Eddie, Quah, Jon & Tong, Chee Kiong. *Religion and Religious Revivalism in Singapore* (Singapore: Ministry of Community Development, 1989).

Kuo, Eddie, Quah, Jon & Tong, Chee Kiong. *Religion in Singapore: An Analysis of the 1980 Census Data* (Singapore: Ministry of Community Development, 1989).

Kuo, Eddie, Quah, Jon & Tong, Chee Kiong. *Religion in Singapore: Report of a National Survey* (Singapore: Ministry of Community Development, 1989).

Lai, Ah Eng. *Beyond Rituals and Riots: Ethnic Pluralism and Social Cohesion in Singapore* (Singapore: Eastern Universities Press, 2004).

Lau, Albert. *A Moment of Anguish: Singapore in Malaysia and the Politics of Disengagement* (Singapore: Times Academic Press, 2000).

Lee, Geok Boi. *The Syonan Years: Singapore under Japanese Rule, 1942–1945* (Singapore: Epigram, 2005).

Lee, Kuan Yew. *From Third World to First: The Singapore Story, 1965–2000* (Singapore: Times Editions, 2000).

Lee, Terence. "Emulating Singapore: Towards a Model for Internet Regulation in Asia", in Gan, Steven, Gomez, James & Johannen, Uwe, eds., *Asian Cyberactivism: Freedom of Expression and Media Censorship* (Singapore: Friedrich Naumann Foundation, 2004) 162.

Leiffer, Michael. *Singapore's Foreign Policy: Coping with Vulnerability* (Abingdon: Routledge, 2000).

Leong, Wai Kum. *Principles of Family Law in Singapore* (Singapore: Butterworths, 1997).

Loughlin, Martin. *Sword and Scales: An Examination of the Relationship between Law and Politics* (Oxford: Hart, 2000).

Low, Kelvin & Tang, Hung Wu, eds., *Principles of Singapore Land Law* (LexisNexis, 2009).

Low, Linda. *The Political Economy of a City-State: Government-Made Singapore* (Singapore: Oxford University Press, 1998).

Lydgate, Chris. *Lee's Law: How Singapore Crushes Dissent* (Melbourne: Scribe, 2003).

McQueen, Rob & Pue, W. Wesley, eds., *Misplaced Traditions: British Lawyers, Colonial Peoples* (Sydney: Federation Press, 1999).

Malik, Waleed Haider. *Judiciary-Led Reforms in Singapore: Frameworks, Strategies, and Lessons* (Washington, DC: World Bank, 2007).

Mauzy, Dianne K. & Milne, Robert Stephen. *Singapore Politics Under the People's Action Party* (London: Routledge, 2002).

McCormick, John P. *Weber, Habermas and Transformations of the European State: Constitutional, Social and Supranational Democracy* (Cambridge: Cambridge University Press, 2007).

Mutalib, Hussin. *Parties and Politics: A Study of Opposition Parties and the PAP in Singapore* (Singapore: Marshall Cavendish International, 2005).

Nelken, David, ed. *Law as Communication* (Dartmouth: Ashgate, 1996).

Neo, Jaclyn Ling-Chien & Lee, Yvonne C. L. "Constitutional Supremacy: Still a Little Dicey", in Thio, Li-ann & Tan, Kevin Y. L. eds., *Evolution of a Revolution: 40 Years of the Singapore Constitution* (Abingdon: Routledge Cavendish, 2009) 153.

Nicholson, Pip. *Borrowing Court Systems* (Leiden: Martinus Nijhoff, 2007).

Nicholson, Pip. "Vietnamese Courts: Contemporary Interactions between Party-State and Law", in Balme, Stephanie & Sidel, Mark, eds., *Vietnam's New Order* (New York: Palgrave Macmillan, 2007) 178.

Neilson, William A. W. "Reforming Commercial Laws in Asia: Strategies and Realities for Donor Agencies", in Lindsey, Timothy, ed., *Indonesia: Bankruptcy, Law Reform and the Commercial Court* (Sydney: Desert Pea Press, 2000) 15.

Pakir, Anne & Tong, Chee Kiong, eds., *Imagining Singapore*, 2nd ed. (Singapore: Eastern Universities Press, 2004).

Patapan, Haig, Wanna, John & Weller, Patrick, eds., *Westminster Legacies: Democracy and Responsible Government in Asia and the Pacific* (Sydney, UNSW Press, 2005).

Peerenboom, Randall. "Varieties of Rule of Law: An Introduction and Provisional Conclusion", in Peerenboom, Randall, ed., *Asian Discourses of Rule of Law* (London: Routledge, 2004) 1.

Peerenboom, Randall. "Competing Conceptions of Rule of Law in China", in Peerenboom, Randall, ed., *Asian Discourses of Rule of Law* (London: Routledge, 2004) 113.

Poh, Soo Kai, Tan, Jing Quee & Koh, Kay Yew, eds., *The Fajar Generation: The University Socialist Club and the Politics of Postwar Malaya and Singapore* (Petaling Jaya: Strategic Information and Research Development Centre, 2010).

Post, Robert, ed. *Law and the Order of Culture* (Berkeley: University of California Press, 1991).

PuruShotam, Nirmala. *Negotiating Language, Constructing Race: Disciplining Difference in Singapore* (Berlin: Mouton de Gruyter, 1998).

Quah, Jon S. T. *Religion and Religious Conversion in Singapore: A Review of the Literature* (Singapore: Ministry of Community Development, 1989).

Quah, Jon S. T. "The 1980s: A Review of Significant Political Developments", in Chew, Ernest & Lee, Edwin eds., *A History of Singapore* (Singapore: Oxford University Press, 1991) 385.

Rahim, Lily Zubaidah. *The Singapore Dilemma: The Political and Educational Marginality of the Malay Community* (Shah Alam: Oxford University Press, 1998).

Rajah, K. S. "Negotiating Boundaries: OB Markers and the Law", in Welsh, Bridget et al., eds., *Impressions of the Goh Chok Tong Years in Singapore* (Singapore: NUS Press, 2009) 107.

Regnier, Philippe. *Singapore: A Chinese City State in a Malay World*, trans. by Christopher Hurst (London: Hurst, 1991).

Rhodes, R. A. W. & Weller, Patrick. "Westminster Transplanted and Westminster Implanted: Exploring Political Change", in Haig Patapan, John Wanna & Patrick Weller, eds., *Westminster Legacies: Democracy and Responsible Government in Asia and the Pacific* (Sydney: UNSW Press, 2005) 1.

Rodan, Garry. *Transparency and Authoritarian Rule in Southeast Asia: Singapore and Malaysia* (London: Routledge Curzon, 2004).

Rodan, Garry. "Westminster in Singapore: Now You See It, Now You Don't", in Patapan, Haig, Wanna, John & Weller, Patrick, eds., *Westminster Legacies: Democracy and Responsible Government in Asia and the Pacific* (Sydney: UNSW Press, 2005) 109.

Rodan, Garry. "Singapore 'Exceptionalism'? Authoritarian Rule and State Transformation", in Friedman, Edward & Wong, Joseph, eds., *Political Transitions in Dominant Party Systems: Learning to Lose* (London: Routledge, 2008) 231.

Root, Hilton L. & May, Karen. "Judicial Systems and Economic Development", in Ginsburg, Tom & Moustafa, Tamir, eds., *Rule by Law: The Politics of*

Courts in Authoritarian Regimes (Cambridge: Cambridge University Press, 2008) 304.

Rutter, Michael. *The Applicable Law in Singapore and Malaysia* (Singapore: Malayan Law Journal, 1989).

Ryan, M. Stanley. *Parliamentary Procedure: Essential Principles* (New York: Cornwall, 1985).

Sai, Siew Min & Huang, Jianli. "The 'Chinese-Educated' Political Vanguards: Ong Pang Boon, Lee Khoon Choy & Jek Yeun Thong", in Lam Peng Er & Tan, Kevin Y. L., eds., *Lee's Lieutenants: Singapore's Old Guard* (St. Leonards: Allen & Unwin, 1999) 132.

Sarat, Austin & Schiengold, Stuart A., eds., *Cause Lawyers and Social Movements* (Stanford, CA: Stanford University Press, 2006).

Shklar, Judith N. "Political Theory and the Rule of Law", in Hutchinson, Allan C. & Monahan, Patrick, eds., *The Rule of Law: Ideal or Ideology* (Toronto: Carswell, 1987) 1.

Silverstein, Gordon. "Singapore: The Exception That Proves Rules Matter", in Ginsburg, Tom & Moustafa, Tamir, eds., *Rule By Law: The Politics of Courts in Authoritarian Regimes* (Cambridge: Cambridge University Press, 2008) 73.

Schiengold, Stuart A. *The Politics of Rights: Lawyers, Public Policy and Political Change*, 2nd ed. (Ann Arbor: University of Michigan Press, 2004).

Schomberg, Rene Von & Baynes, Kenneth, eds., *Discourse and Democracy: Essays on Habermas's "Between Facts and Norms"* (Albany: State University of New York Press, 2002).

Seow, Francis T. *To Catch a Tartar: A Dissident in Lee Kuan Yew's Prison* (New Haven, CT: Yale Southeast Asian Studies, 1994).

Seow, Francis T. *The Media Enthralled: Singapore Revisited* (Boulder, CO: Lynne Reinner, 1998).

Seow, Francis T. *Beyond Suspicion? The Singapore Judiciary* (New Haven, CT: Yale University Southeast Asian Studies, 2006).

Shafir, Gershon. "The Evolving Tradition of Citizenship", in Shafir, Gershon, ed., *The Citizenship Debates: A Reader* (Minneapolis: University of Minnesota Press, 1998) 1.

Sidel, Mark. *Law and Society in Vietnam* (Cambridge: Cambridge University Press, 2008).

Singham, Constance et al., eds., *Building Social Space in Singapore: The Working Committee's Initiative in Civil Society Activism* (Singapore: Select, 2002).

Smith, Rogers M., ed. *Southeast Asia Documents of Political Development and Change* (Ithaca, NY: Cornell University Press, 1974).

Stockwell, Tony. "Forging Singapore and Malaysia: Colonialism, Decolonization and Nation-Building", in Wang Gungwu, ed., *Nation-Building: Five Southeast Asian Histories* (Singapore: Institute of Southeast Asian Studies, 2005) 191.

Strawson, John, ed. *Law after Ground Zero* (London: Glasshouse Press, 2002).

Strong, Tracy B. "Foreword: Dimensions of the New Debate around Carl Schmitt", in Schmitt, Carl, ed., *The Concept of the Political*, trans. by George Schwab (Chicago: University of Chicago Press, 2007) ix.

Strydom, Piet. *Discourse and Knowledge: The Making of Enlightenment Sociology* (Liverpool: Liverpool University Press, 2000).

Tamanaha, Brian Z. *On the Rule of Law: History, Politics, Theory* (Cambridge: Cambridge University Press, 2004).

Tamney, Joseph B. *The Struggle over Singapore's Soul: Western Modernization and Asian Culture* (Berlin: Walter de Gruyter, 1996).

Tan, Kenneth Paul., ed. *Renaissance Singapore? Economy Culture and Politics* (Singapore: NUS Press, 2007).

Tan, Kevin Y. L. "Economic Development, Legal Reform and Rights in Singapore and Taiwan", in Bauer, Joanne R. & Bell, Daniel A., eds., *The East Asian Challenge for Human Rights* (Cambridge: Cambridge University Press, 1999) 264.

Tan, Kevin Y. L. "Understanding and Harnessing Ground Energies in Civil Society", in Koh, Gillian & Ooi Giok Ling, eds., *State–Society Relations in Singapore* (Singapore: Oxford University Press, 2000) 98.

Tan, Kevin Y. L. *Marshall of Singapore: A Biography* (Singapore: Institute of Southeast Asian Studies, 2008).

Tan, Kevin, Yeo, Tiong Min & Lee, Kiat Seng. *Constitutional Law in Malaysia and Singapore* (Singapore: Malayan Law Journal, 1991).

Tan, Chong Kee. "The Canary and the Crow: Sintercom and the State Tolerability Index", in Tan, Kenneth Paul, ed., *Renaissance Singapore? Economy, Culture, and Politics* (Singapore: NUS Press, 2007) 159.

Tan, Jing Quee, Teo, Soh Lung & Koh, Kay Yew, eds., *Our Thoughts Are Free: Poems and Prose on Imprisonment and Exile* (Singapore: Ethos, 2009).

Teo, Soh Lung, *Beyond the Blue Gate: Recollections of a Political Prisoner* (Singapore: Ethos, 2010)

Thio, Li-ann. "Rule of Law Within a Non-Liberal 'Communitarian' Democracy: The Singapore Experience", in Peerenboom, Randall, ed., *Asian Discourses of Rule of Law* (London: Routledge, 2004) 183.

Thio, Li-ann. "Taking Rights Seriously? Human Rights Law in Singapore", in Peerenboom, Randall & Chen, Andrew, eds., *Human Rights in Asia* (London: Routledge Curzon, 2006) 158.

Thio, Li-ann and Tan, Kevin Y. L., eds., *Evolution of a Revolution: 40 Years of the Singapore Constitution* (London: Routledge Cavendish, 2008).

Tong, Chee Kiong. *Rationalising Religion: Religious Conversion, Revivalism and Competition in Singapore Society* (Leiden: Brill, 2007).

Tremewan, Christopher. *The Political Economy of Social Control* (Hampshire: Macmillan Press, 1994).

Trocki, Carl A. *Opium and Empire: Chinese Society in Colonial Singapore, 1800–1910* (Ithaca, NY: Cornell University Press, 1990).

Trocki, Carl A. "David Marshall and the Struggle for Civil Rights in Singapore" in Trocki, Carl A. & Barr, Michael D., eds., *Paths Not Taken: Political Pluralism in Post-War Singapore* (Singapore: NUS Press, 2008) 116.

Trocki, Carl A. & Barr, Michael D., eds., *Paths Not Taken: Political Pluralism in Post-War Singapore* (Singapore: NUS Press, 2008).

Turnbull, C. M. *Dateline Singapore: 150 Years of "The Straits Times"* (Singapore: Times Editions, 1995).

Walzer, Michael. "The Civil Society Argument", in Shafir, Gershon, ed., *The Citizenship Debates: A Reader* (Minneapolis: University of Minnesota Press, 1998) 291.

Whewall, Catherine. "Foreword", in Fong, Hoe Fang, ed., *That We May Dream Again* (Singapore: Ethos, 2009) 6.

Wickham, Gary. "Foucault and Law", in Banakar, Reza & Travers, Max, eds., *An Introduction to Law and Social Theory* (Oxford: Hart, 2002) 249.

Woo, Yen Yen Joyceln & Goh, Colin. "Caging the Bird: TalkingCock.com and the Pigeonholing of Singaporean Citizenship", in Tan, Kenneth Paul, ed., *Renaissance Singapore? Economy, Culture, and Politics* (Singapore: NUS Press, 2007) 95.

Worthington, Ross. *Governance in Singapore* (London: Routledge Curzon, 2003).

Yao, Souchou. *Singapore: The State and the Culture of Excess* (Oxford: Routledge, 2007).

Yao, Souchou. "All Quiet on the Jurong Road: Nanyang University and Radical Vision in Singapore", in Trocki, Carl A. & Barr, Michael D., eds., *Paths Not Taken: Political Pluralism in Post-War Singapore* (Singapore: NUS Press, 2008) 170.

Yeo, Kim Wah & Lau, Albert. "From Colonialism to Independence, 1945–1965", in C. T. Chew, Ernest & Lee, Edwin, eds., *A History of Singapore* (Singapore: Oxford University Press, 1991) 117.

Zahari, Said. *Singapore: Journey into Nationhood* (Singapore: National Heritage Board & Landmark, 1998).

Zahari, Said. *The Long Nightmare: My 17 Years as a Political Prisoner* (Kuala Lumpur: Utusan, 2007).

Zahari, Said. *10 Years That Shaped a Nation* (Singapore: National Archives of Singapore, 2008).

SECONDARY MATERIAL: ARTICLES

Ang, Ien & Stratton, John. "The Singapore Way of Multiculturalism: Western Concepts/Asian Cultures" (1995) 10:1 *Sojourn: Journal of Social Issues in Southeast Asia* 65.

Apel, Karl-Otto. "2 Discourse Ethics, Democracy, and International Law: Towards a Globalization of Practical Reason" (2007) 66:1 *American Journal of Economics & Sociology* 49.

Barr, Michael D. "J. B. Jeyaretnam: Three Decades as Lee Kuan Yew's Bete Noir" (2003) 33:3 *Journal of Contemporary Asia* 299.

Bell, Daniel A. "A Communitarian Critique of Authoritarianism: The Case of Singapore" (1997) 25:1 *Political Theory* 6.

Bernhard, Michael. "Civil Society and Democratic Transition in East Central Europe" (1993) 108:2 *Political Science Quarterly* 309.

Blackburn, Kevin. "Reminiscence and War Trauma: Recalling the Japanese Occupation of Singapore, 1942–1945" (2005) 33:2 *Oral History* 91.

Borkhorst-Heng, Wendy. "Newspapers in Singapore: A Mass Ceremony in the Imagining of the Nation" (2002) 24 *Media, Culture & Society* 559.

Brown, Mark. "Ethnology and Colonial Administration in Nineteenth-Century British India: The Question of Native Crime and Criminality" (2003) 36:2 *British Journal for the History of Science* 201.

Brunnel, Tim. "Intervention – Extending Hospitality, Offshoring Protest – When the International Monetary Fund and World Bank Came to Singapore" (2007) 26 *Political Geography* 493.

Cassady, Simon. "Lee Kuan Yew & the Singapore Media: Purging the Press" (1975) 4:3 *Index on Censorship* 3.

Castells, Manuel. "The Developmental City-State in an Open World Economy: The Singapore Experience" (Berkeley: University of California, 1988), online: <http://brie.berkeley.edu/publications/working_papers.html>.

Chong, Damien. "Enhancing National Security Through the Rule of Law: Singapore's Recasting of the Internal Security Act as an Anti-Terrorism Legislation" (2005) 5 *AsiaRights Journal* 1.

Collins, Alan. "A People-Oriented ASEAN: A Door Ajar or Closed for Civil Society Organisations?" (2008) 30:2 *Contemporary Southeast Asia* 313.

Cover, Robert. "Violence and the Word" (1985) 95 *Yale L.J.* 1601.

Cross, Allen. "Vandalism: An Anglo-American Perspective" (1979) 2 *Police Studies* 31.

Daw, Rowena. "Preventive Detention in Singapore: A Comment on the Case of Lee Mau Seng" (1972) 14 *Mal. L.R.* 276.

de Mello, A. "Eastern Colonies: Review of Legislation, 1934, Straits Settlements" (1936) 18:3 3rd Ser. *Journal of Comparative Legislation and International Law* 156.

Dent, Chris. "Copyright, Governmentality and Problematisation: An Exploration" (2009) 18:1 *Griffith Law Review* 134.

Diamond, Larry. "Thinking about Hybrid Regimes" (2002) 13:2 *Journal of Democracy* 21.

Feket, Liz. "Anti-Muslim Racism and the European Security State" (2004) 46:1 *Race & Class* 3.

Fitzpatrick, Peter. "'Enacted in the Destiny of Sedentary Peoples': Racism, Discovery and the Grounds of Law" (2000) 1:1 *Balayi: Culture, Law and Colonialism* 11.

Froomkin, Michael. "Habermas@Discourse.Net: Towards a Critical Theory of Cyberspace" (2003) 116:3 *Harv. L. Rev.* 751.

George, Cherian. "The Internet's Political Impact and the Penetration/Participation Paradox in Malaysia and Singapore" (2005) 27 *Media, Culture & Society* 903.

George, Cherian. "Consolidating Authoritarian Rule: Calibrated Coercion in Singapore" (2007) 20:2 *Pacific Review* 127.

Gomez, James. "Restricting Free Speech: The Impact on Opposition Parties in Singapore" (2006) 23 *Copenhagen Journal of Asian Studies* 105.

Gomez, James. "Online Opposition in Singapore: Communications Outreach without Electoral Gain" (2008) 38:4 *Journal of Contemporary Asia* 591.

Habermas, Jürgen. "Religion in the Public Sphere" (2006) 14:1 *European Journal of Philosophy* 1.

Harding, Andrew. "The 'Westminster Model' Constitution Overseas: Transplantation, Adaptation and Development in Commonwealth States" (2004) 4 *Oxford Commonwealth Law Journal* 143.

Hewison, Kevin & Rodan, Garry. "The Decline of the Left in Southeast Asia" (1994) *Socialist Register* 235.

Hickling, R. H. "The First Five Years of the Federation of Malaya Constitution" (1962) 4 *Mal. L. Rev.* 183.

Hickling, R. H. "Some Aspects of Fundamental Liberties under the Constitution of the Federation of Malaya" (1963) 2 *M.L.J.* xiv.

Hill, Michael. "Conversion and Subversion: Religion and the Management of Moral Panics in Singapore" (Asian Studies Institute, Working Paper No. 8), online: <http://www.victoria.ac.nz/asiastudies/publications/working/08ConversionandSubversion.pdf>.

Holden, Philip. "A Man and an Island: Gender and Nation in Lee Kuan Yew's Singapore Story" (2001) 24:2 *Biography: An Interdisciplinary Quarterly* 410.

Hor, Michael. "The Freedom of Speech and Defamation" (1992) *S.J.L.S.* 542.

Hor, Michael. "The Presumption of Innocence: A Constitutional Discourse for Singapore" (1995) *S.J.L.S.* 365.

Hor, Michael. "Civil Disobedience and the Licensing of Speech in Singapore" (1999) *Lawasia Journal* 1.

Hor, Michael. "Terrorism and the Criminal Law: Singapore's Solution" (2002) *S.J.L.S.* 30.

Hor, Michael & Seah, Collin. "Selected Issues in the Freedom of Speech and Expression in Singapore" (1991) 12 *Sing. L.R.* 296.

Jayakumar, S. "Emergency Powers in Malaysia, Development of the Law 1957–1977" (1978) 1 *M.L.J.* ix.

Jayasuriya, Kanishka. "The Exception Becomes the Norm: Law and Regimes of Exception in East Asia" (2001) 2:1 *Asian Pac. L. & Pol'y J.* 108.

Kapoor, Ilan. "Deliberative Democracy or Agonistic Pluralism? The Relevance of the Habermas–Mouffe Debate for Third World Politics" (2002) 27:4 *Alternatives: Global, Local, Political* 459.

Kessler, Mark. "Lawyers and Social Change in the Postmodern World" (1995) 29:4 *Law & Soc'y Rev.* 769.

Kuah, Khun Eng. "Maintaining Ethno-Religious Harmony in Singapore" (1998) 28:1 *Journal of Contemporary Asia* 103.

Kluver, Randolph. "Political Culture and Information Technology in the 2001 Singapore General Election" (2004) 21 *Political Communication* 435.

Kluver, Randolph & Soon, Carol. "The Internet and Online Political Communities in Singapore" (2007) 17:3 *Asian Journal of Communication* 246.

Kong, Lily. "Cultural Policy in Singapore: Negotiating Economic and Socio-Cultural Agendas" (2000) 31 *Geoforum* 409.

Lee, Terence. "The Politics of Civil Society in Singapore" (2002) 26:1 *Asian Studies Review* 97.

Lee, Terence. "Internet Use in Singapore: Politics and Policy Implications" (2003) 107 *Media International Australia Incorporating Culture & Policy* 75.

Lee, Terence. "Gestural Politics: Civil Society in 'New' Singapore" (2005) 20:2 *Journal of Social Issues in Southeast Asia* 132.

Lee, Terence. "Internet Control and Auto-regulation in Singapore (2005) 3:1 *Surveillance & Society* 74.

Lee, Terence, & Birch, David. "Internet Regulation in Singapore: A Policy/ing Discourse" (2000) 95 *Media International Australia Incorporating Culture and Policy* 147.

Lim, Fung Chian Mark. "An Appeal to Use the Rod Sparingly: A Dispassionate Analysis of the Use of Caning in Singapore" (1994) 15:3 *Singapore Law Review* 20.

Loughlin, Martin. "Law, Ideologies, and the Political-Administrative System" (1989) 16;1 *J. L. & Soc'y* 21.

Low, Hop Bing. "Habeas Corpus in Malaysia and Singapore" (1977) 2 *M.L.J.* iv.

Lyden, Georgen A. "The International Money Laundering Abatement and Anti-Terrorist Financing Act of 2001: Congress Wears a Blindfold While Giving Money Laundering Legislation a Facelift" (2003) 8 *Fordham J. Corp. & Fin. L.* 203.

Merry, Sally Engle. "Law and Colonialism" (1991) 25:4 *Law & Soc'y Rev.* 889.

Mutalib, Hussin. "Illiberal Democracy and the Future of Opposition in Singapore" (2000) 21 *Third World Quarterly* 313.

Napier, W. J. "An Introduction to the Study of the Law Administered in the Colony of the Straits Settlements" (1898), reprinted in (1974), 16:1 *Mal. L. Rev.* 4.

Oguamanam, Chidi & Pue, W. Wesley. "Lawyers' Professionalism, Colonialism, State Formation and National Life in Nigeria, 1900–1960: 'The Fighting Brigade of the People' " (2007) 13:6 *Social Identities* 769.

Prakash, Gyan. "Subaltern Studies as Postcolonial Criticism" (1994) 99:5 *American Historical Review* 1475.

Prychitko, David L. & Storr, Virgil Henry. "Communicative Action and the Radical Constitution: The Habermasian Challenge to Hayek, Mises and Their Descendents" (2007) 31:2 *Cambridge Journal of Economics* 255.

Qu, Hailin, Li, Lan & Chu, Gilder Kei Tat. "The Comparative Analysis of Hong Kong as an International Conference Destination in Southeast Asia" (2000) 21 *Tourism Management* 643.

Rawlings, H. F. "Habeas Corpus and Preventive Detention in Singapore and Malaysia" (1983) 25 *Mal. L. Rev.* 324

Rodan, Garry. "Civil Society and Other Political Possibilities in Southeast Asia" (1997) 27:2 *Journal of Contemporary Asia* 14.

Rodan, Garry. "The Internet and Political Control in Singapore" (1998) 113:1 *Political Science Quarterly* 63.

Rodan, Garry. "Asia and the International Press: The Political Significance of Expanding Markets" (1998) 5:2 *Democratization* 125.

Rodan, Garry. "Embracing Electronic Media but Suppressing Civil Society: Authoritarian Consolidation in Singapore" (2003) 16:4 *Pacific Review* 503.

Ross, Stanley D. "The Rule of Law and Lawyers in Kenya" (1992) 30:3 *Journal of Modern African Studies* 421.

Sheehey, Benedict. "Singapore, 'Shared Values' and Law: Non East versus West Constitutional Hermeneutic" (2004) 34 *Hong Kong Law Journal* 67.

Sikorski, Douglas. "Resolving the Liberal–Socialist Dichotomy: The Political Economy of Prosperity in Singapore" (1991) 4:4 *International Journal of Politics, Culture and Society* 403.

Silverstein, Gordon. "Globalisation and the Rule of Law: 'A Machine That Runs of Itself?' " (2003) 1:3 *International Journal of Constitutional Law* 427.

Sim, Soek-Fang. "Asian Values, Authoritarianism and Capitalism in Singapore" (2001) 8:2 *The Public* 45.

Sim, Soek-Fang. "Obliterating the Political: One-Party Ideological Dominance and the Personalization of News in Singapore 21" (2006) 7:4 *Journalism Studies* 575.

Tan, Eugene K. B. " 'WE' v. 'I': Communitarian Legalism in Singapore" (2002) 4 *Australian Journal of Asian Law* 1.

Tan, Kevin Y. L. "Lawyers in Politics, 1945–1990", in Kevin Y. L. Tan & Michael Hor, eds., *Encounters with Singapore Legal History* (Singapore: Singapore Journal of Legal Studies, 2009) 529.

Tan, Kenneth Paul. "Singapore's National Day Rally Speech: A Site of Ideological Negotiation" (2007) 37:3 *Journal of Contemporary Asia* 292.

Tan, Kenneth Paul. "Who's Afraid of Catherine Lim? The State in Patriarchal Singapore" (2009) 33 *Asian Studies Review* 43.

Tang, Hang Wu. "The Networked Electorate: The Internet and the Quiet Democratic Revolution in Malaysia and Singapore" (2009) 2 *Journal of Information Law and Technology*.

Tan, Yock Lin. "Some Aspects of Executive Detention in Malaysia and Singapore" (1987) 29 *Mal. L. Rev.* 237.

Tay, Simon. "Human Rights, Culture and the Singapore Example" (1996) 41 *McGill L.J.* 743.

Tey, Tsun Hung. "Confining the Freedom of the Press in Singapore: A 'Pragmatic' Press for 'Nation-Building'?" (2008) *Hum. Rts. Q.* 876.

Tey, Tsun Hung. "Singapore's Jurisprudence of Political Defamation and Its Triple-Whammy Impact on Political Speech" (2008) *Public Law* 452.

Thio, Li-ann. "The Secular Trumps the Sacred: Constitutional Issues Arising from *Colin Chan v Public Prosecutor*" (1995) 16 *Sing. L.Rev.* 98.

Thio, Li-ann. "Working out the Presidency: The Rites of Passage" (1995) *S.J.L.S.* 500.

Thio, Li-ann. "Trends in Constitutional Interpretation: Oppugning Ong, Awakening Arumugam?' (1997) *S.J.L.S.* 240.

Thio, Li-ann. "Lex Rex or Rex Lex? Competing Conceptions of the Rule of Law in Singapore" (2002) 20:1 *Pacific Basin Law Journal* 22.

Thio, Li-ann. "Singapore: Regulating Political Speech and the Commitment 'to Build a Democratic Society' " (2003) 1 *International Journal of Constitutional Law* 516.

Thio, Li-ann. "'Pragmatism and Realism Do Not Mean Abdication': A Critical and Empirical Inquiry into Singapore's Engagement with International Human Rights Law" (2004) 8 *Singapore Year Book of International Law* 41.

Thio, Li-ann. "Control, Co-optation and Co-operation: Managing Religious Harmony in Singapore's Multi-Ethnic, Quasi-Secular State" (2006) 33 *Hastings Const. L. Q.* 197.

Thio, Li-ann. "Beyond the 'Four Walls' in an Age of Transnational Judicial Conversations Civil Liberties, Rights Theories, and Constitutional Adjudication in Malaysia and Singapore" (2006) 19 *Colum. J. Asian Law* 428.

Thio, Li-ann. "The Virtual and the Real: Article 14, Political Speech and the Calibrated Management of Deliberative Democracy in Singapore" (2008) *S.J.L.S.* 25.

Thio, Li-ann. “Legal Systems in Singapore: Chapter 3 – Government and the State”, Legal Systems in ASEAN, online: <http://www.aseanlawassociation.org/legal-sing.html>.

Varvaele, John A. E. “The Anti-Terrorist Legislation in the US: Inter Arma Silent Leges?” (2005) 13 *Eur. J. Crime, Crim. L. & Crim. J.* 201.

Vasoo, S. & Lee, James. “Singapore: Social Development, Housing and the Central Provident Fund” (2001:10) *International Journal of Social Welfare* 276.

Woodier, Jonathan. “Securing Singapore/Managing Perceptions: From Shooting the Messenger to Dodging the Question” (2006) 23 *Copenhagen Journal of Asian Studies* 57.

Worthington, Ross. “Between Hermes and Themis: An Empirical Study of the Contemporary Judiciary in Singapore” (2001) 28:4 *J. L. & Soc'y* 490.

Yang, Anand A. “Indian Convict Workers in Southeast Asia in the Late Eighteenth and Early Nineteenth Centuries” (2003) 14:2 *Journal of World History* 179.

Yao, Su Cho. “The Internet: State Power and Techno-Triumphalism in Singapore” (1996) 82 *Media International Australia* 73.

Zelman, Joshua D. “Recent Developments in International Law: Anti-Terrorism Legislation – Part One: An Overview” (2001–2002) 11 *J. Transnat'l L. & Pol'y* 183.

MEDIA REPORTS

“9 Foreign Students Held for Vandalism”, *Straits Times* (7 October 1993) 25.

“96 Barisans get 4 Months for Contempt”, *Straits Times* (21 December 1967) 4.

“100 US Troops in S'pore for Rest”, *Straits Times* (6 April 1966) 5.

“4,000 Delegates from 120 Countries”, *Straits Times* (16 October 2007).

“A $140, 000 Fountain to Be Opened by Toh on May Day”, *Straits Times* (20 April 1966) 6.

“‘Aid Vietnam’ Display by Barisan”, *Straits Times* (11 April 1966) 4.

“Aid-Vietnam Posters Hint of May Day Violence”, *Sunday Times* (24 April 1966) 1.

“American Teenager Charged with Keeping Stolen Goods”, *Straits Times* (9 October 1993) 1.

“Anti-US Name Campaign”, *Straits Times* (19 May 1966) 11;

“Anti-US Slogans Daubed on Bus Shelters”, *Straits Times* (14 April 1966) 9.

“At Pine Grove: Vandalism on Cars”, *Straits Times* (6 October 1993) 22.

"Barisan Hits 'Phoney Freedom' ", *Straits Times* (10 August 1966) 5.
"Barisan to Hold Meetings Against Police", *Straits Times* (22 May 1966) 3.
"The Barisan Sedition Case Takes New Turn", *Straits Times* (26 April 1966) 1.
"Barricades to Keep Out Trouble at IMF/WB Meet", *Straits Times* (11 September 2006).
"Caning Sentence on Fay to Stay", *Straits Times* (5 May 1994).
"Counsel, DPP Clash over 'Inspiration Day' ", *Straits Times* (8 October 1967) 9.
"Counsel Fails in Bid to Have Case Heard by Another Court", *Straits Times* (25 October 1968).
"Damaging Court Benches: 2 Charged", *Straits Times* (2 August 1967) 8.
"Decision on HK Teen Tomorrow", Straits Times (20 April 1994).
"The Economist Apologises to Lee Kuan Yew", *Bangkok Post* (21 January 2006).
"End of Jury Trials in S'pore", *Straits Times* (23 December 1969).
"Father Denounces Son as 'Incorrigible'", *Straits Times* (15 August 1967) 6.
"Freed, Then Re-arrested", *Straits Times* (1 August 1967) 8.
"A Giant of Singapore's Legal History", *Straits Times* (6 June 2005).
"Girl Fined $200", *Straits Times* (2 August 1967) 11.
"Government Must Act if Law Society Used for Political Ends: PM", *Straits Times* (10 October 1986) 18.
"Govt Rebuts Report Questioning Independence of Singapore Courts", *Channel NewsAsia* (11 July 2008).
"Govt Takes Issue with IHT Article on Civil Society Groups", *Straits Times* (7 October 2006).
HK Youth Denies Charges and Claims He Was Elsewhere", *Straits Times* (23 March 1994) 24.
"Hongkonger Convicted of Vandalism to Get 6 Strokes", *Straits Times* (19 June 1994) 1.
"ISA Detainee Taught MP's Sons", *Straits Times* (3 February 2002).
"Jail, Rotan for Act of Vandalism", *Straits Times* (23 March 1968) 22.
"Judging Singapore's Judiciary", *Wall Street Journal* (15 July 2008).
"The Law Society President Says Lawyers Apathetic About Public Law", *Straits Times* (18 March 2008).
"Lawyers Want Govt to Hear Their Views Before Passing Bill", *Straits Times* (25 September 1986) 18.
"Lesson on Crime from S'pore", *Straits Times* (18 March 1994).
"Malaysia Applauds Lee Kuan Yew's Defamation Win: Report", *Malaysiakini* (19 October 2007).

"May Day: Police on Emergency Alert", *Straits Times* (2 May 1966) 9.

"May Day Rally Approved", *Straits Times* (30 April 1966) 1.

"Mobs Out for US Blood", *Straits Times* (9 April 1966) 1.

"Other Branches of Law Need Reform", *Straits Times* (16 December 1969).

"Our Case Proved Beyond All Doubt – Minister", *Straits Times* (23 December 1969).

"PM: It's My Job to Stop Politicking in Professional Bodies", *Straits Times* (10 October 1986) 14.

"Police Asked Me to Persuade Son to Plead Guilty: Witness", *Straits Times* (18 March 1994) 31.

"Police Officers Hit Me, Says Hongkong Student", *Straits Times* (17 March 1994) 25.

"The Police Stand", *Straits Times* (13 September 2006).

"Political Podcasts, Videocasts Not Allowed during Election", *Straits Times* (4 April 2006).

"Putting Up Posters: 23 Charged", *Straits Times* (4 May 1966) 4.

"Reasons Behind the Vandalism Bill ...", *Straits Times* (25 August 1966) 4.

"Reinstate Expelled Students", *Straits Times* (19 April 1966) 5.

"Security Men Raid Barisan Office", *Sunday Times* (7 August 1966).

"Singapore Arrests Opposition Members in Myanmar Protest", *Reuters* (8 October 2007), online: Reuters.com <http://www.reuters.com/article/newsOne/ idUSSIN30196720071008>.

"Singapore Has an Independent Judiciary", *Wall Street Journal* (24 July 2008).

"Singapore Judges Its Juries", *Straits Times* (20 December 1969).

"SM Urges SBC Drama Head to Stay Despite Son's Vandal Conviction", *Business Times [of Singapore]* (1 August 1994).

"Society Illegal, Dr Lee Warned", *Straits Times* (10 April 1966) 2.

"S'pore–Qatar Pact to Study Legal Systems", *Straits Times* (19 November 2009).

"S'pore 'Right to Blacklist Activists' ", *Straits Times* (7 October 2006).

"S'pore, Through Foreign Eyes", *Straits Times* (16 September 2006).

"Teens Vandalism Trial Postponed", *Straits Times* (24 February 1994) 17.

"Teen Vandal Gets Jail and Cane", *Straits Times* (4 March 1994) 1.

"The Law Must Run Its Course", *Straits Times* (4 March 1993) 25.

"Thumbs up for S'pore Service Standards", *Straits Times* (29 March 2007).

"Today Paper Suspends Blogger's Column", *Straits Times* (7 July, 2006).

"Troops for Border", *Straits Times* (11 August 1966) 1.
"Two Barisan Leaders Arrested on Sedition Charge", *Straits Times* (16 April 1966) 1.
"Two Bloggers Jailed for Making Seditious Remarks Online", *Channel News Asia*, (7 October 2005).
"Two Foreign Students Admit Vandalism, Mischief", *Straits Times* (1 March 1994) 3.
"Two Girls Remanded", *Straits Times* (11 July 1967) 6.
"Two Remanded on Vandalism Charge", *Straits Times* (8 July 1967) 5.
"Two Teenagers 'to Plead Guilty' ", *Straits Times* (26 February 1994) 30.
"US Reaction to Fay Case Shows It Dare not Punish Criminal", *Straits Times* (13 April 1994) 3.
"Vandal Case: HK Boy Gave Names of Others", *Straits Times* (16 March 1994) 2.
"Vandal Charge: Bail Refused to Girl, 18", *Straits Times* (11 August 1967) 11.
"Vandalism Case: American Teen Faces more than 40 Charges", *Straits Times* (15 October 1993) 3.
"Vietnam to Bolster Singapore Ties, Particularly on Law", *Thai News Service* (21 Aug 2007).
"Warning for Blogger Who Posted Cartoons of Christ", *Straits Times* (21 July 2006).
"We Don't Tango with the Govt: Michael Hwang", *Straits Times* (25 July 2008).
"World Bank Accuses S'pore of Breaching Formal Agreement", *Straits Times* (14 September 2006).
"Worst Week in Air War for US", *Straits Times* (15 August 1966) 1.
"Youth Gets Four Months for Vandalism", *Straits Times* (18 July 1968) 6.
"Youths on Vandalism Charges: Judge Orders Joint Trial", *Straits Times* (3 February 1994) 24.

Ahmad, Rosnah. "Govt Rebuts Human Rights Accusations", *Today* (10 July 2008).
Au Yong, Jeremy. "Singapore Takes Flak for Ban on Protests", *Straits Times* (10 September 2006).
Au Yong, Jeremy. "Singapore Govt Wins Kudos for Smart PR", *Straits Times* (24 July 2008).
Bhavani, K. "Distorting the Truth, Mr Brown?" *Today* (3 July 2006).

Boey, David. "28 Activists Who Pose Security Risk Are Banned", *Straits Times* (12 September 2006).

Boo, Krist. "Event Was a Success, Says Lim Hwee Hua", *Straits Times* (21 September 2006).

Boo, Krist. "Pat on the Back for S'pore as Event Organiser Retires", *Straits Times* (22 September 2006).

Chan, Fiona. "Many Thanks and Well Done Singapore, Say delegates", *Straits Times* (21 September 2006).

Chan, Beng Soon. "10 Die in Thai Border Ambush", *Straits Times* (9 August 1966) 1.

Chan, Heng Weng. "PM Goh Remains Committed to Consultation and Consensus Politics", *Straits Times* (4 December 1994).

Chan, Heng Weng. "There Are Limits to Openness", *Straits Times* (29 December 1994).

Chew, Xiang. "IP Rights, Rule of Law Our Competitive Edge: MM Lee", *Business Times* (20 October 2009).

Chia, Sue-Ann. "New Media, Same Rules", *Straits Times* (15 April 2006).

Chia, Sue-Ann. ""Self-radicalised" Law Grad, 41 JI Militants Held", *Straits Times* (9 June 2007).

Chong, Elena. "Accused Had No 'Noble Aim' in Exposing Lapses", *Straits Times* (26 June 2010).

Chua, Mui Hong. "PM: No Erosion of My Authority Allowed", *Straits Times* (5 December 1994).

Dwyer, Michael. "Singapore's Accidental Exiles Leave a Damning Vacuum", *South China Morning Post* (2 September 2004).

Ee, Ming Chong, Derek. "Be Strict, Not Harsh, on Vandals – Local or Foreign", *Straits Times* (9 October 1993).

Elms, Deborah K. "Let Them Hear the Message of the Masses: IMF/World Bank Meetings", *International Herald Tribune* (30 September 2006).

Evans, Rachel. "Singapore Leader Rejects Amnesty", *International Financial Law Review* (18 October 2007), online: <http://www.iflr.com/Article/1983342/ Singapore-leader-rejects-Amnesty.html>.

Fong, Leslie. "Three Newsmen Held", *Straits Times* (3 May 1971).

George, Cherian. "The Cause Celebre of the Chattering Classes", *Straits Times* (29 December 1999).

Harun, Said Osman Hj Mohd Ali, Sam, Jackie, Khoo, Philip, Cheong, Yip Seng, Fazil, Abdul, Pestana, Roderik, & Lee, Gabriel, "Terror Bomb Kills 2 Girls at Bank", *Straits Times* (11 March 1965).

Hussain, Zakir. "Blogger Who Posted Cartoons of Christ Online Being Investigated", *Straits Times* (14 June 2006).
Hussain, Zakir. "No Go for Gay Picnic, Run at Botanic Gardens", *Straits Times* (8 August 2007).
Hussain, Zakir. "No Change to Act Governing Law Society", *Straits Times* (14 July 2008).
Hussain, Zakir. "Raffles, MM Lee and the Rule of Law: CJ", *Straits Times* (28 October 2009).
Jacob, Paul. "Existing Laws Adequate, Says Law Society", *Straits Times* (22 May 1986).
Jacob, Paul. "The Man at the Centre of the Controversy", *Straits Times* (9 October 1986) 16.
Kirkpatrick, M. "Jeyaretnam's Challenge", *Asian Wall Street Journal* (17 Oct 1985).
Kor, Kian Beng. "Myanmar Activists 'Defied Our Laws' ", *Straits Times* (18 September 2008).
Kor, Kian Beng. "Ex-activists Pen Memoirs for New Book", *Straits Times* (14 November 2009).
Lee, Kuan Yew. "Why Singapore Is What It Is", *Straits Times* (15 October 2007).
Leong, Hong Chiew. Letter to the editor, *Straits Times* (8 October 1993).
Leong, Weng Kam. "Biggest Crisis Has Brought Family Even Closer", *Straits Times* (7 August 1994).
Li, Xueying. "A Well-Oiled Event – Thanks to Team S'pore", *Straits Times* (22 September 2006).
Li, Xueying. "Meetings Showed Singapore Can Do It", *Straits Times* (22 September 2006).
Li, Xueying. "Govt Reviewing Public Order Laws", *Straits Times* (17 January 2009).
Liaw, Wy-Cin. "S'pore 'Can't Take Chances' with Security", *Straits Times* (11 September 2006).
Lim, Catherine. "The PAP and the People: A Great Affective Divide", *Straits Times* (10 September 1994).
Lim, Catherine. "One Government, Two Styles", *Straits Times* (20 November 1994).
Lim, Lydia. "20 Years On: Impact of Marxist Plot on S'pore", *Straits Times* (7 July 2007).
Loh, Chee Kong. "What Price, This Success? MM Asked Whether Singapore Sacrificed Democracy", *Today* (15 October 2007).

Loh, Chee Kong. "Tough Words for Protestors and Anarchists: DPM Wong", *Today* (16 April 2009).

Long, Susan. "Been There, Done That, and Thrived", *Straits Times* (14 December 2001).

Low, Aaron. "Penal System Works", *Straits Times* (19 Jan 2009).

mr brown. "S'poreans Are Fed, Up with Progress!" *Today* (30 June 2006).

Nathan, Dominic. "15 Nabbed Here for Terror Plans", *Straits Times* (6 January 2002).

Ng, Ansley. " 'Prostituting' Too Strong a Word", *Today* (18 September 2008).

Oon, Clarissa. "MM Rebuts NMP's Notion of Race Equality", *Straits Times* (20 August 2009).

Oon, Clarissa. "Law Society Head Revives Issue of Role in Reform", *Straits Times* (13 September 2009).

Osman, Ahmad. "Ex-Fateha Chief Investigated for Net Comments", *Straits Times* (4 July 2002).

Pang, Stephanie. "Protest Singapore Style; 3 Marchers, 19 Media, 1,000 Police", *Bloomberg* (19 November 2007), online: Bloomberg.com. <http://www.bloomberg.com/apps/news?sid=aHKiTH1ny.7Q&pid=20601080>.

Peh, Shing Huei & Kwek, Ken. "14 Civil Society Groups Call for Event Boycott", *Straits Times* (13 September 2006).

Peh, Shing Huei. "Activists on S'pore Turnaround: 'Too Little, Too Late'", *Straits Times* (16 September 2006).

Pereira, Marcel Lee. "Many Spin-off Benefits with Mega-Events", *Straits Times* (11 January 2007).

Soh, Natalie. "Big Changes to Penal Code to Reflect Crime's Changing Nature", *Straits Times* (18 September 2007).

Sua, Tracy & Fong, Tanya. "Singapore Stands by Decision to Bar Some Activists", *Straits Times* (9 September 2006).

Suhaimi, Nur Dianah. "Pink Event Draws 1,000", *Sunday Times* (17 May 2009).

Tan, Ooi Boon. "Vandalism Spree Provokes Outraged Reaction from Public", *Straits Times* (8 October 1993).

Tay, Erica. "PM Thanks S'poreans for Making Meetings a Big Success", *Straits Times* (21 September 2006).

Vijayan, K. C. "Law Society Call for Decriminalisation of Homosexuality", *Straits Times* (5 April 2007).

Vijayan, K. C. "Global Law Meeting Will Tackle Heavy Issues", *Straits Times* (12 October 2007).

Wong, Sher Maine & Chua, Min Yi. "Condemn JI Terrorists – Yaacob", *Straits Times* (22 September 2002).

WEB SITES

About the IBA <http://www.ibanet.org/About_the_IBA/About_the_IBA.aspx>.
Bryan, Kelley. "Rule of Law in Singapore: Independence of the Judiciary and the Legal Profession in Singapore" (22 October 2007); Lawyers' Rights Watch Canada, < http://www.lrwc.org/pub1.php >.
Bryan, Kelley & Rubin, Howard for Lawyers Rights Watch Canada. "The Misuse of Bankruptcy Law in Singapore: An Analysis of the Matter of Re Joshua Benjamin Jeyaretnam, ex parte Indra Krishnan" (October 2004): <http://www.lrwc.org/documents/Misuse%20of%20Bankruptcy%20Law.Bryan&Rubin.22.10.04.pdf>.
Davidson, Gail & Rubin, Howard, Q.C. for Lawyers Rights Watch Canada. "Defamation in Singapore: In the Matter of J. B. Jeyaretnam" (July 2001): <http://www.lrwc.org/news/report2.php>.
Governance Matters 2009: <http//info.worldbank.org/governance/wgi>.
Members of the Presidential Council for Religious Harmony: <http://app.sgdi.gov.sg/mobile/agency.asp?agency_id=0000000898>.
Ministry of Law <http://app2.mlaw.gov.sg>.
"National Day Rally Address by Prime Minister Goh Chok Tong, Speech in English, August", Speech-Text Archival and Retrieval System: <http://stars.nhb.gov.sg/ stars/public>.
Howard Rubin for Lawyers Rights Watch Canada, "In the Matter of an Addendum to the Report to Lawyers Rights Watch on the trial of J. B. Jeyaretnam as a Result of Observations on the trial of Chee Soon Juan" (March 2003): <http://www.lrwc.org/documents/Addendum.Chee.Soon.Juan.trial.Mar.03.pdf>.
'Penalty Notices', U.K. Home Office <http://www.homeoffice.gov.uk/anti-social-behaviour/penalties/penalty-notices/>.
"Police Declare Joggers an 'Illegal Assembly' " <http://www.yawningbread.org/>.
Reporters Without Borders: <http://www.unhcr.org/refworldpublisher,RSF,SGP,0. html>.
Singapore Statutes Online <http://statutes.agc.gov.sg/>.
"SDP Writes to International Bar Association About Its Conference in Singapore": <http://www.singaporedemocrat.org/articleiba.html>.
Supreme Court of Singapore: <www.supcourt.gov.sg>.

MISCELLANEOUS

Speeches

Chief Justice Chan Sek Keong. "Keynote Address to New York State Bar Association Seasonal Meeting" (27 October 2009), online: Supreme Court of Singapore: <www.supcourt.gov.sg>.

Jeyaretnam, J. B. "The Rule of Law in Singapore", in *The Rule of Law and Human Rights in Malaysia and Singapore: A Report of the Conference Held at the European Parliament* (Limelette, 1989) 37.

Lee, Kuan Yew. "Address by the Prime Minister at the Seminar on Communism and Democracy", 28 April 1971.

Lee, Kuan Yew. "The Mass Media and New Countries", Paper presented to the General Assembly of the International Press Institute, 9 June 1971.

Lee, Kuan Yew. "For Third World Leaders: Hope or Despair?" Delivered at JFK School of Government, Harvard University, 17 October 2000, online: <http://www.gov.sg/sprinter/search.htm>.

Transcript of the Question-and Answer Session Following the Address to the 20th General Assembly of the International Press Institute at Helsinki by the Prime Minister (9 June 1971).

Reports

1858 Proclamation of Queen Victoria, *Straits Government Gazette* no. 47 (19 November 1858) 245.

Amnesty International. *Report of an Amnesty International Mission to Singapore, 30 November to 5 December 1978* (London: Amnesty International, 1980).

Asia Watch. *Silencing All Critics: Human Rights Violations in Singapore* (Washington, DC: 1989).

Cassady, Simon. "Lee Kuan Yew & the Singapore Media: Purging the Press" (1975) 4:3 *Index on Censorship*.

International Bar Association Human Rights Institute. "Prosperity versus Individual Rights? Human Rights, Democracy and the Rule of Law in Singapore" (July 2008), online: <http://www.ibanet.org/Article/Detail.aspx?ArticleUid=0081C460–4B39–4ACB-BB40–8303FCEFDB31>.

International Press Institute. *IPI Report*, June/July 1971.

Lawyers Rights Watch Canada. "Singapore: Independence of the Judiciary and the Legal Profession in Singapore" (17 October 2007).

"Report of the Special Rapporteur on the Independence of Judges and Lawyers", UN Commission on Human Rights, 52nd Sess., UN Doc. E/CN.4/1996/37.

World Bank. *The East Asian Miracle* (New York: Oxford University Press for World Bank, 1993).

World Economic Forum Global Competitiveness Report 2008, online: <http://www.weforum.org>.

Unpublished Conference Papers

Austin, Ian. "Singapore in Transition: Economic Change and Political Consequences", Paper presented to the 17th Biennial Conference of the Asian Studies Association of Australia, July 2008.

Tan, Kevin Y. L. "Lawyers in Singapore Politics, 1945–1990", Paper presented at *Paths Not Taken: Political Pluralism in Postwar Singapore* (2005).

Tang, Hsiang-yi. "Surviving on the Edge in Singapore: Mr Brown's Satirical Podcasting Finds a Way Out", Paper presented at *Convergence, Citizen Journalism & Social Change: Building Capacity*, University of Queensland, March 2008.

Tey, Tsun Hung. "Singapore's Jurisprudence of Defamation and Scandalising the Judiciary", Paper presented at the *Centre for Media and Communications Law Conference*, Melbourne Law School, November 2008.

Wade, Geoff. "Suppression of the Left in Singapore, 1945–1963: Domestic and Regional Contexts in the Southeast Asian Cold War", Paper presented at the 5th European Association of Southeast Asian Studies (EUROSEAS) Conference, University of Naples 'L'Orientale', Italy, 12–15 September 2007.

Unpublished Papers

Dent, Chris. "The Administrativist State and Questions of Governmentality" (2009).

Wade, Geoff. "Operation Cold Store: A Key Event in the Creation of Malaysia and in the Origins of Modern Singapore", Paper presented at the 21st Conference of the International Association of Historians of Asia, 21–25 June 2010.

INDEX

Books in the series (continued from page iii)

Autonomy and Ethnicity: Negotiating Competing Claims in Multi-Ethnic States
Yash Ghai

Constituting Democracy: Law, Globalism and South Africa's Political Reconstruction
Heinz Klug

The Ritual of Rights in Japan: Law, Society, and Health Policy
Eric A. Feldman

The Invention of the Passport: Surveillance, Citizenship and the State
John Torpey

Governing Morals: A Social History of Moral Regulation
Alan Hunt

The Colonies of Law: Colonialism, Zionism and Law in Early Mandate Palestine
Ronen Shamir

Law and Nature
David Delaney

Social Citizenship and Workfare in the United States and Western Europe: The Paradox of Inclusion
Joel F. Handler

Law, Anthropology and the Constitution of the Social: Making Persons and Things
Edited by Alain Pottage and Martha Mundy

Judicial Review and Bureaucratic Impact: International and Interdisciplinary Perspectives
Edited by Marc Hertogh and Simon Halliday

Immigrants at the Margins: Law, Race, and Exclusion in Southern Europe
Kitty Calavita

Lawyers and Regulation: The Politics of the Administrative Process
Patrick Schmidt

Law and Globalization from Below: Toward a Cosmopolitan Legality
Edited by Boaventura de Sousa Santos and Cesar A. Rodriguez-Garavito

Public Accountability: Designs, Dilemmas and Experiences
Edited by Michael W. Dowdle

Law, Violence and Sovereignty among West Bank Palestinians
Tobias Kelly

Legal Reform and Administrative Detention Powers in China
Sarah Biddulph

The Practice of Human Rights: Tracking Law between the Global and the Local
Edited by Mark Goodale and Sally Engle Merry

Judges beyond Politics in Democracy and Dictatorship: Lessons from Chile
Lisa Hilbink

Paths to International Justice: Social and Legal Perspectives
Edited by Marie-Bénédicte Dembour and Tobias Kelly

Law and Society in Vietnam: The Transition from Socialism in Comparative Perspective
Mark Sidel

Constitutionalizing Economic Globalization: Investment Rules and Democracy's Promise
David Schneiderman

The New World Trade Organization Knowledge Agreements, 2nd edition
Christopher Arup

Justice and Reconciliation in Post-Apartheid South Africa
Edited by François du Bois, Antje du Bois-Pedain

Militarization and Violence against Women in Conflict Zones in the Middle East: A Palestinian Case-Study
Nadera Shalhoub-Kevorkian

Child Pornography and Sexual Grooming: Legal and Societal Responses
Suzanne Ost

Darfur and the Crime of Genocide
John Hagan and Wenona Rymond-Richmond

Fictions of Justice: The International Criminal Court and the Challenge of Legal Pluralism in Sub-Saharan Africa
Kamari Maxine Clarke

Militarization and Violence against Women in Conflict Zones in the Middle East: A Palestinian Case-Study
Nadera Shalhoub-Kevorkian

Conducting Law and Society Research: Reflections on Methods and Practices
Simon Halliday and Patrick Schmidt

Planted Flags: Trees, Land, and Law in Israel/Palestine
Irus Braverman

Law, Violence and Sovereignty Among West Bank Palestinians
Tobias Kelly

Culture under Cross-Examination: International Justice and the Special Court for Sierra Leone
Tim Kelsall

Cultures of Legality: Judicialization and Political Activism in Latin America
Javier Couso, Alexandra Huneeus, Rachel Sieder

Courting Democracy in Bosnia and Herzegovina: The Hague Tribunal's Impact in a Postwar State
Lara J. Nettelfield

Law, Society, and History: Themes in the Legal Sociology and Legal History of Lawrence M. Friedman
Robert W. Gordon and Morton J. Horwitz

After Abu Ghraib: Exploring Human Rights in America and the Middle East
Shadi Mokhtari

Adjudication in Religious Family Laws: Cultural Accommodation, Legal Pluralism, and Gender Equality in India
Gopika Solanki

Water on Tap: Rights and Regulation in the Transnational Governance of Urban Water Services
Bronwen Morgan

Elements of Moral Cognition: Rawls' Linguistic Analogy and the Cognitive Science of Moral and Legal Judgment
John Mikhail

A Sociology of Constitutions: Constitutions and State Legitimacy in Historical-Sociological Perspective
Chris Thornhill

Mitigation and Aggravation at Sentencing
Julian V. Roberts

The Gacaca Courts, Post-Genocide Justice and Reconciliation in Rwanda: Justice without Lawyers
Phil Clark

Institutional Inequality and the Mobilization of the Family and Medical Leave Act: Rights on Leave
Catherine R. Albiston

3316930R00195

Printed in Great Britain
by Amazon.co.uk, Ltd.,
Marston Gate.